Cross-Cultural Exchange and the Colonial Imaginary

Cross-Cultural Exchange and the Colonial Imaginary

Global Encounters via Southeast Asia

Edited by
H. Hazel Hahn

NUS PRESS
SINGAPORE

Published by:

NUS Press
National University of Singapore
AS3-01-02, 3 Arts Link
Singapore 117569

Fax: (65) 6774-0652
E-mail: nusbooks@nus.edu.sg
Website: http://nuspress.nus.edu.sg

ISBN 978-981-3250-06-2 (paper)

National Library Board, Singapore Cataloguing in Publication Data

Names: Hahn, H. Hazel, editor.
Title: Cross-cultural exchange and the colonial imaginary: global encounters via Southeast Asia / edited by H. Hazel Hahn.
Description: Singapore: NUS Press, [2019] | Includes bibliography and index.
Identifiers: OCN 1089121221 | ISBN 978-981-32-5006-2 (paperback)
Subjects: LCSH: Southeast Asia--Civilization--Colonial influence. | Southeast Asia--Civilization--Western influences. | Southeast Asia--Social life and customs--Colonial influence. | Southeast Asia--Social life and customs--Western influences.
Classification: DDC 303.4820959--dc23

Cover image: Screen from the Fort Council Room, Batavia, early 18th century, teak, 297 x 231 cm, Museum Sejarah, Jakarta, inv. No. 3724 D.L.

Typeset by: Ogma Solutions Pvt Ltd
Printed by: Markono Print Media Pte Ltd

Contents

List of Illustrations

Acknowledgments

The editor, H. Hazel Hahn, wishes to thank the following colleagues and friends at Seattle University, who contributed to the development and completion of this volume through their encouragement and intellectual engagement. The names mentioned are in no particular order: Theresa Earenfight, Tom Taylor, Jacquelyn Miller, Kan Liang, Bill Kangas, Charles Tung, Naomi Hume, Ken Allan, David Madsen, Molly Hilliard-Clark, Susan Meyers, Marco Zangari, Nova Robinson, Onur Bakiner, Randy Souza, Harriet Phinney, and Margaret Chon. Heartfelt thanks are also due to Judith Henchy, William Clay, Holly Woodsen, Ray Jonas, Imran bin Tajudeen, Jiat-Hwee Chang, Zoltán Biedermann, Philippe Peycam, Jessica Riskin, Chris Kutz, Stefanie Von Clemm, and Damien Barnecutt. Peter Schoppert, the director of NUS Press, and his editorial team, in particular Lena Qua, have helped make the process of publishing this volume smooth and effective. Last but not least, the editor is grateful for the bountiful collegiality and patience that the contributors to this volume have shown through the long journey we have had together.

Introduction

H. Hazel Hahn[1]

How can a controversy about forms of deference (show of respect to the elite) in Java reveal tensions around colonial policies and the rise of nationalism? How were monumental screens created by Chinese craftsmen in Batavia used in ways that rendered them uniquely Batavian objects? What was Vietnamese about the French colonial governor's palace in Hanoi, and how did the Vietnamese design partially French rural houses? What can the circulation of jazz in Asia tell us about changing meanings of jazz, circuits of exchange, colonial culture, and its appropriation? Such questions point us to the evolving meanings of objects and practices that can be interpreted and resituated in numerous ways. *Cross-Cultural Exchange and the Colonial Imaginary* provides such multi-layered interpretations with a fresh perspective. It approaches the study of objects and cultural practices by closely analyzing their contexts—such as changes in settings, participants, audiences, or time periods—as well as their representations in a trans-imperial framework.

The history of colonization looms large for the cultural history of Southeast Asia in the modern era, in particular the period from the mid-nineteenth to the mid-twentieth centuries, when imperial expansion was at its peak. For this reason, it is unusual to focus on the topic of exchange for the modern period. For long, the standard narrative of colonial culture has been one of domination and imposition of the colonizers' cultures on colonized societies and subsequent erosion of local cultures due to "modernization" seen as Westernization. In spite of significant inroads made in revising such approaches, cultural flow has continued to be seen largely as being in one direction, from the universalized "West"—which most frequently signifies Western Europe and the US—to other parts of the world, particularly in the modern era.[2] In architecture history, the way "vernacular" architecture is considered to be "local" and somehow outside the march of ("Western") architectural progress in the world is a prominent and much-debated example.[3] Such interpretations were in many ways a direct legacy of the colonial era itself. Colonizers had emphasized superiority and domination, and also insisted on clear distinctions between the colonizer and colonized, as well as between the metropole (center) seen as impervious to influences from the colonies and periphery (colony). During the subsequent period of decolonization, the Cold War, and the Vietnam War, political history—and to a less extent social and economic history—were valued in seeking to understand turbulent contemporary situations, and the history of everyday culture was neglected in comparison. Political history emphasizing the agency of the colonized, in examining anti-colonial struggles and independence, also maintained the above binaries.[4]

This interdisciplinary volume emphasizes the contested nature of colonial domination, which was necessarily always a process.[5] In exploring colonial culture, power relations, and circuits of exchange as the core themes of this volume, we highlight the interplay of different groups, offering in-depth examinations of shared spaces and cultures that produced strategies of integration, adaptation, and appropriation as well as resistance. We underline a wide range of actors, their motivations, and interactions, as well as local specificities, and in this way, we complicate the binary of the colonizer-colonized. And we seek to illuminate the multi-linear trajectories (rather than binary exchange between two continents) of the flow of objects, cultural practices, and cultural knowledge, through a trans-imperial framework.

The complex exchange networks of goods, people, and ideas of many parts of Southeast Asia in relation to the broader world in the modern period is not well understood, especially in comparison to the early-modern era.[6] A case in point providing a tantalizing glimpse of such exchange networks is Vietnamese influence on Senegalese cuisine.[7] In examining the patterns of flow, it is also necessary to set aside the precolonial-colonial and colonial-postcolonial binaries as logical organizing principles.[8] Regime changes have been transformative in many ways. However, periodization along precolonial-colonial-postcolonial regime changes can provide an exaggerated sense of such transformations, including false images of the monolithic power of the state (whether precolonial, colonial, or postcolonial). Such periodization can also overshadow continuities including those in the material infrastructure.[9]

Further, the cultural influence of Southeast Asia on Europe has been hardly studied compared to the intersections of British and Indian cultures in Britain.[10] Laurie Sears presents an important counter-argument in *Shadows of Empire: Colonial Discourse and Javanese Tales* (1996), showing that Javanese shadow theater "developed within an atmosphere where nineteenth-century discourses of science and progress" both contributed to and drew from "Javanese and Dutch intellectual exchanges," resulting in Javanese cultural influence on Dutch thought.[11] Leslie Barnes presents another counter-argument against established views, by examining in *Vietnam and the Colonial Condition of French Literature* (2014) the influence of colonial and postcolonial Vietnam on French literature. In order to utilize such novel approaches, this volume also sets aside a clear division between metropole and periphery. As Julie Codell attests, this distinction "has evaporated as we have come to understand how interconnected and interdependent these spatial entities are for their geographical, historical, political and cultural identities."[12] In short, aiming to contribute in providing a fuller picture of exchange networks, the chapters in this volume, through choices in geographical, temporal, and inter-group frameworks, collectively re-assess longstanding interpretive divisions: metropole-periphery, colonizer-colonized, precolonial-colonial, and colonial-postcolonial.

Cross-Cultural Exchange: Evolution of a Concept and Approaches

"Cross-cultural exchange" is defined here as a fluid, multi-linear and multi-layered exchange, what Pierre-Yves Manguin describes as "trans-cultural, mutual processes that took place within complex sets of networks, in terms of chronology, of directionality, of quality and of intensity."[13] Cross-cultural exchange is a phenomenon perhaps as old as the history of human settlements. Therefore, descriptions of instances of cross-cultural exchange have been an integral part of the historical enterprise.[14]

The view of cross-cultural exchange as salient themes in themselves, as a central focus of scholarly effort, has emerged in recent decades. Prior to the 1990s, "cultural exchange" was used mostly to refer to academic exchange (such as exchange sponsored by the Fulbright Program) or other contemporary public and private institution-based exchange.[15] Then the term was adopted for historical investigation, with nations or regions as distinct units.[16] The notion of cultural exchange in such studies reflects the longstanding interpretive framework highlighting civilizational differences for all historical periods, even as these studies, through their sheer choice of subject matter, emphasize shared elements across cultures rather than civilizational clashes.[17] In this regard Anthony King's *The Bungalow* (1984) is a pioneering work on "the production of a global culture" that showcases, through an interdisciplinary approach, how a dwelling originating from rural India became a cross-cultural house-type found around the world.[18]

"Cross-cultural exchange" is often used to draw transnational frameworks beyond nation-states or national cultures. Frameworks for thriving water-centered studies, for example, override continental boundaries and necessarily encompass multi-state regions, whether the Atlantic World, the Mediterranean, or the Indian Ocean World.[19] This volume draws on the approaches of world history, transnational history, "connected history," "entangled history," "new imperial history," and the "global turn" in architecture history and art history, which have explored exchange networks in broad regions.[20] Through such approaches, the notion of cross-cultural exchange contributes to a dynamic understanding of culture as continuously evolving.

Related to "cross-cultural exchange" is a matrix of concepts such as inter-cultural exchange, trans-cultural exchange, transculturation, cultural exchange, cultural transfer, *histoire croisée*, cultural mediation, and cultural mobility. Unlike "cross-cultural exchange" which implies a dynamic receiver, "cultural transfer"—cultural infusion from the outside—implies a passive one.[21] The idea of "Indianization" of ancient Southeast Asia, advanced by George Coedès and others, can connote such a passive receiver.[22] The notion of "transculturation," related to "hybridity," has been fruitfully applied to interpret patterns of cultural flow and connections. Wolfgang Welsch sees transculturality today as integral to globalization leading not to homogeneity but to further heterogeneity, so that in every culture there is "no longer anything absolutely foreign."[23] Thomas DaCosta Kaufmann and Michael North utilize "cultural mediation" as appropriate for the early modern period.[24]

Empire and the Predicament of Cross-Cultural Exchange

Compared to Western Europe, Southeast Asia is a much more diverse region when considering geography, languages, ethnicities, religions, and cultures, in no small part due to the large waterborne areas. There is no clear scholarly consensus on whether and how Southeast Asia forms a cohesive region in a historical perspective.[25] However, one of the distinctive characteristics of the region is a long-established trade network for both the mainland and seaborne areas, most notably the Silk Road and spice-trade routes.[26] This network has not only played an important role in connecting the region to the broader world but made many parts of the region centers of cross-cultural exchange for much of history, due to the movement of goods, ideas, and people.

Although European traders, missionaries, and colonizers were latecomers in the area compared in particular to Arabs, Indians, and Chinese (not to mention populations migrating within the region), their presence commenced a long period of interaction—foremost in the Philippines and Java—compared to other regions of Asia. Since the early modern era, the history of cross-cultural exchange in Southeast Asia has been intertwined with the history of the expansion and collapse of empires: European, also American in the case of the Philippines, and Japanese during World War II. The eventual colonization of most of the region by various empires resulted in highly complex processes of cultural changes in the modern era. The Philippines stands out as something of a case apart from the global Spanish empire most of which lay in Latin America, rendering it simultaneously an imperial outpost of sorts ruled much of the time by Mexican governors, and a valuable player in the global Manila Galleon trade (1565–1815). Its subsequent colonization by the US then linked it to North America, Hawai'i, and other places. The British (especially), French, and Dutch empires were also global in formal and informal ways. A major under-studied aspect in colonial societies is inter-Asian migration of varied populations, notably Chinese, which overlapped with and in many cases was part of colonial dynamics. Through a lens across imperial boundaries, this volume underscores the diversity, as well as common strands, of colonial interactions in an already highly diverse region.

Names of Continents and Their Purported Identities

In this regard, a word on continental names and identities is necessary. While we do have to use terms such as "Southeast Asia," "Europe," "East" or "West," we understand such terms to be historical constructs that are much too often used with exaggerated senses of clarity regarding collectively understood geographical or cultural boundaries. We do not consider Southeast Asia or Europe as politico-cultural monoliths. We prefer to emphasize that the conceptual division of Eurasia into two distinct continents of Europe and Asia has been a gradual process orchestrated largely by Europeans and that over the last few centuries came to be accepted by the world as somehow a geographically logical phenomenon.[27] Not only has Asia itself largely been a gradual cartographic construct with evolving borders from the perspective of Europe, the region known as "Southeast Asia" today was a relatively unknown area in European cartography and geography until the nineteenth century, with subsequently continually evolving boundaries and names.

The term "Southeast Asia" was not coined until World War II, and like many other geographic regions, is necessarily an artificial construct.[28] The new designation of the region, and its initial scholarship as part of newly established Area Studies, were motivated by military concerns.[29]

The chapters in this volume cover the Dutch East Indies, French Indochina, British Malaya, the Philippines under American rule, and British Ceylon, while George Dutton's and Sarah Moser's chapters treat pre- and postcolonial perspectives respectively. While the volume's primary framework is delineated by Southeast Asia and Western Europe, routes of exchange treated here frequently connected these regions to the broader world. Matthew Schauer shows that intellectual societies' knowledge-exchange circuit was global. Dawn Odell highlights the circulation of people and materials among the Netherlands, China, and colonial Java. Frederick Schenker traces the circulation of jazz, which originated in North America, as well as the circulation of Filipino musicians, through colonial Asia and elsewhere. Cross-cultural exchange among Vietnam, India, and France is the focus of Hazel Hahn's chapter. And Benita Stambler charts the dissemination of photographs taken in British Ceylon to Britain and other regions.[30]

The circuit of exchange treated here should thus be seen as a series of complex networks within Southeast Asia and nearby regions extending to parts of Europe and other parts of the world, networks overlapping with imperial spheres of influence but far from neatly determined by them. Local inhabitants, Arabs, Chinese, and Europeans circulated in this broad region, bringing with them objects, information, and people. The concept of *histoire croisée,* first formulated by Michael Werner and Bénédicte Zimmermann, is helpful here. Thomas DaCosta Kaufmann and Michael North write that *histoire croisée* designates "multilateral entanglements that occur in a temporal and spatial framework where many actors interact together on different levels, in different directions," illuminating "the synchronic tangle of political, economic, intellectual, artistic and human dynamics involved in processes of cross-cultural exchange."[31]

Another issue to clarify concerns the term "Europe." This volume covers several specific Western European powers. One of the indications of the vagueness of "Europe" is that in common parlance today what is most often designated as "Europe" by non-Europeans signifies Western, Central, and Northern European countries understood to belong to the "West" (as opposed to Eastern European countries that were in the Soviet bloc seen as being on the fringes of democratic and "advanced" Europe). The sense of "Europe" is much more modulated within Europe than without. For one, the question whether the UK belongs to the "Continent" seems to be a perennial one that extends to the country's place in the European Union and the looming "Brexit." And in Italy (which completed unification in 1870), divisions between the northern and southern regions are historically strong, and racial theories held that Southerners were of "Mediterranean or African stock" unlike "Germanic or Aryan" Northerners.[32] The seeming power and cohesiveness of "Europe," in light of the history of European colonization in Southeast Asia, should not be exaggerated. In this respect approaches to imperial history have been moving away from the view of all-powerful empires towards a more dynamic interpretation of "entangled" history.[33]

Paradoxically, in the modern era much of Europe continued to undergo great changes in boundaries. Among European empires that held sway in Southeast Asia, Great Britain and post-Napoleonic France had relatively stable boundaries (the changes of Alsace and Lorraine being exceptions, and although France underwent regime changes in 1815, 1830, 1848, 1852, 1870, and 1940 as well as the establishment of the Fourth and Fifth Republics in 1946 and 1958). In contrast, the Netherlands underwent significant border changes as well as regime changes in the early nineteenth century; the turbulence of the Napoleonic Wars was followed by the establishment of the Kingdom of the Netherlands in 1815, from which Belgium seceded in 1830. We are used to the idea that the majority of new nation-states in the world resulted from the turbulence of World War II and decolonization, thus forming the major part of "Third World" as a result of the dynamics unfolding within and emanating from Europe. However, it is easy to forget that Europe has seen, even in the modern era, numerous regime and boundary changes and not just in Eastern Europe, as Norman Davies examines in *Vanished Kingdoms: The Rise and Fall of States and Nations* (2012). *Cross-Cultural Exchange and the Colonial Imaginary* emphasizes the fragmented nature of exchange, instead of exchange between two clearly definable continents.

Clothing and Luxury Goods as Examples of Cross-Cultural Exchange

Cross-cultural exchange is much more than a trade of objects or information. It can entail an implantation of new lifestyles, ways of thinking, and formations of new cultural identities. Whether a cultural practice is considered to be "foreign" or not has much to do with complex processes of cultural change.[34] For example, something that might have once been considered foreign could years, decades, or centuries later no longer be viewed as foreign or even claimed to be of local origins. Today, no one considers silk to be "Chinese" or Arabic numerals to be a "foreign" way of writing numbers (the adjective "Arabic" is used only so that it can be distinguished from other ways of writing numbers, such as Roman numerals). And few people in Southeast Asia consider "Western" clothes as such because they are simply seen as clothes.

If we go back generations, however, we find that the introduction of such clothes often provoked controversies and debates, as Arnout H.C. van der Meer's chapter shows about colonial Java.[35] And today traces of tension sometimes remain as they are considered the norms of suitable clothes that civilized population should wear, whereas at one time, in many places in Southeast Asia, naked upper part of the body was considered the norm.[36] Meanwhile, older types of clothes have become re-defined as "traditional," "national" or "regional costumes," in spite of the fact that such clothes continued to evolve, in part through colonization, as Benita Stambler's chapter shows regarding colonial Ceylon. Such costumes became part of exotic spectacle consumed by Europeans as Stambler's and Susie Protschky's chapters demonstrate. The phenomenon of the evolution of the meaning of different clothes is an example of how certain cultural practices have come to be seen as "Western," with the connotation of "modern," and, most often "universally applicable," while the "traditional" is considered to be particular to a local culture.[37] However, in everyday practices today one person could wear these clothes in a neutral manner most of the time, but could also, in various times and settings, be aware of different meanings of wearing the clothes, depending on the context. This phenomenon could illustrate Welsch's argument that individuals have "multiple attachments and identities."[38] We might therefore say that these clothes are today neutral, as they have been firmly integrated into everyday life.[39]

The phenomenon of "Western" clothes becoming "universal" can be ironic, as much as "non-Western" clothes being seen as "exotic," since many components of modern European-style clothes in fact originated outside of the "West," jeans (dungarees originating in seventeenth-century Bombay) and the paisley pattern originating in third-century Persia being just two of myriad examples.[40] Whereas the cotton manufacturing and trade in the industrial era, centered in England and the US, is well known, the earlier history of the manufacturing and trade of cotton textile is not. *The Spinning World: A Global History of Cotton Textiles, 1200–1850*, edited by Girogio Riello and Prasannan Parthasarathi, emphasizes both the longevity and the global nature of such trade, with India as the center.[41] In many parts of the world women wore trousers long before they became acceptable for European women. These phenomena exemplify how memories of cross-cultural exchange are selectively preserved and interpreted.

Moreover, many luxury goods in early modern Europe such as porcelain, wallpaper, and other textiles came from Asia. Much of the items were identified in Europe as "Chinese," "Indian," "Japanese" and such. However, those objects were also manufactured in Europe in *chinoiserie* styles, which have continued to impact a broad range of modern designs of porcelain, furniture, gardens, clothing and so on. This phenomenon resulted in a deep integration of patterns and motifs from Asia into European goods, so that much of the time it cannot be easily discerned or identified which part of a European textile, ceramic, or wallpaper was originally "Asian." And given the complex interweaving of regionally circulated patterns and styles within Asia, identifying them as being originally emerging from a particular country is a very complicated task that should be considered largely moot.[42] Historical origins of the use of indigo in textiles, for example, cannot be easily traced as indigo plant has been widespread around the world for thousands of years.[43] In the Provence region of France cotton textile patterns from India, as well as Persia, have become thoroughly integrated over several centuries into famed local textiles, so that most people simply regard them as "Provençale" textiles.[44] In the examples of the circulation of clothing and luxury goods, we see that they are not only continually re-interpreted (and origins are remembered or forgotten in varying degrees) but are also subject to much changes, leading to further complex processes of adaptation and exchange.

Dutton's chapter in this volume shows that a Vietnamese priest's gift of silk cloth to the nineteenth-century Portuguese royal court was received very positively, so much so that a Portuguese princess had dresses made in this fabric. Other Portuguese women, in turn, sought to emulate this practice. This episode provides a rare glimpse (rare because of the parties involved in the exchange) into how fashion trends could be sparked by the introduction of exotic goods, much like the fashion of Indian cashmere shawls in France in the early nineteenth century.[45] Such phenomena were part of broad, long-established, and accelerating patterns of the global circulation of goods.

Key Themes and Aims

Colonial societies were ethnically and culturally much more diverse than what a simple "colonizer" and "colonized" divide might indicate. Official colonial definition of the colonized collectively as undifferentiated "natives" had profound consequences. However, in reality colonized subjects' social position and status varied widely and continuously evolved. Colonized subjects are rendered here as possessing complex motivations, diverse worldviews, and varying degrees of agency. In addition, colonizers are also revealed to be a relatively diverse group, as recent scholarship suggests.[46]

We argue that notable shifts in the alignment of ideologies and cultural practices through time are often highly complex. In the early period of colonization, colonizers tended to adopt local customs in manifesting signs of power through interior decoration, clothing, deference rituals, or architectural practices, as Odell, van der Meer, and Caroline Herbelin show. In other words, colonizers sought to create distinction through the adaptation and assimilation of the practices of the local, indigenous elite. During the heyday of colonial power in the late nineteenth century, in the Dutch East Indies hybrid styles of architecture continued to be widely used by colonial officials. In the same period in French Indochina, although French physicians recognized that indigenous straw huts were much more salubrious than European-style housing,[47] European styles of architecture functioned as signs of imperial power. However, as both Herbelin and Hahn emphasize, what were "European," "French," "local" or "indigenous" were all much more complicated than initially appear.

In the late colonial era, by around 1900, culturally sensitive or "ethical" imperial policies came to be seen as crucial for shoring up imperial holds in both Dutch East Indies and British Malaya, as van der Meer and Schauer argue. In French Indochina such sensibility emerged by the 1920s, as seen in the effort to cultivate an "Indochinese Style" of architecture as Herbelin discusses. By this period local, "traditional" culture of the colonized was often seen as fragile and in need of protection. At the same time, the evolving hybrid cultural modernity posed challenges to the colonizers for maintaining distinction, especially given that the rhetoric of the "civilizing mission" seemed to encourage modernization seen as Europeanization. A case in point is jazz, which, Schenker argues, was crucial for the strengthening of imperial structures, through the cultivation of distinction. The emergence of Asian jazz professionals, however, tended to bolster the sense of their capacity for independence, creating further need for the colonizers to reinforce distinction. The integration and appropriation of practices by the colonized are also investigated by Herbelin, Moser, Hahn, and van der Meer, while nationalism and anti-colonial movements are explored by van der Meer and Schauer.

Colonial governments' policies frequently reinforced or exacerbated cultural differences and social divides among ethnic groups by imposing policies particular to each ethnic group. In the Dutch East Indies, for instance, the ethnic Chinese were under a separate and elaborate legal system.[48] In French Indochina, the ethnic Chinese were required to join a congregation, yet the Chinese continued to evade French attempts to control them and also were able to take advantage of the congregation system.[49] In each of the two cases the Chinese themselves were a very diverse group that did not for the most part share a common language.[50] Also in French Indochina, a group of Tamil Indians as French citizens had a much more privileged position than the vast majority of the colonized.[51] Yet such Christian Tamil Indians also frequented Hindu Tamil temples in Saigon, as Hahn's chapter shows. And "Montagnards" of the Central Highlands were identified by the French as a minority group with specific attributes.[52]

Each empire created its own distinct dynamics. Dutch colonial Java provides a unique case study in colonial history because, as van der Meer emphasizes, for over three centuries the Dutch in Java encouraged cultural and social mixing to legitimize and maintain colonial authority. And compared to the British and Dutch empires, French Indochina was relatively isolated in terms of transportation networks and tourism circuits.

This volume collectively emphasizes the role of amateurs—whether ethnographers, collectors, or aficionados—as important intermediaries in the circulation of knowledge and goods. Finally, a number of chapters in the volume—by Schauer, van der Meer, Hahn, Herbelin, and Moser—address the topic of cultural heritage as dynamic processes. What was, and is to be, valued as part of heritage entail evaluation, selection, and contestation through potentially competing narratives within national, regional, or local frameworks, as the concept of shared heritage is necessarily a part of modern construction of collective identity.[53] These processes in turn often entail re-interpretations of the past.[54] This volume provides cases modifying perceived colonial-postcolonial dichotomies. The regaining of national sovereignty through independence, while marking a fundamentally new era, did not entail discontinuity in all aspects of daily life. In regards to architecture and the built environment, as Moser demonstrates, the colonial past has continued to play a significant role.

Section One: Knowledge Exchange

The three chapters of the first section highlight cases of the collection and exchange of cultural knowledge. In Chapter 1, "Nineteenth-century Portugal

Through Other Eyes: The Diaries of Philiphê Bỉnh," George Dutton considers observations of life in Lisbon in the early nineteenth century from the perspective of a young Vietnamese Jesuit priest who was a long-term resident of Lisbon. Bỉnh's account provides a rarely glimpsed perspective, of someone who appreciated the comparative material abundance of Lisbon and made unique observations in impressively non-judgmental ways. Bỉnh transmitted the information to the public in highlighted everyday material culture including food consumption, tea-drinking rituals, reception of Vietnamese silk cloth, the mail service, and religious worship.

Chapters 2 and 3 are both on knowledge collection and imperial policies. In Chapter 2, "Collecting Malay Heritage: Scholarly Societies and Imperial Policy in British Malaya in the Early Twentieth Century," Matthew Schauer illuminates the role played by a network of local and global intellectual societies in the imperial mission, through their active collection and sharing of ethnological information, to the mutual aim of cultural preservation and appropriation. These amateur scholarly relationships often superseded imperial political rivalries, and involved open exchange of both academic knowledge and ideas concerning imperial governance, leading to a significant collection of "heritage." Such efforts were to prevent the erosion of the culture of the colonized, and to lead to a culturally sensitive and less exploitive form of imperial governance.

Whereas Schauer's chapter focuses on the collecting of heritage, van der Meer in Chapter 3, "Rituals and Power: Cross-Cultural Exchange and the Contestation of Colonial Hegemony in Indonesia" emphasizes heritage as a contested, lived issue regarding forms of deference—including rituals and sartorial practices—in interactions between Javanese and Europeans. This chapter examines the roots of colonial hybridity in Indonesia, the construction of a symbolic-cultural constitution that legitimized colonial authority, beginning with the profound influence Javanese aristocratic culture had in the nineteenth century on the architecture, dress, language, and entertainment of European civil servants and entrepreneurs, and ensuing changes and their repercussions.

Section Two: Material and Architectural Exchange

The four chapters in the second section treat material and architectural exchange. In Chapter 4, "'Chinese' Screens in the Dutch East Indies," Dawn Odell investigates tensions between place as a site for imagery and place as a subject of representation in the late eighteenth-century material world as objects and individuals moved with increasing ease between the Netherlands and its colonies. Odell's chapter explores how the architectonic, monumental screen, and its painted or carved picture functioned together to guide forms of social engagement between Batavian elites, producing new meanings that made the screen a uniquely Batavian object.

In Chapter 5, "Absent Narratives and Missing Jewels: Cultural Heritage of a Tamil Temple in Ho Chi Minh City," Hazel Hahn presents another case of a wide network of cross-cultural exchange, extending from colonial Saigon to India and France, and, as does Odell, underlines the production of new meanings when objects are situated in new settings to new audiences. On the *vimana* (tower over the sanctum) of the Sri Thendayuthapani Temple are some extremely unusual figurines—boys in European clothes—amidst the usual iconography of Hindu deities and other religious symbols. This chapter reconstructs the history of this obscure temple through historical research as well as a visual analysis of material culture, and also discusses its contemporary status.

Material and architectural exchange in colonial Vietnam is also the topic of Caroline Herbelin in Chapter 6, "French *Nhà Rường* and a Vietnamese Palace for the Governor?: Architectural Exchange in Colonial Vietnam." Herbelin draws upon, first, the relationship between architecture and power as materialized in the Governor General's palace in Hanoi, and second, Vietnamese uptake of French architectural styles as demonstrated through the houses of rich Vietnamese constructed in a "French style" in rural Cochinchina in the 1930s. Arguing that a wide array of cultural borrowings was governed by comparable social mechanisms that defined specific instances of practices and uses, Herbelin proposes a method for capturing the diversity and the meaning of these exchanges by considering their social and technical contexts.

In Chapter 7, "Rejecting and Reproducing Colonial Urbanism in Putrajaya, Malaysia," Sarah Moser argues that recent state urban planning and architecture, as seen in Putrajaya—Malaysia's new capital city—reproduce aspects of British colonial urbanism in several key ways. Colonial-era values and ideology are embedded in new urban developments in the form of ethnic districts and exoticized Orientalist styles. Also incorporated are early twentieth-century British planning philosophies such as English garden suburbs, botanical gardens, and "New Towns." The architecture and planned environment of Putrajaya are meant to produce new meanings emphasizing a smooth blending of urban and technocratic "modernity" and "Islamic tradition."

Section Three: Leisure Exchange

In the third section, three chapters focus further on colonial cultural forms, this time ones that provided leisure and entertainment, such as photography, dance, transgressive dressing, and music. Benita Stambler in Chapter 8, "Context and Content: Colonial Photographs from Kandy, Ceylon," employs a multi-layered approach for examining photographs from Ceylon. The photographs later took on additional importance and impact through postcards, engravings, and illustrations in the press, contributing to global interactions. Stambler explores the representation of sartorial practices and other customs, the tension between image and text, and modifications of images, whether intended or unintended.

Sartorial practices and photography are also the key themes of Chapter 9. Susie Protschky's "Slipping into Something More Exotic: Transgressive Dress in Early Twentieth-century Java" examines cultural encounter between Europeans and Javanese through two vignettes on racially transgressive dress. The first vignette is on a photograph of two Dutch girls dressed in Javanese clothes, and the second is on a memoir of a racially "mixed" Indo-European woman who appeared in public dressed in a Javanese court-dancer outfit, when such dressing garnered much attention in Europe. Examining colonial notions of femininity, Protschky provides insights into the nature and limits of encounter between Europeans and Asians, and argues that the change in audience was a key factor in the production of new meanings.

In Chapter 10, "Jazz and the British Empire: The Rise of the Asian Jazz Professional," Frederick Schenker's point of departure is the global circulation of US popular song, in particular jazz, in the early twentieth century. The British Empire created a market for jazz performances. By playing jazz for European audiences throughout Asia, Filipino musicians were able to take advantage of the imperial entertainment circuit to gain mobility, financial profit, and become cosmopolitan. This chapter explores the influence of British imperialism and the circulation of jazz throughout colonial Asia and argues that one of the legacies of European empire was the creation of a new labor category in Asia, the professional jazz musician. Schenker charts the changing meanings of jazz as it circulated globally. While in colonial Asian societies jazz stood for modernity and European-ness, the participation of Asian musicians generated new significances.

Notes

1. Thanks to Vimalin Rujivacharakul, Aaron Freundschuh, and Nova Robinson for their comments and suggestions on the Introduction.
2. See Edward Said, *Orientalism* (New York: Pantheon Books, 1978). On the construction of the "East" and "West" by "non-Westerners," see Arif Dirlik, "Chinese History and the Question of Orientalism," *History and Theory* 35, no. 4 (Dec. 1996): 96–118; "Is There History after Eurocentrism?: Globalism, Postcolonialism, and the Disavowal of History," *Cultural Critique* 42 (Spring 1999): 1–34. On the decentering of Europe, see Dipesh Chakrabarty, *Provincializing Europe: Postcolonial Thought and Historical Difference* (Princeton: Princeton University Press, 2000).
3. See Marcel Vellinga, "The End of the Vernacular: Anthropology and the Architecture of the Other," *Etnofoor* 23, no. 1 (2011): 171–92.
4. In Vietnamese history, the tendency to project back into the past from the point of view of the political revolution has been a salient tendency and a point of contention. On the critique of this, see Patricia M. Pelley, *Postcolonial Vietnam: New Histories of the National Past* (Durham: Duke University Press, 2002), 208–9.
5. On contested colonial dynamics see, for example, Brenda S.A. Yeoh, *Contesting Space in Colonial Singapore: Power Relations and the Urban Built Environment* (Honolulu: University of Hawai'i Press, 2003); Jean Gelman Taylor, *Indonesia: Peoples and Histories* (New Haven: Yale University Press, 2004).
6. On cross-cultural exchange in the early modern era, see Thomas DaCosta Kaufmann and Michael North, eds., *Mediating Netherlandish Art and Material Culture in Asia* (Amsterdam: Amsterdam University Press, 2014); Karina Corrigan et al., eds., *Asia in Amsterdam: The Culture of Luxury in the Golden Age* (New Haven: Yale University Press, 2016); Benjamin Schmidt, *Inventing Exoticism: Geography, Globalism, and Europe's Early Modern World* (Philadelphia: University of Pennsylvania Press, 2015).
7. This resulted from the movement of Senegalese soldiers to Vietnam and back to Senegal, many of who brought Vietnamese wives. Samantha Spooner, "A tale of two countries; the unlikely love story between Senegal and Vietnam," *Mail & Guardian Africa*, 17 March 2015. <http://mgafrica.com/article/2015-03-15-a-tale-of-two-countries-the-unlikely-love-between-senegal-and-vietnam> [accessed 6 July 2015].
8. On a theme-based cultural history treating both colonial and postcolonial periods, see for example Van Nguyen-Marshall, Lisa B. Welch Drummond, and Danièle Bélanger, eds., *The Reinvention of Distinction: Modernity and the Middle Class in Urban Vietnam* (Heidelberg: Springer, 2011).
9. As can be seen in the historiography of post-World War II Germany, even a collective zero-hour type of resolve for conscious change did not result in a thoroughgoing reform of society in all spheres. See Rebecca Boehling, *A*

Question of Priorities: Democratic Reforms and Economic Recovery in Postwar Germany (New York: Berghahn Books, 1996).

10. On the influence of Indian culture in Britain see, for example, Antoinette Burton, *At the Heart of the Empire: Indians and the Colonial Encounter in Late-Victorian Britain* (Berkeley: University of California Press, 1998).
11. Laurie Sears, *Shadows of Empire: Colonial Discourse and Javanese Tales* (Durham: Duke University Press, 1996), 13. On cultural exchange between regions in Southeast Asia and Europe that focus on material culture, see also Susie Protschky, *Images of the Tropics: Environment and Visual Culture in Colonial Indonesia* (Leiden: KITLV Press, 2011); Caroline Herbelin, *Architectures du Vietnam colonial. Repenser le métissage* [Architectures of Colonial Vietnam. Rethinking Hybridity] (Paris: INHA, 2016); Caroline Herbelin, "Introduction," special issue on Southeast Asia, *ABE Journal* 11 (2017). On cross-cultural influence through personal relations, see among others Jean Gelman Taylor, *The Social World of Batavia: European and Eurasian in Dutch Asia* (Madison: University of Wisconsin Press, 1983); Frances Gouda and Julia Clancy-Smith, eds., *Domesticating the Empire: Race, Gender, and Family Life in French and Dutch Colonialism* (Charlottesville: University of Virginia Press, 1998); and Ann Stoler and Frederick Cooper, eds., *Tensions of the Empire: Colonial Cultures in a Bourgeois World* (Berkeley: University of California Press, 1997).
12. Julie F. Codell, "The Art of Transculturation," in *Transculturation in British Art, 1770–1930*, ed. Julie F. Codell (Farnham, UK: Ashgate Publishing, 2012), 1.
13. Pierre-Yves Manguin, "Introduction," in *Early Interactions Between South and Southeast Asia: Reflections on Cross-Cultural Exchange*, ed. Pierre-Yves Manguin, A. Mani, and Geoff Wade (Singapore: ISEAS Publishing, 2011), xvii.
14. The history of places isolated for long periods, such as that of the Easter Island, is an exception, whereas the well-known view of the isolation of early-modern Japan has been exaggerated at times. Kenneth Pyle, *Japan Rising: The Resurgence of Japanese Power and Purpose* (New York: The Century Foundation, 2007), 35.
15. An example of "cultural exchange" in this sense is "In Search of Meaningful Cultural Exchange: Southeast Asia and Japan," Proceedings of the Second International Symposium on Cultural Exchange Between Japan and Southeast Asian Countries, held in Tokyo from 22 to 30 March 1979 (Tokyo: Japan Foundation, 1980).
16. For example, see Masao Watanabe, *Science and Cultural Exchange in Modern History, Japan and the West* (Uppsala: Academiae Upsaliensis, 1997); Michele Marrapodi and A.J. Hoenselaars, eds., *The Italian World of English Renaissance Drama: Cultural Exchange and Intertextuality* (Newark, DE: University of Delaware Press, 1998).

17. A widespread example of civilizational clashes deals with the interpretation of the Mongol Empires. Recent revisionist interpretations highlight the role of cultural exchange. See Thomas T. Allsen, *Culture and Conquest in Mongol Eurasia* (Cambridge: Cambridge University Press, 2001); Thomas T. Allsen, *Commodity and Exchange in the Mongol Empire: A Cultural History of Islamic Textiles* (Cambridge: Cambridge University Press, 1997).
18. Anthony D. King, *The Bungalow: The Production of a Global Culture* (London: Routledge & Kegan Paul, 1984).
19. Maria Fusaro, Mohamed-Salah Omri, and Colin Heywood, eds., *Trade and Cultural Exchange in the Early Modern Mediterranean: Braudel's Maritime Legacy* (New York: Taurus Academic Studies, 2010); David Richardson and Filipa Ribeiro da Silva, eds., *Networks and Trans-Cultural Exchange: Slave Trading in the South Atlantic, 1590–1867* (Leiden: Koninklijke Brill NV, 2015); on Indian Ocean Studies, see for example Ashin Das Gupta, *India and the Indian Ocean World: Trade and Politics* (Uttar Pradesh, India: Oxford University Press, 2004); Kenneth R. Hall, ed., *Secondary Cities and Urban Networking in the Indian Ocean Realm, c.1400–1800* (Lanham: Lexington Books, 2008).
20. On problematizing the us/them binary, see Nicholas Thomas, *Entangled Objects: Exchange, Material Culture, and Colonialism in the Pacific* (Cambridge, MA: Harvard University Press, 1991); Joseph Shatzmiller, *Cultural Exchange: Jews, Christians, and Art in the Medieval Marketplace* (Princeton: Princeton University Press, 2013). Brian A. Catlos in *Infidel Kings and Unholy Warriors: Faith, Power, and Violence in the Age of Crusade and Jihad* (2014) refutes the model of civilizational clashes and emphasizes instead pragmatic sharing among Muslims, Christians, and Jews in the Mediterranean region of the eleventh and twelfth centuries. On world history, see for example C.A. Bayly, *The Birth of the Modern World, 1780–1914* (Oxford: Wiley-Blackwell, 2003); Geoffrey C. Gunn, *History Without Borders: The Making of an Asian World Region, 1000–1800* (Hong Kong: Hong Kong University Press, 2011). On connected history, see Sanjay Subrahmanyam, "Connected Histories: Notes towards a Reconfiguration of Early Modern Eurasia," *Modern Asian Studies* 31, no. 3 (1997); Tansen Sen, *India, China, and the World: A Connected History* (Lanham: Rowman & Littlefield, 2017). On new imperial history, see for instance Kathleen Wilson, ed., *A New Imperial History: Culture, Identity and Modernity in Britain and the Empire, 1660–1840* (Cambridge: Cambridge University Press, 2004); Antoinette Burton, ed., *After the Imperial Turn: Thinking with and through the Nation* (Durham and London: Duke University Press, 2003); Catherine Hall and Sonya O. Rose, eds., *At Home with the Empire: Metropolitan Culture and the Imperial World* (Cambridge: Cambridge University Press, 2006). On the global production of culture, see Kristin L. Hoganson, *Consumers' Imperium: The Global Production of American Domesticity, 1865–1920* (Chapel Hill: The University of North

Carolina Press, 2007); Daniel Savoy, ed., *The Globalization of Renaissance Art: A Critical Review* (Leiden: Brill, 2017).

21. Bernd Roeck favors "cultural exchange" over "cultural transfer" as a process "in which the differentiation between ['giver' and 'receiver'] blurs quickly whenever two or even more cultures participate in the processes." Bernd Roeck, "Introduction," in *Cultural Exchange in Early Modern Europe vol. 4, Forging European Identities, 1400–1700,* ed. Herman Roodenburg (Cambridge: Cambridge University Press, 2007), 2–4.
22. The general consensus is that Indian culture was brought to Southeast Asia by a group of traders and priest-scholars. Milton Osborne, *Southeast Asia: An Introductory History* (Crows Nest, Australia: Allen & Unwin, 2010), 34. Peter Skilling criticizes the "unidirectional" view that Buddhism traveled from India and Sri Lanka to Southeast Asia, rendering the latter as a "passive recipient of Indian 'influence'." Peter Skilling, "Buddhism and the Circulation of Ritual in Early Peninsular Southeast Asia," in *Early Interactions Between South and Southeast Asia*, ed. Manguin, Mani, and Wade, 371.
23. Wolfgang Welsch, "Transculturality: The Puzzling Form of Cultures Today," in *Spaces of Culture: City, Nation, World*, ed. Mike Featherstone and Scott Lash (London: Sage, 1999), 198. On cultural "mélange," see Jan Nederveen Pieterse, *Globalization and Culture: Global Mélange*, 3rd edition (Lanham, MD: Rowman & Littlefield, 2015).
24. Thomas DaCosta Kaufmann and Michael North, "Introduction: Mediating Cultures," in *Mediating Netherlandish Art and Material Culture in Asia*, ed. Kaufmann and North, 18–19.
25. See a helpful survey of the idea of Southeast Asia as a region in Geoffrey C. Gunn, *First Globalization: The Eurasian Exchange, 1500 to 1800* (Lanham: Rowman & Littlefield, 2003), 10–12. Anthony Reid sees a cohesiveness of Southeast Asia in terms of geography and population in *Charting the Shape of Early Modern Southeast Asia* (Bangkok: Silkworm Books, 1999). Also see Barbara Watson Andaya and Leonard Y. Andaya, *A History of Early Modern Southeast Asia, 1400–1830* (Cambridge: Cambridge University Press, 2015), 14–16. Milton Osborne emphasizes the diversity of the region especially in regard to religion but also shared themes in political history. Osborne, *Southeast Asia*, 24. Benedict Anderson highlights colonial intervention in drawing precise borders in the region subsequently ratified by international law in *The Spectre of Comparisons: Nationalism, Southeast Asia and the World* (New York: Verso, 1998), 318.
26. On the Silk Road in Southeast Asia, see Ian C. Glover, "The Southern Silk Road: Archaeological Evidence of Early Trade between India and Southeast Asia," in *The Silk Roads: Highways of Culture and Commerce*, ed. Vadime Elisseeff (Oxford: Berghahn Books, 2000).
27. See Edward Said's emphasis on the forgetting of shared Eurasian culture in *Orientalism* (1978).

28. On the origins of the term Southeast Asia, see Donald K. Emmerson, "'Southeast Asia': What's in a Name?," *Journal of Southeast Asian Studies* 15, no. 1 (1984): 1–21; Martin Lewis and Kären Wigen, *The Myth of Continents: A Critique of Metageography* (Berkeley: University of California Press, 1997); H. Hazel Hahn, "Abstract Spaces of Asia, Indochina and Empire in the French *Imaginaire*," in *Architecturalized Asia: Mapping a Continent through History*, ed. Vimalin Rujivacharakul et al. (Hong Kong and Honolulu: Hong Kong University Press and University of Hawai'i Press, 2013).
29. John Bowen, "The Development of Southeast Asian Studies in the United States," *The Politics of Knowledge: Area Studies and the Disciplines,* ed. David L. Szanton (Berkeley: University of California Press, 2004), 391.
30. By including a chapter on British Ceylon in this volume we are in no way suggesting that Sri Lanka "belongs" to Southeast Asia. It is notable in this regard that the region of "Southeast Asia" initially included Sri Lanka but not the Philippines or eastern Indonesia until 1945. See Emmerson, "'Southeast Asia': What's in a Name?," 7–8.
31. Michael Werner and Bénédicte Zimmerman, "Beyond comparison: Histoire croisée and the challenge of Reflexivity," in *Religion and History* 45 (2006): 30–50; "Penser l'histoire croisée: entre empire et réflexivité," [Rethinking crossed history: between empire and reflexivity] in *Annales H.S.S.* 58 (2003): 7–36; *De la comparaison à l'histoire croisée* [From comparison to crossed history] (Paris: Seuil, 2004); Thomas DaCosta Kaufmann and Michael North, "Introduction—Artistic and Cultural Exchanges between Europe and Asia, 1400–1900: Rethinking Markets, Workshops and Collections," in *Artistic and Cultural Exchanges Between Europe and Asia, 1400–1900*, ed. Michael North (Farnham, UK: Ashgate Publishing, 2010), 2.
32. Alfredo Niceforo, *Italiani del nord e italiani del sud* [Northern Italy and Southern Italy] (Torino: Fratelli Bocca, 1901), cited in Chiara Mazzucchelli, *The Heart and the Island: A Critical Study of Sicilian American Literature* (Albany: State University of New York, 2015), 5.
33. On the concept of "entangled" history, see Gyan Prakash, "Introduction," in *After Colonialism: Imperial Histories and Postcolonial Displacements*, ed. Gyan Prakash (Princeton: Princeton University Press, 1995), 11–12.
34. See Lydia Liu's critique of "cultural translation" in *Translingual Practice: Literature, National Culture, and Translated Modernity—China, 1900–1937* (Stanford: Stanford University Press, 1995), 1–3.
35. See also in the case of Korea, Hyung Gu Lynn, "Fashioning Modernity: Changing Meanings of Clothing in Colonial Korea," *Journal of International and Area Studies* 11, no. 3 (2004): 75–93.
36. On the perception of European practice as the civilizational norm, see Thongchai Winichakul, "The Quest for 'Siwilai': A Geographical Discourse of Civilizational Thinking in the Late 19th and Early 20th Century Siam," *Journal of Asian Studies* 59, no. 3 (Aug. 2000): 528–49.

37. On the traditionalization of the kimono following the introduction of Western clothes, see Liza Dalby, *Kimono: Fashioning Culture* (Seattle: University of Washington Press, 2001), 64–7.
38. Welsch, "Transculturality," 198.
39. *The Social Life of Things: Commodities in Cultural Perspective* (New York: Cambridge University Press, 1986) edited by Arjun Appadurai, demonstrates that social meanings of objects change and vary widely across space and time, that the life of things across cultures can be traced. Appadurai's argument has influenced anthropology and social history in particular and subsequently also art history and cultural history. Jonathan Gil Harris criticizes the new variety of New Historicism for treating objects as portals of synchronic, unchanging meanings unlike Appadurai's diachronic analysis. Jonathan Gil Harris, "The New New Historicism's *Wunderkammer* of Objects," *European Journal of English Studies* 4, no. 2 (2000): 111–23. Stephen Greenblatt calls to examine the sensation of rootedness. Stephen Greenblatt, "A Mobility Studies Manifesto," in *Cultural Mobility: A Manifesto,* ed. Stephen Greenblatt (Cambridge: Cambridge University Press, 2009), 250–3.
40. See Bonnie Smith's forthcoming book on the global production of the West.
41. Giorgio Riello and Prasannan Parthasarathi, eds., *The Spinning World: A Global History of Cotton Textiles, 1200–1850* (Oxford: Oxford University Press, 2009).
42. On modern *chinoiserie*, see Andrew Bolton et al., *China through the Looking Glass* (New York: Metropolitan Museum of Art, 2015).
43. On indigo dye, see Catherine Legrand, *Indigo: The Colour that Changed the World* (London: Thames & Hudson, 2013).
44. On Indian textiles in France, see Josette Brédif, *Toiles de Jouy. Classic Printed Textiles from France 1760–1843* (London: Thames & Hudson, 1989); Melanie Riffel and Sophie Rouart, *Toile de Jouy: Printed Textiles in the French Classic Style* (London: Thames & Hudson, 2003); Starr Siegele, *Toiles for all Seasons: French and British Printed Textiles* (Boston: Bunker Hill Publishing, 2004); George Bryan Souza, "The French Connection: Indian Cottons and Their Early Modern Technology," in *How India Clothed the World: The World of South Asian Textiles, 1500–1850,* ed. Giorgio Riello and Tirthankar Roy (Leiden: Koninklijke Brill NV, 2009).
45. On the fashion of Indian cashmere shawls in France, see Monique Lévi-Strauss, *Cashmere: A French Passion 1800–1880* (London: Thames & Hudson, 2013); Susan Hiner, *Accessories to Modernity: Fashion and the Feminine in Nineteenth-Century France* (Philadelphia: University of Pennsylvania Press, 2010); H. Hazel Hahn, *Scenes of Parisian Modernity: Culture and Consumption in the Nineteenth Century* (New York: Palgrave Macmillan, 2009), 29–31.
46. On the diversity of colonizers in Dutch East Indies, see Taylor, *Indonesia*; Kerry Ward, *Networks of Empire: Forced Migration in the Dutch East India Company* (New York: Cambridge University Press, 2009). In the case of

French Indochina, Marie-Paul Ha emphasizes the diversity of French women in respect to class, ethnicity, geographical origins, education, marital status, and work, and Natasha Pairaudeau highlights the role of Tamil Indians, many of who were French nationals. Marie-Paul Ha, *French Women and the Empire: The Case of Indochina* (Oxford: Oxford University Press, 2014); Natasha Pairaudeau, *Mobile Citizens: French Indians in Indochina 1858–1954* (Copenhagen: NIAS Press, 2015).

47. Ha, *French Women and the Empire*, 57.
48. Charles Coppel, *Ethnic Chinese in Indonesia* (Singapore: Singapore Society of Asian Studies, 2002), 136–50, 157–68.
49. Tracy C. Barrett, *Chinese Diaspora in South-East Asia: The Overseas Chinese in IndoChina* (New York: I.B. Tauris & Co. Ltd., 2012), 11–15.
50. Barrett, *Chinese Diaspora in South-East Asia*, 116.
51. See Pairaudeau, *Mobile Citizens.*
52. Eric Jennings, *Imperial Heights: Dalat and the Making and Undoing of French Indochina* (Berkeley: University of California Press, 2012).
53. On heritage, see Michael Hitchcock, Victor T. King, and Michael Parnwell, eds., *Heritage Tourism in Southeast Asia* (Honolulu: University of Hawai'i Press, 2010); Patrick Daly and Tim Winter, eds., *Routledge Handbook of Heritage in Asia* (Abingdon, UK and New York: Routledge, 2012).
54. On the critique of the rhetoric of common "folk" heritage constructed by the cultural elite, see Michael Herzfeld, *Anthropology Through the Looking-Glass: Critical Ethnography in the Margins of Europe* (Cambridge: Cambridge University Press, 1987).

SECTION ONE
Knowledge Exchange

CHAPTER 1

Nineteenth-century Portugal Through Other Eyes: The Diaries of Philiphê Bỉnh

George Dutton

The eighteenth and early nineteenth centuries saw the continuation of a well-established pattern of travel and travel writing across Europe. Poets, philosophers, adventurers, and dilettantes—increasingly representing emerging middle classes—crisscrossed the continent, exploring its grand monuments and backwater towns. Many wrote as they traveled, and upon returning home published journals, diaries, letters or miscellaneous anecdotes describing their experiences. It was a grand age of travel writing and accounts appeared in numerous languages including German, Spanish, English, and French. These works were translated frequently, further extending their audience.[1] Among the popular destinations for these travelers, most of them northern Europeans, was Portugal in the extreme southwestern corner of the continent. For those visiting from northern Europe, and most notably the English, Portugal represented a kind of exotic world, a place that lay beyond the ordinary and yet retained elements of the civilization that was part of the shared European culture. Reports of Portugal's charms as well as its shortcomings became part of the travel lore of this period.

Most travelers to Portugal of this era came from various parts of northern Europe, but its long-extant links to the wider world also brought in a small trickle of visitors from more distant lands. Notable among them was a Vietnamese priest by the name of Philiphê Bỉnh (1759–1833), who arrived in Lisbon in 1796 accompanied by three traveling companions. He had been sent by Vietnamese Christians to petition the Portuguese court to appoint a bishop to lead their community. During his lengthy stay in Portugal, Bỉnh kept journals and wrote letters home recording his observations and experiences of turn-of-the-century Lisbon in an early form of romanized Vietnamese, which had been developed by European missionaries and slowly taken up by literate Vietnamese Catholics. In this respect, his written legacy places Father Bỉnh squarely into the tradition of early modern travel writing about Portugal. At the same time, his perspective was, unsurprisingly, radically different from that of the German, English, or French visitors to that country. His observations of Portuguese customs, practices, and institutions were very much shaped by the late eighteenth-century Vietnamese society he had left behind, but were also influenced by his position within the Catholic Church, and by the fact that his residence in Lisbon would eventually extend nearly four decades into the 1830s.

This chapter examines Philiphê Bỉnh's writings on early nineteenth-century Portuguese society as a part of the travel literature of this era, while illustrating the ways in which his writings represented a unique manifestation of this genre. Although Bỉnh's writings were never published, and thus failed to achieve the broad circulation of accounts penned by his European traveling counterparts, they were written with a public audience in mind and with a similar purpose, to pass on observations and reflections on life in Portugal. The particular value of Philiphê Bỉnh's observations of early nineteenth-century Portuguese life and society lies in their being a very detailed and thus very rare early Asian description of European life. This chapter shares the emphasis on material exchange addressed elsewhere in this volume, in the treatment of everyday material culture, whether tea ceremony, clothing, or the postal system. The emphasis on cross-cultural exchange is also central here particularly regarding the collection and interpretation of knowledge about everyday practices and rituals. The main purpose of Bỉnh's knowledge collection—done in an era prior to the colonization of Vietnam—was the education of fellow Vietnamese Catholics whom he had left behind.

It is true that in Father Bỉnh's writings we are left more with the inference of "cross-cultural exchange" than concrete evidence of this process. For as much writing as he left behind, evidence of Father Bỉnh's impact upon those in his adopted Portuguese homeland is quite limited, in particular because we have no Portuguese descriptions of him or the excitement he may have sparked. Thus, Bỉnh represents a challenge to the historian, for he is a man known to us almost exclusively by his own account. At the same time, by situating his writings about Portugal within the larger context of travel narratives from the turn of the nineteenth century, I argue that he was part of a broader pattern of cross-cultural engagement centered upon this place. Like all visitors to Lisbon, and perhaps more than most, Bỉnh's presence there provoked ideas and questions about the elsewhere from which he came. By Bỉnh's own accounts, his arrival and subsequent interactions sparked some measure of interest in his person and the culture he represented. He reports that the priests in his new religious community asked a great many questions about his homeland, while some rushed to the library to seek further background information on their new resident.[2] Moreover, while he gradually adapted to his new home, Father Bỉnh remained a Vietnamese man and a representative of distant people and culture, and did so in a distinctly self-conscious way. He was always a figure who straddled the two cultural worlds of Portugal and Vietnam, and the lack of concrete evidence of his impact upon the Portuguese cultural landscape does not change this.

Ultimately, this is the story of an encounter that appears to have shaped Father Bỉnh far more than the Portuguese with whom he interacted, yet there were distinct ways in which Bỉnh left his mark, not least in raising awareness in numerous circles of the state of Christianity in the distant reaches of the Portuguese-influenced world. Furthermore, Bỉnh's observations resonate and contrast with later forms of knowledge collection by colonizers treated especially by Mathew Schauer and Arnout van der Meer in this volume. Finally, the case of Father Bỉnh is instructive for illustrating a concrete vector of the transmission of ideas. In his descriptions of life in Portugal and reflections on events of his era, we have a window into the ways in which a particular Asian individual encountered and interpreted the European world at the turn of the nineteenth century. This makes Bỉnh's writings one of the earliest extended representations of Europe by an Asian traveler.[3]

European Traveler Accounts of Portugal at the Turn of the Nineteenth Century

In writing about his journey to Portugal, Bỉnh took part in one of the great eras of travel writing on southern Europe. A partial list of European accounts includes: Charles François Du Périer Dumouriez, *État présent du royaume de Portugal, en l'année MDCCLXVI* (1775); Robert Southey, *Letters Written During A Short Residence in Spain and Portugal* (1797); J.-B.-F. Carrère, *Voyage en Portugal, en particulierement a Lisbonne* (1798);

James Cavanah Murphy, *A General View of the State of Portugal; containing a topographical description thereof* (1798); Henry Frederick Link, *Travels in Portugal* (1801); George Downing Whittington, *Travels through Spain and part of Portugal, with commercial, statistical, and geographical details* (1808); Richard Barnard Fisher, *A Sketch of the City of Lisbon and its environs; with some observations on the manners, disposition, and character of the Portuguese nation* (1811); Marianne Baillie, *Lisbon in the Years 1821, 1822, and 1823* (1825); A.P.D.G., *Sketches of Portuguese Life, Manner, Costume and Character* (1826); and William Morgan Kinsey, *Portugal Illustrated* (1828). As this lengthy list suggests, there was a ready market for such descriptions of southern European states, a fact confirmed by one author who reported: "Since my return to England, I have found the public curiosity so excited by, and such an apparent interest seemingly taken in, everything that relates to Spain and Portugal."[4]

To northern Europeans, southern Europe was an exotic place of balmy climates, restorative waters, and cultural distinctiveness. For visitors from places like England or Germany, or even France, Portugal represented part of an imagined "south," which was not merely a geographical referent, but was also a term freighted with broader cultural significance. This imagined "south" included several notable features: Catholicism in its various forms, which was a strong contrast to the Protestantism that dominated northern Europe; dirt and poverty, which were certainly not absent in northern Europe, but which had become associated with the southern reaches of the continent in a more explicit way; finally "backward" customs and a sense of sloth or indolence were also often associated with the "south" in contrast to the hard-working, industrious societies of northern Europe.[5] These European travelers brought with them a particular set of expectations about Portugal that substantially shaped how they viewed and wrote about the country and its people. While on the one hand, one might attribute their common descriptions of Lisbon as dirty and overrun by priests to a certain reality, it is equally likely that it was precisely this that they expected to find, and that their subsequent writings chose to focus on these features that reinforced their preconceptions.

Based in part on these preconceptions, northern Europeans' accounts of Portugal, and notably of Lisbon, painted a portrait of a city and a country that lay not only at the geographical but also at the cultural margins of Europe. This depiction was in part colored by the writers' views of Portugal as a heavily Roman Catholic country, one where religious fervor remained very strong and manifested itself publicly on a regular basis in the form of processions, robed clerics walking through the streets, and beggars and collectors of charity all invoking religion. This very visible Catholicism clearly marked Portugal as different from the predominantly Protestant religious traditions in their home countries, which were practised in more subdued fashion. The Church and its institutions in Portugal were seen as almost medieval in some respects, and the seeming ubiquity of priests, processions, and mendicants employing religious appeals was regarded as a sign of the backward nature of Portuguese society. A British soldier during the Peninsular Wars of 1807–15 commented of religious manifestations he witnessed: "What an ignorant, superstitious, priest-ridden, dirty, lousy set of poor Devils are the Portuguese," and noted of the city that it "swarms with monks, friars and ecclesiastics of all ages, sorts and kinds."[6] Another British soldier remarked after arriving in Portugal in 1810: "Nobody can have visited Lisbon without being struck with the frequency and magnitude of the religious processions which are there conducted."[7]

While religion and its manifestations attracted the attention of northern European visitors, the city of Lisbon in a larger sense also drew comment, both for its cityscape and for its lack of cleanliness. While a few visitors were impressed with Lisbon, and conceded that the city might have some attractions that merited praise, most were highly critical or disparaging in their comments.[8] Among these critics was Francis Collins, who in 1809 observed that while Lisbon might appear attractive at first glance, closer inspection revealed the city's many flaws:

> Lisbon itself, when viewed from the river, appears beautiful and magnificent rising gradually from the banks of the river Tagus . . . but [admiring] sentiments are materially lessened on a nearer inspection, for this place is far from having that regularity in its buildings, that cleanliness in its inhabitants, or that order and industry throughout, which its distant appearance seemed to promise. . . .[9]

Others were more directly dismissive of the cityscape, like Dumouriez who wrote: "The houses are irregular, poorly built, and uncomfortable. The mosquitoes, and bugs, and insects of every type are born from the blood of Lisbonne and other cities, making it impossible to reside there."[10] Like many, Dumouriez also bluntly critiqued the city's basic sanitation: "The streets are full of trash."[11] An 1800 guidebook provided another typically overwrought description of Lisbon's dirt:

> Misery and filth meet the eye in every disgusting shape, while the nose is assailed by the mingled effluvia of *sardinhas* frying in rancid oil, and of the remains of filth putrefying in the streets upon mounds of filth of a still worse description.[12]

Finally, perhaps the most critical view was that offered by a British soldier during the military campaigns to drive out the Napoleonic armies and then defend the city against future invasions: "Without seeing [the Portuguese] it is impossible to conceive there exists a people in Europe so debased. The filthiest pigs sty is a palace to the filthy houses in this dirty, stinking city."[13] In short, there was a common view that dirt and squalor were defining features of Lisbon's urban condition.

The rather unflattering view of Lisbon that emerges from this small sampling of travel accounts is one shaped by a general consensus that the place was dirty, architecturally commonplace, and beset by (depending on the author) too many priests, too many beggars, too many bandits, or excesses of all three. While there were some favorable comments to be sure—praise for some of the grand architecture, admiration for some of its finer vistas, and in some accounts acknowledgement of the accomplishments of the Portuguese people and state—the general sense was of a place that compared poorly to its northern European counterparts. Were one to rely strictly upon these particular accounts, Portugal of the late eighteenth- and early nineteenth-century period would appear an unappealing destination of limited interest. It is here where the accounts by Father Bỉnh provide a useful counterpoint and alternative way of thinking about Portugal, one that is less critical and reminds us that one's angle of vision makes all the difference in how one understands a given place.

Philiphê Bỉnh's Views of Portugal

At first glance, Bỉnh's comments on life in Lisbon and aspects of the city share some commonalities with those of the European travelers who overlapped with him during his residence in the city between his arrival in 1796 and his death in 1833. The content of Bỉnh's writings echoes that of his northern European contemporaries, for he also wrote about notable sites in the city and its surroundings. Like other visitors, he described the famous Necessidades Gardens behind the Palace of the same name, with their lush, fruit tree-lined walkways.[14] Like some of them, Bỉnh admired the fountains of the King's palace at Queluz.[15] He wrote about some of the more renowned churches of the city, in particular the Church of Saint Rock (São Roque), the home Church of the Jesuit Order in Lisbon.[16] He also described the hot springs in the near-by town of Caldas da Rainha and their purported healing qualities.[17] In addition, like his fellow visitors, Bỉnh commented at length on the many manifestations of religion in Lisbon, and the role of the

Catholic Church in the larger society of Portugal. In these respects, Bỉnh's travel writings on Portugal have much in common with the travelers from northern Europe.

Bỉnh's writings also paralleled those of European visitors to Portugal in terms of their format. Like many of the published European travel records, Bỉnh's writings were initially composed as private observations, taking the form of both personal journals and letters to friends.[18] Similar to some of these European travel accounts, Bỉnh's were written with a particular audience in mind. Although Bỉnh had no intention of publishing his writings, he was not merely keeping a written account for his own sake. Rather, because he had been sent as an envoy of a particular community of Vietnamese Christians, these men and women represented the real audience for his letters and the imagined audience for his journals. When it became increasingly obvious in the late 1810s that he would be unlikely ever to return to his homeland, Bỉnh stipulated that were he to die in Europe, he wanted his journals sent back to his homeland and those he had left behind.[19]

Although they shared some commonalities with the writings of other observers, Bỉnh's writings were also distinctive in several important respects, and it is here that he offers a significant counterpoint to the more familiar travelogues of Portugal in this period. First, and most importantly, Bỉnh brought with him a radically different perspective, one that profoundly shaped how he understood and contextualized the Portugal that he saw. Most obviously, Bỉnh's geographical vantage point was far removed from that of northern Europeans writing about Lisbon. For Bỉnh, coming from Asia, Portugal lay in the "west," a term that he frequently invoked in an unselfconscious way using the Vietnamese word for "west"—*phương Tây*.[20] For Bỉnh there was certainly no sense of Portugal as a "south" in contradistinction to any kind of "north."[21] Rather, for this Vietnamese visitor Portugal represented a kind of undifferentiated "west" juxtaposed to the "east" he had left behind. That which he was seeing and describing in Portugal stood in for all of the "west." Given his vantage point this made an enormous amount of sense. The degree of cultural, linguistic, and religious difference between Lisbon and London, for instance, would have been substantially less marked than that between Lisbon and Thăng Long (Hà Nội), the only true urban space of any sort in the Tonkin he had left behind. While Bỉnh never described his expectations of the "west" before arriving in Lisbon, he probably anticipated built-up urban spaces featuring a substantial number of religious buildings, whether churches or religious order houses. He had made several earlier trips to the Portuguese outpost at Macao in the early 1790s, and what he saw there likely shaped his expectations of Europe.

The degree to which Bỉnh's frame of reference was shaped by his Vietnamese background is nicely illustrated in a brief comment he made on early nineteenth-century European political events:

> In 1804, on the 2nd day of January, a person like Quang Trung by the name of Bonaparte, who had been born in Corfu in the country of Italy was elevated to the [position of] Emperor of the countries of France and Italy.[22]

Bỉnh drew on the recent history of Vietnam to find an analog to explain the stature of Napoleon to his readers, and so to explain the Corsican's imperial ascendance, the French military leader became "like Quang Trung." Quang Trung was a Vietnamese military leader who, like Napoleon, had risen from obscurity at the geographical margins of the realm to become briefly the Emperor of the united Vietnamese territories between 1788 and 1792. This was a figure whose exploits Bỉnh would have seen firsthand, for he had lived in Tonkin during the 1780s, when Quang Trung invaded the northern Vietnamese realm no less than three times. It was, in any case, a very apt comparison, and would have had enormous resonance for Bỉnh's intended audience.[23]

Later, Bỉnh used a similar comparative framework when he discussed the restrictions placed upon Lisbon's residents in 1808 during the short occupation of the Napoleonic forces: "This is like the year 1785 all over again, when Quang Trung went up into Đàng Ngoài (Tonkin) and there banned all the villages from beating their drums, because he feared that the people would come together to resist him. This year, when the French invaders arrived in Portugal, they similarly banned all of the churches from ringing their bells, because over here (in Europe) they do not have drums. . . ."[24] Bỉnh followed this with a discussion of the role that church bells played in Portuguese society. In short, Bỉnh's account demonstrates how a fresh perspective can shift the ways in which one considers European history—using it not as the source of analogies, but rather as the subject of analogies grounded elsewhere, in this case Vietnam.

While his place of origin profoundly influenced his views of Portugal, a second point of departure from the perspectives of European visitors was that unlike so many of them Bỉnh had become a long-term resident of Lisbon. Most European visitors stayed anywhere between a few days and a few months. Bỉnh, however spent nearly four decades in the Portuguese capital before his eventual death in 1833. His perspective was that of a man who had seen many of the inner workings of Portuguese (or at least Lisbonite) society over an extended period of time. Thus, rather than merely visiting the Necessidades gardens, he actually lived in the adjacent palace for more than a decade. He saw Lisbon as it was slowly transformed from the late 1790s through the departure of the royal family in 1807, the Napoleonic invasions, the British occupation, their aftermath, the Constitutionalist upheavals of the 1820s and beyond. In addition to these large-scale issues, he became intimately acquainted with many of the quotidian elements of life in Lisbon. From food preparation to café culture, and child-raising to medical treatment, Bỉnh had first-hand experience that became fodder for his observations. In this regard, he became more akin to a particular "insider" albeit one with a personal history that gave him a unique perspective.

Third, Bỉnh was clearly unique as a commentator on turn of the nineteenth-century Portugal because he had come on a mission for a Catholic community and had settled into a role in Lisbon as an ordained Catholic priest. Indeed, Bỉnh was clearly, himself, the product of an earlier cultural exchange in his Tonkinese homeland, to which European Catholic missionaries had brought new conceptions of religious belief and practice. Father Bỉnh had grown up in a place where the complex mediations of the encounter between existing Vietnamese beliefs/practices and newly introduced conceptions were in constant and dynamic tensions. Indeed, his trip to Portugal grew out of the tensions produced by this very specific cultural exchange. By the time he arrived in Lisbon, Father Bỉnh was already a veteran of the cultural clashes and accommodations that such encounters produced. In any case, as an ordained Catholic observer of life in Lisbon, he clearly had a substantially different understanding of the attitudes toward the Catholic church in Portugal, and of the role of priests in Portuguese society.[25] As a priest, Father Bỉnh was obviously far more sympathetic to the clergy. Even more importantly, his personal experience as a Catholic in Vietnam profoundly shaped his view of the church. He had come from a realm in which Catholicism was a beleaguered and semi-clandestine faith, and now found himself in a place where Catholicism was not merely practised openly, but served as the very cornerstone of social and state institutions. Although there had been periodic conflicts between the state and certain religious orders in Portugal over the course of the eighteenth century—particularly with the Jesuits—the state's support for and embrace of Catholicism more generally was never in question.

Finally, it is worth noting that unlike the northern Europeans who wrote primarily to satisfy curiosity about an exotic place, Bỉnh wrote to educate his readers with a very practical purpose. He wrote to offer a guide to the ins and outs of life in Lisbon for any Vietnamese who might in the future undertake a similar trip to the west. By detailing his experiences of Portugal and the ways in which its society functioned, Bỉnh sought to ease the way for future Vietnamese visitors. Thus, one might see Bỉnh's writings as less akin to travelogues like Robert Southey's *Journal of a Residence in Portugal*, and more similar to guidebooks such as *The Lisbon Guide* (1800) and the later *Baedeker's*. Indeed, in anticipation of their use as a kind of guidebook, Bỉnh included a series of indexes for several of his notebooks to facilitate tracking down particular pieces of information, noting in the prefaces that this would make his journals more useful to his readers.[26]

The combination of his Vietnamese background, his lengthy stay in Lisbon, and his status as a priest ensured that Bỉnh's perspective would be a radically different one. I now shift to an examination of Bỉnh's encounter with Portugal. I begin with a brief comment on how Bỉnh was received by the royal court, an episode that illustrates his early impact upon the local imagination, before turning to a closer examination of the viewpoints that Bỉnh offered on aspects of Portuguese life and events in Lisbon. To illustrate Bỉnh's vantage point I look briefly at his descriptions of various institutions that he observed in Portugal, and also one aspect of Portuguese social practice, namely foodways. Some institutions, like the Catholic church, were ones with which he was well acquainted, albeit under radically different circumstances in Vietnam. Others, like postal networks, national lotteries, and medical establishments were ones he had never previously encountered. Bỉnh's descriptions of each of these institutions hint at the particularities of his perspective and suggests different ways of thinking about them.

Portugal Encounters Bỉnh

Before examining Bỉnh's responses to the Portuguese world in which he found himself, I turn briefly to Portugal's reception of him. Portugal had for centuries been a state heavily engaged with far-flung corners of the globe, and while many of these ventures had faded into memories, some, like its Brazilian colony, continued to have an enormous impact on the "motherland." Despite this long engagement with the globe, the arrival in Lisbon of visitors from remote regions of the world still excited some measure of interest. Indeed, Bỉnh almost certainly counted on this reaction to his arrival to help in gaining access to the royal court. As was noted earlier, he carefully emphasized his delegation's distinctiveness by donning Vietnamese attire in their meetings with officials and then the prince regent. When the Vietnamese envoys finally had their first formal audience with the Portuguese ruler, they brought with them a few simple gifts from

Asia (probably purchased in Macao). These were presented to the ruler during this first meeting on a sultry afternoon in August at the royal palace of Queluz on the outskirts of Lisbon. The gifts consisted of some hand fans, a few hair combs, an ivory betel nut box, and 15 bolts of a flower-patterned silk cloth.

This presentation of a set of simple goods was clearly part of the protocol for foreign visitors, but as always in such encounters, it was tinged with uncertainty. Bỉnh was self-conscious about what he considered the inadequacy of these gifts, having no idea of how they would be received or how they might shape the ruler's reaction to himself, his delegation, and ultimately his mission. As such, he was forced to attempt to read the nuances of the aftermath of the gift giving ceremony. Thus, he took it as a good sign that the ruler accepted the gifts directly from their hands, rather than delegating the acceptance process to a subordinate. When Bỉnh noticed that the gifts remained out, and had not been put away, he also took this as a positive indicator. He was further pleased when during the course of their subsequent stroll through the royal gardens with the ruler's party, the prince regent and his wife each took out a newly-presented hand fan to cool themselves in the sweltering heat. Whether this was merely politeness or good manners was unknown to Bỉnh, but he took each of these indications to suggest that the gifts (if not necessarily ideal) had been suitable for the occasion.[27]

While the hand fans, combs and ivory box were likely promptly stored away with such similar gifts from official delegations, the silk cloth presented by the Vietnamese visitors had a greater impact. Indeed, it had a result that Bỉnh certainly had not anticipated. Shortly after having received the flower-patterned silk cloth that Bỉnh had brought, the prince regent's wife, Princess Carlota, ordered that it be used to make several outfits for herself. She was soon seen at court events wearing dresses sewn from this Asian silk. Seeing the Princess wearing clothes sewn from this exotic new fabric, the other ladies in her entourage were eager to acquire some of their own to emulate the new royal fashion. Several of them subsequently made their way to the Necessidades convent house where Bỉnh was staying, and requested that he sell them some of this cloth so that they might make their own dresses. Bỉnh had to explain to them that first of all he was not a merchant or trader, and thus he was the wrong person to approach. Secondly, he informed them that he no longer had any of this fabric, and that even if he had, he would not want them to imitate the styles being worn by the Queen.[28] Clearly, although the gifts brought by the Tonkinese envoys were quite modest, they made a brief splash at the court, which was probably not much used to the kinds of exoticism represented either by these gifts, or by the Vietnamese envoys themselves.

In the aftermath of this sequence of events, Bỉnh and his companions continued to represent exotic figures at court, at their residence, and sometimes in the streets of Lisbon. Unfortunately for Bỉnh, however, the initial excitement surrounding his arrival as an envoy from a remote land waned as time passed. Although Bỉnh was instructed to continue to wear his Vietnamese robes at court audiences, the ruler himself was no longer impressed, but rather sought to impress other visitors by the presence of exotic visitors from Asia. There was a brief revival in public interest in the Vietnamese men's exotic presence when one of them died in 1802. The event became something of a public spectacle in which the ruler paid for masses for the man's soul, and his body was laid out in traditional Vietnamese robes for public viewing prior to burial. Bỉnh noted that many Lisbonites came to see the body on display, attracted by the exotic element of the man's death and garb.[29] This proved, however, to be a fleeting revival of public interest. Soon Bỉnh and his two remaining companions drifted back into their largely invisible routines. As Bỉnh's star dimmed and he himself faded into the background of life in Lisbon, what increasingly came to matter for him in this cross-cultural encounter was his own understandings of Portuguese society and its elements, for they would ultimately shape him more than he did them. In what follows I explore Father Bỉnh's descriptions of Portuguese civic institutions to suggest the ways in which he sought to comprehend their functions and significance and to write about these in language and imagery that would convey them to his intended Vietnamese audience.

Bỉnh's Accounts of Portuguese Institutions

Given his situation and mission, it is hardly surprising that Bỉnh's view of the church in Lisbon was far more salutary than that of the Protestant visitors from northern Europe. He spent the majority of his life in Lisbon as a working priest who routinely said an average of three masses a week over the 20-year period between 1807 and 1827. He neither questioned the role of priests nor their substantial public profile, and was not interested in questions about the degree to which the church impinged on public life. This was something that he took for granted, and probably relished. Rather than acerbic criticism of Portugal's Catholic culture, Bỉnh's extensive commentary on the church matter of factly described the ways in which the lives of priests and lay Catholics in Lisbon differed from those of his home in Tonkin. For example, Bỉnh devoted two pages to a survey of the different types of religious images that were to be found in the various houses of worship around Lisbon, remarking on how crosses seemed to be found everywhere, "because every parochial church as well as every religious order house must be able to bring out a cross as well as a portable statue of their own saint."[30] He noted that the statues of saints found in Portugal tended to be very large and heavy, in contrast to those found in Vietnam, which were always a great deal lighter. Again, there were practical reasons for this difference: namely, that Vietnamese Catholic religious figures had to be light so they could be easily carried away and hidden in the event of a renewal of religious persecution, while Portuguese ones would be (and could be) of a more substantial nature to be publically paraded with pomp through the streets. In this regard, the religious structures he found in Lisbon also differed markedly from those he had left behind in Tonkin. Like the religious images, Vietnamese churches were usually lightweight wooden structures that often could be disassembled in the event of a crackdown on Catholics, and either relocated or hidden until the danger had passed.

While the Catholic church loomed large for Bỉnh, he was also a keen observer of urban life in its many forms, and he became the first Vietnamese to offer a detailed description of the many day-to-day practicalities of life in a European city. He wrote in considerable detail on elements of urban society and urban infrastructure including the postal system, the national lottery, fire brigades and public security, and the Portuguese healthcare system, virtually all entirely alien to him. Thus, rather than comparing them (usually unfavorably) with the counterparts found in his home country, Bỉnh took a very matter-of-fact approach in which he offered detailed explanations of the institutions, their structures and functions. The Vietnam that he had left behind had very little in the way of an urban tradition or the types of infrastructure often associated with it. The country had several very small seaports, a growing market town at Saigon, and a somewhat more elaborated imperial capital at Thăng Long. Even Thăng Long, however, was primarily a royal center to which had been attached an artisanal community and market area to support the court and its populations.[31]

Among the Portuguese institutions that particularly impressed Bỉnh was the postal system for which there was no real counterpart in Vietnam. While messages could be carried in Vietnam between government offices, this was strictly a royal institution with an extremely circumscribed purpose. In Portugal he encountered a system that was open to the public as well, one that systematically linked Lisbon to the rest of Portugal and Europe beyond. Given the importance of this system, it is perhaps not surprising that Bỉnh provided a careful tutorial on how it functioned. Bỉnh described a system in which every residence had a house number on the door, enabling mail to be properly directed. There was postal delivery and pickup twice a week all around the country, with postal carriers traveling by horseback to transport the mail between cities. He noted that the vast majority of the letters were simply conversational, as was the custom of the "west." He discussed the central post office in Lisbon as having a great range of tasks as it sorted the mail to its many different destinations. He noted that they sorted it all out, then put it into leather sacks, put it on the back of a horse and rode day and night, no matter the weather, in order to get it to its destination. He even commented on how mail at his residence was sorted, providing a practical example: "for example, if my name were Antaõ, then one would look for the letter 'A,' and if my name were Bảo Lộc (Paul), then one would look under the letter 'B,' etc. And if one saw one's name then one could go to get his letter, otherwise not. And if you did not get your letter on the day it came, then you could come to check the next day to see if it was still there."[32]

At one level this seems mundane information. Modern postal systems are taken for granted, and those who use them do not give them a second thought. None of the European travel accounts bothered to talk about it. But through Bỉnh's account, we can look at this institution with fresh eyes and consider the perspective of a man who had come from a society in which something of this type did not exist, and perhaps would have been largely superfluous. Vietnamese were certainly able to communicate with one another in the early modern period, but their worlds were, in some regards, much smaller. Furthermore, extremely limited literacy would have made a postal system largely unnecessary. But here was a system that worked, and worked very logically, and perhaps just as importantly, to which Vietnam was linked. The letters that Bỉnh received from the community back home would have passed through this system before they reached his hands.

A second institution that fascinated Bỉnh was the Portuguese lottery system, which also had no equivalent in Tonkin. As he described it, the system was run as a concession from the king to private entities who had the right to run the contest by printing and then selling tickets, which were paper chits with numbers on them. Bỉnh reported that princesses of the royal court would sometimes purchase as many as 20 tickets, wealthier commoners might purchase between five and ten tickets, while the poor would pool their resources to purchase and share a single ticket. In such cases, the ticket was apparently torn into parts and distributed amongst the people who had contributed to its purchase. When the numbers were announced these people would come together and compare their ticket sections to see if they had won, and would then go together to collect the prize. He noted that some people would even buy tickets every day, because the more you bought the greater your chances of winning, and that once all tickets were sold, the drawing would be held. In case his reader was still unclear on how the system worked, Bỉnh wrote that you would win if your number was drawn, and if not you would have lost the money you spent to buy the ticket. Prizes for the contest were as high as 50,000 silver *crusados* for first place, 40,000 for second, followed by a graduated series of lesser prizes.[33] The remainder of Bỉnh's description involved the mechanisms for distributing the prizes, including printed announcements regarding the winning numbers. He noted that there was an army of young children that was involved in the lottery system, first as tickets sellers and later in tracking down winners, for which they often collected a modest finder's fee. While Bỉnh had clearly never seen anything like the lottery in Vietnam, he tried to provide a useable frame of reference for this, and he came up with the Vietnamese civil service examination system. As with the lottery, those who wished to participate in these rigorous examinations had to make a modest investment of three coins of cash (*các kẻ đi thi sinh đồ ba quan*) as an administrative fee. Then, as with the lottery in Portugal, the vast majority would fail and thus lose their investment, while only a very few would succeed.[34] While there are clear limits to the usefulness of this analogy, it again revealed the distinct perspective that Bỉnh provided for thinking about this particular Portuguese institution.

A third civic institution that caught Bỉnh's attention was the organized system of public safety, represented by both police and fire departments. His lengthy description of the fire prevention service is worth quoting:

> In the capital houses burn very quickly, especially in the summer time when there are sometimes two or three fires every day. Even though the streets are so crowded, it is still easy to determine quickly where the fire is so no harm is caused. The first task is to protect individuals by ringing the bell in order to waking the sleeping so they can immediately flee the house, while the second is to call the troops who bring the water, because they will come out night and day. They sleep in places near water sources, and [when there is a fire] they immediately bring several water carriages, together with a vehicle carrying ladders in order to reach the upper windows, and they then travel quickly to the location of the fire.

After this he described the various water sources around the city and how water was taken from them, and the ways in which bucket brigades could be set up. He concluded by observing:

> Any time there is a fire in a house, all of the churches ring their bells as a signal for people to come out to try to save the house; there were times when the fire would be on the upper story, and times when the fire would be on the lower story. [This is because] in these apartment houses there were kitchens on every floor. Oftentimes the fires began not in the kitchen, but outside, caused by the [oil] lamps which had to be lighted throughout the night while one slept. . . .[35]

As a long-term resident living in the middle of the dense urban core, Bỉnh obviously had a vested interest in the functionings of this system, which he must have witnessed first hand over the many years of his residence.

The final institution that Bỉnh came to know quite well during his time in Lisbon was the medical establishment and its manifestations in the form of physicians, pharmacists, and the treatment regimens they prescribed. Encounters with the medical establishment had become one of the major realities for Bỉnh and his companions who came to suffer from various ailments during their earlier years in Lisbon, with some of the conditions becoming chronic for at least two of the men. Thus, doctors had to be brought in, and a wide variety of remedies attempted, which Bỉnh described in considerable detail. He talked about the various times when they called doctors to come to treat the men. He discussed the numerous instances in which he and his companions were told to send for more doctors, of their coming in to discuss the case, and of their prescribing medicines. If the medicines did not work, the doctors would meet to discuss the case further and consider using other medicine. Then he discussed the costs of hiring more doctors.[36]

He noted that during the early years of their residence, these costs were covered by the head of the religious house where they were staying because of the belief that they would be staying at most a year or two. As it turned out, the stay of the Vietnamese delegation extended into years and then decades, and their illnesses, especially that of his companion Brother Ngẩn, lingered for years as well. Bỉnh directly compared the Portuguese doctors that he worked with to those in Tonkin. He noted that the European doctors seem to be less compassionate and less attentive, but far more persistent than their Vietnamese counterparts. He wrote that if Vietnamese doctors could not affect a cure they would simply leave for fear of being embarrassed by their failure. The doctors in the "west," however would not leave if things did not go well. Instead, they would advise their patients to call additional doctors to consult on the matter, while the original doctor would remain as well. When illnesses became too severe, patients were referred to hospitals, a concept with no equivalent in Vietnam where all medical care would have taken place at the patient's home. Bỉnh was greatly impressed by the concept of the hospital, which he translated as "Houses of Compassion" [*nhà thương xót*] to which seriously ill patients could be brought, and where they would be given not only medical care, but also provided with meals and beds. He observed that in the west such institutions were not only found in the largest cities, but also in smaller towns, and reported that Lisbon itself had many hospitals. He wrote about the fees associated with hospitalization, noting that it was sometimes more economical to send a patient to the hospital than to call specialists to a private residence.[37]

Bỉnh on Portuguese Foodways

While institutions drew Bỉnh's attention, he was also particularly fascinated with Portuguese food practices with which he became intimately acquainted through years of shared meals with his fellow clerics in his two religious residences. For the most part, the customs and foodways he experienced were substantially different from the ones to which he had been accustomed in Vietnam. It is striking that Bỉnh seems to have accepted these in a matter-of-fact fashion. He expressed no sense of revulsion at foods that he encountered, nor did he regard any of the items that were eaten as being culturally repugnant. Rather, his perspective was that of a dispassionate (if not exactly disinterested) observer. This again distinguishes him from the few Europeans travelers who did comment on food, among them Richard Fisher who in 1811 wrote: "I have occasionally dined with a Portuguese family, but Portuguese and English tastes do not much agree in the culinary art. Besides their poultry and game, there is nothing else to recommend on their tables, but their bread, their wine, and their fruit."[38]

When he first arrived, Bỉnh, like Fisher, was conscious of the degree to which people's relationships to food were shaped by their experiences and local customs. He wrote:

> This is a matter that I know very clearly because [when I first arrived] I did not wish to eat or drink things in the manner of the West no matter how they were made, and as for the people of the West they also do not wish to eat things prepared in the manner of Annam regardless of how they are cooked. [This is] because people in this country or that country

> are acquainted with the customs and manners of eating and drinking in their own country from the time that they are young.[39]

Bỉnh was able to overcome his initial resistance to local foodways, and his subsequent descriptions show the experience of many years of dining in the Oratorian Order houses in which he made his home. The communal meals that were served to him at these houses gave him the opportunity to see a wide range of food and food preparation styles, which he reported in great detail.

Having come from a country long embroiled in civil war and its attendant chaos, Bỉnh was used to relatively modest amounts of food at meals. Indeed, typical Vietnamese meals were simple affairs, consisting primarily of rice, perhaps some collected greens, and supplemented sporadically by meat or fish when available or affordable. In stark contrast, the meals that were prepared for Bỉnh and his companions at his Order residence represented a kind of lavish and perpetual feast. Unlike in Tonkin, such meals always included meat of some kind, either in the form of beef, pork, chicken, or lamb, or seafood such as fish or shellfish. Meals were also always accompanied by starches, including both Western style bread and the rice to which Bỉnh had been accustomed in Vietnam. Wine was set out for every meal as liberally as water and each person could simply help himself. Bottles of condiments were also placed on trays on each table, which included oil, vinegar, salt, and pepper.[40] There was also fruit with each meal, most often oranges, which the mild Portuguese climate made available six months each year, and which were grown in the gardens of the Necessidades house where Bỉnh lived for the first decade of his residence in Lisbon. When oranges were served each person usually ate two or three, though as Bỉnh points out to his readers this was a variety for which one did not eat the peel (unlike the varieties or practice back in Tonkin). In fact, he compared the Portuguese oranges with the "bởi" fruit of China (probably akin to pomelos), noting that these are easier to peel and grew quite readily.[41] He reported that on feast and mass days various other kinds of fruits would also be set out.

Bỉnh wrote in detail of the numerous foods he was served, including descriptions of the ways in which they were prepared. He wrote of various kinds of bread, salads, boiled eggs, nuts, raisins, and figs. On special days there would even be a kind of dessert made from sweet rice boiled with milk, sugar and flour, and then sprinkled with cinnamon powder, perhaps something like a bread pudding.[42] He observed that Portugal did not have water buffalo, but rather cows, which were much larger than Vietnamese water buffalo. He went into considerable detail about the parts of the cow that were served, from tongue to leg to tripe. He even wrote about the fluctuating cost of beef, which he compared to the cost of beef back in Tonkin.[43] Bỉnh described the preparation processes of some of the dishes he encountered. In one section he provided detailed instructions for the bread-baking process, which he had never seen. Elsewhere he described the process by which fish were pan-fried, noting the dredging of the fish in flour, cooking it in hot oil, flipping it over twice to ensure that both sides were sufficiently browned. Again, this type of information was not to be found in the European travelogues of Portugal, but was included by Bỉnh for his readers as possible future residents in Portugal.

Although much of what he saw in Portuguese foodways was alien to Bỉnh, there was one habit that was already very familiar to him, namely the drinking of tea. In Vietnam, as in Portugal, tea was commonly imported from China and consumed as a regular part of meals or other social interactions. The one major cultural difference between these two practices was the way in which tea was prepared:

> The tea that the merchants brought back to the West was truly good tea, but they put sugar into both the good and the bad [teas], and then it would always smell and taste very sweet. . . . For this reason [the first few times] when I went out to visit people and they invited me to drink the tea I did not say anything but remained silent and drank the tea in the same way that they did. [Eventually] there came a time when I had to say something, and I asked them not to put sugar into my tea, which they regarded as very odd. Then I told them that in my country of Annam, and in the country of China, when one drinks tea one does not put sugar into so that one might know the scent of the tea. But in the West when merchants come back from the East, and people buy the tea . . . they [first] look at it and smell it, but immediately thereafter they put sugar into it to make it sweet. . . . From that time forward, when I would go to visit people, they would know not to put sugar into my teacup, because they now knew my preference.[44]

In this regard, Bỉnh was able to compare directly two very different tea-drinking practices. He laid out detailed descriptions of the European methods for preparing and serving tea, not merely as a point of information for his imagined audience, but also as a primer in what to expect when anyone, like him, arrived from Vietnam.

Conclusion

While Bỉnh wrote about European life for himself and for a future readership in Tonkin, the priests in his residence also urged him to write for the local public as well. This reflected their own curiosity about this unusual visitor in their midst, but certainly also the larger European interest in the exotic. In 1818, Bỉnh wrote of the pressure he felt when his fellow clerics urged him to write about his homeland:

> At that time the priests of the Order of Saint Philip asked me to write about all of these thing in the country of Annam over these past thirty years, in order that I might produce a book which could be sold, because everyone wanted to know of [such] unusual things.[45]

This episode reminds us that Bỉnh was aware of the European appetite for the exotic, an awareness he had himself exploited during the early years of his residence when he deliberately appeared at the royal court in elaborate Vietnamese regalia. For northern Europeans, Portugal was the exotic land about which they wrote. For the Portuguese, Bỉnh himself represented the exotic, and they hoped that he might produce an account of his homeland for Lisbonites, eager to learn more about distant Tonkin. But Bỉnh wrote that he was not inclined to do so. After being approached about the possibility of writing such an account, he concluded: " . . . I did not write this, because I did not want these people to know about the affairs in my country."[46] Bỉnh's answer is enigmatic, for it is not entirely clear what aspects of life in Tonkin he was trying to hide. Indeed, part of his mission was to describe to the Portuguese ruler the state of life in his homeland as part of his calculated appeal on behalf of the Portuguese Catholic communities. It is possible that he feared that anything he wrote about his homeland might be misconstrued by his political enemies and somehow used against him in his mission to secure further missionaries.

Whatever the reason for refusal to write such an account, it does suggest that Bỉnh did not see himself as a person whose role was to make the "east" somehow more legible to the "west." On the contrary, Bỉnh's writings were designed to demystify the "west" for those he had left behind in Tonkin. In doing so, Bỉnh left behind a distinctive reading of the "west" as represented by Portugal. As a different type of visitor to early nineteenth-century Lisbon, Philiphê Bỉnh offers a useful alternative way to think about that city and how it appeared to an outsider. This visitor from a distant land and a different culture brought with him a fresh lens on Portuguese society of this period, reminding us of the ways in which multiple perspectives help us to rethink the object of examination. Like the northern European visitors to Lisbon between the 1760s and the 1820s, Bỉnh was an outsider for whom Lisbon represented an exotic land. Bỉnh's perspective, however, was a substantially different one, a function both of his point of origin and of the nature of his encounter with Lisbon. For him Lisbon stood in for an exotic "west," a place far removed in most respects from the Tonkin he had left behind. Its physical appearance, its institutions, its foodways and customs were all novel to him, and he reflected his interest in these things in his writings.

Furthermore, Bỉnh distinguished himself by the length of his stay in Portugal, and by the fact that he spent much of his time there as a working Catholic priest, who immersed himself in the religious culture of Lisbon. Thus, rather than viewing Lisbon as a place of religious excesses and Catholic superstitions, he regarded it as a place of religious freedoms in which priests played crucially important roles for a devout population. At the religious level, Lisbon was both familiar and strange. It was familiar precisely because of this Catholic culture, for it was in this culture that Bỉnh himself had grown up, and to which he had dedicated his life. The language of Roman Catholicism was one in which he was fluent, and its rituals, imagery, and beliefs were his own. It was strange, however, for he came from a land and a time where such practices were barely tolerated, if at all. In Tonkin he was part of an oft-persecuted minority that was frequently forced to hide its rituals and beliefs from an often hostile state. In Portugal he found a Catholicism that was not merely tolerated, but publically embraced and directly supported by the state. Thus, his perspective on Catholicism in Lisbon was that of a man liberated from the hardships of life as the practitioner of an underground faith to the status of a member of the institutional mainstream. His vantage point was also that of a man who had come from a homeland of limited infrastructure, and highly attenuated financial circumstances. He found himself for nearly four decades in a land that, for all its difficulties, offered food in abundance, elaborately decorated houses of worship, and institutions ranging from hospitals and post offices to libraries and fire houses. It was a different world for Bỉnh, and yet he never lost his ability to report on what he saw in a matter-of-fact way, while also offering useful analogies for the audience he had left behind.

Notes

1. While the tradition of the "Grand Tour" had developed for members of the aristocracy and elite beginning in the middle of the seventeenth century, by the late eighteenth century the exploration of Europe and attendant published writings by travelers had expanded to include other segments of society, members of the middle class and professionals. Early in the nineteenth century, British soldiers joined this mix during their participation in the Iberian campaigns against Napoleon's armies, and some wrote about their

experiences. See, for example Jeremy Black, *Italy and the Grand Tour* (New Haven: Yale University Press, 2003), 1.

2. Philiphê Bỉnh, *Truyện Anam Đàng Ngoài, Quyển I* [Tales of Annam, the Outer Region, vol. 1], ms. Borgiana Tonchinese 1. Biblioteca Apostolica Vaticana. 1822: 576–7. [Hereafter TADN]
3. Although a small number of Asian visitors had been arriving in Europe during the early modern era—from China, Siam, and Japan, for example—few left any kind of record of their visits.
4. Richard Barnard Fisher, *A Sketch of the City of Lisbon and its environs; with some observations on the manners, disposition, and character of the Portuguese nation* (London: J. Ridgway, 1811), 1.
5. While a detailed examination of the origins of these sorts of stereotypes lies beyond the scope of this chapter, it seems clear that such conceptions were at the very least reinforced (if not initiated) by the relatively recent publication of Montesquieu's highly influential 1748 work *L'esprit des loi*, in which he discussed the putative link between climate and temperament. Baron de Montesquieu, *The Spirit of the Laws*, trans. Thomas Nugent (Kitchener, Ontario: Batoche Books, 2001), 246–60.
6. Gavin Daly, "A Dirty, Indolent, Priest-Ridden City: British Soldiers in Lisbon during the Peninsular War, 1808–1813," *History* 94, no. 316 (2009): 467, 477.
7. Ibid., 477.
8. Among the few that were positive were James Cavanah Murphy, *A General View of the State of Portugal; containing a topographical description thereof* (London: Cadell and Davies, 1798) and Fisher, *A Sketch of the City*.
9. Francis Collins, *Voyages to Portugal, Spain, Sicily, Malta, Asia Minor, Egypt, &c. from 1796 to 1801: With an Historical Sketch, and Occasional Reflections* (London: Richard Phillips, 1809), 25–6.
10. Charles François Du Périer Dumouriez, *État présent du royaume de Portugal, en l'année MDCCLXVI*] (Lausanne: François Grasset & Comp, 1775), 174.
11. Ibid., 32.
12. *The Lisbon guide; containing directions to invalids who visit Lisbon; with a description of the city, and tables of the coin, weights, and measures of Portugal* (London: Printed for J. Johnson by J. Crowder, 1800), 26.
13. Cited in Daly, "A Dirty, Indolent, Priest-Ridden City," 461–82.
14. TADN, 562–3.
15. Ibid., 572–3.
16. Philiphê Bỉnh, *Sách Sổ Sang Chép Các Việc* [Notebook that Records and Transmits All Matters], ms. Borgiana Tonchinese 3. Biblioteca Apostolica Vaticana, 1822–32: 415–6. [Hereafter *Sach So*]
17. *Sach So*, 130ff; *TADN*, 721ff.
18. Examples of travel accounts that began as letters include Robert Southey's *Letters Written During a Short Residence* (1799) and Marianne Baillie's *Lisbon in the Years 1821, 1822, and 1823* (1825).

19. *Sach So*, 599.
20. Bỉnh routinely used the formulation "phương tây," a terminology and concept that was introduced by European missionary priests over the course of the seventeenth and eighteenth centuries.
21. If anything, the reverse would have been true for Hanoi lies at the 16th parallel and Lisbon the 39th.
22. Philiphê Bỉnh, *Nhật Trình Kim Thư Khất Chính Chúa Giáo* [Daily Records, Current Letters (Pertaining to) the request for a Primary Bishop], ms. Borgiana Tonchinese 7. Biblioteca Apostolica Vaticana, 1796–1826: 45; emphasis added. [Hereafter *Nhat Trinh*]
23. The particular irony of this comparison is that nearly a century and a half later, in the 1940s, Vietnamese historians writing about Quang Trung would compare him to Napoleon, rather than the other way around. Writing in 1940, Phan Trần Chúc referred to Quang Trung as "the Napoleon of Việt Nam." This was of course a radically altered context: literate Vietnamese would have been fully aware of the Napoleonic reference as a result of their French-inflected education. Furthermore, of course, Bỉnh had been a contemporary of Napoleon, who had been dead for 120 years by the time Chúc was writing. See Phan Trần Chúc, *Vua Quang Trung Nguyễn Huệ (Lịch Sử)* [1940], Sài Gòn: Chí Ký Xuất Bản, 1957 reprint, 1.
24. Ibid., 52.
25. Fisher's 1811 account is also quite positive toward the clergy, in part because he was housed at the Convent of Saint Vincente. There he had very positive interactions with the resident Augustinians who suitably impressed him. Fisher, *A Sketch of the City*, 25.
26. *Sach So,* n.p. (preface).
27. Bỉnh's account of his first audience with the ruler is taken from *Sach So*, 164–7; *TADN*, 570–3, and *Nhat Trinh*, 9–10.
28. *Sach So,* 167–8.
29. *TADN*, 718. The entire description of the man's death and the rituals surrounding it are found in pp. 714–18.
30. *Sach So*, 121.
31. On Thăng Long as a capital, see William Logan, *Hanoi: Biography of a City* (Seattle: University of Washington Press, 2000).
32. *Sach So*, 455–8.
33. The *crusado* was a coin commonly used in eighteenth-century Portugal.
34. *Sach So*, 458–60.
35. *Sach So*, 451ff.
36. *Sach So*, 153–4.
37. While Bỉnh and his companions were generally cared for at the Order houses where they lived, hospitals were not entirely an abstraction for him. One of his co-religionists, Brother Liễn had been left behind in Macao in 1796, and when he fell ill in 1800 he was taken to one of the religious hospitals in

Macao, where he received exemplary care, though it placed a severe financial burden on the dwindling financial resources of the ex-Jesuits awaiting Bỉnh in Macao. *TADN*, 706–7.

38. Fisher, *A Sketch of the City*, 27–8.
39. *Sach So*, 564.
40. Ibid., 551–2.
41. Ibid., 135–6.
42. Ibid., 552–3.
43. Ibid., 554–5.
44. Ibid., 552–3.
45. *TADN*, 597.
46. Ibid.

CHAPTER 2

Collecting Malay Heritage: Scholarly Societies and Imperial Policy in British Malaya in the Early Twentieth Century

Matthew J. Schauer

In the late nineteenth century, the imperial administration in British Malaya sought to expand their influence in the less populated and more isolated areas of the Malay Peninsula. British administrators initially gathered their knowledge of indigenous culture and languages by informally interviewing residents and receiving non-standard training from local teachers.[1] As a result of the colony's growing economy and this intensifying Western presence, members of the colonial government perceived there to be an increased need for codified cultural and historical knowledge concerning the peoples of the region. This knowledge, which was pursued in the form of amateur scholarly societies, was to be used to aid the expansion of the colony by facilitating trade and daily interactions, and also to provide a more culturally sensitive form of empire. As Arnout H.C. van der Meer examines in his chapter on the power and complexity of the system of courtly respect and deference (*hormat*) in Dutch-controlled Java, social interactions were often imbued with great political, social, and political weight. In order to educate the civil servants and expatriates living in British Malaya, scholars created guides to the ethnology, history, social, and cultural practices of the

Malays. This informal education aimed to help the British to avoid cultural misunderstandings, facilitate increased cooperation, and help convey to the indigenous populations of British Malaya the theoretical benevolence and benefits of British imperial control.

During the late nineteenth and early twentieth centuries, European scholarly societies began to increase in popularity in colonial Southeast Asia. These intellectual clubs were often tied to sister societies in other colonies and to parent societies in the metropole. This scholarly network allowed for the exchange of material pertaining to the culture and history of indigenous people across imperial political divides. Many of the members of these societies were civil servants and administrators, who were also amateur scholars. They used these societies as a way to bolster their own academic reputation, gain information that helped to inform their own perceptions of the indigenous people they attempted to control, and to provide an insight into their own form of imperial governance.

These societies were established in colonial holdings such as French Indochina, British Malaya, and the Netherlands East Indies. They shared common goals as well as members and information. These colonial intellectual clubs aimed to collect, preserve, and promulgate cultural, historical, and archaeological information related to the indigenous populations in their respective colonies.[2] By preserving these cultural traditions from the perceived threat of increasing modernity and cultural incursions from outside the colony, these societies saw themselves as custodians of ethnological knowledge. European attempts to protect indigenous cultural heritage from degeneration served the imperial mission as a propagandistic exercise of imperial altruism, and afforded administrators the opportunity to appropriate or alter the practices and records of indigenous cultural heritage to serve their own purposes. An example of this process in action in British Malaya was the inclusion of Malay traditional literature in government textbooks as a way to improve Malay literacy and expand government education programs in rural portions of the Peninsula in the early twentieth century.

The information collected and published under the auspices of these intellectual societies was added to the contemporary corpus of Western scholarly knowledge concerning specific localities and groups of indigenous people. This corpus of knowledge was used subsequently to facilitate and influence academic characterizations of indigenous populations and inform imperial governmental policies. These policies included the implementation of educational initiatives that were meant to increase the economic productivity of rural Malays, to manage social mobility through the institution of vocational programs, and improve public health in the colony. These educational programs were part of a larger initiative to modernize the colony, solidify ties between the Malays and the British government, reinforce the role of Malays as a "privileged race," and protect them from the "aggressive" and "politically mature" Chinese.[3]

This scholarly knowledge was disseminated primarily through published journals and volumes, which were purchased by libraries and collections in both Europe and North America, and often exchanged for the publications of other local scholarly societies in Southeast Asia. These publications served as a primary source of academic information pertaining to the specific colony for researchers in other areas of the globe. The academic writings in these journals often contained pro-imperial rhetoric, but were in general much more focused on an elite audience and less overtly propagandistic than the pro-empire colonial exhibitions that were assembled in Europe in the early twentieth century. These exhibitions were rife with characterizations of the indigenous populations of Southeast Asia as exotic and inferior, and also served as a demonstration of the competitive nation of global imperialism, as has been examined by the historians Frances Gouda and Marieke Bloembergen. Although these journals aimed at a far smaller audience than the colonial exhibitions, the work of these academic societies served as an influential, albeit still often racialized and exoticized, "on-the-ground" source of imperial knowledge for scholars and readers in the metropole.[4]

In addition to the information that was sent out of the colony through publications and exchanges, these societies often possessed museums, libraries, and archives in which they preserved artifacts, manuscripts, and published volumes within the colonies. For example, the L'Ecole française d'Extrême-Orient had a large library in Hanoi specializing in collecting publications and manuscripts relating to the region, as well as museums in Hanoi, Saigon, and Phnom Penh.[5] The Royal Batavian Society of Arts and Sciences and the Straits Branch of the Royal Asiatic Society had similar libraries and museums. These institutions served as both an archive to aid researchers and a protective repository of the artifacts and manuscripts that were seen as being "threatened" by the inability of the indigenous populations to preserve them. In many cases, these societies were literally purchasing and preserving the history of these populations.

The growth of these colonial scholarly societies was in many ways a reaffirmation of the Victorian sensibilities that influenced the increase in popularity of amateur historical research, antiquarianism, and archaeology in mid-nineteenth century Great Britain. According to historian Philippa

Levine, nineteenth-century Britons became interested in constructing historical narratives for their nation to reinforce "a heritage legitimized by the contemporary."[6] When these ideas were exported to the colonial setting of British Malaya, the amateur scholars' focus on "British" heritage shifted to a vague and malleable conception of "Malay heritage." As in Britain, these amateur scholars' goals were to collect and preserve knowledge, history, and culture, but in the colony, this knowledge was used to reinforce a common identity embedded in a conception of British imperial dominance. The British hoped to utilize this knowledge not to only train civil servants, but to aid governance through the appropriation, reinterpretation, and reinforcement of selected Malay cultural traditions. This use of indigenous cultural heritage within the structures of imperial control was in some ways similar to the methods used by the British in India that have been examined by Bernard Cohn and Nicholas Dirks.[7] The ethnological work of these civil servant scholars was also seen as a reservoir of information as the British embarked on a campaign to increase the modernization and efficiency of the colony during the early twentieth century.

This chapter will specifically examine two colonial scholarly societies, the Royal Batavian Society of Arts and Sciences (*Koninklijk Bataviaasch Genootschap van Kunsten en Wetenschapen*) and the Straits Branch of the Royal Asiatic Society (SBRAS), as being demonstrative of these trends focusing on the collection and preservation of indigenous culture knowledge in Southeast Asia. These Societies also displayed the type of interaction and cooperation that was found routinely between members of these colonial intellectual societies, even though they resided in competing colonial entities.[8] The chapter will then analyze British colonial administrator and ethnologist R.J. Wilkinson's *Papers on Malay Studies* project, which was compiled as a source of scholarly knowledge for the average reader, and as a tool to be used to educate imperial civil servants.

The *Papers on Malay Studies* project serves as an example of the perceived utility of "Malay heritage" as a tool of information and imperial governance. Wilkinson's work on the project also conveys an insight into a broader British conception of Malay traditions and history as a potential unifying cultural base. Wilkinson saw the bedrock of Malay traditions as potentially providing the political and social stability necessary to transform British Malaya into a more modern and profitable colony. Ultimately Wilkinson hoped to use his knowledge of Malay culture and history to shape Malay traditions to fit within the cultural and economic framework of modern imperialism.

A Community of Scholars: The Straits Branch of the Royal Asiatic Society and the Royal Batavian Society of Arts and Sciences

The Straits Branch of the Royal Asiatic Society was part of a network of scholarly research on science, history, and the humanities that extended from Western Europe to a number of different colonial centers. The Society was originally founded by a group of high-ranking colonial administrators and magistrates in Singapore in 1877. It was affiliated a year later with the prestigious Royal Asiatic Society in Calcutta founded by William Jones in 1784. A number of other branches of the Asiatic Society were also established throughout Asia in the nineteenth century: the Bombay branch in 1824, the Ceylon branch in 1845, and the Japan branch in 1872. The first major society in Southeast Asia was the Dutch Royal Batavian Society of Arts and Sciences in Batavia (Jakarta), which was founded in 1778 and revitalized by Stamford Raffles during the British Occupation of Java from 1811 to 1816. These Societies had very cordial relationships. In 1929, the Malayan Branch of the Royal Asiatic Society even presented a bust of Stamford Raffles to the Batavian Society as a "token of friendship [...] and esteem."[9]

These local colonial intellectual societies had similar missions and membership, and also shared some members directly. The SBRAS was created as a result of the increasing British economic and political presence in the Malay Peninsula after the 1874 Treaty of Pangkor. With this expansion of influence, the British had an increased need for information pertaining to the people, history, botany, and geography of the Peninsula.[10] Archdeacon G.F. Hose wrote in the inaugural address of the society that:

> A careful study of the religious opinions and practices of the people would not be interesting only, but directly useful ... [demonstrating to missionaries] the real errors to be eradicated and the real defects in faith and morals that have to be supplied, and useful to the governing class too, as discussing the true character and nature of the people to be governed.[11]

The Royal Batavian Society had similar goals nearly one hundred years earlier:

> The Genootschap [Society] ... will attempt to stimulate all arts and sciences and will eagerly receive anything which deals with natural history, antiquities, customs, and mores of the peoples. However, its principle goal is to make such matters the subject of its investigations

> which can be beneficial to the agricultural, trade, and particular welfare of these settlements.[12]

These missions coincided with the goals of colonial civil servants and administrators, as well as expatriate businessmen, merchants, and entrepreneurs.

At first, the work of the Royal Batavian Society was primarily focused on the natural sciences. Stamford Raffles' influence and his seminal studies of Java helped to shift the academic focus of the Society. After Raffles, members' works trended more towards the study of linguistics and antiquities, such as the analysis of ancient Javanese texts.[13] In conjunction with these linguistic studies came a trend of the preservation and translation of native texts, in order to compile translated or at least transcribed Malay myths and history. These ideas of preservation were expanded to the preservation of ancient ruins on Java, such as Borobudur, and ultimately included the recording of native practices such as farming and arts and crafts. In the latter half of the nineteenth century and early twentieth century, the Batavian Society began to trend towards ethnology in conjunction with the Dutch government's continuing military expeditions to Aceh and Bali, as well as through the new policies of "Ethical" imperialism. These broad policies, which were formally instituted from 1907 to 1927 are covered in a chapter in this volume by Arnout van der Meer. The cultural policies of "Ethical imperialism" hoped to preserve ancient culture and archaeological sites as representative of a sense of Javanese Malay ethnic unity. This sense of Malay unity, as supported by the government, was also manufactured in British Malaya through the use of traditional Malay literature and culture in government schools.

The SBRAS like the Royal Batavian Society published the work of its members in a variety of forms. Papers that were read at the Society's lectures and meetings were often published in the Society's *Journal*, along with changes to the by-laws, membership rolls, and meeting minutes. The Royal Batavian Society published papers in its own *Verhandelingen* (the Society's proceedings), its minutes in separate volumes entitled *Notulen*, and a *Tijdschrift* that was published typically every year. Both societies also funded and published monographs on a variety of subjects, as well as reprints and translations of historic texts or inscriptions. The SBRAS's academic domain was a bit more clearly demarcated than that of the Royal Batavian Society, in that it emphasized three major topical categories of academic enquiry:

> Natural History (Fauna, Flora, Ethnology, Anthropology, Geology, and Meteorology), Malay Studies (Malay language, classics, customs,

folklore, artifacts etc.) and Malayan History (history of modern day Malaysia and Singapore). [14]

This wide variety of topics included papers by civil servants of many different areas, many of them eventually garnered an academic career in some capacity. Notable members were Malay historian/ethnologists R.J. Wilkinson, Richard Winstedt, and C.O. Blagden, naturalist and museum curator Robert Shelford, and archaeologist/ethnologist Tom Harrisson. In addition to Stamford Raffles, the RBS's membership rolls included well-known Dutch governmental figures/scholars such as B.J.O Schrieke, G.A. Wilken, A.W. Nieuwenhuis, and C. Snouck Hurgronje.

Membership was initially relatively small in the SBRAS, but it did contain a number of powerful colonial administrators and political figures such as Frank Swettenham and W.E. Maxwell, and it eventually grew to 150 members during its founding year of 1877. It also welcomed a number of members of the Sultan's families, local elites, and businessmen on its early membership rolls. The Royal Batavian Society drew members from similar social classes: colonial administrators, wealthy merchants, and planters. Its first five Indonesian members joined in 1860, but the society generally restricted members to the Indonesian royal elite until the 1930s when nearly 10 per cent of the Royal Batavian Society's members were of native descent.[15] In the 1930s and 1940s the Society's museums and journals became popular due to the rise in Indonesian nationalism, but the Society eventually folded and was integrated within the auspices of the Indonesian National Museum (*Museum Nasional*). The SBRAS was renamed the Malaysian Branch of the Royal Asiatic Society and continues to exist today. As of 1995, the Society had nearly a thousand members.[16]

At the end of the nineteenth century, the contents of the publications of the Royal Batavian Society of Arts and Sciences (Bataviaasch Genootschap van Kunsten en Wetenschappen) and the SBRAS reflected a greater push by local intellectuals towards the collection, protection, and analysis of cultural and historical knowledge relating to the Malays. The *Transactions of the Royal Batavian Society* or the *Verhandelingen* was published from 1779 to 1950 in 79 volumes.[17] Until 1860, the vast majority of the articles published in the *Verhandelingen* were related to the natural sciences, including articles covering ichthyology, botany, zoology, and geology. Of the articles that did not cover the natural sciences, 10 were on anthropology and ethnology, 25 were travel narratives, and 20 covered local history. Out of the 189 articles published before 1860, only 22 of them covered folklore, literature, archaeology, and linguistics and only 3 specifically examined religion.[18]

From 1860 to 1889, the natural sciences were completely absent from the *Verhandelingen* with only 32 articles in total published on these topics. The majority of these essays covered literature and folklore, local history, or were travel narratives. In 1890, a major shift occurred that would continue to the end of the journal's publication run in 1950. From 1890 onwards, 77 of the 99 articles published were related to languages, folklore, local literature, or archaeology, and antiquities. Previously, these articles would likely have been published in the Society's *Tijdschrift*, but these fields had such an increase in popularity that they dominated the bulk of the *Verhandelingen*'s pages. The majority of the remaining articles covered history, anthropology, sociology, and ethnology. There is an overlap as some of the articles examining mythology and native literature also connect with historical ideas.[19] Articles included those covering the translation or study of specific inscriptions or manuscripts, and those examining archaeological sites and artifacts. For example, K.F. Holle published a study of Kawi records that were inscribed and copied on copper plates, which dealt with land gifts, taxation, and religion from 856 and 1369 AD, and J. Ph. Vogel analyzed Borobudur in his article that contextualized reliefs in the temple using different Hindu myths.[20] Both of these projects tapped into the legacy of Stamford Raffles, who studied Borobudur extensively and also spent time examining Kawi inscriptions in copper plates.[21] There were also attempts to give the reader a more comprehensive view of local languages such as S.J. Esser's article on the dialects of Javanese spoken in Banjumas, Purbolinggo, and Purwokerto; or local beliefs, such as an article by W.L. Steinhart on religious beliefs and chants of the peoples of the island of Nias.[22]

This shift from a focus on the natural sciences to ethnography and archaeology was reflective of the gradual solidification of anthropology as an emerging academic discipline apart from the natural sciences in Europe in the late nineteenth century. For example, English amateur ethnologists began using "guides" for collecting information and observations during their travels in the first half of the nineteenth century, similar to the ways that they would have collected and catalogued exotic flora and fauna. The British Association for the Advancement of Science published a guide to help travelers organize their information using a questionnaire in 1841. The best known of these guides, *Notes and Queries on Anthropology*, was first published in 1874 and reissued several times, the last being in 1951.[23] *Notes and Queries* guided the traveler in the collection of both physical and cultural data, and included sample questions that the traveler should ask "natives," rulers for measuring subjects, and guides to skin color. This shift from the natural sciences to ethnology was in many ways a very contentious process, and was in part pushed by a perceived need for a cultural data concerning the indigenous peoples of newly conquered colonies.

In nineteenth-century France, the Société d'ethnographie specialized in studying different races using ideas concerning the "philosophy of human history" including Orientalism, linguistic ideas, and literary examination.[24] Its rival society, the Société d'anthropologie, used materialist and positivist methods for data collection, anthropometry, and biology and had a large number of physicians on its membership rolls.[25] It was not until the early twentieth century that within French intellectual circles ethnology began to be commonly used in its more modern-day definition, highlighted cultural differences, and combined with fieldwork and the production of ethnography.[26]

French scholars began to eschew earlier forms of physical anthropology based in the natural sciences, as the creation of ethnographies began to be perceived as a much more useful enterprise for gaining an understanding of the indigenous populations of France's colonial holdings in Asia and Africa.[27] A similar phenomenon occurred in the Netherlands Indies, particularly during the "Ethical Policy" era (c. 1901–27). During this period, "Indologists" began to be more extensively employed by the colonial government as both imperial administrators and advisors, as part of their initiatives to push for a more culturally sensitive and less exploitive form of imperial governance. In British Malaya in the early twentieth century, the use of ethnology to bring about a more benevolent form of governance manifested itself through the previously described attempts to educate civil servants, and the implementation of Wilkinson's vernacular education policies. Malays were taught a British imperial version of their own language, history, and handicraft skills as a way to foster cultural rebirth and greater economic independence outside of the dominant rubber trade.

In the British Empire, anthropology still remained primarily the purview of amateurs for the majority of the late nineteenth and early twentieth centuries.[28] With the exception of their colonies in West Africa, British colonial governments did not begin to widely employ professional anthropologists until the years before the Second World War.[29] Even though the government was generally not the primary source of funding, amateur ethnological information, collected by administrators in the field, and published in intellectual societies such as the SBRAS, was a tool utilized by colonial civil servants.

Much like the *Verhandelingen,* the *Journal of the Straits Branch of the Royal Asiatic Society* (JSBRAS), first published in 1878, tended to publish work that specialized on the collection and translation of ancient documents, artifacts, and folklore. The *Journal* also included a variety of articles on the natural sciences, such as a large number of submissions by the prolific botanist H.N. Ridley on entomology, biology, and botany, which included such titles as "The Bird Dropping Spider in Johor," "An Insectivorous Squirrel," and an ongoing series titled "New and Rare Malayan Plants."[30] In the early twentieth century the *Journal* had a much more pronounced focus on local beliefs, customs, and ethnology. Much of this work was focused on linking the customs and beliefs of the present-day Malay people to ancient traditions and a literary past, as will be examined in greater depth in later sections in this chapter. For example, Hans Overbeck (1842–1942), a German merchant and expert on Malay languages and culture who would be imprisoned during both World Wars by the British and Dutch, published a three-part series from 1924 to 1925 entitled "Malay Customs and Beliefs as Recorded in Malay Literature and Folklore."[31] Scholars also compiled and reevaluated ancient and recent histories of the Peninsula, such as C.O. Blagden's work on the *Sejarah Melayu* or *Malay Annals*, a sixteenth-century romanticized literary history of Malacca Sultanate.[32]

The journals of the Straits Branch of the Royal Asiatic Society and the Royal Batavian Society of Arts and Sciences were widely distributed around the world. In 1877, the Royal Batavian Society had academic connections with 158 sister organizations, in countries such as their fatherland of the Netherlands, the United States, Egypt, Denmark, Portugal, Japan, Australia, Denmark, and Norway, including the Straits Branch of the Royal Asiatic Society.[33] In 1923, The SBRAS recorded exchanges of printed materials with 83 institutions and societies in 22 countries in Europe, Asia, and the Americas, including the Royal Batavian Society and several in the Dutch East Indies. The Society also received donations from 26 private collectors and institutions such as the Ministry of Public Works in Cairo, The University of Montana in Missoula, the Ornithological Society of Japan, and civil servant Richard Olaf Winstedt.[34] Richard Winstedt and Wilkinson's *A History of Perak*, was also given as an "exchange" to the L'Ecole française d'Extrême-Orient in 1933 for its library.[35] These exchanges allowed these societies to create libraries as colonial reservoirs of global scholarly knowledge, as well as archives of indigenous artifacts and ancient manuscripts.[36]

The members of each Society tended to be interested in their respective colonies. The British, more often than the Dutch, crossed imperial boundaries to do their research, with British scholars studying Dutch-controlled areas of Sumatra and Kalimantan. This is likely due to the increase in the focus of Dutch scholars on specific areas of indigenous resistance in the Indies. For example, the Dutch undertook military campaigns in Aceh from 1873 to 1904 and completed a decisive and brutal campaign against the kingdoms in southern Bali in 1906. During the same period, the British were able to generally maintain their system of indirect rule, and eliminate any large-scale radical political movements in the Malaya.

These scholars in the Straits Branch of the Royal Asiatic Society and the Royal Batavian Society did share a common corpus of literature from which to draw analyses, such as the *Sejarah Melayu*, a common inspirational founder in the person of Stamford Raffles, and similar scholarly goals. Collaborative efforts were frequent and took the form of members publishing in the other Society's journal, scholars participating in joint projects (such as the *Malay Subjects* project which will be discussed in the later section), and cooperative publishing through presses such as E.J. Brill of Leiden. For instance, Richard Winstedt published an outline of a paper on "The Early History of Singapore, Johore, and Malacca" in the *Journal of the Straits Branch of the Royal Asiatic Society* on behalf of Dutch ethnologist G.P. Rouffaer in 1922.[37] Winstedt also published his own article on a version of the *Ramayana* found in Patani, an ancient Malay kingdom, in the Royal Batavian Society's *Feestbundel* in 1929.

Leiden-based publishing house E.J. Brill helped to facilitate this intellectual exchange by publishing and promulgating a large number of both Malay- and Javanese-language books, as well as the most important works of Dutch-language scholarship on the Indies and Malaya. Brill became known worldwide as one of the finest publishers of "Oriental printed editions," winning gold medals at the World Exhibition in Vienna in 1873 and the Paris World Exhibition of 1878, and established itself in the field of ethnology by publishing the works of Dutch scholar Snouck Hurgronje, including his seminal books on his visit to Mecca (1888) and the peoples of Aceh (1906).[38]

R.J. Wilkinson came into contact with E.J. Brill after he wrote an index and helped translate Hurgronje's two-volume work on Aceh. When he began his project to compile pamphlets into volumes to serve as a handbook for the general reader, he began by publishing his first volume *Malay Beliefs* with E.J. Brill in 1906. These two groups of active scholars, and the history of collaboration between them, would help set the stage for R.J. Wilkinson's *Malay Subjects* project, which hoped to be a comprehensive regional compendium on Malay culture and history. Ultimately G.A. Wilken, who studied matrilineal descent, was the only Dutch scholar to have his work published in the volumes, but the pamphlets do include numerous citations of the work of German and Dutch scholars. The *Malay Subjects* project was the product of the desire to harness the wide-ranging expertise that could be found among the amateur scholars of the colonies, particularly in the civil service.

R.J. Wilkinson and the *Malay Subjects* Project

Richard James Wilkinson (1867–1941), like many of his contemporaries, did not set out from Cambridge with the intention to serve in Malaya. He ended up joining the Straits Settlement Civil Service after being excluded from the Indian Civil Service for failing his mandatory riding exam.[39] He showed a great aptitude for languages and passed proficiency exams in the Malay and Hokkien Chinese languages.[40] William Maxwell, the secretary of the Straits Settlement, persuaded Wilkinson to begin work on a comprehensive Malay-English dictionary project. It is during his work on the dictionary, that he met and began to collaborate with Walter Skeat.[41] The dictionary would be published in 1901 and served as an extremely influential work of scholarship, in that it revolutionized the Malay language and alphabet, and made both Malay culture and the study of it more accessible to the English-speaking world. It is from this precedent that Wilkinson began to envision a greater cohesion between the Malay and English worlds. This goal of greater cultural connections between the British and Malay would manifest itself in his educational policies and scholarship.

Wilkinson's most significant work was a compendium of ethnological and historical information about the Malay. This compendium, titled the *Papers on Malay Subjects*, was in many ways a response to a call for the gathering and preservation of knowledge relating to the Malay, so that the imperial administration had a reservoir of knowledge that could inform their policies. This project also tapped into the scholarly trends arising from local amateur intellectual societies, as it attempted to provide a broad base of knowledge for the general reader and focused on ethnology and history as opposed to the natural sciences.

There had been calls by earlier scholars for a comprehensive work on Malay culture, which could be utilized by the imperial government. For example, in the introduction to Walter Skeat's work *Malay Magic*, fellow amateur ethnologist/ civil servant C.O. Blagden pointed to the utility of this sort of knowledge, which might seem superfluous to the "practical men," by harkening back to the events of 1857 in India: "If, for instance, in 1857, certain persons, whose concern it was, had paid more attention to the facts of this kind, possibly the Indian Mutiny could have been prevented, and probably it might have been foreseen."[42] He also stated the general importance of having a reservoir of knowledge as a tool of governance by declaring that "there can be no doubt that an understanding of the ideas and modes of thought of an alien people in a relatively low stage of civilisation facilitates very considerably the task of governing them."[43]

Walter Skeat also pleaded to the colonial government to enact a "thorough survey of the Peninsula as a whole, from the point of view both of geographical and ethnological science and of industrial and economic development."[44] He stated that unlike in the Netherlands Indies, British India, and the American-controlled Philippines, the government in British Malaya had avoided undertaking anything in the way of a large-scale government-sponsored program focused on "intimately studying and carefully considering the peculiarities of the alien and less civilized races committed to their care."[45] Aside from aiding global scholarship on the region, Skeat believed that "A more intimate study of the people of the country and their habits of life and thought is urgently required in order to avoid the growing danger of estrangement and want of sympathy between the rulers and the ruled." Skeat saw the colonial government's culturally insensitive methods as hindering cooperation between the government and the indigenous people:

> A dangerous tendency to elaborate and Europeanise administrative and judicial machinery … to lose touch with native ideas and customs, to push the native gently but firmly aside, and to impose upon him all manner of well-meant but complicated regulations, which he cannot in the least understand, and which often run counter to his social and religious principles.[46]

This theme of the utility of creating a comprehensive collection of knowledge, in order to lead to a more culturally specific and sensitive forms of governance and education, was of primary importance to R.J. Wilkinson and his work on the *Papers on Malay Subjects* project.

The *Papers on Malay Subjects* project grew out of the specific recommendations of E.W. Birch, the resident of Perak, and D.G. Campbell, the Resident of Negri Sembilan, who saw the need for a comprehensive compendium of cultural and historical knowledge in order to allow residents and expatriates to cultivate greater cultural sensitivity. E.W. Birch, the

Resident of Perak from 1904 to 1911, was one of the members of the civil service at the forefront of what civil servant C.W. Harrison would refer to as the "pro-Malay campaign."[47] This campaign was a push towards moving away from the pure economic exploitation of the colony and its people, by integrating the Malays more fully into the colonial economy and its benefits, and protecting and preserving Malay culture.[48] As a response to these ideas, the colonial administration, led by Birch, proposed to show support for the Malays by compiling a handbook on Malay history, law, and customs, in order to ensure that the members of the civil service demonstrated a greater sympathy towards Malay cultural institutions as a way to gain their trust.[49]

The hope was that this newfound sensitivity would also then demonstrate to the Malay people that the colonial government supported them culturally, politically, and economically. One focus was preventing the innumerable errors in protocol that were interpreted as rudeness by the Malays, and led the Malays to immediately cultivate a sense of mistrust towards the British. This was particularly a problem when civil servants had transferred from another colony.[50] Birch wrote:

> It is generally admitted that there is no shyer, prouder, more sensitive race than the Malays. They do not lightly accord their confidence to officers whom they do not know, who are moreover actually ignorant of traditions which are a commonplace amongst the people whose interests they try to serve. The Malays are not pushful persons like the Chinese, they are not parasites on the white man like the Indians in these States, so they are apt to go unheard. But education is spreading amongst them, and their needs will be more insistently put forward soon.[51]

Civil servants in Malaya had also demonstrated a lack of proficiency when it came to a variety of subjects relating to Malay culture and daily life, making it particularly difficult for them to understand the Malays' "needs." There had been poor performances by cadets on the Civil Service exam in 1904, particularly in the fields of "elementary rules of law as to marriage, divorce, and intestate succession … land tenure and succession among the Menangkabau Malays … Malay Life and Customs … Malay Industries."[52] The preexisting textbooks, of which Walter Skeat's *Malay Magic* was the recommended reading on "Malay Life and Customs," were perceived to be inadequate.[53]

E.W. Birch hoped to connect this project to educate the civil service to a larger policy of inculcating the British in Malaya with a greater sensitivity to Malay customs, and he wrote:

> It is very desirable that more open recognition should be accorded to Malay sentiment and susceptibility on this subject [the governmental support of Malay culture] than is afforded at present. There can be no better way of ensuring this than to cause the rising generation of officers to be instructed in such matters.[54]

After the Council of Residents meeting in December 1906, it was decided that Birch's recommendation that the project be handed over to a single expert within the civil service, and Campbell's proposal that they utilize "several gentlemen in collaboration, each contributing the knowledge he has acquired during a lengthened period of residence amongst the community about whom he writes" be combined. Also, one single editor was to be appointed to compile essays by specific local experts.[55]

R.J. Wilkinson, who was seconded to be director of the project, saw that the model of several authors had its limitations in terms of lacking a "unity of design," but hoped to overcome this by keeping the collection organized topically.[56] Wilkinson hoped to compile "this little series of books" so that they would be "written for beginners," but also contain reference materials in the form of "concise notes and appendices suitable for the more advanced student to refer to."[57] The model for this plan would be Wilkinson's pamphlet *Malay Beliefs* published in 1906. *Malay Beliefs* examines a number of different topics generally relating to "Malay Muhammadanism" and pre-Islamic religion and culture, including Malay science, origin myths, and concepts of the soul and magic.[58]

Wilkinson envisioned *Malay Beliefs* as the first pamphlet in the series that would become the *Papers on Malay Subjects* project. Of his goals for *Malay Beliefs*, Wilkinson wrote:

> This little book is intended to help Civil Service Cadets studying for that part of their examination which deals with the Malay people.... The book was originally prepared as a section or sub-division of a larger work on 'the Peninsular Malays'; but owing to the likelihood of delay.... I have decided to publish each section as a pamphlet complete in itself. The other pamphlets in the series will deal with Malay Literature, Malay Life and Customs, Malay Government and Law, Malay History, and Malay Industries. Each little book is designed for beginners only and is of an elementary or introductory character.[59]

These potential pamphlet titles would ultimately form the categories used in the first series of the *Papers on Malay Subjects* project, which would be compiled between 1907 and 1910.

The *Papers on Malay Subjects* project is significant in that it reflects global imperial intellectual trends in ethnology and a common trans-imperial project to collect and codify information about indigenous populations within a Western scholarly framework. The subsequent publication of the volume was widely promulgated, and it remains in print today. *Paper on Malay Subjects* served as one of the most important texts for providing background on these various topics not only to members of the British civil service in Malaya, but also to scholars and readers worldwide. This project also demonstrates the prevailing preoccupation not only with collecting ethnological information, but also "preserving" this knowledge from the cultural onslaught of forces such as global religious movements and Westernization. Wilkinson put these ideas into practice during his tenure as the Inspector of Schools from 1898 to 1900 in the Straits Settlements, 1903 to 1906 in the Federated Malay States, and later as governor of the Straits Settlements in 1911 and 1914. The final section of the chapter will examine how Wilkinson's ideas concerning imperial policy in British Malaya were influenced by his desire to protect and revitalize Malay culture and traditions.

Wilkinson's Ideas Concerning the Preservation of Malay Culture and Empire

Wilkinson stressed that, in order to rule effectively, the British government needed to contextualize its laws with the beliefs of both Islam and pre-Islamic religious practices, and take into account the rippling cultural effects of their decisions. Wilkinson perceived Malay culture to be an extremely complex mixture of religious syncretism, superstition, and elaborate protocol that was influenced by an individual's ancestry, profession, and social class. European scholars perceived Malay culture to be fluid and constantly adapting to local influences, as it was formed out of numerous religious and cultural legacies. This sense of Malay cultural malleability fit in well with Wilkinson and Birch's conception of "culturally sensitive" empire, one that would allow the British administration to rule within a framework of aspects of Malay culture. Wilkinson's concept of national "Malay character" was generally rooted in rich cultural traditions, but he predicted the eventual decline of the Malays due to the cultural encroachment of the British and the growth of the influence of orthodox Pan-Islamic movements.

Wilkinson viewed Islam, pre-Islamic religious beliefs concerning magic and superstition, and systems of politeness and protocol as the building blocks of Malay culture. He supported Dutch scholar C. Snouck Hurgronje's ideas that Islamic fundamentalism was the natural enemy of progress for the Malay. Wilkinson saw Pan-Islamism as a threat to the political control of the British colonial government, and Islamic orthodoxy as being a force that could potentially eradicate the rich culture of the region and make the Malays resistant to modern Western ideas of science and ways of life.[60]

Wilkinson viewed certain aspects of the nature of Islam in the Peninsula as becoming incompatible with the goals of creating a modern British colony in Malaya. For instance, he stated that the observance of Islam caused the position of women in Malay communities to regress to one in which they had an "absolute dependence on the male sex."[61] Wilkinson perceived an increase in male domination as challenging Malay women's traditionally prominent economic roles within the marketplace.[62] He also stated that:

> The fact remains that Malays are most prosperous, most intelligent and most industrious in those parts of the Peninsula (such as the Menangkabau States) where they have kept to their traditional customs in opposition to the doctrines of Muhammadan Law.[63]

Wilkinson also saw traditional culture as being limited by Muslim restriction, which was causing gradual loss of Malayan scholarly traditions:

> On the whole, however, the subjects that used to occupy the thoughts of the Malays of old are losing ground except in the domain of theological study. The native of the Peninsula is becoming less of a Malay and more of a Mussulman; his national ceremonies are being set aside, and his inherited superstitions are opposed to Moslem belief as much as to Western science.[64]

Islam's role as a nationalistic and cultural power, that often superseded traditional Malay culture, challenged Wilkinson's desire for a colony that could grow into Westernized modernity based upon the traditional culture of the Malay Sultanates. Pan-Islamic nationalism had the potential to challenge the authority of the Sultans, as they were able to transcend local politics, were distinctly non-Western, and in some instances strongly supported anti-colonial *jihad*.[65]

This is not to say that Wilkinson's ideas of a future colony unified by Malayan culture were completely devoid of Islamic influence. Wilkinson instead focused on Islam as an aspect of the complex literary traditions of Malaya. These literary traditions, which included epics like the *Sejarah Melayu*, provided a traditional record of Malayan history and culture, as opposed to the ideas gleaned from anthropological fieldwork. He saw great value in the *Quran* as a moral guide, but lamented that due to the Malays' obsession with form instead of meaning in Islam, the *Quran* was seldom read and never in the vernacular, which effectively stripped the document of its meaning and value.[66] He stated that in Malaya the "devout Moslem" is the man who says many prayers rather than the man of upright or moral life.[67]

Wilkinson saw Malay traditions as fading away, and ultimately degrading the culture that would be essential for forging a new British-guided Malay nation. Besides his criticisms of Islam, Wilkinson was cognizant of the fact that his own British colonial government was also responsible for the loss of ancient cultural traditions. He lamented that the study of the courtly literature, poetry, and art, was falling out of favor, as British cultural influence subsumed ancient Malay practices. Wilkinson wrote:

> The study of palace-language and ceremonial is now dying out, as the introduction of new European elements into the etiquette of Sultan's courts is destroying the importance of a knowledge of precedents; evidence of the former popularity of this branch of research is visible in historical books such as the 'Malay Annals' where the author dwells lovingly even on such minor details as the proper way of wearing a shoulder-cloth (tetampan) and the exact number and nature of the different musical instruments that went to make up a royal band.[68]

Outside of the Sultan's court, British law became the most powerful form of legality and superseded much of ancient Malay customary law, eliminating hundreds of years of tradition.[69] Wilkinson believed that the British government was basing its control of law and order too much on "mere force," and he recommended instead creating laws that extended farther into Malay society.[70] This essentially undercut the strict system of protocol and social status, on which political and social power rested in the Malay world.

Wilkinson's overarching criticism of the British colonial regime in Malaya focused primarily on the human and political effects of their lack of cultural sensitivity towards the Malay people. Wilkinson believed in the mission to improve and modernize the Peninsula as a more efficient colony. He also hoped to revitalize Malayan culture and, as a result, strengthen the cultural bond between Malays and the British. He saw a distinct lack of compassion among civil servants, whom he saw as counteracting any progress that they brought to the colony due to their inability to connect with the Malays on a human level. Even in the case of the diffusion of Western forms of medicine, he believed that the doctors' work was losing some of its value since they "in ignorance, offend terribly against native custom."[71] He also compared and contrasted the "character" of the Malays, whom he saw as an intelligent race with rich history, literature, and culture, with the exploitive nature of many of the civil servants meant to administer the colony and win the Malays' support. He described these civil servants as "petty officials who have no belief in their work and simply take it up in order to prey upon native householders ignorant of what is wanted and only too willing to pay to be left alone."[72] He wrote that "racial dominion rests upon character—not upon wealth, nor even upon intelligence," and without Englishmen of the proper moral fiber, the colonial mission would be a failure.[73]

Wilkinson saw the strong "character" of the Malays, which was personified by the political stability of the Sultanate, as the basis for the modernization of the Peninsula. To Wilkinson, this character was manifested outwardly through the Malays' literature, arts, and language, which he saw as being threatened by the imperial government's focus on its solely economic interests. Wilkinson described how "the very natural love of the people for their own language is combated or discouraged by individual Englishmen in order that it may not interfere with the spread of English," and how the Malays' devotion to the Sultan, their history, and literary traditions, were seen at worst as potential threats to the government or at best as superfluous.[74] Wilkinson wrote:

> It is a matter of real regret that the patriotism of the Malays, their self-respect, their reverence for immemorial law, their loyalty to their rulers, their traditions of courtesy, and their love of study for its own sake—things that contain the germs of national progress—should be continually depreciated and dishonoured as not being 'business.'[75]

Wilkinson stressed that these cultural traditions were not incompatible with British dominion, and that they demonstrated a long legacy of traditional structures in the form of traditional politics, law, and art. This structure, if revitalized and supported by the British government, would lead to an artistic and cultural renaissance, embedded within the growth of modern progress through the cultivation of the Malays' intellect through new educational policies.

These educational policies would involve cultivating a culturally hybridized elite ruling class and providing rudimentary vocational training for rural Malays. Wilkinson's desire to maintain stability through the preservation of Malay heritage would then be achieved by maintaining distinct class divisions between the extensively Western-educated "traditional elites" and the Malays in rural villages, or *kampongs*. These education policies were perceived as theoretically leading to increases in literacy and social welfare among rural Malays, providing political stability in the form of a British-educated Malay ruling class, and ultimately increasing the efficiency of the colony by keeping rural Malays from migrating to the cities in search of work. Wilkinson's ultimate hope was to expand Western education as the colony modernized. Wilkinson's ideas would be partially integrated, but put on hold after the Depression, in favor of policies that continued to limit government-sponsored Western education to only urban elites.

Conclusion

The ethnological information collected and shared by scholarly societies, and these societies' mutual goals of cultural preservation and appropriation, reveal a sense of the changing nature of imperialism in Southeast Asia in the early twentieth century. With the push towards the "Ethical Policies" in the Netherlands Indies and a British focus on "more culturally sensitive" imperial governance, colonial governments in Southeast Asia began to see indigenous cultural knowledge as both a tool of governance and a way to convey a broad sense of the benevolence of the imperial mission. The cooperation between these intellectual societies stands contrary to the hyper-competitive nature of empire in the late nineteenth century, and conveys an increased sense of imperial stability in Southeast Asia on a broad European scale.

On the level of the individual colony, the collection of this "heritage," through informants and interviews, and the gathering of manuscripts and objects to be preserved in European museums and archives, were characterized by the Europeans as an attribute of imperial policies that focused on an increased stake for indigenous populations in the goals of empire. The colonial government characterized the protection of these artifacts, manuscripts, and cultural practices as an act of goodwill in service of the later generations that would become imperial subjects within the colony. In both the Netherlands Indies and British Malaya, access to this information was controlled and indigenous cultural heritage was coupled with imperial initiatives towards education and pro-imperial propaganda, such as in textbooks assigned in government schools.[76]

Indigenous cultural preservation remained the purview of these intellectual societies and their archives, libraries, and museums until decolonization. Some of these intellectual societies still exist today, and many of them shifted from a focus on cultural preservation in service of the empire, to one on preserving knowledge for use within the new post-colonial nation. This is reflected in the increase in indigenous membership in societies like the Malaysian Branch of the Royal Asiatic Society, and the assimilation of colonial institutions such as museums, into the framework of the new nation, as in Indonesia. In effect, cultural heritage in Indonesia and Malaysia was reclaimed by Southeast Asian nationalists from imperial structures, and used to bolster common sentiments of Indonesian and Malaysian nationalistic identity. For instance, the number of Indonesian visitors to the Museum of the Royal Batavian Society in Batavia doubled as nationalist sentiments began to rise in the late 1930s and 1940s.[77]

In many ways, Wilkinson's hopes of stabilizing Malaya along the lines of Malay tradition did eventually come to fruition, although this occurred within the independent state of Malaysia. The members of the Sultanates and "traditional elites" validated their rule by coupling Malay history and traditions and appropriating pre-existing British imperial political structures. They conveyed stability to the British government through their integration in Western social circles and forms of education, and characterized themselves as fulfilling their "traditional" roles as the ruling class. By focusing on revitalizing "traditions" within colonial policy, Malay cultural heritage was used to effectively reinforce the political, social, and economic power of "traditional" Malay elites, and informed the greater policies of "Malay privilege" that restricted the ability of many non-Malays to effectively gain meaningful official political power.[78]

These intellectual societies then served an important role in the imperial mission. Not only do they give us a sense of common cooperation between colonial entities during the early twentieth century, but also they can provide us a sense of what topics were deemed to be academically and politically important to those expatriates and civil servants working in colonies in Southeast Asia. Further research will examine the extent to which the different colonial powers in the region used this information to directly inform governance, or if these projects were more reflective of a general academic trend in imperial culture and knowledge collection for the sake of "imperial" science in the early twentieth century.

Notes

1. T.N. Harper, "Globalism and the Pursuit of Authenticity: The Making of a Diasporic Public Sphere in Singapore," *Sojourn: The Journal of Social Issues in Southeast Asia* 12, no. 2 (Oct. 1997): 267.
2. For an overview of intellectual societies in Southeast Asia, see Su Lin Lewis, "Between Orientalism and Nationalism: The Learned Society and the Making of 'Southeast Asia'," *Modern Intellectual History* 10, no. 2 (2013): 353–74.

3. Richard Winstedt, *Annals of the American Academy of Political and Social Science* 226, Southeastern Asia and the Philippines (Mar. 1943): 99.
4. These exhibitions are examined extensively in the Dutch case by Frances Gouda in *Dutch Culture Overseas: Colonial Practice in the Netherlands Indies 1900–1942* (Amsterdam: Amsterdam University Press, 1995) and by Marieke Bloembergen in *Colonial Spectacles: The Netherlands and the Dutch East Indies at the World Exhibitions 1880–1931* (Singapore: NUS Press, 2006).
5. Anon., "L'Ecole francaise d Extreme-Orient," *Pacific Affairs* 25, no. 3 (Sept. 1952): 293. The article was based on Georges Coedés and Louis Malleret, "L'Ecole française d'Extrême-Orient," *Cahiers français d'information* (15 April 1951).
6. Philippa Levine, *The Amateur and the Professional: Antiquarians, Historians, and Archaeologist in Victorian England, 1838–1886* (Cambridge: Cambridge University Press, 1986), 4.
7. For example, the British administration hoped to use Malay traditional literature and histories in the classroom as a way to foster increased literacy, and to institute classes instructing Malays in their own traditional crafts, such as basketry and silverwork, in order to help Malays find a more productive economic niche. See Matthew Schauer, "Industrious Women and Lost Traditions: Gender, Imperial Exchange, and Handicrafts Education in British Malaya 1916–1932," *Journal of World History* 28, nos. 3–4 (2017): 493–524.
8. Harper, "Globalism and the Pursuit of Authenticity," 267.
9. "Stamford Raffles and the Netherlands East Indies: Historic Ceremony in Batavia," reprint of an article published in *British Malaya* (May 1930): 15–16, 22. Reprinted in *Journal of the Malaysian Branch of the Royal Asiatic Society* 68, Part II (1995): 142.
10. There were other intellectual societies in Singapore, such as the Straits Philosophical Society, which was founded in 1893. According to historian Jim Jose, the SPS's journals did publish 14 articles on anthropology, but generally focused on debating topics ranging from philosophy, religion, economics, politics, and imperialism. See Jim Jose, "Imperial Rule and the Ordering of Intellectual Space: The Formation of the Straits Philosophical Society," *Crossroads: An Interdisciplinary Journal of Southeast Asian Studies* 12, no. 2 (1998): 26.
11. G.F. Hose, "Inaugural Address," *JSBRAS* 1 (1878): 6 as cited in Choy Chee Meh nee Lum, "History of the Malaysian Branch of the Royal Asiatic Society," *JMBRAS* 68, Part II (1995): 88.
12. "Programma" in *Gedenkboek* vol. I, Appendix A, ii–ix. As cited in Lian The and Paul van der Veur, *The Verhandelingen van het Bataviaasch Genootschap: An Annotated Content Analysis* (Athens, Ohio: Ohio University Press, 1973), 3.
13. Ibid., 6.
14. H.N. Ridley, "The Scientific Exploration of the Peninsula," *Journal of the Straits Branch of the Royal Asiatic Society* 75 (1917): vii–xi, as cited in Choy Chee Meh nee Lum, "History of the Malaysian Branch," 91.

15. The and van der Veur, *The Verhandelingen van het Bataviaasch Genootschap*, 16.
16. Choy Chee Meh nee Lum, "History of the Malaysian Branch," 86.
17. The and van der Veur, *The Verhandelingen van het Bataviaasch Genootschap*, 19. The Society's *Tijdschift* was published from 1853 until 1955, with a break during the Second World War, and was primarily devoted to the study of local cultures and languages.
18. Ibid., 22.
19. Ibid., 23.
20. The original article is K.F. Holle, "Kawi-oorkonden; facsimiles met transcriptie van een inscriptie op koperen platen van 782 en 1295 van Çaka (A.D. 856 en 1369)," [Kawi Documents: Facsimiles with transcriptions of an inscription on copper plates from 782 and 1295 (Çaka Calendar) A.D. 856 and 1369] *Verhandelingen* 39, pt. 2, sec. 3 (1880): 1–9. Vogel's article is: J. Ph. Vogel, "Het verhaal van den wijzen Vidhura afgebeeld op den Barabudur," [The story of the sage Vidhura as it is depicted on Barabudur] *Feestbundel* II (1929): 412–17.
21. See Thomas Stamford Raffles, "Copies of two ancient inscriptions on copper plates dug up in the vicinity of Surabaya," *Verhandelingen* 8, sec. 8 (1826): 327–31.
22. S.J. Esser, "Het dialect van Banjoemas, inzonderheid zooals dit in de regentschappen Poerbolinggo, en Poerwokerto gesproken wordt," [The dialect of the Banjoemas regency, as it was spoken particularly in Poerbolinggo and Poerwokerto] *Verhandelingen* 68, sec. 1 (1926): 1–77; W.L. Steinhart, "Niassche priesterlitanieen," [Priestly Litanies from Nias] *Verhandelingen* 74, sec. 1 (1938): i–x, 1–63.
23. Henrika Kuklick, "The British Tradition," in *A New History of Anthropology*, ed. Henrika Kuklick (Oxford: Blackwells, 2008), 53–4.
24. Sibeud, "Ethnology in France 1839–1930," 99.
25. Ibid., 98–9.
26. Ibid., 100–1.
27. Ibid., 106–9.
28. Anthropology was taught in British universities in a variety of forms in the late nineteenth century, but was generally relegated to departments dealing with the natural sciences and not often integrated within undergraduate programs. Oxford formed the first school of anthropological studies in 1906, but did not have a permanent chair of the school until 1936. See Henrika Kuklick's excellent book, *The Savage Within: The Social History of British Anthropology 1885–1945* (1993), for an overview of the professionalization of British anthropology.
29. Kuklick, "The British Tradition," 61. According to Kuklick, the first government anthropologist in Africa was Northcote Thomas, who served in Nigeria and Sierra Leone from 1908–12. The first full-time government anthropologist who came from the colonial civil service was R.S. Rattray who was appointed in the Gold Coast Colony in 1921.

30. Henry Nicholas Ridley (1855–1956), who is most famous for his work fostering the rubber industry in the Malay Peninsula, was published 105 times in the *Journal.* See Lim Huck Tee and D.E.K. Wijasuriya, *Index Malaysiana* (Kuala Lumpur: Malaysian Branch of the Royal Asiatic Society, 1970), 120–3 for a full index of Ridley's articles for the Journal. H.N. Ridley, "The Bird-dropping spider (Orinthos-catoides) in Johor," *JSBRAS* 25 (Jan. 1894): 172–3; H.N. Ridley, "An Insectivorous Squirrel," *JSBRAS* 32 (June 1899): 217. H.N. Ridley's "New and Rare Malayan Plants" article series ran in some form from 1907 to 1922.
31. See Hans Overbeck, "Malay Customs and Beliefs as Recorded in Malay Literature and Folklore. Part I," *JMBRAS* 2, issue 3 (Dec. 1924): 280–8; Part II: *JMBRAS* 3, issue 1 (Apr. 1925): 53–7; Part III: *JMBRAS* 3, issue 3 (Dec. 1925): 22–30.
32. See C.O. Blagden, "Sejarah Melayu, An Unpublished Version of the 'Malay Annals'," *JMBRAS* 3, issue 1 (Apr. 1925): 10–52.
33. The and van der Veur, *The Verhandelingen van het Bataviaasch Genootschap,* 17.
34. Anon., "List of Members, Exchanges and Donations," *The Journal of the Malayan Branch of the Royal Asiatic Society* (1924): xxviii xxxvi.
35. "Ecole Française d'Extrême-Orient," *Bulletin de l'Ecole française d'Extrême-Orient* 34 (1934): 709–50.
36. The majority of the SBRAS's archives were ceded to the Raffles Library, and the remaining items are presently in the National Archives and National Library of Singapore. The RBS archives have been assimilated into the National Museum of Indonesia in Jakarta. For more on the library see, Wai Sin Tiew, "The History of the Library of the Straits Branch of the Royal Asiatic Society (SBRAS) 1877–1923," *Sekitar Perpustakaan* 28 (1999): 1–10.
37. G.P. Rouffaer, "The Early History of Singapore, Johore, and Malacca; an outline of a paper by G.P. Rouffaer," R.O. Winstedt, *JSBRAS* 86 (Nov. 1922): 257–60.
38. Sytze van der Veen, *Brill: 325 Years of Scholarly Publishing* (Leiden: Brill, 2008), 63, 66.
39. J.M. Gullick, "Wilkinson, Richard James (1867–1941)," *Oxford Dictionary of National Biography* (Oxford: Oxford University Press, 2004), 1.
40. Ibid., 1.
41. Ibid.
42. C.O. Blagden, "Introduction," in Walter William Skeat, *Malay Magic* (Singapore: Oxford University Press, 1984 [1900]), viii.
43. Ibid., ix.
44. Walter Skeat, "Introduction," in Walter Skeat and C.O. Blagden, *The Pagan Races of the Malay Peninsula* (London: Macmillan, 1906), x.
45. Ibid., x.
46. Ibid., xi.

47. "C.W. Harrison to E.W. Birch, 3 May 1907," Papers of Sir Ernest Birch, as cited in P.L. Burns, "Introduction," in *Papers on Malay Subjects*, ed. R.J. Wilkinson, selected by P.L. Burns (Kuala Lumpur: Oxford University Press, 1971), 2.
48. R.J. Wilkinson, "Statement," in Memorandum by E.W. Birch, "The Malay Race in the FMS," 28 May 1906, Papers of Sir Ernest Birch. As cited in Burns, "Introduction," 2.
49. E.W. Birch, cited in "Preface," in R.J. Wilkinson, "Malay Literature Part I: Romance, History, and Poetry," *Papers on Malay Subjects*, general editor R.J. Wilkinson (Kuala Lumpur: J.L. Wallace at the F.M.S. Government Press, 1924), iii–iv.
50. Ibid., iv.
51. Ibid., iv–v.
52. Ibid., iii.
53. Ibid.
54. Ibid., iv.
55. Wilkinson, "Malay Literature Part I," v.
56. Ibid., vi.
57. Ibid.
58. R.J. Wilkinson, *Malay Beliefs* (Leiden: E.J. Brill, 1906), 47.
59. Ibid., i.
60. Ibid., 80
61. Ibid., 17.
62. Ibid.
63. Ibid.
64. Ibid., 80.
65. Ibid., 18.
66. Ibid., 14.
67. Ibid.
68. Ibid., 79.
69. Ibid.
70. Ibid., 80.
71. Ibid.
72. Ibid., 80–1.
73. Ibid., 81.
74. Ibid.
75. Ibid.
76. For the Malayan case, see Naoki Soda, "Indigenizing Colonial Knowledge: The Formation of Pan-Malay Identity in British Malaya," unpublished Dissertation, Kyoto University Graduate School of Asian and African Area Studies, 2008. John Darwin's *The Empire Project: The Rise and Fall of the British World System* (Cambridge: Cambridge University Press, 2011) makes the argument that "nation building" within the British colonies, particularly in India, were part of a larger, often unintentional system of British imperialism.

There are parallels that can be drawn between the system of privilege and education in British India and British Malaya, which I am in the process of exploring.

77. The and van der Veur, *The Verhandelingen van het Bataviaasch Genootschap,* 14.
78. For a contemporary description of the British government's reasoning behind the British governments policies relating to "Malay Privilege," see Richard Winstedt, *Annals of the American Academy of Political and Social Science* 226, Southeastern Asia and the Philippines (Mar. 1943): 97–111.

CHAPTER 3

Rituals and Power: Cross-Cultural Exchange and the Contestation of Colonial Hegemony in Indonesia

Arnout H.C. van der Meer

In the spring of 1913 Raden Soemarsono, a young Javanese public prosecutor, was on his way to report to his new European superior, the Assistant-Resident J.C. Bedding of Purwakarta (West Java). Soemarsono had just been transferred from the Dutch East Indies cosmopolitan capital, Batavia, to the backward provincial town of Purwakarta. On his arrival at the local police court he was shocked to see that his fellow countrymen were crouching before the European civil servant, sitting on the floor, and addressing Bedding in high Javanese. After each sentence they also brought their hands together in a gesture of respect and obedience (*sembah*). These longstanding Javanese forms of deference, known collectively as *hormat* (respect), were viewed as a thing of the past by the Western-educated and Europeanized Soemarsono. When Assistant-Resident Bedding noticed that Soemarsono was dressed in European fashion (trousers, jacket, and a headscarf), a clash between tradition and progress (*kemajuan*) ensued. Bedding demanded that Soemarsono change his European trousers for a Javanese *sarong* (wraparound skirt) and take his place on the floor. The Javanese public prosecutor refused. He had attended a European secondary school, spoke fluent Dutch, sat on chairs in the presence of Europeans, and was used to being treated as an equal. Grudgingly, Bedding allowed Soemarsono to attend the meeting. However, he provided him no chair, and the prosecutor could not sit on the floor because he wore Western trousers and that would represent submission to Javanese deference forms. Thus, Soemarsono would have been forced to stand throughout the meeting. Rather than submit to that humiliation, he excused himself to attend to the pile of paperwork that came with his new office.[1]

Due to Soemarsono's connections with powerful Dutch administrators, and through them to the Governor General, the aftershocks of this seemingly minor confrontation in the small provincial town of Purwakarta soon reverberated throughout colonial Indonesia. The confrontation was the latest example of a European civil servant deliberately acting against government stipulations that prohibited Dutch officials from demanding traditional Javanese forms of deference in their contacts with the indigenous people of Java. At the peak of the progressive Ethical Policy (c. 1901–27), the colonial government could not tolerate this kind of behavior any longer. Consequently, Governor General Idenburg promulgated a stern circular—which quickly became known as the *hormat*-circular of 1913—that sought to end these practices once and for all. Contemporaries referred to the circular as the "most curious piece of Indies legislation" in history as it went much further in condemning the behavior of European administrators than similar circulars in the previous decade and led to increased support of the colonial government for the nascent nationalist movement.[2] This seemingly contradictory consequence illustrates that at times the interests of the colonial government and nationalist movement aligned. The circular's enactment resulted in a colony-wide debate on the importance of cross-cultural exchange and hybridity for the maintenance of colonial rule on the one hand, and Javanese and European identities on the other hand.

The conflict between Bedding and Soemarsono was rooted in nineteenth-century colonial policy aimed at establishing colonial cultural hegemony over Java. During this formative period of the colonial state, the Dutch aligned themselves with the traditional Javanese aristocracy, known as the *priyayi* class. The system of indirect rule that ensued was beneficial to the Dutch and Javanese elite alike and left the Javanese peasantry under the governance of their own aristocracy and social-cultural institutions. Crucially, the Dutch embarked on a process of cultural accommodation to legitimize colonial authority and correspondingly assumed the highest rank in the Javanese social order. By adopting Javanese symbols of power, deference rituals, dress, architecture, food, and even social customs, the Dutch colonizers embedded themselves into Javanese society in a clearly recognizable manner.[3] As Matthew Schauer and Caroline Herbelin also demonstrate in this volume, hybrid cultures were thus not merely accidental side effects of colonialism in Southeast Asia, but essential to its functioning.[4]

This cultural project of control became contested as the result of the Ethical Policy, which from 1901 onward intended to legitimize colonial authority and hegemony on more modern grounds. Initiated in the Netherlands, but strongly supported by influential high colonial officials, this new attitude towards the colonial relationship stimulated the development of Java under Dutch leadership and in accord with Western ideas about modernity, civilization, science, and technology. This policy shift is akin to the conception of a more culturally sensitive and morally grounded policy as Schauer examines.[5] The existing scholarship has focused primarily on the socio-economic, political, and technological aspects of the Ethical Policy and only paid scant attention to the changes in the outward appearance of colonial authority that occurred simultaneously. In contrast, here it is argued that these changes were in fact essential to the functioning of colonial rule, the implementation of the Ethical Policy, and the shifting grounds of colonial authority.[6]

Numerous historians have agreed that the legitimacy of colonial regimes often depended upon the preservation of traditional local elites.[7] Although the institution of indirect rule in the Netherlands Indies has been the subject of excellent historiographical studies, the actual rituals, displays, and social conventions that made colonial power visible have received scant attention.[8] This is a bit surprising, since both contemporaries and historians have often referred to the myth of Dutch colonialism. This entailed that the small Dutch nation could not rule its large empire through force alone and needed to rely on a degree of consent. However, these studies have considered cultural accommodation as the byproduct of interactions with the Javanese elite, not as constitutive of them. I seek to turn this argument around by stating that material culture and outward appearance were crucial instruments in the maintenance of colonial authority, beginning with the adoption of rituals and symbols of power of the Javanese elite.

The Trappings of Colonial Power

Arguably the most visible and sensitive adaptations from Javanese aristocratic culture by the Dutch were deference rituals that encompassed social behavior, dress codes, a stratified language system, honorific titles and regulations regarding the make-up of an official's entourage, and symbols of power.[9] For instance, the Javanese had to approach Dutch officials, as they would their own aristocracy, in a crouching walk (*jongkok*), sit cross-legged on the ground (*sila*) in their presence, and make a *sembah* gesture (placing hands together while bringing thumbs to the upper lip) after speaking out of respect for one's superiors. Traditionally, these rituals were combined with the strict linguistic protocols that prescribing a superior was to be addressed in high Javanese (*krama*), while he or she would respond in low Javanese (*ngoko*). Additionally, the various ethnic groups in Java were forced to dress according to their ethnicity. The only exceptions to this rule were the Dutch, who were, interestingly enough, allowed to wear Javanese-inspired clothing in the semi-private sphere. This was true especially of the large Eurasian segment of the European population. And finally, one's social position was often reflected in certain symbols of power (*ampilan*), of which the most famous and important was the Javanese *payung* (ceremonial parasol). The color of the *payung* represented the office or birth of its bearer. Those of highest rank were gilded; those of lesser rank were gilded to some extent or had other coloring (see Fig. 3.1).[10]

By adopting these deference rituals and symbols, the Dutch essentially tried to manipulate the Javanese concept of power in order to legitimize colonial authority. Benedict Anderson has argued that the Javanese concept of power differs from that in the Western world. Javanese power, he suggested, is concrete (it exists outside of its bearers), homogenous (all of the same type), its quantity is constant (zero-sum game) and is not morally ambiguous ("power simply is").[11] Where wealth and technology might increase the power of an individual in the Western world, in Java power was obtained and enhanced through asceticism. Thus, spiritual purity helped maintain or increase power, whereas impurity diffused power. While personal ascesis was the fundamental way to accumulate and absorb power, this process could be furthered by the possession of certain objects or persons regarded as being filled with power. For this reason Javanese rulers gathered as many heirlooms (*pusaka*) as possible, including *krisses* (Javanese spiritual daggers), spears, and musical instruments. Anderson concluded that the "Javanese tradition of political thought, therefore, typically emphasizes the signs of Power's concentration, not the demonstration of its exercise or use."[12] This suggests that by adopting Javanese rituals and symbols of power, the Dutch tried to adopt the corresponding concept of power that made them relevant. This in effect minimized the Dutch reliance on the Western concept of power, which depended more on coercion and force.

Figure 3.1: Dutch Resident of Semarang P. Sijthoff with a servant holding his golden ceremonial *payung* in 1904, just before the prohibition of its usage. Leiden University, Collections KITLV Digital Image Library [UBL-KITLV], Image Code 2603.

The adaptation to Javanese society to legitimize colonial rule was not only the result of an unconscious cultural exchange, but also a conscious policy.

By the end of the nineteenth century, Dutch civil servants stood at the apex of the social hierarchy of colonial society and enjoyed a seigniorial lifestyle on Java. The plethora of deference rituals and symbols of power deployed by these officials constantly reminded the Javanese aristocracy and masses as well as European residents of their inferior social position. In their interactions with the Javanese these officials demanded to be addressed as *kandjeng tuan*, a title traditionally the prerogative of *Bupati* (traditional Javanese district heads) and royalty, meaning "your highness." Similarly, European residents were accompanied by a plethora of servants, one of whom carried a golden *payung*—historically the privilege of Javanese royalty—as a symbol of his power. The official Residency houses on Java also radiated a sense of power. While the Roman columns on their verandas gave these houses a Western appearance, their ground plans, structures, and high-hipped roofs were architectural adaptations of the Javanese *pendopo*. Just like the Dutch official whom it provided with shelter, the house was a significant hybrid product of the colonial age, similar to the ways the French colonizers of Indochina in the early colonial period in particular integrated local architectural forms as Herbelin demonstrates in this volume.[13]

An essential part of the deference rituals that upheld colonial hierarchy was the Javanese language stratification. It was customary that a person of high rank addressed his or her social inferiors in *ngoko* (low Javanese) and that the reply was given in *krama* (high Javanese).[14] According to the Dutch Orientalist, linguist and colonial Advisor for Native Affairs G.A.J. Hazeu, the subdivision of both language types was so highly refined, that "all nuances of rank of a feudal society could be expressed therein."[15] The Dutch consciously adopted the Javanese language stratification to legitimize their position as rulers. With the exception of high indigenous officials, such as *Bupatis* and *Patihs*, all Javanese were to be addressed by Dutch officials in *ngoko*, and expected to reply in high Javanese. However, by the turn of the century an increasing number of Javanese aristocrats were enjoying Western education in the Dutch language. Consequently, a significant addition was made to the colonial Javanese language hierarchy. Dutch officials addressed the Western-educated Javanese in Dutch, although they still expected the latter to reply in *krama*. Remarkably, Dutch replaced *ngoko* in these conversations, supposedly an "inferior" language. However, it simply would not do for the Dutch to speak *ngoko* to the Javanese and have them answer in Dutch.

The refusal by European civil servants to converse in Dutch with their colleagues in the indigenous civil service (in contrast, for example, to the practices in French Indochina) was the topic of many spirited debates in the decades around 1900. Knowledge of the Dutch language brought with it a certain level of social prestige. In a sense it allowed the speaker to distance him or herself from traditional society and achieve a more equal footing with Europeans. As early as 1890, the government had encouraged European civil servants to communicate in Dutch with their Western-educated indigenous counterparts. The fear of losing prestige and weakening colonial rule prevented many Europeans from acting on this circular. Instead they demanded compliance with the "traditional" Javanese language stratification, albeit with modifications involving the insertion of the Dutch language. The fear of offending Dutch civil servants was still too great, even for high Javanese aristocrats, to challenge the social order and refer to the existence of the circular.[16]

In the Indonesian national heroine Kartini we encounter a voice of reason, a voice that protested against the conformity of traditional Javanese society, a voice that even challenged the Dutch adaptation of Javanese forms of deference. Kartini was fully aware of the oppressiveness of Javanese deference rituals, which she considered a burden. In a letter to her friend Stella Zeehandelaar in 1899, Kartini described how deeply the *hormat*-etiquette dominated even her private life in which even her younger siblings had to bow and crouch when passing her, sit on the floor in her presence, address her in high Javanese, and finish each sentence with a *sembah*.[17] In Kartini's opinion, these deference rituals were an abomination. Interestingly, she declared that she would not withhold from her elders due deference, but that beginning with herself she would propagate the dismissal of all ceremony.

In Kartini's correspondence, it becomes clear that she detested showing deference to Europeans even more than showing it to other Javanese. For instance, in 1900 Kartini wrote how she was amused, could not suppress a smile, and had to bite her lips to prevent herself from laughing outright at the manner in which Dutch officials preserved their prestige over the Javanese. In a sarcastic letter she mocked the emphasis that the Dutch placed on their so-called prestige. Kartini clearly did not buy into the "ridiculous spectacle" that Dutch colonizers maintained was crucial to legitimizing their authority in the eyes of the Javanese population. She even went so far as calling the Dutch prestige imaginary, in essence undermining the cultural grounds on which colonial rule was constructed. However, although Kartini presented herself as a modernizer in most of her writings, here we also find a woman defending the rights of her class. She clearly resented the Dutch adoption of Javanese deference customs to which in her eyes only the Javanese rulers were entitled. In this respect her criticism was not unique.

A year before, in 1899, an anonymous author critiqued the Dutch reliance on Javanese deference traditions and symbols of power and the accompanying loss of power of the Javanese aristocracy. The author was particularly bothered by the propensity of lower Dutch civil servants, whom he branded petty kings, for demanding deference of lower Javanese aristocrats. Like Kartini, he distinguished between the right of the Javanese aristocracy to demand deference and the lack of justification for the Dutch to do the same.[18] According to a report by the *Bupati* of Demak Hadiningrat in 1893, however, this increased concern with *hormat*-etiquette reflected the changing balance of power between both branches of the colonial civil service. The *Bupati* argued that during the last decades of the nineteenth century the prestige of the Javanese branch of the colonial civil service had suffered from increased direct contact between the general population and European civil servants. In addition, while these European officials had to comply with higher educational standards, their Javanese counterparts did not. Consequently, the prestige and stature of the Javanese aristocracy was diminished in the eyes of the Javanese people and Europeans alike. To compensate for their reduced power, Hadiningrat believed, many indigenous civil servants demanded more deference from the Javanese people while showing more to their European superiors in the hope of having some measure of influence. Hadiningrat argued that only more Western-style education could remedy this imbalance and bring real prestige back to the indigenous civil service.[19]

One of the earliest Dutch opponents of the use of Javanese deference rituals by colonial civil servants was H.E. Steinmetz. A young controller himself, he was well aware of the deference practices pervasive on Java. In a book he wrote under a pseudonym in 1888, he severely criticized the behavior of European civil servants towards their Javanese subordinates in general, specifically their abuse of *hormat*-etiquette. Steinmetz sarcastically described the first years of the career of a civil servant as the "*hormat*-period," a period when he was most susceptible to acquiring a taste for Javanese deference rituals. It was not surprising then, he argued, that young civil servants quickly learned to be "angered when an indigenous person passes him or his house without uncovering his head nor dismounts his horse; when a lower ranking civil servant dares to address him in Malay; a *Wedana* or tax collector enters his home with footwear, etc."[20] Failure to modernize the colonial relationship by leadership through example, Steinmetz cautioned, also made the Dutch more susceptible to manipulation by Javanese civil servants, who, by showing exaggerated *hormat* could try to improve their career opportunities.

Early in his career Steinmetz already noticed that an increasing number among the Javanese considered it humiliating to show traditional deference in general, but especially towards Europeans. He believed that because Europeans were located outside the Javanese system they did not fully understand that the reception of deference required a certain approachable attitude in return. Steinmetz essentially argued that the nineteenth-century policy of cultural adaptation to legitimize colonial authority had either failed, or worse, never worked. He asserted that continued use of *hormat*-etiquette was degrading, time consuming, and did little to further European prestige. To those who believed that Dutch colonial rule depended on Javanese deference and status symbols, he retorted that they should worry more about Dutch men's tendency of living with indigenous concubines, as well as their alcoholism and godlessness. In his opinion those habits were far more detrimental to colonial prestige than the lack of *hormat*-etiquette. Steinmetz therefore proposed that the colonial government prohibit European civil servants from demanding traditional deference and using Javanese status symbols. However, in 1889 few were receptive yet to the young official's radical plea.[21]

This changed in the following decade when the first official Advisor for Native Affairs, Christiaan Snouck Hurgronje, joined Steinmetz's cause. Originally trained as an Arabic and Islamic scholar in the Netherlands, Snouck Hurgronje found his way to the colonies after a research visit to Mecca. He believed that understanding Islam in general and local cultures specifically could improve the effectiveness of Dutch colonial policy. From 1898 until 1907 he filled the post of Advisor for Native Affairs, a position reflective of the changing times. Crucially, the Advisor's office was independent from the Department of the Interior (responsible for the conservative civil service) and enjoyed a direct and personal connection to the Governor General. His task was twofold, namely to serve as a barometer of distress suffered by the indigenous population and to advise the Governor General thereof. Moreover, the Advisor acted as an ombudsman for the growing number of "educated natives." Snouck Hurgronje personally tutored several young Javanese of high birth and provided them with Western education. Most of his students went on to hold prominent positions in colonial society in the following decades.[22]

As an Advisor, Snouck Hurgronje drew attention to the contradictory government policy of continued reliance on Javanese forms of deference while seeking to modernize the colonial relationship. After almost a century of indirect rule, many of the Javanese traditions regarding ranks, titles, entourage, social deference conventions and the like had become outdated and difficult to maintain due to changing historical circumstances. Technological, political, social, and economic changes resulted in a society that was rapidly becoming less in harmony with its aristocratic core of ritual and deference. These diverging tendencies were reflected in growing tensions between various social groups, old and new, in colonial society. It was not until the promulgation of the Ethical Policy in 1901, however, that there was finally enough political support to attempt to resolve the uncertainties, hence anxieties, caused by these dualistic policies by modernizing the outward appearance of colonial rule.

Throughout the period of the Ethical Policy it was the office of the Advisor of Native Affairs that took the initiative in dismantling the Javanese aristocratic façade of Dutch colonial rule. For instance, in 1903 Snouck Hurgronje instigated change by advising the Governor General to prohibit the use of large retinues for European civil servants and *Bupatis* while touring their districts. These honorary retinues, he argued, were a waste of time and money and had no purpose other than fulfilling the European desire for display. Snouck Hurgronje therefore proposed to prohibit the use of retinues for high-ranking civil servants when touring in a carriage and only requiring an escort of Javanese civil servants whose presence had an actual purpose. Four months later Snouck Hurgronje's counsel was turned into an official government circular that prohibited the use of escorts and honorary retinues for European civil servants. It was the first sign of things yet to come.[23]

The onset of the Ethical Policy as well as Snouck Hurgronje's presence prompted Steinmetz to argue for abolishing Javanese deference rituals and status symbols once again. Despite the publication of his critical book in 1888, Steinmetz had successfully passed through the hierarchy of the colonial civil service and was appointed as the president of the "Diminished Welfare Committee." The Committee was an institutional icon of the Ethical Policy founded in 1904 with the task of examining the causes of poverty in Java and recommending ways to remedy the situation. It was against this background that Steinmetz officially proposed to prohibit European officials from demanding traditional Javanese deference, titles, honors, and servitude; in other words, that *hormat*-abuses should be brought to an end. Presented with this proposal, Snouck Hurgronje concurred with Steinmetz. In a letter to the Governor General, he stated that the broadening horizons of the modern age, due to improved modes of transport and communication, had laid bare the backwardness of Javanese *hormat*-etiquette, which needed to be replaced with less stilted cosmopolitan forms of deference. Snouck Hurgronje cited Japan and Siam (Thailand) as examples of more modernized Asian societies to follow.[24]

Just a few days after taking office, Governor General van Heutsz was presented with the recommendations of Steinmetz and Snouck Hurgronje. The infamous general had "pacified" Aceh in the previous years and was rewarded with the highest office in the colony. With military decisiveness he dealt with the issues discussed in the recommendations in front of him. These suggestions of his advisors convinced him that the legitimacy of colonial rule should not depend on Javanese symbols of power and traditional deference. In November 1904, he signed and promulgated two circulars with the intention of modernizing colonial rule and the relationship between the European civil service and Javanese society. The so-called *payung* circular of 3rd November prohibited the use of *payungs* by European civil servants, which was followed on 16th November by the more elaborate *hormat*-circular, prohibiting most other forms and rituals of deference.[25] In his private correspondence with the Minister of Colonial Affairs Idenburg, van Heutsz boasted about how with the stroke of his pen he had prohibited European civil servants from demanding traditional Javanese deference, surrounding themselves with large retinues of Javanese subjects, being received and honored with triumphal arches and fireworks, and crucially from carrying a golden *payung* as a symbol of their power.[26] In short, van Heutsz had launched an almost all-encompassing attack against what he described as the "foolishnesses" of the nineteenth-century colonial order.

The language of the *hormat*-circular of 1904 revealed the underlying concerns and beliefs shared by Snouck Hurgronje and van Heutsz—who had previously worked together during the pacification of Aceh—with regard to the future development of the colony. The circular explicitly stated that more modern international forms of respect should replace the Javanese traditional forms of deference to stimulate increased participation of the Javanese in modern society. According to the circular, traditional *hormat*-etiquette was outdated, time-consuming, and humiliating for those whose sense of dignity had just been awakened, and adverse to the development of trust between the colonizer and colonized. In a sense, the circular intended to align the exterior appearance of colonial rule with the more modern interior institutions and developments encapsulated by the Ethical Policy. Consequently, the *hormat*-circular articulately ended the nineteenth-century belief that Javanese traditions were necessary to legitimize colonial authority:

> It is a false notion indeed to think that the authority, through simplification of indigenous social formalities, would be endangered and that maintenance of customs such as appearing before superiors without foot wear, sitting on the floor, accompanying discussions with *sembah* etc. would involve an interest of state.[27]

This was a judiciously worded warning to those who maintained that the circular would diminish European prestige and colonial authority.

Nonetheless, the *hormat*-circular of 1904 left conservatives some wiggle room, since it stated that the process of change should be most strongly encouraged in areas of modern development (for example, urban settings), leaving most of colonial Java open to a less urgent interpretation.[28] In addition, in the Netherlands Indies circulars were instructions that fell somewhere between strong advice and binding laws. This meant that compliance with these instructions was expected, but most of the time it was not monitored or enforced by the colonial government. Consequently, the theory and practice of colonial rule as reflected in government circulars could be miles apart. It depended on the local civil service representatives to execute these circulars and enforce compliance. Snouck Hurgronje acknowledged as much in 1904, stating "the lips of a civil servant fold into a smile when pronouncing the word 'circular.'"[29] The promulgation of multiple government circulars against the aristocratic character of colonial society was a challenge to that order but by no means meant its end.

The Appearance of Colonial Rule Contested

The *payung*- and *hormat*-circulars of 1904 triggered a fierce debate in colonial society on the appearance and grounds of colonial authority that lasted until the end of the Dutch rule. Although supporters of the new progressive Ethical Policy could be found, its opponents were far more prominent in the colonial press. The two positions within this debate can be illustrated by the contrasting editorials of two colonial newspapers. Among the few who applauded the decision of the Governor General to prohibit the use of *hormat* as well as the *payung* was the editor of the largest European newspaper in Surabaya. He argued that as long as *hormat* kept the Javanese stuck in past traditions it would be impossible to uplift them into strong, self-conscious economical individuals. More importantly, he stated, colonial rule should not be based on traditional Javanese deference but on virtuousness and moral superiority of the colonizer. In other words, he interpreted the circulars as measures to redefine the grounds of cultural hegemony in the colony.[30]

In stark contrast, the editor of Batavia's largest newspaper completely rejected the reasoning of his colleague by perceiving the circulars and the Ethical Policy in general, as a severe threat to the existence of the Netherlands Indies. In his opinion, the Javanized appearance of Dutch colonial rule was absolutely essential in maintaining peace and order. The abrupt changes to this exterior, he cautioned, could force the authorities to become more reliant on coercion. According to the conservative argument, *hormat*-etiquette and the *payung* were essential parts of the Javanese social fabric that could not be so easily discarded. He concisely summarized this sentiment by stating that: "payungs are cheaper than bayonets and less cruel."[31] It was the prohibition of the *payung*, the nineteenth-century symbol of Dutch colonialism on Java, which was foremost lamented by the colonial press. What angered conservatives most was that Javanese civil servants were still entitled to their *payungs*, leading them to wonder how European and colonial prestige could be maintained. Van Heutsz's conviction that the Dutch should rule through moral superiority and example instead of Javanese deference rituals was rejected as being too naïve.

In February 1906, Governor General van Heutsz requested Snouck Hurgronje's opinion on the effectiveness of the *payung*- and *hormat*-circulars. In his response, Snouck Hurgronje explained that the *payung* circular had been quite successful, as it concerned such a strong visual symbol that was hard to ignore. However, the *hormat*-circular he considered an utter failure. Apparently, European civil servants still demanded that their Javanese counterparts sit on the ground in the *sila* posture, present a *sembah* each time they spoke, and converse according to the Javanese language hierarchy. Snouck Hurgronje therefore pressed upon van Heutsz "that a renewed, strong inculcation of the intentions of the Government in this regard seems anything but redundant."[32] Van Heutsz concurred with his Advisor and rather quickly issued a new *hormat*-circular in April 1906.[33]

Through the *hormat*-circular of 1906, Governor General van Heutsz expressed his sincere discontent with the continued use of Javanese *hormat*-etiquette by his European civil service. Civil servants who acted in accordance with the spirit of the circular were the exception instead of the rule. This resulted in the perseverance of the traditional character of colonial society and undermined the authority of the Governor General. The new circular emphasized that the days of the seigniorial civil servant were over and that colonial officials needed to follow orders of the central bureaucracy in Batavia. The circular also provided explicit examples of undesired behavior, such as the adherence to the Javanese language hierarchy by European civil servants. Furthermore, European civil servants were reminded that Javanese civil servants remained entitled to ceremonial *payungs*. This remark suggested that the response of European civil servants to the *payung* circular had been to force their indigenous counterparts to give up theirs.[34]

The *hormat*-circular of 1906 exacerbated the differences of opinion over how to maintain cultural hegemony—as opposed to reliance on coercion—even further. Within this debate, European civil servants represented those who argued in favor of maintaining Javanese traditions, whereas central bureaucrats, such as the Advisor for Native Affairs, advocated the Ethical Policy and modernization of the colonial relationship. According to a conservative Batavian newspaper, this was also a conflict between "men of reality," the civil servants, and "men of theory," Batavian bureaucrats such as van Heutsz and Snouck Hurgronje.[35] Public opinion and the majority of the colonial press supported the more "realistic" conservative position, which indicated anxiety over uplifting and modernizing the colonized and the accompanying social changes. It therefore came as no surprise that in the last year of van Heutsz's tenure, he once more needed to challenge the persistent reality of European civil servants demanding deference from the Javanese. The language of the circular of 1909 was permeated with a sense of anger and disappointment. It stated bluntly that the Governor General "can and will not allow that his clear orders be considered unwritten."[36] Civil servants who refused to comply with the previous *hormat*-circulars were threatened with dire consequences (although those remained undefined). The 1909 circular reflected, more clearly than its predecessors, the frustration of the progressive colonial elite with the predominant conservatism among Europeans in the colony. It became clear that the supporters of modernization of the colonial relationship needed help from the Javanese themselves.

The *hormat*-debate between 1904 and 1909 coincided with the birth of a nationalist movement in the Indies. This was not accidental since both can be considered consequences of the Ethical Policy. The emergence of the "young Javanese," Western educated and often employed in non-traditional professions, reignited the debate on Javanese deference traditions and changed its dynamic drastically. Where previously the question was to what extent Europeans could demand Javanese deference forms, the young

Javanese questioned the pervasiveness of traditional deference in general. In other words, they did not just want to modernize the interactions between Europeans and Javanese, but among all members of colonial society. Interestingly, most of the young Javanese themselves originated from the privileged *priyayi* class, but as a result of their education and work outside the traditional civil service, many came to consider themselves as a class of new intellectuals. The appearance of the young Javanese as new participants in the *hormat*-debate led to the forging of new cross-ethnic alliances. The protagonists of the Ethical Policy and the young Javanese together opposed the coalition of European civil servants and Javanese aristocrats.[37]

The diverging opinions within Javanese society on the matter of *hormat* were apparent in the rapidly expanding vernacular press. For instance, in January 1912, an anonymous author in the *Pemberita Betawi* urged his fellow countrymen to stop showing old-fashioned forms of deference, such as crouching, to their superiors. He stated that these practices had their use in the past, but did not belong in the present century of progress. In the same month champions of *hormat* traditions voiced their concerns in the *Pantjaran Warta.* They presented deference as a product of civilization and development, without which society would fall apart. To prevent this degeneration from occurring, vocal young Javanese needed to be taught to be more, not less, respectful of their social superiors. This sense of a generational divide permeated many vernacular press articles. Often, the young Javanese were accused of hypocrisy, for on the one hand opposing *hormat*-etiquette in their dealings with superiors (mostly members of the traditional elite), while on the other hand continuing to exact deference from their own inferiors. The *hormat*-debate thus divided both European and Javanese communities.[38]

This development did not come as a surprise to the office of the Advisor for Native Affairs. In 1908, soon after the foundation of Boedi Oetomo, the first Javanese political organization in the Indies, Hazeu reported that he had seen the divide within the Javanese elite coming. Only to the untrained observer, he argued, did the Javanese appear unchangeable and static—a sneer to his conservative adversaries—but in part due to the educational policies of the colonial government the opposite was true. The young Javanese consisted of low-ranking civil servants as well as those trained in modern professions, such as medicine and teaching. In essence, they formed a new social group, which distanced itself from the traditional aristocracy by increasingly emphasizing merit over birth. Their rapid organizational development was crucial to the foundation of the Sarekat Islam, Indonesia's first mass movement, in 1912. Its rise made it clear to Hazeu that the era when the docile Javanese simply accepted everything unpleasant was gone for good. The young Javanese, who in their daily life still had to squat in the presence of *Bupatis*, present him with a *sembah*, and depended on him for career advancement, applauded the *hormat*-circulars. Moreover, the new generation was in favor of ending the hereditary character of the office of the *Bupati* and instead have merit not birth determine appointment.[39] Just as the nineteenth-century Vietnamese priest Philiphê Bỉnh in George Dutton's chapter in this volume, the encounter with European culture, both material and immaterial, made the young Javanese question what it meant to be Javanese and modern without becoming Dutch.

The rise of the nationalist movement caused great anxiety among the Javanese as well as the European population. In several letters by Governor General Idenburg (van Heutsz's successor), one can find mention of "nervous anxiety," "fear," and "a nauseous panic" among the European and Chinese groups in the Indies. Idenburg alluded to the clear schism that developed within the European community between the protagonists of the Ethical Policy and those supporting the conservative policies of the previous century. According to Idenburg, at stake was the question of whether the Dutch were "sincere in uplifting the natives both mentally and materially or whether everything remains the same and exploitation by the state is merely replaced by exploitation by private enterprise."[40] In fact, what occurred in the Indies was a great fragmentation of political order and society. Several groups came forth to advocate their plans for the future direction of colonial society. The accompanying anxiety resulted in conflicts that were unthinkable a decade earlier. One of the most influential of those conflicts was the one between Raden Soemarsono and Assistant-Resident Bedding in 1913.

A Turning Point: Soemarsono, Bedding, and the *Hormat*-circular of 1913

The small and dusty provincial town of Purwakarta seemed like an unlikely place for the confrontation between Assistant-Resident Bedding and *Jaksa* Soemarsono. Although Purwakarta was part of the Residency of Batavia, life in the town hardly resembled the hustle and bustle of the cosmopolitan colonial capital. Its relative isolation gave the town an aura of backwardness, at least according to Hazeu, and seemingly shielded it from modern developments such as the Ethical Policy and the nationalist movement. It was precisely because time seemed to have moved more slowly in Purwakarta that made it into a prime location for a clash between a protagonist of *kemajuan* (progress) and defenders of the old order.

Purwakarta was a typical nineteenth-century colonial town, in that its layout clearly reflected the duality of colonial governance. The centers of Javanese and colonial rule were separated from each other, seemingly leaving the traditional center of power intact. Still to this day, a large pond lies at the heart of Purwakarta. Located on its southern shore was the large residence and office of the Assistant-Resident. Constructed in the empire style it bore most of the traits of a typical Indies colonial house, with its columned porches, high-hipped roof, and typical ground plan based on Javanese architectural designs. The small European community lived to the south and east of the residence, forming a self-contained neighborhood. Purwakarta's center, the town square (*alun-alun*) with two holy banyan trees, could be found to the west of the pond. The square was surrounded by the residence and office of the *Bupati* (*Kabupaten*), the local mosque, and a prison building. Looking out over the *alun-alun* was the *pendopo* of the *Bupati* where most civil servant meetings were held. This was most likely where Bedding and Soemarsono met and squared off for the first time.

The different paths of the two civil servants that led to their encounter shed a light on the anxiety and difference of opinion between them. Bedding arrived on Java in 1893, almost a decade before the promulgation of the Ethical Policy, embarking on a 32-year-long career in the European civil service. While passing through the civil service hierarchy, starting at the bottom as an Aspirant-Controller and ending at the top as Resident, he lived and worked all over Java.[41] The Krawang regency, of which Purwakarta was the capital, held special meaning for him. From 1900 until 1906, he was placed in Purwakarta as an Aspirant-Controller, unaware that he would eventually return as the Assistant-Resident from 1911 to 1916. From his personal photo album, it is possible to sketch an image of his life in Purwakarta (Fig. 3.2). The architectural style of his residence as well as the clothing his family wore indicated how the life of the Bedding family was suspended in the nineteenth century. In private his wife still wore the *sarong* and *kebaya*, an adaptation of Javanese dress, and he himself the typical white colonial suit (*jas tutup*), which contrasted with the more clearly recognizable Western fashion adopted by Europeans in the large colonial cities. Bedding not only was, but also lived the seigniorial life of a European civil servant of *tempo doeloe* (the good old days).

Figure 3.2: Assistant-Resident Bedding and his family on the front porch of their colonial empire style home in Purwakarta (circa 1911). UBL-KITLV 119332.

In contrast, Raden Soemarsono was among the first Javanese of noble descent—*Raden* is an aristocratic title that means "of noble blood"—to receive a Western education in the Indies. In 1901, he was one of just three Javanese who took part in and passed the admissions exam for the European secondary school in Batavia. After finishing his European education, he first held the office of Assistant-Wedana (assistant-district head) within the indigenous civil service in Bogor, before being appointed as *Jaksa*—prosecutor—of Batavia in 1911. Finally, he was reassigned to Purwakarta in 1913. In the words of Hazeu, Soemarsono thus made the transfer from "Grosz-Stadt Batavia" and the Residence of the Governor General to an "old-fashioned provincial town." Soemarsono also stood out because of his involvement in the nascent nationalist movement. He was an active member of Boedi Oetomo (1908), considered the first political organization in colonial Indonesia, and eventually even held a commissioner's position within the organization. In addition, he was also active as an advisor to the Sarekat Islam (1911), the first broad nationalist political movement in Indonesian history. He balanced his private activities in these associations with his work as *Jaksa*. This was a precarious combination, since while he worked for the regional colonial administration he also critiqued the colonial system. This made him, and many others like him, vulnerable to accusations from both European civil servants and more traditional Javanese aristocrats.[42]

However, the young Soemarsono did have influential allies in government circles. It was Snouck Hurgronje who tutored many of the leaders of the first wave of nationalists, and his successor Hazeu continued with his work. The position of the Advisor of Native Affairs actually grew in importance with the increasing anxieties surrounding the "nationalist awakening." Like Soemarsono, this placed Hazeu in a risky position. On the one hand, he had direct access to the Governor General through his advice on all matters relating to indigenous developments, and on the other hand, his contacts with the indigenous movements made him vulnerable to criticism from conservative forces. One of Hazeu's contacts was Soemarsono, and their relationship was the indirect cause of the explosion of public debate on the importance of culture in legitimizing colonial authority.

Towards the end of July 1913 Soemarsono appealed to his mentor Hazeu for support. In his letters to Hazeu he explained that Assistant-Resident Bedding and the Resident of Batavia had accused him of incitement and revolutionary mindedness. Additionally, Soemarsono was suspected of having transgressed the Indies press law, a grave offense that in previous years had resulted in several Javanese being exiled. Soemarsono realized he faced serious charges, and going through his plea for help one gets the distinct impression that Soemarsono expected to be suspended, fired even, or worse. He clearly looked to Hazeu for a way out of his predicament. Although Soemarsono admitted he had a difficult personality because of his honesty and sincerity, he assured Hazeu that his "consciousness still tells him he did nothing wrong."[43] Hazeu reassured his mentee, promised he would look into the matter and kindly asked him to send all the relevant information that could help him in doing so.[44]

From the correspondence between Soemarsono and Hazeu we can reconstruct a chronicle of events in Purwakarta and their relationship to the final *hormat*-circular of 1913. According to Hazeu, Soemarsono was an educated young man who had a strong sense of mission to modernize his compatriots, to compete with the Chinese, and to unite the Javanese. He corresponded regularly with better-known early nationalists such as Dr.

Wahidin and Tjipto Mangkoenoesoemo. This progressive worldview was reflected in his aversion to Javanese aristocratic culture, which was reflected in his refusal to either demand or submit to *hormat* customs. In Batavia and Bogor this progressive attitude was more or less accepted. There he was able to express his opinion, but when he was transferred to Purwakarta this posture became a real challenge. According to Hazeu, among the small town's European and indigenous civil services a "tradition of rigid conservatism" was prevalent. The clash between Bedding and Soemarsono was only a precursor of things to come. Soemarsono's behavior not only came as a shock to Bedding, but also to the Javanese civil servants in the district. The latter, Hazeu stated, feared that they would lose their traditional influence over the local population if they tolerated the behavior of Soemarsono.[45]

Officially, Soemarsono acted within his rights and the boundaries drawn up by the various *hormat*-circulars of the previous decade. Given his association with the nascent nationalist movement, Bedding and the traditional Javanese elite in Purwakarta found pretense to blacken the *Jaksa*. In Purwakarta, Soemarsono took it upon himself to aid the local branch of the Sarekat Islam in gaining legal recognition. He found himself diametrically opposed by the traditional *Bupati* and his family, who perceived the Sarekat Islam as a threat to their prestige and rank. In May 1913, the *Bupati* even ordered the Sarekat Islam to cease the acceptance of new members because it only encouraged estrangement instead of unity among the common people.[46] The order was to no avail: in part due to Soemarsono's support, the Purwakarta branch of the Sarekat Islam grew to 15,000 members before the end of the year.[47]

In this period, Soemarsono also lectured on the occasion of the five-year anniversary of Boedi Oetomo. He proposed that the Javanese had to come together as one people and one nation and that their nationalism should be both economical and political. This was not a new or revolutionary lecture; Soemarsono had presented it before in Batavia. In the environment of Purwakarta it was received differently. A newspaper report on the lecture stated that something was "fermenting" in Purwakarta. The European citizens even organized a secluded meeting in the local club to discuss countermeasures. Finally, the attitude and activities of Soemarsono were turned against him. Bedding summoned Soemarsono and warned him that he needed to restrain himself from using any language inciting criticism of the colonial government or suffer the consequences.[48]

Soemarsono was not one to be put in place that easily. Within weeks of the lecture he helped spread Soewardi Soerjaningrat's famous pamphlet in

Dutch titled *If I were a Dutchman*. In the pamphlet, Soewardi imagines what it is like to be a Dutchman who celebrates hundred years of independence from Napoleon's France, while being an oppressor in Asia. Soewardi finds the whole notion of a celebration an insult to the indigenous people, even more so since they are expected to participate and help finance the whole occasion. The only right thing that a "liberty-loving Dutchman" should do, he argues, is to democratize the Indies. Soewardi turned his Western-style education and knowledge against the colonizers. It resulted in the exile of Soewardi and by association reflected very badly on Soemarsono. Assistant-Resident Bedding was quick to accuse Soemarsono of incitement and transgression of the press law for illegal distribution of political pamphlets.[49]

Hazeu was not convinced of Soemarsono's harmful intentions. Instead he focused on his complaints about the deference traditions that were still commonplace in Purwakarta, which convinced Hazeu that something was rotten in the culture of the civil service. Hazeu based his opinion on correspondence between Bedding and the *vice-Jaksa* of Purwakarta, which Soemarsono had given him. Apparently, the *vice-Jaksa* had dared to sit on a chair during a meeting of the police court in the absence of the Assistant-Resident (who normally presided). Bedding suspected that Soemarsono had encouraged his friend to do so and wrote the following letter to restore order to his police court:

> Considering you are expected at the session of the police court tomorrow, I notify you, that I do not allow you to sit on a chair, since that is a preference I have personally only granted to *Jaksa* R. Soemarsono. You always used to sit on a mat and without my permission, you allowed yourself to sit on a chair. There is no reason for that.[50]

According to Soemarsono, this short notice illustrated the relationship between the modern and educated Javanese on the one hand and those "European and indigenous civil servants, who still place value in the old worn-out *hormat*-customs within the civil service"[51] on the other.

The correspondence made a lasting impression on Hazeu, who immediately contacted Governor General Idenburg about the matter. According to Hazeu, the contrast between the education of the young Javanese, during which they were trained as equals, encouraged to converse in Dutch, make European friends, and state their opinion freely, contrasted greatly with the reality of their careers in the colonial bureaucracy where "they are confronted with a European superior with a completely different mentality." Since Hazeu believed that the new generation of Javanese no longer tolerated every humiliation as they used to, he urged the Governor

General to promulgate a new, but even tougher, *hormat*-circular. The new one, Hazeu argued, should make it impossible for someone like the "Assistant-Resident Bedding, to have the power to decide individually if a native of modern development and civilization is allowed to sit on a chair in the company of European civil servants."[52] For the maintenance of peace and order in the Indies, Hazeu argued, this step was absolutely necessary. The Governor General agreed completely and issued another *hormat*-circular within less than a month from Soemarsono's first appeal for help from Hazeu.

The resulting *hormat*-circular of 22nd August 1913 was far more threatening than all its precursors. Hazeu's hand is clearly recognizable in the text of both the circular and an accompanying confidential attachment. The circular opened with an extensive overview of the preceding *hormat*-circulars, after which it concluded that these had been willfully ignored by a considerable part of the European and indigenous civil service. In essence, the circular stated that all who continued to diametrically oppose government policies would face severe punishment. The circular was a clear product of the Ethical Policy, since it reiterated that there was no reason to be afraid of the national awakening of the Javanese, which "instead, should be interpreted as the first result of the long lasting attempts to uplift the natives."[53] Finally, it emphasized that civil servants were there for the people, not the other way around.

Just as important as the circular itself was an attached confidential document that elaborated on the changing relationship between the European civil service and the indigenous people. Its message was clear: No longer could Europeans be considered the superiors of the growing number of highly-educated young Javanese. Consequently, the attitudes towards these Javanese intellectuals needed to adapt to the times. Three case studies were provided to show how not to proceed, and although these were anonymous, the example of the encounter between Soemarsono and Bedding stood out. The occasional recourse to harsh language in this document showed the dissatisfaction of the government and seemed to promise a strong move towards modernizing the colonial relationship. However, when this confidential note was leaked to the press and the judgment of the government on its own civil servants became public, an unprecedented debate in both the European and the vernacular press erupted. This time however, all groups in colonial society participated in the escalating debate.[54]

Unsurprisingly, the fiercest criticism of the new circular derived from European civil servants, who were angry and humiliated after receiving a public reprimand. The civil servants completely rejected the accusations of the circular and placed the blame squarely at the feet of the Advisor of Native Affairs, a mere man of theory rather than practice, and the Javanese themselves, who simply wanted to show Javanese deference to their European superiors out of a sense of politeness.[55] A completely different interpretation of the circular could be found in the vernacular press, where the old-fashioned deference demands of both European civil servants and Javanese aristocrats were fiercely criticized and ridiculed. For instance, in the periodical *Doenia Bergerak,* an author imagined what he would do if he were a *Bupati*. He would ignore the *hormat*-circular, be unmoved by the misery of his subjects, befriend European capital, and crush natives who refused to squat before him.[56] Publications like these demonstrated that the discussion regarding the culture of colonial rule was no longer merely a debate regarding the relationship between Europeans and Javanese: it now incorporated all of colonial society. This in turn resulted in the forging of new alliances.

In October 1913, the Adjunct Advisor for Native Affairs, D.A. Rinkes, offered the support of the colonial government to Tjokroaminoto, then president of the Sarekat Islam, with the founding of local branches of its organization. While the central government supported the Sarekat Islam, many European and indigenous civil servants opposed the growth of the organization (the situation in Purwakarta comes to mind). Tjokroaminoto accepted Rinkes's offer, after which both men toured Java together. These shared presentations by Rinkes and Tjokroaminoto represent the precarious coalition between the protaganists of the Ethical Policy and the nationalist movement. On behalf of the government, Rinkes spoke at Sarekat Islam gatherings and told the audience that civil servants were there for the people, not the other way around. Moreover, he presented the latest *hormat*-circular as evidence of the sincere intentions of the government to develop the Indies and its inhabitants. The servile deference traditions were considered an obstacle in the way of progress. The Javanese were no longer obliged to crouch or make the *sembah*.[57]

That the message of Rinkes was well received can be seen in the many referrals to the *hormat*-circular in the vernacular press and at Sarekat Islam meetings. The circular provided the new generation with ammunition in defending itself against unjust treatment and demands by social superiors. The Sarekat Islam helped disseminate this information quickly all over Java.

During a gathering in Semarang in 1914, for example, the supporters of the local Sarekat Islam branch carried around a banner stating: "We, Javanese do no longer want to be trampled upon." Even more to the point: "The Javanese does not want to squat like a frog."[58] Meanwhile, the vernacular press pledged to monitor the abuse of power in colonial society and report any offence against it. Indeed, from 1913 onwards the vernacular press is filled with examples of abuses of power.

Contested Hegemony

The promulgation of the *hormat*-circular in 1913 was a turning point in the struggle over cultural hegemony in the Indies. Since 1901 the main challenge had come from European protagonists of the Ethical Policy—like Snouck Hurgronje and Hazeu. From August 1913 onwards the nationalist movement became involved and eventually took over. A strong conservative reaction, led by European civil servants and elements within the traditional Javanese aristocracy, mirrored the dynamic growth of the nationalist movement after 1913. These conservative voices pushed back against the increased Europeanization of the Javanese and modernization of the colonial relationship, which they believed could only result in open rebellion when the colonized discovered they could never become truly equal to Europeans. Instead, the Javanese and their culture should be protected from negative European influences.[59] Whenever tensions in colonial society mounted, for example following the murder of a European civil servant in Toli-Toli in 1918 and the eruption of violence in Garut in 1919, conservative voices called for a restoration of the traditional aura of the colonial civil services as counterweights to the derailed nationalist movement. As a prominent civil servant put it: "a modern police force costs several millions more than the old Asian instrument of power: *Hormat*."[60]

Similar sentiments emerged in the wake of the communist revolts of 1926 and 1927 in West Java and Sumatra. For conservative civil servants as well as the Javanese aristocracy, the revolts proved that they had been right all along: the *hormat*- and *payung*-circulars had severely undermined colonial authority and prestige. The only solution was to reinstate certain symbols of power and deference forms. A great sense of nostalgia for the autocratic rule of yesteryear came over the colony. This naïve longing for the past ignored the profound changes that had altered colonial society completely. The symbols of power and deference forms had in fact lost their meaning and importance. They had become relics of a bygone past. The progressive *Bupati* Achmad Djajadiningrat understood this well enough when he argued in 1929 that the "glory of the *payung*" was irreparable.[61]

Conclusion

The seemingly minor confrontation between a Javanese subordinate and a Dutch colonial official over deference-etiquette and dress in 1913 illuminates the various ways in which cross-cultural exchange both supported and undermined Dutch colonial legitimacy in late colonial Java. The encounter was illustrative of how the Dutch adopted and employed elements of Javanese culture, like dress, symbols of power, and architecture as well as deference traditions, to legitimize colonial authority around the turn of the twentieth century. This enduring system of cultural hegemony was first challenged by the implementation of the Ethical Policy, which aimed to modernize the colonial relationship. As Soemarsono's experience demonstrated, by 1913 this policy had not yet been successful. It took the emergence of the Indonesian nationalist movement to finally reverse the current of cultural exchange and modernize the grounds of colonial authority. Soemarsono, with his Western education, Dutch language skills, and familiarity with European culture and society, personified this change. Like many other young Javanese, he refused to squat, crouch, sit on the floor, present *sembah*, and conform to the Javanese language hierarchy. For Soemarsono and the nationalist movement in general, the right to converse in Dutch, sit on chairs, shake hands, and wear European clothes, became symbols of emancipation. Even when violent outbursts associated with the nationalist movement in the colony (that is, in 1918, 1919, 1926, and 1927) provided a strong conservative reaction with ammunition, the earlier reversal of this most peculiar pattern of cultural exchange remained in place. The non-conformism in outward appearance and deference rituals of Western-educated young Javanese like Soemarsono, their associations, beginning with the Sarekat Islam and the newspapers they printed, disseminated, and read, proved to be incredibly contagious.

Notes

1. Leiden University Library (UBL), Collection Hazeu, H 1083, no. 29, correspondence Advisor for Native Affairs G.A.J. Hazeu and *Jaksa* Soemarsono.

2. P.H. Fromberg, "De Inlandsche Beweging op Java," [The Indigenous Movement on Java] *De Gids* 78 (1914): 28–9.
3. Benedict Anderson, "The Language of Indonesian Politics," in Benedict R. O'G. Anderson, *Language and Power: Exploring Political Cultures in Indonesia* (Ithaca, NY: Cornell University Press, 1990), 123–51. John M. Brownlee, "Colonial Knowledge and Indigenous Power in the Dutch East Indies," *Explorations in Southeast Asian Studies* 2, no. 1 (1998): 19–29. Leslie H. Palmier, *Social Status and Power in Java* (London: University of London, Athlone Press, 1960), 1–36.
4. See the chapters in this volume by Matthew Schauer and Caroline Herbelin.
5. See Schauer's chapter.
6. Elsbeth Locher-Scholten, *Ethiek in Fragmenten: Vijf Studies over Koloniaal Denken en Doen van Nederlanders in de Indonesische Archipel, 1877–1942* [Ethics in Fragments: Five Studies on Dutch Colonial Theory and Practice in the Indonesian Archipelago, 1877–1942] (Utrecht: HES Publishers, 1981); Marieke Bloembergen and Remco Raben, *Het Koloniale Beschavingsoffensief: Wegen Naar het Nieuwe Indie* [The Colonial Civilizing Mission: Avenues towards the New Indies] (Leiden: KITLV Press, 2009); Steven Wedema, *"Ethiek" und Macht: Die Niederländisch-Indische Kolonialverwaltung und Indonesische Emanzipationsbestrebungen, 1901–1927* [Ethics and Power: The Netherlands Indies' Colonial Administration and the Indonesian Emancipation Movement, 1901–1927] (Stuttgart: F. Steiner, 1998); Suzanne Moon, *Technology and Ethical Idealism: A History of Development in the Netherlands East Indies* (Leiden: CNWS Publications, 2007); Susie Protschky, ed., *Photography, Modernity and the Governed: Re-viewing the 'Ethical' Era in Late-Colonial Indonesia* (Amsterdam: Amsterdam University Press, 2014).
7. C.W. Newbury, "Patrons, Clients, and Empire: The Subordination of Indigenous Hierarchies in Asia and Africa," *Journal of World History* 11, no. 2 (2000): 227–63.
8. H.W. van den Doel, *De Stille Macht: Het Europese Binnenlands Bestuur op Java en Madoera, 1808–1942* [Soft Power: The European Colonial Administration on Java and Madura, 1808–1942] (Amsterdam: Bert Bakker, 1994). Heather Sutherland, *The Making of a Bureaucratic Elite: The Colonial Transformation of the Javanese Priyayi* (Singapore: Heinemann Educational Books, 1979).
9. *Hormat* can either be translated as a noun, meaning respect or respectful, or as a verb, in which case it refers to showing or receiving someone's respect.
10. Benedict Anderson, *Language and Power: Exploring Political Cultures in Indonesia* (Ithaca, NY: Cornell University Press, 1990), 194–237.
11. In contrast, Anderson argued that Western power is abstract, heterogeneous, has no limits and is morally ambiguous. Anderson, *Language and Power*, 17–77.
12. Anderson, *Language and Power*, 28.
13. *Het Nieuws van den Dag voor Nederlandsch-Indië* [Netherlands Indies' Daily News] 9, no. 246 (24 Oct. 1904).

14. Anderson, *Language and Power*, 131–2.
15. Leiden University Library (UBL), Collection Hazeu, H 1083, no. 29, G.A.J. Hazeu to the Committee "Mangajoe Basa Djawa," 6 Dec. 1918.
16. *Bijblad op het Staatsblad van Nederlandsch-Indië* [Addition to the Government Gazette] 40, no. 6496 (Batavia: Landsdrukkerij, 1907), 265–8.
17. Kartini to Mejuffrouw Zeehandelaar, 18 Aug. 1899, in *Kartini, Letters of a Javanese Princess* (Kuala Lumpur: Oxford University Press, 1976), 13.
18. "Nota Betreffende de Verhouding tusschen het Europeesch en het Inlandsch Bestuur," [Memorandum on the Relationship between the European and Indigenous Colonial Administration], 1521–4.
19. Hadi Ningrat, "De Achteruitgang van het Prestige der Inlandsche Hoofden en de Middelen om daarin Verbetering the Brengen," [The Decline of the Prestige of Indigenous Administrators and Ways to Improve it] *Tijdschrift voor het Binnenlandsch Bestuur* 17 (1899): 367–85.
20. Eckart [pseudonym of H.E. Steinmetz], *Indische Brieven aan een Staatsraad* [Indies' Letters to the Council of State] (Haarlem: De Erven F. Bohn, 1888), 181–2.
21. Ibid.
22. van den Doel, *De Stille Macht,* 181–2.
23. Snouck Hurgronje to Governor General Roosenboom, 16 Aug. 1903, in *Ambtelijke Adviezen* 2: 1027–8. This resulted in an official circular: *Bijblad op het Staatsblad* 37, no. 5946 (Batavia: G. Kolff & Co, 1904), 395–7.
24. Snouck Hurgronje to the Director of the Administration of the Interior, 26 May 1904, in *Ambtelijke Adviezen* 2: 1028–35.
25. *Bijblad op het Staatsblad* 38, no. 6118 (Batavia: Landsdrukkerij, 1905): 314–16. The *payung* circular was dated 3 Nov. 1904, but not published in *Bijblad.*
26. The Historical Documentation Center for Dutch Protestantism (HDC), Collection A.W.F. Idenburg, Inventory no. 129, Governor General J.B. van Heutsz to Minister of Colonial Affairs A.W.F. Idenburg, 13 Mar. 1905.
27. *Bijblad op het Staatsblad* 38, no. 6118: 315.
28. Ibid., 314–16.
29. Snouck Hurgronje to the Directeur van Binnenlandsch Bestuur, 20 April 1904, in *Ambtelijke Adviezen* 1 (1957): 525.
30. *Soerabaiasch Handelsblad*, 26 Nov. 1904.
31. *Het Nieuws van den Dag voor Nederlandsch-Indië* 9, no. 278 (30 Nov. 1904).
32. Snouck Hurgronje to Governor General Van Heutsz, 1 Mar. 1906, in *Ambtelijke Adviezen* 2: 1037–8.
33. *Bijblad op het Staatsblad* 40, no. 6496 (Batavia: Landsdrukkerij, 1907): 265–8.
34. Ibid.
35. *Het Nieuws van de Dag voor Nederlandsch-Indië* 11, no. 92 (23 Apr. 1906).
36. *Bijblad op het Staatsblad* 43, no. 7029 (Batavia: Landsdrukkerij, 1910): 120–1.
37. Akira Nagazumi, *The Dawn of Indonesian Nationalism. The Early Years of the Budi Utomo, 1908–1918* (Tokyo: Institute of Developing Economies, 1972);

A.P.E. Korver, *Sarekat Islam 1912–1916: Opkomst bloei, en structuur van Indonesië's eerste massabeweging* [Sarekat Islam 1912–1916: Rise, Efflorescence, and Structure of Indonesia's First Mass Movement] (Amsterdam: Historisch Seminarium van de Universiteit van Amsterdam, 1982); Robert van Niel, *The Emergence of the Modern Indonesian Elite* (The Hague and Bandung: W. Van Hoeve Ltd., 1960).

38. *Koloniaal Tijdschrift (KT)* 1 (1912): 219, referring to *Pemberita Betawi*, 17 Jan. 1912. *KT* 1 (1912): 229–30, referring to *Pantjaran Warta*, 18 Jan. 1912. *KT* 1 (1912): 724, referring to *Bintang Soerabaja*, no. 82.
39. D.A. Rinkes, "Oude en Nieuwe Stroomingen onder de Bevolking," [Old and New Currents among the Indigenous Population] *Indisch Genootschap. Verslagen der Algemene Vergaderingen over de Jaren 1915–16–1920* (18 Nov. 1916), 55–78.
40. Governor General Idenburg to H.H. van Kol, 7 July 1913, in S.L. van der Wal, *De Opkomst van de Nationalistische Beweging in Nederlandsch-Indie: Een Bronnenpublicatie* [The Rise of the Nationalist Movement in the Netherlands Indies: A Source Publication] (Groningen: J.B. Wolters, 1967), 297–8.
41. In 1893, Bedding began his career as an Aspirant-Controller, became Controller in 1898, was promoted to Assistant-Resident in 1911, and finally made it as Resident of Banten in 1922. Bedding retired and repatriated in 1925.
42. UBL, Collection Hazeu, H 1083, 29, G.A.J. Hazeu to the Governor General, 18 and 20 Aug. 1913.
43. UBL, Collection Hazeu, H 1083, 29, Soemarsono to G.A.J. Hazeu, 28 July 1913.
44. UBL, Collection Hazeu, H 1083, 29, Soemarsono to G.A.J. Hazeu, 28 July 1913 and 17 Aug. 1913. Soemarsono to D.A. Rinkes, 8 Aug. 1913.
45. UBL, Collection Hazeu, H 1083, 29, G.A.J. Hazeu to Governor General A.W.F. Idenburg, 18 August 1913.
46. *Het Nieuws van den dag voor Nederlandsch-Indië* 18, no. 113 (19 May 1913).
47. Nationaal Archief, Den Haag (NL-HaNA), Ministerie van Koloniën: Openbaar Verbaal, 1901–52 [hereafter Koloniën / Openbaar Verbaal], 2.10.36.04, 1076, Verbaal (Vb.) 22 Aug. 1913. NL-HaNA, Ministerie van Koloniën: Geheim Archief, 1901–40 [hereafter Koloniën / Geheim Archief], 2.10.36.51, 153, Vb. 9 August 1913, B13. Soewardi Suryaningrat, "Staat de Regeering werkelijk sympathiek tegenover de S.I.?," [Is the Government Really Sympathetic towards the S.I.?] *De Indiër* 1, no. 4 (13 Nov. 1913): 48.
48. *Het Nieuws van den dag voor Nederlandsch-Indië* 18, no. 125 (2 June 1913).
49. Soewardi Surjaningrat, "Als ik eens Nederlander was,...," *Uitgave van het Indische Comite tot Herdenking van Neerlands Honderjarige Vrijheid* ["If I were a Dutchman,...." *Publication of the Indies Committee for the Commemoration of One Hundred Years of Dutch Independence*] (Bandung, 1913). A complete translation of the pamphlet can be found in Savitri Prastiti Scherer, "Harmony and Dissonance: Early Nationalist Thought in Java," unpublished Masters Thesis, Cornell University, 1975.

50. UBL, Collection Hazeu, H 1083, 29, J.C. Bedding to Wirasaputra, 7 July 1913.
51. UBL, Collection Hazeu, H 1083, 29, Soemarsono to G.A.J. Hazeu, 17 Aug. 1913.
52. UBL, Collection Hazeu, H 1083, 29, G.A.J. Hazeu to Governor General A.W.F. Idenburg, 20 Aug.1913.
53. *Bijblad op het Staatsblad* 48, no. 7939 (Batavia: Landsdrukkerij, 1914). The confidential attachment can be found in UBL, Collection Hazeu, H 1083, 29, "Nota bij de hormatcirculaire van 22 Augustus 1913."
54. UBL, Collection Hazeu, H 1083, 29, "Nota bij de hormatcirculaire van 22 Augustus 1913."
55. W.T.L. Boissevain, "Protestbeweging van de Vereeniging van Ambtenaren bij het Binnenlandsch Bestuur," [Protest Movement of the Association for Civil Servants of the European Colonial Administration] *KT* 3, no. 1 (1914): 69–78. "De zevende hormat-circulaire en de uitlatingen van Dr. Rinkes," [The Seventh Hormat-Circular and the Commentary of Dr. Rinkes] *KT* 3, no. 1 (1914): 365–7. Tertius, "Geef acht, B.B.!," [Salute, European Colonial Administrators!] *KT* 3, no. 1 (1914): 376–80. G.Th. Stibbe, "Nog een Protest," [Another Protest] *KT* 3, no. 1 (1914): 493–5.
56. *KT* 3 (1913): 682–3, referring to *Doenia Bergerak*, no. 32.
57. D.A. Rinkes to Oemar Said Tjokjroaminoto, 25 Oct. 1913, in *De Opkomst van de Nationalistische Beweging in Nederlands-Indië*, 346–53 [The Rise of the Nationalist Movement in the Netherlands Indies: A Source Publication] *KT* 3 (1913): 519, referring to *Oetoesan Hindia*, no. 24. *KT* 3 (1913): 526, referring to *Djawa Tengah*, no. 7.
58. *KT* 3 (1913): 1410, referring to *Kaoem Moeda*, no. 165.
59. M.B. van der Jagt, "Ethische Koers en Bestuursambtenaar," [The Ethical Policy and Colonial Administrators] *KT* 4, no. 2: 1191–215 and 1328–45.
60. J.W. Meijer Ranneft, *De toekomst van het Binnenlandsch Bestuur* [The Future of the European Colonial Administration] (Buitenzorg: Archipel, 1922), 10.
61. van den Doel, *De Stille Macht*, 387–94. Achmad Djajadiningrat's comments can be found in R.A.A. Djajadiningrat, "De positie van de regenten op Java en Madoera in het huidige bestuursstelsel," [The Position of the Indigenous Regents on Java and Madura in the Current Administration] *Indisch Genootschap* (15 Nov. 1929): 90.

SECTION TWO
Material and Architectural Exchange

CHAPTER 4

"Chinese" Screens in the Dutch East Indies

Dawn Odell

What does it mean to be "Chinese" in the context of eighteenth-century Batavia? Even by the standards of an early modern world in which formerly distant cultures were increasingly brought into contact with one another through trade and other endeavors, Batavia (present-day Jakarta, Indonesia) had a diverse population, one that its European residents organized into a number of permeable and unstable categories based upon religion, country of origin, and freed or enslaved status, among other markers of difference.[1] Historians often interpret the art produced in this complex environment through a framework that stresses relationships between a work and the norms of its presumed maker's cultural home, assessing an object's ability to translate its meaning from one fixed social, architectural, and geographic context into another. In this chapter, I consider a work, a monumental carved screen (Fig. 4.1) that initially appears to be an example of this successful cross-cultural translation, an object presumed to have been created in Batavia by Chinese craftsmen in the employ of Dutch colonists, in order to resituate and repurpose an Asian object within a colonial European interior.[2] However, closer examination suggests that contrary to expectations, this "Chinese" screen functioned in ways that oppose its presumed models, revealing instead the social and ecological particularities of Batavia. Ultimately, the chapter posits that the screen's material presence—its role in configuring and responding to the space it inhabits—is key to understanding its status

Figure 4.1: Screen from the Fort Council Room, Batavia, early eighteenth century, teak, 297 x 231 cm, Museum Sejarah, Jakarta, inv. No. 3724 D.L. Author's personal collection.

as a specifically Batavian, rather than Chinese, object. This chapter's subject matter, the carved screen, is similar to the types of "hybrid" architectural and material creations discussed by Caroline Herbelin, H. Hazel Hahn and Arnout H.C. van der Meer in this volume. In conversation with their contributions, this chapter argues that the screen's meaning stems from its uniquely Batavian form and function, and highlights both local specificities and the diversity of patterns of cross-cultural exchange also emphasized by the other authors.

Although more opulent than most and better known, this screen is just a single example of a type that commonly decorated the interiors of domestic and civic spaces within the city of Batavia.[3] The form and decoration of the screens varied from relatively small-scale, undecorated single panels to highly wrought, multi-panel room dividers, and they were used not only in the Dutch East Indies but also in other Dutch colonial contexts including South Africa.[4] In an earlier effort to understand these screens within the larger context of specifically Batavian material culture, I suggested that the screens might be seen as mediating between two competing social spaces, the busy streets, squares, wharfs and canals of seventeenth-century Batavia, the Dutch East India Company's administrative and commercial capital in Asia, and the more intimate, interior spaces of the colonists' homes and civic chambers.[5] With its Dutch canals, imposing fort and protective walls, Batavia was an overt manifestation of the Dutch political presence in Asia and also, in the arrangement of its neighborhoods within a hierarchy of racialized identities, a diagram of the social complexities of colonial life.[6] As one of the world's great trading centers, Batavia was inhabited by individuals from regions as far flung as Portugal, Germany, India, China, and north Africa, in addition to those from Java and other Indonesian islands. Andries Beeckman's (?–1664) ca. 1661 oil painting of Batavia (Fig. 4.2) has become the canonical visual representation of the city's diversity.[7] Among dozens of other figures pictured in this image, a viewer finds in the background at the far right, men in dark, European suits processing on horseback away from the walls of Fort Batavia. In the mid-ground, male figures in Chinese and Japanese robes walk among other men dressed in fitted striped jackets and ballooning trousers, the stripes an indication, perhaps, of the figures' status as freed slaves.[8] Near them, two women sit on stools beside carpets, upon which fruits are displayed for sale. They wear long, patterned skirts; one has no covering above the waist and the other is dressed in a loose white blouse. A man with a moustache and wearing a turban and long white robes, scarf thrown over one shoulder, strolls past a group of men who are barefoot, wearing long skirts and close-fitting white caps, and engaged in kicking a ball between them. The variation of the population on display here and the celebration of the city's bustling outdoor activity is similar to many seventeenth- and early eighteenth-century depictions of Batavia, in that the activities of the urban inhabitants are presented unfurling out of doors and across spaces bounded and defined by the city's architecture.

Figure 4.2: Andries Beeckman, *The Castle of Batavia*, 1661, oil on canvas, h 108 cm x w 151.5 cm, Rijksmuseum, Amsterdam, object number SK-A-19.

Johan Nieuhof (1618–72), Beeckman's contemporary and one of the most popular European travel book writers of the seventeenth century, illustrated his 1682 account of a visit to Batavia with prints that, similar to Beeckman's painting, display a range of individuals moving across stage-like architectural backgrounds. His representation of the city's Latin School, for example, shows figures in European and Asian dress walking before shuttered windows and a blank white wall, pierced only by the hint of a view into an interior colonnaded courtyard (Fig. 4.3). As in the Latin School, the majority of images from Nieuhof's Batavia text (including depictions of the Chinese hospital, Church of the Cross, Orphanage, Chinese Temple, and Tiger Canal) focus on exterior views of architecture. The text does include several single-page, closely observed depictions of human and plant "types," presented separately from the main travel narrative, but the work contains not a single representation of figures in a Batavian interior. Instead, the Batavian population, whether of European, Asian or African origin, is always depicted out of doors.

Nieuhof's representation of his Batavia visit as a sequence of exterior views is in marked contrast to his contemporaries' depiction of life at home in Europe. In representing Dutch urban experience, artists frequently position the viewer as an "insider," who glimpses urban spaces from within domestic

Figure 4.3: Illustration of the Latin School from Johan Nieuhof, *Gedenkwaerdige Zee en Lantreize, door verscheide gewesten van Oostindien: behelzende veele zeltzaame en wonderlijke voorvallen en geschiedenissen. Beneffens een beschrijving van lantschappen, steden, dieren, gewassen, draghten, zeden en godsdienst der inwoonders en inzonderheit een wijtloopig verhael der stad Batavia...* Jacob van Meurs, 1682, engraving with later hand-coloring, image size 15.4 cm x 13 cm. Author's personal collection.

interiors, through open doors and windows. Pieter de Hooch's (1629–after 1684) oil painting of *The Bedroom* (Fig. 4.4), for example, places the viewer within a series of telescoping doorways through which adjacent houses may be glimpsed. In contrast to Nieuhof's blank walls, de Hooch's painting emphasizes the permeable boundary between interior and exterior spaces, and the role of women in guarding transitions between the two, creating a form of representation that was recognized even in the seventeenth century as a particularly Dutch visualization of domesticity.[9]

In Batavia, domesticity was less securely tied to "Dutchness." Figures in the foreground of Beeckman's canvas help to explain why. Here a man wearing a suit of European design and a large lace collar strolls with a woman, presumably his wife or domestic companion, dressed in a Javanese loose-fitting white blouse, long vest, and patterned skirt. A diminutive servant

Figure 4.4: Pieter de Hooch, *The Bedroom*, 1658/60, oil on canvas, 51 x 60 cm, The National Gallery of Art, Washington, DC, Widener Collection, accession number 1942.9.33.

accompanies the processing couple and shades them with a large parasol. The couple is a visual representation of what had by this period become a conventional domestic relationship for male European colonists in Batavia. Many Dutch men married or cohabitated with Asian women because few European women traveled to or lived in Batavia in the seventeenth and eighteenth centuries.[10] Marriage between European men and Asian women was tolerated and in some periods even encouraged by the VOC, but European visitors to Batavia rarely failed to describe these relationships as anything other than unnatural and unwholesome; they focused particular disdain on the women, their "dingy complexions" and boorish manners.[11] These textual descriptions, however precise in their critiques, were not reinforced by visual depictions. Following the model of Nieuhof and Beeckman, artists visiting the colony rarely represented the interior life of the city.[12] In concert, perhaps, with the artists' unwillingness to depict life behind walls, the screen further obscured the colonial domestic interior from a viewer's scrutiny, separating the polyglot commercial life of the city from its less celebrated domestic realm.

An engraving from Johan Wolfgang Heydt's (1738–c. 1800) *Description of Africa and the East Indies* (Fig. 4.5) clarifies the screen's placement within the Council Chamber of Batavia Castle and its role in protecting a view and framing a movement from street (or in this case corridor) to nested interior.[13] As Heydt's text explains:

> In front of the entrance or door stands a room divider [g] or *schützel* as the Dutch used to call it. When the door is opened it prevents people looking too far into the hall. The divider is well carved from wood with nice foliage and statues mostly gilded. These room dividers are very common in European houses in the Indies, they stand in front of entrances at the doors. This fashion has been adopted from the Chinese. They invest a lot of money for it, one more than the other to make their houses more attractive.[14]

Placed directly inside of and horizontal with the chamber's central doorway, the screen prevented those passing by the entry from seeing deeper into the interior and acted as a kind of portable wall, blocking not only the viewer's eyes but also the visitor's body from moving straight through the entrance directly into the space beyond. The screen's presence forced visitors to stop, pause, mark the threshold, and conceive a transition before moving sideways around the screen and entering the space of the interior.

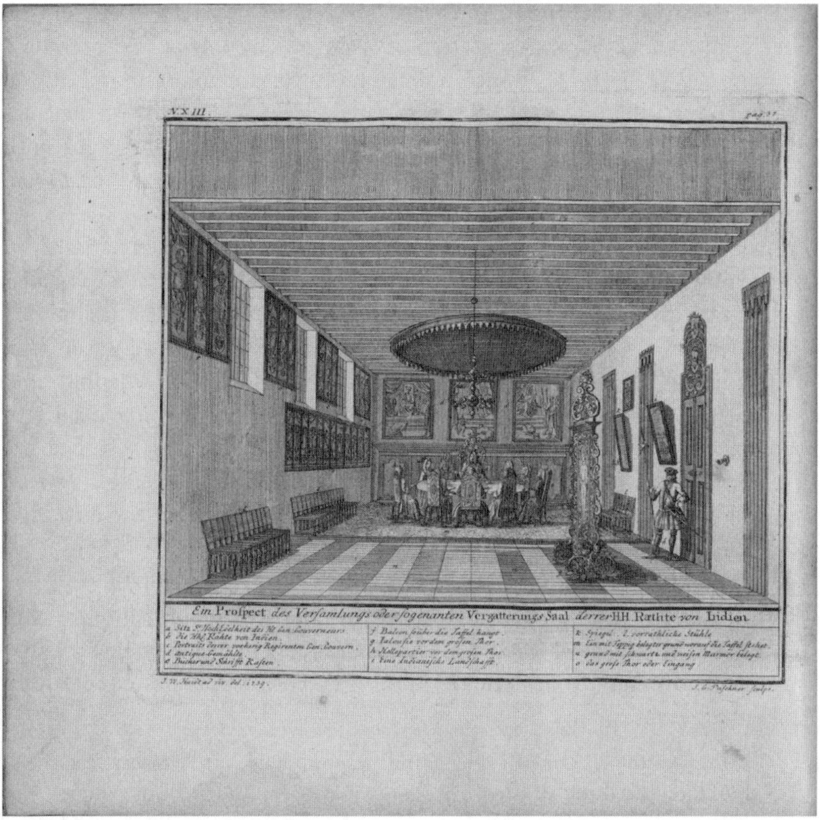

Figure 4.5: Illustration from Johann Wolfgang Heydt, *Allerneuester geographisch und topographischer Schauplaz von Africa und Ostindien oder ausführliche und wahrhafte Vorstellung & Beschreibung der Holländisch-Ost-Indischen Compagnie zugehörigen Länderen* (Wilhermsdorf: Tetschner, 1744), engraving.

As Heydt states, in form and function the inspiration for these Batavian screens was thought to be Chinese, but in terms of function the Chinese model for our Batavian screen is not a piece of furniture but an element of architecture, a freestanding wall that in a traditional Chinese home would be located just inside of and horizontal to the primary entrance. Traditional multi-generational residences in China were composed of individual rooms arranged around the perimeter of a courtyard. Larger homes might be composed of three or more courtyards, which the visitor would encounter sequentially via a progression along a horizontal axis. The movement through the courtyards and past individual halls and chambers was also a movement from more public to more private, sequestered, nested spaces. In addition, a high windowless wall surrounded the compound. The entire residence was thus screened from public view, and a visitor to a house such as this would move from the street, through the single doorway, piercing the otherwise unbroken expanse of exterior wall, to be stopped by a freestanding wall, which would force a pause and a movement sideways into the first and most public of the home's courtyards.[15] Beyond Heydt's unique illustration of the screen standing within the VOC Council Room, our best evidence for the placement of screens in Dutch colonial interiors is derived from domestic architecture in South Africa. Extant eighteenth-century examples of the "Cape screen" indicate that they were constructed opposite the front door and were the most striking feature of the *voorhuis* or entrance hall.[16] The screens regulated the flow of air, light, and visitors between the entrance hall and the *agterhuis* behind and were often embellished with carved designs that echoed the decoration found on the fanlights above the front door, creating a visual pairing similar to the decorative relationship between the screen and doorway in Heydt's print.

Unlike the moveable Batavian screen that is the subject of this chapter, "Cape screens" are not pieces of freestanding furniture but were built into the fabric of the house. The difference in nomenclature between different types of Chinese screens, specifically screen walls (*yingbi*) versus painted screens (*huaping*), helps to clarify the distinction between the form and the function of "Cape screens" and our Batavian example.[17] For unlike the *yingbi*, which was perhaps the inspiration for the "Cape screens" and which in China originated as a wall of rammed or pounded earth, the Batavian screen provides more than protection and concealment; it also serves as a site of ornamentation. Richly carved with decoration that aids in defining and demarcating place, the Batavian screen acts as an honorific and in this way has a function more akin to a *huaping* than a *yingbi* screen. However, once again the relationship between the Chinese prototype and its Batavian descendant is complex and imperfect. In the East Asian tradition, a *huaping* screen is most often conceived as a painted representation inconspicuously supported by a wooden frame. It confers status on its owner not by blocking access to interior spaces but by opening and framing spaces within which the owner is presented to the viewer. For example, as Wu Hung has argued, the fifteenth-century portrait of the Ming dynasty Hongzhi emperor (Fig. 4.6) shows how the *huaping* instantiates particular qualities to the space it creates and reflects those qualities onto the person who sits before it.[18] In this painting the screen draws attention to the emperor's uniquely elevated position in Chinese society by juxtaposing his static portrayal with the writhing form of the five-clawed dragon behind him. By opposing the clearly portrait-like qualities of the emperor's frozen and iconic representation with the more animated qualities of the dragon twisting in space, the painting also makes the viewer aware of tensions within the fiction of representation: the screen's image appearing more lifelike than the emperor's. Qiu Ying's sixteenth-century depiction of a scholar examining two fan paintings, part of a larger art collection that surrounds him (Fig. 4.7), provides another example of how, in China, moveable screens could be used to create and contextualize space. Here, two standing screens form a protective outdoor chamber for the gentleman to appreciate his rare and precious objects. In conjunction, the screens not only form a space but also comment upon that space; they create a "room" that as Wu Hung argues, differentiates and juxtaposes the spheres of nature and culture.[19] The landscape paintings on the screens' surface reference both the subject matter most popular among elite scholar artists and present the viewer with images of the natural environment that challenge the reality of the garden environment surrounding the screens.

The iconographical implications of the moveable painted Chinese screen, the screen's ability to establish through its decoration the meaning of the space it creates, resonates with our Batavian example (Fig. 4.1), which is decorated at its top with the coats of arms of Batavia and, to the left and right of the Batavian arms, the coats of arms of the six Dutch cities where the VOC had chambers at home in the Netherlands (to the left: Amsterdam, Rotterdam, Delft; to the right: Middelburg, Hoorn, Enkhuizen). In addition, the screen's central figure, surmounted by a canopy, is believed to represent the Greek hero Perseus holding the shield that allowed him to defeat Medusa.[20] Perseus is a particularly appropriate figure to decorate a screen that marks a private space within an outpost of the Dutch mercantile empire, for although Perseus eventually came to greatness and founded Mycenae, as an infant the hero was forced to brave the seas in a wooden chest, an experience akin to making the many months-long voyage from Amsterdam to Batavia and, worse, a reminder of the potential for shipwreck. Similar to the peripatetic lives of many of the VOC company employees, Perseus traveled the world too, in his case searching for Medusa, and visited Ethiopia among other extra-European places. However, his martial costume and conquering stance emphasize his role as a warrior rather than a voyager, and project apotropaic qualities similar to those of the Chinese screen wall (*yingbi*).

Figure 4.6: Portrait of the Hongzhi Emperor, fifteenth century, Ming dynasty, hanging scroll, ink and color on silk, 6 ft. 10 1/8 inches x 5 feet 3/4 inches, National Palace Museum, Taipei, Taiwan.

Figure 4.7: Qiu Ying, *Ranking Ancient Works in a Bamboo Court*, album leaf, ink and color on silk, 41.2 x 33.7 cm, Palace Museum, Beijing.

By focusing on Perseus, I have diverted attention from the screen as a whole and left unexplored one of the qualities that is most striking when the object is viewed in person: the screen's insistent three-dimensionality, its presence as a sculptural form. Walking around the screen, we find ourselves confronted with a view of Perseus's posterior (Fig. 4.8), a somewhat surprising representation that would never have been depicted on a Chinese screen. For although Chinese screens might thematically link the front and back surfaces (for example, placing a calligraphic text on one side and an image related to the text's content on the other), the two sides do not form a sculptural whole. They do not aim to represent a three-dimensionally unified figure or object. The materiality of the screen, its presence or "thingness," is in fact a quality central to the methodology of this chapter which began by asking what it means to be "Chinese" within the context of an early modern colonial city and attempts to answer that question by thinking through claims that the Batavian screen is itself "Chinese," that it imitates Chinese prototypes and is made by Chinese craftsmen. But as this chapter aims to show, under closer examination, a coherent and symmetrical relationship between the two—Chinese "original" and Batavian "imitation"—quickly breaks down as the physical presence of the screen forces the viewer toward an interaction quite different from those established by *yingbi* or *huaping* screens. Instead, the screen becomes an example of an unresolved imitation, an incoherent translation, and suggests the possibility that failure might be an aspect of cross-cultural encounter and exchange. As John Plotz notes when teasing out the methodology of "thing theory:"

> Thing theory, then, is not a theory about the cultural significance of objects. There is a familiar rationale for appraising evocative objects, the eloquent signifiers by which a culture makes itself known to itself.... The logical objection to such work is that it generally hears the objects saying nothing that the ambient culture has not carefully instilled. From Mauss to Strathern, the aim has been to unpack what the culture meant objects to mean, rather than to reflect on failures of meaning, or on slippages that occur between the intended meaning and the actually embodied substance....[21]

If the model for our Batavian screen is a moveable, painted Chinese screen, then a comparison between the two has shown the ways that Batavian screens do not do what their Chinese models can. The Batavian screen does not create "rooms" for study, contemplation, or imperial audience but instead stops the viewer in a liminal space that is neither inside nor outside. It also demands that the viewer confront the image of the screen before moving

Figure 4.8: Detail of illustration from Johann Wolfgang Heydt, *Allerneuester geographisch und topographischer Schauplaz von Africa und Ostindien oder ausführliche und wahrhafte Vorstellung & Beschreibung der Holländisch-Ost-Indischen Compagnie zugehörigen Länderen* (Wilhermsdorf: Tetschner, 1744), engraving.

past the object. This is in contrast to Chinese screens that frame the living subject within a painted representation and control the beholder's reception of that subject, becoming backdrops and scene-setters to reflect upon the person or object placed in front of it. For this reason, it is uncommon to find Chinese representations of viewers standing directly in front of screens and looking at them, for screens are not typically appreciated in isolation as large-scale paintings but rather are paired with figures and objects that, backs to the screen, are presented frontally to the viewer. An early twentieth-century photograph of the board of the Royal Batavian Society of Arts and Sciences (Fig. 4.9) demonstrates such an arrangement, as it shows the board members seated before the screen in a manner that is more akin to a viewer's ideal encounter with a *huaping* screen (Fig. 4.6, for example) and quite different from the Batavian screen's original placement and the viewer's original encounter with it in the Council Chamber. Rather than confronting the screen as they pass through a doorway, the board members sit with their backs to the screen, allowing the screen to set the scene and to add luster to their status as intellectuals and administrators. The placement is precise even

Figure 4.9: Photograph of the Board of the Royal Batavian Society of Arts and Sciences, detail, Batavia, 1925, photographic collection, KITLV, Leiden.

down to the location of the centrally seated board member, whose head is in perfect alignment with Perseus's.

This photograph reflects both a later period and different kind of engagement with the screen. In the eighteenth century the Batavian screen was not displayed in a manner that would have allowed it to function as a *huaping*, but it also did not function as a *yingbi*. For it is not a sight-blocking courtyard wall, but a filigree web that allows light and glimpses of rooms beyond to shimmer through its carved net. Rather than preventing views of activities behind it, the screen's transparency makes those sights even more pleasant and more tantalizing, as they dance into view between the screen's scrollwork and tracery. When photographed in natural light, another example of a Batavian teak screen (Fig. 4.10), of similar dimensions to the example on which this chapter focuses, shows glimpses of the starkly white wall that stands behind it, as the light moves around and through the screen's lacelike form. In contrast to a Chinese courtyard *yingbi*, what stands behind the Batavian screens is not obscured by but incorporated into the screen's imagery. Coupled with the fact that these screens are intended to be viewed three-dimensionally and engaged as one might view a sculpture (consider again the posterior view of Perseus), then the Batavian screens not only create a spatial demarcation but also assert a figural presence, a presence that can be absorbed simultaneously as substance and representation.

The materiality of the Batavian screens, their insistent "thingness," may be a reason that, although the screens traveled widely throughout the Dutch colonial world, including to locations in Africa and the Americas, their particular combination of form and function never translated to interiors back home in the Netherlands. This may be related to the Dutch insistence on clear visibility between interior and exterior, discussed briefly above (see Fig. 4.4), and on a form of civic voyeurism that became a metaphor for Dutch nationalism as well as Dutch domesticity. Instead of utilizing East Asian screens in ways that would translate their form and function from a colonial to a local setting at home in Europe, the Dutch decorated their interiors by deconstructing multi-panel Asian screens and displaying individual boards flat across the surface of walls.[22] Screens displayed in this wallpaper-like manner were often decorated with scenes of landscapes and cityscapes, affirming the two-dimensional surface as a site for representation and eliding a more embodied confrontation with the screen as a presence, thus constituting another "failure" of translation between a Chinese, a colonial, and a European vocabulary.

Figure 4.10: Screen, early eighteenth century, teak, National Museum of Indonesia, Jakarta. Author's personal collection.

This chapter has argued that the Batavian screen does not adhere to a Chinese model in its form or function, that it acts neither like an architectural wall nor like a painted surface, and instead reconfigures East Asian conventions for separating and differentiating space into a specifically Batavian (that is colonial, neither wholly Dutch nor Asian) object. But our understanding of these screens can be complicated yet further by expanding their placement and context beyond a consideration of how a viewer confronts a screen as an entry point between architectural space, and examining the larger ecological environment surrounding the object. As even a casual reader of travel texts relating to Batavia will soon discover, a central concern of any seventeenth- or eighteenth-century European description of the city is its overwhelming heat. Charles Peter Thunberg (1743–1828), who visited Batavia in the last quarter of the eighteenth century recounts:

> The heat of the climate has that influence likewise on the Europeans who arrive here, that in time they become heavy, inactive, and less lively, than they are in the colder climates; so that the most industrious man,

> against his inclination, frequently sinks into a state of inactivity and idleness.[23]

John Splinter Stavorinus (1739–88), a Dutch naval officer who, like Thunberg, traveled widely in the East Indies, concurs that the climate is unpleasant and diminishes the energy and even the mental health of its European inhabitants:

> Most of the people who live here [Batavia], and even many rich ones, who, it might be supposed, had attained the summit of their wishes, have something in their countenances expressive of discontent and dejection, and which seems a certain sign, that all is not right within. The climate, may, undoubtedly, contribute much to this appearance; the animal spirits do not flow in that free circulation, nor do the powers of the mind possess that strength and elasticity, which animate the human frame, and give energy to the exertions of the soul, in more temperate climes.[24]

The climate was not simply detrimental to health; it could also be fatal, as Stavorinus writes:

> What, however, is the most disagreeable circumstance attending residence at Batavia, is the insalubrity of the climate, and the great degree of mortality which prevails there, especially among transient visitors, or people that first arrive; this apparent to such a degree, that the English, who circumnavigated the globe (1768–1770), and had experienced almost every vicissitude of climate, declared that Batavia was not only the most unhealthy place they had seen, but that this circumstance was a sufficient defence or preservative against any hostile attempts, as the troops of no nation would be able to withstand, nor would any people in their senses, without absolute necessity, venture to encounter this pestilential atmosphere.[25]
>
> It is supposed, that of the Europeans of all classes, who come to settle in Batavia, not always half the number survive the year. The place resembles, in that respect, a field of battle, or a town besieged. The frequency of death renders familiar the mention of them, and little signs are shewn of emotion and surprise, on hearing that the companion of yesterday is today no more.[26]

Thunberg makes these statistics personal and piercing when he recounts:

> Among other kind friends, whom I now missed on the island, was Dr. Hoffman's lady, who had departed from this world during my absence. This recalled to my remembrance, how I had, shortly before my departure to Japan, sat down to dinner in this very house with thirteen persons, eleven of whom, my friend now informed me, had been carried

> off by the fevers which usually prevail here, in the space of three weeks, in so much, that the whole thirteen, he and myself were at this time the sole survivors. This furnishes an irrefragable proof of the mortality and unhealthy climate of this spot, where a great number of humid vapours fill the heated atmosphere, render the body sluggish, and apt readily to receive the seeds of putrification.[27]

I quote Thunberg and Stavorinus at length to convey the degree to which the inhabitants of Batavia felt themselves to be at war with their environment. Indeed, Stavorinus describes Batavia as "a field of battle." Although the inhabitants of Batavia were not yet aware that deadly malarial fevers were carried by mosquitoes, they did understand in some ways that the "bad air," rising from stagnant and polluted canals, was the cause of the illness that weakened and killed so many of the city's inhabitants.[28]

The quality of the air, the movement of air, is a constant theme among writers who visit Batavia, and the inhabitants' ability to circulate air, and to encourage breezes to flow through a property, both to cool it and to refresh "bad air" with good air, was vitally important when designing and constructing houses. As Stavorinus notes, "in several [residences] the windows are closed with a lattice-work of rattans, in the place of being glazed, for the sake of air."[29] In aid of circulation, fanlights became one of the most interesting architectural features of homes built for elites such as Renier de Klerk, Director General of the Dutch Council of the Indies. His house, constructed in what was originally the countryside around Batavia, is designed to allow healthy air to move freely between its rooms. The fanlights (Fig. 4.11), which decorate both interior and exterior doors, were carved in a manner similar to the Batavian screens (Fig. 4.10) into a delicate filigree that allowed air to easily move between them.

The images depicted in these fanlights often worked in concert with other aspects of the interior—floor and skirting tile, furniture, textiles—to create a unified decorative program that tied the boundaries marked by fanlight and screen to the home as a whole in a manner that would have been familiar in Europe. However, the particular environment of Batavia, and especially the fear of allowing its dangerous air to stagnate, fostered a dematerialization of doors, windows, and even the fabric of the screen itself. The result was an object, a Batavian object, that resists simple classifications, and instead stands as an example of a thing that pushes and pulls at the problem of where meaning and materiality meet.

Figure 4.11: Fanlight over interior door, *Huis Renier de Klerk*, 1760, Jakarta. Author's personal collection.

Notes

1. Based upon the Batavia *Dagh-Register* of 1674 (J.A. van der Chijs, ed. ['s-Gravenhage: Nijhoff, 1902], 94–5), Susan Abeyasekere lists the following population counts for the city of Batavia: Dutch 2,024; Eurasian 726; Chinese 2,747; Mardijkers (freed slaves, often Christian and originating from territories colonized by Portugal) 5,362; Moors (Indian Muslims) and Javanese 1,339; Malayans 611; Balinese 981; slaves 13,278. Susan Abeyaskere, *Jakarta: A History* (Oxford: Oxford University Press, 1987), 19.
2. Kees Zandvliet, *The Dutch Encounter with Asia, 1600–1950* (Amsterdam: Rijksmuseum; Zwolle: Waanders, 2002), 37, and Marieke Bloembergen and Martijn Eickhoff, "Travelling Far on Rather Short Legs," *The Focus: Postcolonial Dialogue, The Newsletter*, no. 59 (Spring 2012): 30 both state that the screen is of Chinese manufacture. Zandvliet also writes that the market in cabinet making was "dominated by Chinese" around 1700, and that the "manufacture and use of wooden screens—usually called a *schutsel* in contemporary inventories—was East Indies," a use which "had been adopted from the Chinese." Jan van Campen, "The Hybrid World of Batavia," in *Asia in Amsterdam: The Culture of Luxury in the Golden Age*, ed. Karina H.

Corrigan et al. (Salem, Massachusetts: Peabody Essex Museum; Amsterdam: Rijksmuseum, 2015), 44 explains that the screen "is more in line with the local production by Chinese furniture makers" and ties the screen to both "local Asian custom" and "Chinese tradition."

3. Batavia was an important trading post for the Dutch East India Company (*Vereenigde Oostindische Compagnie*, hereafter VOC). For a detailed analysis of the role of Batavia in VOC trade between Asia and Europe, see Robert Parthesius, *Dutch Ships in Tropical Waters: The Development of the Dutch East India Company (VOC) Shipping Network in Asia 1595–1660* (Amsterdam: Amsterdam University Press, 2010). The screen that is the focus of this chapter was one of the highlights of a 2009 exhibition at the Victoria and Albert Museum. See Michael Snodin and Nigel Llewellyn, eds., *Baroque Style in the Age of Magnificence, 1620–1800* (London: V&A Publishing, 2009). It was also featured in Karina H. Corrigan, Jan van Campen, and Femke Diercks, eds., with Janet C. Blyberg, *Asia in Amsterdam: The Culture of Luxury in the Golden Age* (Peabody Essex Museum, Salem, Massachusetts, and the Rijksmuseum, Amsterdam, the Netherlands, 2015).
4. Discussions of Dutch colonial furniture, including screens, are found in Titus M. Eliëns and Monique van de Geijn-Verhoeven, *Domestic Interiors at the Cape and in Batavia, 1602–1795* (Zwolle; Waanders; Den Haag: Gemeentemuseum, 2002); Dave van Gompel, Joost Hoving and Reinier Klusener, *Furniture from the Netherlands East Indies 1600–1900: A Historical Perspective based on the Collection of the Tropenmuseum* (Amsterdam: KIT Publishers, 2013); Victor Ido van de Wall, *Het hollandsche koloniale barokmeubel; bijdrage tot de kennis van het ebbenhouten meubel omstreeks het midden der XVIIde en het begin der XVIIIde eeuw* [Dutch colonial baroque furniture; a contribution to the knowledge of ebony furniture from the middle of the seventeenth to the beginning of the eighteenth centuries] (Antwerpen, De Sikkel; 's-Gravenhage: M. Nijhoff, 1939); Michael North, "On Art and Material Culture in the Cape Colony and Batavia in the Seventeenth and Eighteenth Centuries," in *Mediating Netherlandish Art and Material Culture in Asia*, ed. Thomas DaCosta Kaufmann and Michael North (Amsterdam: Amsterdam University Press, 2014); and J. Terwen-De Loos, *Het Nederlands-koloniale meubel : studie over meubels in de voormalige Nederlandse koloniën Indonesië en Sri Lanka* [Dutch colonial furniture: a study of furniture in the former Dutch colonies of Indonesia and Sri Lanka] (Franeker: T. Wever, 1985).
5. Dawn Odell, "Public Identity and Material Culture in Dutch Batavia," in *Crossing Cultures: Conflict, Migration and Convergence: The Proceedings of the 32nd International Congress of the History of Art*, ed. Jaynie Anderson (Melbourne: Miegunyah Press, 2009).
6. Marsely L. Kehoe, "Dutch Batavia: Exposing the Hierarchy of a Dutch Colonial City," *Journal of Historians of Netherlandish Art* 7, no. 1 (Winter

2015) doi:10.5092/jhna.2015.7.1.3 explains how distinctions between ethnic identities were incorporated into Batavia's city plan.

7. In preparatory drawings, Beeckman labeled the "types" of people represented in his Batavia painting, see Menno Jonker, Erlend de Groot, and Caroline de Hart, *Van velerlei pluimage: Zeventiende-eeuwse waterverftekeningen van Andries Beeckman* [Of all sorts of people: Seventeenth century watercolor drawings by Andries Beeckman] (Nijmegen: Uitgeverij Vantiilt/NKA, 2014).
8. For more on freed slaves or *mardijkers* and their status in Batavia, see Hendrik E. Niemeijer, *Batavia: Een koloniale samenleving in de 17de eeuw* [Batavia: A colonial society in the seventeenth century] (Amsterdam: Balans, 2005).
9. Much has been written about the relationships between gender, genre painting, and Dutch identity, among others see: Elizabeth Alice Honig, "The Space of Gender in Seventeenth-Century Dutch Painting," in *Looking at Seventeenth-Century Dutch Art: Realism Reconsidered*, ed. Wayne Franits (Cambridge: Cambridge University Press, 1997) and Nanette Salomon, *Shifting Priorities: Gender and Genre in Seventeenth-Century Dutch Painting* (Stanford: Stanford University Press, 2004).
10. For more on Batavia domestic relationships, see Leonard Blussé, *Strange Company: Chinese settlers, mestizo women and the Dutch in VOC Batavia* (Dordrecht, Holland and Riverton, NJ: Foris Publications, 1983); Jean Gelman Taylor, *The Social World of Batavia: Europeans and Eurasians in Colonial Indonesia* (Madison: University of Wisconsin Press, 2009); and Eric Jones, *Wives, Slaves and Concubines: A History of the Female Underclass in Dutch Asia* (DeKalb: Northern Illinois University Press, 2010).
11. John Barrow, *A Voyage to Cochinchina in the Years 1792–1793…* (London: T. Cadell and W. Davies, 1806), 209.
12. An exception is the work of Jan Brandes [1743–1808]. Brandes's sketchbooks contain dozens of watercolor drawings of his home and other Batavian interiors. Unlike Nieuhof, Beeckman, and other artists discussed in this chapter, Brandes work was never publicly distributed. For more on Jan Brandes, see *The World of Jan Brandes, 1743–1808: Drawings of a Dutch Traveler in Batavia, Ceylon, and Southern Africa* (Zwolle: Waanders, 2004).
13. Batavia Castle housed the residence of the Governor General, the highest-ranking VOC official in Asia, chair of the Council of the Indies, and the VOC's judicial and administrative head. The castle was located at the north of the city along an estuary formed by the Ciliwung River.
14. Johann Wolfgang Heydt, *Allerneuester geographisch- und topographischer Schau-Platz von Africa und Ost-Indien, oder, Ausführliche und wahrhafte Vorstellung und Beschreibung von den wichtigsten der Holländisch-Ost-Indischen Compagnie in Africa und Asia zugehörigen Ländern, Küsten und Insulen* [The most recent geographical and topographical scenes of Africa and East India, or, a detailed and true image and description of the most important lands belonging to the Dutch East India Company in Africa and Asia, associated countries, coasts, and islands] (Willhermsdorff, 1744), translation from Adolf Heuken SJ,

Translation of and commentary on all pages concerning Batavia in J.W. Heydt's "Allerneuster Geographisch- und Topographischer Schau-Platz von Africa und Ost-Indien," [The most recent geographical and topographical scenes of Africa and East India, or, a detailed and true image and description of the most important lands belonging to the Dutch East India Company in Africa and Asia, associated countries, coasts, and islands] *Wilhermsdorff, 1744* (Jakarta: Cipta Loka Caraka and Kartini Collection, 2013), 8. In Heydt's illustration, the screen is labeled "g" and titled "Ialousie vor dem grosen Thor," which Heuken translates as "room divider in front of the great door."

15. The Chinese screen wall, sometimes referred to as a "spirit wall," may have had an apotropaic function as well in that it prevented evil spirits, thought to travel only in straight lines, from entering the home. Ronald G. Knapp, *China's Living Houses: Folk Beliefs, Symbols, and Household Ornamentation* (Honolulu: University of Hawai'i Press, 1999), 68. For an example of the placement of a screen wall in a home constructed at the turn of the eighteenth century, see the Huang family Yin Yu Tang house at the Peabody Essex Museum <www.pem.org/yinyutang>.
16. A.M. Obholzer, M. Baraitser, and W.D. Malherbe, *An Inquiry into the Sources of Cape Architecture and A Survey of Built-In Early Cape Domestic Woodwork* (Grosvenor House Edition Number One, 1985), 175. Victor Ido van de Wall, *Oude Hollandsche Buitenplaatsen van Batavia* [Old Dutch Country Houses in Batavia, Java] (W. Van Hoeve, 1943) and C. de Bosdari, *Cape Dutch Houses and Farms: Their Architecture and History, Together with a Note on the Role of Cecil John Rhodes in their Preservation* (A.A. Balkema, 1953) also suggest Asian sources for Dutch colonial architecture in South Africa, including the construction of the screen wall.
17. For a discussion of these terms, see Michael Sullivan, "Notes on Early Chinese Screen Painting," *Artibus Asiae* 27, no. 3 (1965): 239 and Sarah Handler, *The Austere Luminosity of Chinese Classical Furniture* (Berkeley: University of California Press, 2001), 271–85. The canonical work on the screen in Chinese art is Wu Hung, *The Double Screen: Medium and Representation in Chinese Painting* (1997).
18. Wu Hung, "The Painted Screen," *Critical Inquiry* 23 (Autumn 1996): 41–3.
19. Ibid., 52–4.
20. Frederick de Haan, *Oud Batavia. Platenalbum druk II* (Bandoeng, 1935); Michael Snodin and Nigel Llewellyn, eds., *Baroque Style in the Age of Magnificence, 1620–1800* (London: V&A Publishing, 2009).
21. John Plotz, "Can the Sofa Speak," *Criticism* 47, no. 1 (Winter 2005): 110.
22. The "Chinese Room" of the palace of the Orange-Nassau stadholder court in Leeuwarden is an example of this form of interior design. The panels decorating the room were installed in 1695 under the guidance of Princess Albertine Agnes van Nassau, daughter of Frederik Hendrik and Amalia van Solms, and were acquired by dismantling lacquered Chinese standing screens.

23. Charles Peter Thunberg, M.D., *Travels in Europe, Africa, and Asia, vol. II, contains two expeditions to the interior part of the country adjacent to the Cape of Good Hope and a Voyage to the Island of Java performed in the years 1773, 1774, 1775* (London: Printed for and sold by W. Richardson, 1793), 297.
24. John Splinter Stavorinus, *Voyages to the East-Indies: by the late John Splinter Stavorinus, esq*. (London: Printed for G.G. and J. Robinson, 1798), 388.
25. Ibid., 394.
26. Ibid., 399ff.
27. Thunberg, *Travels in Europe, Africa, and Asia*, 129.
28. For more on the causes for the rise of malaria in the eighteenth century, see Peter H. van der Brug, "Unhealthy Batavia and the decline of the VOC in the eighteenth century," *Jakarta-Batavia: Socio-cultural Essays*, ed. Kees Grijns and Peter J.M. Nas (Leiden: KITLV Press, 2000), 43–74.
29. Stavorinus, *Voyages to the East-Indies*, 261.

CHAPTER 5

Absent Narratives and Missing Jewels: Cultural Heritage of a Tamil Temple in Ho Chi Minh City[1]

H. Hazel Hahn

The Sri Thendayuthapani Temple is one of three major Hindu, Tamil temples located in Ho Chi Minh City, and dates from the 1880s.[2] The temple's *vimana* (tower over sanctum), built in 1936, features some extremely unusual figurines, namely boys in European clothes, amidst the usual iconography of Hindu deities and other religious symbols. What explains such an unusual set of figurines? Using this question as a point of departure, this chapter explores this little-studied temple's history, patterns of cross-cultural exchange, and the politics of cultural heritage from the late nineteenth century to the present.[3] I focus especially on the interwar period, a time of intensive and pivotal changes in colonial Vietnam, delving into Vietnamese perceptions of the temple and the impact of Rabindranath Tagore's visit of Saigon in 1929. Then I assess recent accounts of the temple's history from present-day Indian perspectives, and compare contemporary perceptions and usage of this temple and those of the Mariamman Temple. In the face of the scarcity of sources written by Tamils in Vietnam, reconstructing the history of this temple through sources in French, Vietnamese, English, and Tamil, plus a visual analysis of the *vimana*, reveal a rich and complex legacy of cross-cultural exchange that helps understand the broader history of colonial Saigon as well as the permutations of the present-day politics of cultural heritage in Vietnam and India. Through the lens of a single temple we can see the vagaries of cultural diversity in the interwar period, a time of accelerating identity-formation of the "Vietnamese" and "Indian." Through a focus on an ethnic and religious minority group and its pattern of cross-cultural exchange, this chapter seeks to complicate, as Caroline Herbelin also does in her chapter in this volume, the binaries of the colonizer-colonized and European-Asian and emphasize patterns of exchange in the Asian region. Similar to the ways that Dawn Odell demonstrates that monumental carved screens created by Chinese craftsmen in Batavia should be seen as "Batavian" rather than "Chinese," I seek to show that the unique *vimana* produced unique meanings specific to its locale.

Tamil Migration

The more recent migration of Tamils, mostly from Bengal or Tamil Nadu, into various parts of today's Southeast Asia began in the 1830s. Following the abolishment of slavery throughout the British Empire in 1834, Tamils went to work at sugar, tea, and other plantations under a system of indentured servitude. French and Dutch plantation owners recruited cheap labor under similar agreements in 1846 and 1873 respectively.[4] Other Tamils, who emigrated on a more voluntary basis, arrived later.[5]

The establishment of the French colonial regime in Cochinchina in the 1860s began a new phase of Indian migration into the region.[6] Many Tamils from the French possessions of Pondicherry, Karaikal, and Mahe coming into French Indochina were middle or low-ranking civil servants, petty traders, moneylenders, brokers, textile merchants, barbers, tailors and such.[7] Following the decree of 21 September 1881 issued by the French colonial government regarding "Indian renouncers (*renonçants*)," some Indians renounced their Hindu or Muslim status and adopted the French Civil Code in order to receive the French nationality.[8] Although small in number, renouncers made up a significant portion of the Indians who migrated to Indochina and held the right to vote in local elections.[9] They were majority Christians but also included Hindus, Muslims, and Sikhs.[10] In population statistiques renouncers were counted among "Europeans and assimilated," and not as "Indians." Saigon's local government ran a school where the children of renouncers who knew no French were taught in Tamil and French for entry into French-language schools.[11] Natasha Pairaudeau emphasizes that the Tamil migrants formed a diverse group beyond "the stereotyped Chetty moneylenders."[12] Tamils in Indochina encompassed Hindus (among whom were Chettiar bankers and moneylenders as well as merchants of textiles and diary products); Muslims (who worked in commerce); and Christians (who were functionaries of the colonial state).[13] Fred Clothey, in a study on the Tamil diaspora, also emphasizes the sheer diversity of the Tamils—Brahmin, merchant, Dalit (untouchables), Hindu, Muslim, and Christian.[14] In 1910 there were about 1,000 Indians (called "*Malabars*") in French Indochina.[15] The number of "Indians and Malays" in Cochinchina, according to a 1926 census, was 8,777, the majority of whom lived in Saigon and Cholon—the population of which was predominantly ethnic Chinese.[16] According to government estimates the number of "Indians" in Cochinchinese provinces (excluding Saigon and Cholon) grew from 619 in 1926 to 1,026 in 1929.[17] The number of "Indians (English subjects)" in Hanoi grew from 60 in 1926 to 147 in 1929 and 200 in 1931.[18] According to the 1937 census, about 1,000 of the Indians hailed from the French colonies in India; the majority lived in Saigon and other cities of Cochinchina, engaging in textile trade, brokerage, and moneylending.[19] Often, French functionaries whom the indigenous population of Cochinchina dealt with were Tamils from Pondicherry or Karikal.[20] The self-identified "French from India" played a significant role in local elections. In 1929, 70 members of the Hindu Mutual Aid Association of Cochinchina protested against a group of Indian French seeking to use the Association to influence local elections.[21] The Governor of Cochinchina Pierre Pagès noted in his report to the Governor General René Robin in 1935 that the Indian French played a very important role in Saigon's electoral politics.[22]

Nonetheless Chettiars, although small in number, were the most visible group of Indians in French Indochina, receiving the most government attention and also press—mostly negative press—due to their financial activities in banking and moneylending, wealth, and power. The Chettiars, or Nattukkottai Nagarathars of Chettinard mostly from Tamil Nadu, were originally salt traders who expanded into pearl fisheries.[23] After the mid-nineteenth century they became bankers who built operations in Southeast Asia, playing a role in financing the opium trade.[24] In French Indochina, as in Burma, southern India, British Malaya, Thailand, and the Dutch East Indies, the financial activities of the Chettiars formed a small-scale global financing system which, from 1880 to 1939, was separate but linked to a system of European and American international banks.[25]

In French Indochina the Chettiars were singled out among Indians as moneylenders despised by both the Vietnamese and the French. In 1915 members of the Cochinchinese Colonial Council stated that the Bank of Indochina lent out great sums at an interest rate of 8 per cent to Chettiar bankers, who in turn operated at interest rates of between 36 per cent and 50 per cent.[26] The French often described Chettiars as a "real plague," who brought to the administration little revenue and contributed nothing to the country.[27] In 1934, of the total of 71.9 million piasters of motgaged land debt in Cochinchina, Chettiars owned 14.5 million piasters or 20 per cent.[28] In 1937 Chettiars owned about 22,204 hectares of ricefields in the Mekong River Delta. Although the French attempted to increase credit to villagers, over half of peasants in Indochina, unable to secure loans from financial institutions, borrowed from Chettiars.[29] That unlike the Chinese (some of who were moneylenders as well), Chettiars sent the majority of their profits back to India highlighting their allegiances and cultural differences from the Vietnamese.[30]

Hindu Temples in Saigon

It was the Tamil Chettiars who built the Tamil temples in colonial Saigon.[31] Religion was the basis of the community organization of Chettiars, who were devotees of Shiva.[32] By the early twentieth century there were three main Tamil temples in Saigon: the Sri Thendayuthapani Temple at 66 Rue Ohier (Tôn Thất Thiệp Street); the Subramanian Swamy Temple known in Vietnamese as Chùa Ông at 98 Rue McMahon (Nam Kỳ Khởi Nghĩa Street); and the Mariamman Temple known in Vietnamese as Chùa Ba Mariamman at 45 Rue Amiral Roze (Trương Định Street). All three were centrally located in Saigon.

The Mariamman Temple (Fig. 5.1), built in the early twentieth century, is consecrated to Mariamman (Khali), a southern Indian goddess.[33] Like the other two temples, it has a large hall (*mandapams*) and inner and outer circumferences. This temple increasingly attracted devotees from both the Vietnamese and Khmer populations in the first half of the twentieth century.[34] Mariamman, a "dark" goddess believed in southern India to prevent the spread of smallpox, became, in the eyes of the Vietnamese in Cochinchina, the Indian embodiment of the Black Lady [Bà Đen], a goddess of popular Vietnamese religious belief.[35] Khmer practices of Hinduism also influenced the Vietnamese, who had adopted Khmer deities, enabling the Vietnamese to associate Bà Den with the Indian Hindu goddess.[36] Some Vietnamese did not view this phenomenon in a favorable light. The reporter Nguyen-Hoang wrote in 1929 that practising Buddhism was better than "mixing with half-naked Hindus of the Amiral Roze Street," referring to the devotees at the Mariamman Temple (also called the "Amiral Roze Street Temple").[37]

Figure 5.1: Mariamman Temple. Author's personal collection.

The Sri Thendayuthapani Temple[38] was dedicated to Thenday Yutthapani (Subrahmanya or Dandayuthapani), a son of Shiva and popularly known as Murugan, like the Subramanian Swamy Temple and most Tamil temples of Singapore, Penang, Rangoon and elsewhere in Southeast Asia.[39] Murugan, often referred to as *Tamil Kadavul* (God of Tamils), is worshipped primarily in areas with Tamil influences. The six mountains in Tamil Nadu are considered Murugan's homes, and the building of a Tamil temple symbolizes an attempt to recreate the sacred space related to Tamil homeland.[40] Murugan is a symbol of Tamil homeland and culture, and the temple dedicated to Murugan a place of common Tamil identity.[41]

The Sri Thendayuthapani Temple was widely known, and self-identified, in colonial Saigon as the "Chetty temple" ("Chùa Chetty" in Vietnamese; "Pagode Chetty" or "Pagode des Chettys" in French), where the Nattukottai Chettiars' religious, business, and social lives revolved.[42] A guidebook published in Saigon in 1934 listed a "Pagode des Chettys" as well as a "Pagode de Chua-Ba," showing how the Sri Thendayuthapani Temple and the Mariamman Temple were respectively known in the colonial period.[43] These names show that the former was distinctly associated with Chettiars and the latter with Mariamman. Near the temple on the Rue Ohier were a number of Chettiar banking firms.[44] However, the street was a center of a Tamil community broadly and not just the Chettiars; a number of renouncer policemen, jewelers and other Tamils lived on the street, as shown by street directories of 1912 and 1913.[45] A number of moneylenders and bankers were Tamils not belonging to the Nattukottai Chettiar corporation.[46]

For a while Hindu temples of colonial Saigon were officially referred to as "Buddhist," strangely enough. The 1881 government decision allowing the construction of a temple referred to "Indians followers of Brahma."[47] However, when the legal status of both Mariamman Temple and the Subramanian Swamy Temple was jointly approved in 1918, the members of the Administrative Council overseeing both these temples referred to themselves as "Buddhist Indians," and the temples as "Buddhist temples (*pagodes buddhistes*)," although it is plainly clear that the French knew that the Indians in question were not Buddhists but rather Hindus ("Brahmanistes").[48] These strange designations can be explained by the fact that a place of worship was classified in colonial Indochina as a church, pagoda (for Buddhism and all the related cults), Chinese temple (temple of congregations), or a *đình* (communal house for the village genie), and that identifying a temple as "Buddhist" could facilitate government authorization.[49]

There were divisions and conflicts among Hindu devotees. In 1918 a group of Tamil Indians wrote to the Head of the Division of Immigration and Identity of the colonial government, protesting against what they saw as mismanagement and dilapidation of funds of the Administrative Council of the Mariamman Temple and the Subramanian Swamy Temple, and requesting that the head of the Council be elected each year. One of the reasons for the tension among the devotees was, according to the Central Commissioner Maroselli, that the head of the congregation of "Indian Buddhists" was an English subject from northern India who spoke Hindustani and not Tamil.[50]

The Chetty community organized a popular Thaipusam festival each year.[51] A large crowd watched a street procession featuring a famous silver chariot (Fig. 5.2), and also enjoyed fireworks. *L'Echo annamite*, an influential reformist newspaper written in French by Vietnamese journalists, reported on these festivals in an ambivalent tone. In 1921, announcing the annual festival of the "temple of Chetty bankers," the paper noted that Chettiars hesitate to make this extravagant spending in anticipation of a new National Loan bonds. Having been pressed into service during previous loans, the

Figure 5.2: Sri Thendayuthapani Temple. Author's personal collection.

paper noted, Chettiars now carefully hide their wealth and would even wish to hide the silver float as well.[52] In 1925, *L'Echo annamite* reported that the annual festival of Chettiars attracted an immense crowd, enchanted by the procession featuring the silver float and brilliant fireworks, organized "by the black barons of the local finance."[53] In 1926, *L'Echo annamite* reported on another successful festival, commenting that "our Chettiars know how to liven up the public and calculate the interest of their loans at 36% with equal skill."[54] In 1931 a chair was brought from India for carrying a Murugan statue in festival processions.[55] Pure-breed zebuses from southern India were carefully kept at the temple away from other animals.[56]

Tagore's Visit

In spite of the clear identification of the Sri Thendayuthapani Temple with Chettiars, the temple served as a focal point of community activities representing not only Chettiars but Tamils of all stripes in the Saigon-Cholon region, encompassing Hindus, Christians, and Muslims.[57] This phenomenon fits into the pattern of Christians in India, almost all untouchables, frequenting Tamil temples.[58] In fact, one Administrative Council, with a director elected each year, oversaw both the Sri Thendayuthapani Temple and the Tamil mosque located at Rue Amiral Dupré (Saigon Central Mosque, 66 Đông Du Street).[59] In July 1924, anticipating a visit by the Bengali poet Tagore, who had won the Nobel Prize in 1913, a group of Indians of Saigon and Cholon gathered at the "Chetty Temple" and elected members of a welcome committee. The committee was headed by a renounced Indian and included "four Chettys, two Muslims, four Indian French subjects, four Bombay merchants, four Hindus and three Parsis."[60] The committee sent a program, including a planned procession with elephants and music to various Saigon newspapers. Tagore was also to visit Angkor. For the occasion "each Hindu element" ("Hindu" here refers to Indian) of Saigon and Cholon contributed funds totaling 4,719 piasters. The breakdown of the donation was:

Renouncers	1,308 piasters
Chettiars:	1,500
Muslims:	1,000
Non-renouncers (Saigon):	361
Non-renouncers (Cholon):	250
Sindhi merchants:	300[61]

Both Tamils of different religions and non-Tamils (Sindhi merchants) participated. This chart shows that all the Indian groups rallied together to honor Tagore, and also that the temple was a center of the efficient communication network of the Tamil community and the broader Indian community. *Réveil Saigonnais*, a paper for Indian French subjects, urged Indians of Saigon to unite and welcome Tagore properly, seeing Tagore's visit as an occasion for asserting the notion of Greater India, Indian influence in Asia in ancient times.[62]

Tagore ended up not visiting in 1924 but did so in 1929. On the day of his arrival in Saigon on 21 June 1929, he had a public lunch at the City Hall. In the evening at a reception at the Municipal Theater, Tagore was presented by Bùi Quang Chiêu, a leader of the Constitutionalist Party who first invited him, and Tagore spoke as well.[63] The following day, Tagore was to visit the Botanical and Zoological Garden, museums, several schools, a Chinese temple and a Vietnamese temple in Cholon, and two art schools in the outskirts. That evening, at the Eden Cinema documentaries on Indochina were presented in Tagore's presence.[64] On the third and final day of his sojourn, Tagore visited the Sri Thendayuthapani Temple and also met with the Governor General Pierre Pasquier (1928–34).[65] At the temple, Tagore participated in a religious ceremony (the opening ceremony of the Institute of Poetry Murugananda Vasagasala), along with Bùi Quang Chiêu and Lefebvre (a French member of the welcome committee for Tagore's visit).[66] A girl chanted a song by the poet Passecarane. The Indians presented 2,101 piasters to Tagore, and Xavier, a Vice President of the welcome committee, made a speech.[67]

Tagore's visit sparked a debate among Vietnamese intellectuals and journalists regarding Tagore's ideas and their applicability *vis-à-vis* nationalist and reformist movements. Here, what interests us is the ideas of Tagore and Vietnamese regarding cultural heritage and identity. In his speech at the Municipal Theater, Tagore evoked the legacy of the influence of Indian civilization in this region, "the vision of a life that has left a signature on this land, and that still flows in her blood." He invoked an "encounter that awoke the soul of this country, to thread her into a new path of accomplishment [...] in Arts and Ideas." While the memory of this age "lies in magnificent ruins only," he declared himself to be "a messenger from the Past" seeking to renew an association "rich in the length of duration and in its accomplishments."[68] In his concluding remarks he said he brings "the greetings of that radiant India, who lavished her light on this land, as well as the message of sympathy and brotherhood of present India who lives separated from [the people of

Indochina] by geographic distance and by the dead solitude of her own darkness."[69] Thus Tagore invoked the shared cultural heritage of India and Indochina, but also in the last sentence made a discreet reference to the shared fate of the two regions as colonies. Tagore's aim of stopping over in French Indochina was actually visiting Angkor, which he wound up not doing due to his fragile health.[70] Whereas Tagore was well known for his universalism, a sort of syncretism bringing together all religions,[71] the "magnificent ruins" in the unspecified Indochina region likely referred to the monuments of Angkor. If so, this reference underlines Tagore's vision of Angkor as a site of Hindu civilization, which fits with the tenor of the rest of his speech that highlighted the influence of ancient Indian, that is to say Hindu, civilization. For Tagore it was Hinduism that provided India, marked by a great diversity of races, with a unity in the realm of ideas.[72] Tagore's visit occasioned Bùi Quang Chiêu and other like-minded Vietnamese reformists to also highlight the influence of ancient Indian civilization on Vietnamese civilization. One of the most concrete manifestation of the influence of Tagore's ideas was on Cao Dai, a syncretic religion with a nationalist character formally established in 1926 in Cochinchina.[73]

The Sanctuary and *Vimana* of the Sri Thendayuthapani Temple

While Tagore's visit instigated debates on civilizational interactions, left undiscussed by the Vietnamese was the influence of French (and European) culture on the region. Sri Thendayuthapani Temple's architecture and material culture shed some light on the shared cultural heritage of Vietnam and India as well as French influence.

At the center of the temple is a closed sanctuary. The central shrine is dedicated to Murugan. Tiles representing a peacock, Murugan's vehicle, are placed above the shrine. Other tiles, with flower or geometric patterns widely seen in southern India, are used around the shrine and other walls and columns in the main hall as well. To the right is a shrine for Krishna. The presence of Krishna here is very unusual, in that there would be no shrine to Krishna in a temple consecrated to Murugan in India. This indicates that some minority members were devotees of Krishna and gave him a place of honor, but as subordinate to Murugan, not at the center where he would normally be. On the left side of the sanctuary is a shrine dedicated to Shiva. The presence of three different deities makes this temple very popular in southern India, in which various deities are worshipped together, and indicates that the Chettiars were motivated to build this temple to represent all that they could.[74] On some of the columns in the main hall are images of Krishna, Ganesh (a brother of Murugan), and other deities; these images are in more modern styles than the rest of the temple. In addition there are two statues of Buddha and one of Quan Am in the back of the temple. This can perhaps be explained by the original classification of the temple as "Buddhist" as discussed above; the presence of Buddha statues at this temple adds to the somewhat syncretic characteristics of the Tamil temples of Ho Chi Minh City.

In 1936 a *vimana* (Fig. 5.3) was built on the roof terrace of the Sri Thendayuthapani Temple, by artisans brought from Tamil Nadu.[75] A *vimana*, characteristic of Tamil temples in southern India,[76] represents the energy emanating from the sanctum, whose axis goes through the *vimana*. In the form of a stepped pyramid, a *vimana* is relatively smaller in size compared to a gopuram at the entrance of the temple, which is barrel-shaped and more rectangular.[77]

The *vimana* of the Sri Thendayuthapani Temple is composed of four tiers. On the bottom tier Murugan is represented along with his consorts. Under his feet is his vehicle, the peacock that symbolizes the deity's radiance and beauty. On the second tier from the top, the six-headed Murugan and consorts are represented again, along with the peacock. In addition, this *vimana* includes some exceedingly enigmatic sculptures. On the third tier from the top are eight boys or young men, two on each of the four sides of the tower. All eight have *tilaks* or red dots on their foreheads, indicating that they are Hindu. They appear to be humans looking out onto the world from where they are perched. On traditional *vimanas* and gopurams devotees, as well as deities, these are commonly represented. So appearing to be human is not the unusual part; rather it is the European clothes that stand out as very rare. All have light skin, dark hair, and dark eyes.

This *vimana* strikingly resembles a *vimana* at the famous sixteenth-century Kapaleeswarar Temple built in a Dravidian style in Mylapore, Tamil Nadu. The two *vimana*s share the four-tier structure and nearly identical architectural elements, as well as very similar placements of figurines. Located within the Kapaleeswarar Temple complex dedicated to Shiva, this small shrine is dedicated to Brahma, represented with four heads (one of which is invisible) and sitting on a lotus while holding a rosary and a pot. His two female attendants are treated as generic goddesses on this *vimana* (rather than Saraswati, his usual spouse).[78] Two bearded sages flanking the trio are Brahma's typical companions. The nandi bull, Shiva's vehicle, is on the

Figure 5.3: Sri Thendayuthapani Temple. Author's personal collection.

second tier from the top. Below the bulls are *Kopurantanki* (supporters of the Gopuram), even though here this is a *vimana*, not a gopuram.[79] This *vimana* most likely served as a model for that of the Sri Thendayuthapani Temple. We see, then, that the only unusual features on the latter are the boy figures, who take place of the *Kopurantanki* and were likely conceived as a variant of *Kopurantanki*. This placement also shows that the boys are the least sacred or important figures on the *vimana*.

Such European or Europeanized-looking *Kopurantanki* are, although scarcely documented or studied, not as rare as one might think in southern India and date from the colonial period, according to Samuel K. Parker. A photograph of a gopuram at a Tamil temple taken by Parker shows European *Kopurantanki*, a male and female pair on each corner, wearing European

Figure 5.4: Sri Thendayuthapani Temple. Author's personal collection.

underwear.[80] Such integration of European-looking figures acknowledged the power of Europeans but at the same time made them subordinate to Hindu deities.

Of the eight boy figures on the *vimana* in question, the ones (see Fig. 5.3) that bear the most resemblance to traditional Hindu figures are two bare-chested boys, each holding a dagger and wearing a necklace. The iconography of a figure holding a dagger on a gopuram or *vimana* is relatively rare. On the gopuram of the Sri Mariamman Temple in Singapore (244 South Bridge Road), seemingly just one of some 72 figurines of deities, devotees and so on, the gopuram holds a dagger. Next (see Fig. 5.3), we have two boys or young men in European shirts and shorts, one with a moustache, looking out onto the world holding a book each. They indicate more of a sense of formality than the other figures. They look like schoolboys waving cheerfully. Finally we have two boys (Fig. 5.4) or young men with moustaches looking like circus performers or bicyclists, holding on to the *vimana*, functioning as *Kopurantanki*.

These figurines do not recall any other figurines or works of fine art. Rather, I would argue that they recall late nineteenth-century French images of young men featured in posters. The boys looking like circus performers recall posters (Fig. 5.5) by the French poster artist Jules Chéret that conveyed a sense of physicality and entertainment.[81] The boys on the *vimana* are actively engaging with the world; they seem to be visually surveying the horizon from their high vantage viewpoint. They convey senses of curiosity, enthusiasm, education, physicality, and openness towards the world, as opposed to an orientation towards the inner, spiritual, otherworldly realm. Thus they are profoundly transgressive. Not only do they collectively express a distinctly late nineteenth-century French sensibility, they seem to symbolize the ideal of late nineteenth-century French boyhood adapted for Hindu boys: education, sports, and a sense of curiosity and optimism about the world. What could also be problematic (from present-day Hindu perspective) is that the figurines seem to be drawn not from fine art or architecture but rather from popular cultural imagery circulating in commercial posters.

Contemporary Hindu temples were not the purview of the Ecole Française de l'Extreme Orient (EFEO) which focused on archaeology, as well as ancient architecture and art that were little-differentiated from archaeology. Hence EFEO seems to have never studied this temple. On the cover of the 1943 issue of *Indochine hebdomadaire illustré*, a photo of a Tamil mosque of Saigon was published, but with a caption "Chetty temple" which further indicates that the history of the temple is obscure.[82] I have not located any sources from the Tamil perspective or any other perspective from the colonial period describing the *vimana*. I approach these figurines as part of material culture. Similar to the ways Odell articulates about the screens crafted by Chinese artisans in Batavia, this *vimana* is the type of artifact that took on a unique set of meanings—that continue to evolve—through its spatial relocation. It should be seen as a uniquely "Indochinese" object in a way akin to the way the carved screen in Batavia should be considered a uniquely "Batavian" rather than "Chinese" object, specific to its location and its variegated, evolving contexts. There are differences between the screens and the *vimana* in that the screens were located in interiors and thus the spatial practices around them did much to generate new meanings, while the *vimana* had a fixed location on the top of the temple. However, their functions are similar in that they do not "make sense" if seen in isolation. It is clear that the figures in question, as very unusual *Kopurantanki*, modernized the *vimana*, making it a hybrid of sorts. The figurines could be interpreted as Indians or Europeans. If Indians, they appear to be Europeanized Hindus. If Europeans, they would be Europeans who became Hindus. Some questions can be asked. Were the figures meant to represent a process of

Figure 5.5: Jules Chéret, "Cirque d'hiver. L'homme obus" (1878), *Les affiches illustrées* (1886–95). Author's personal collection.

Europeanization, including European-style education, so that the dagger-holding boys get transformed into boys in Western clothing, a process seen as beneficial? Were the figures meant to represent simultaneous, multiple identities for Hindu boys, so that they could be European-looking boys familiar with European culture, while also remaining Hindu and retaining Hindu culture? Were they meant to be European boys represented as subordinate to Hindu deities? Were they meant to represent humans who climbed onto the *vimana*, mixing with deities and thus showing much daring and adventurous spirit? However, such a "hybrid" *vimana* or gopuram is rare, since no other relatively well-known Tamil temple in Southeast Asia—mainly in Singapore and Malaysia—or Ceylon, seems to have one. What could be safely said about the figurines is that whatever is represented, whether Europeanization, Hinduization or the cultivation of cross-cultural identities, the process was seen as beneficial at the time, and that the *vimana* thus overtly refers to the interaction with and influence of European culture. They thus implicitly refer to the positive effects of the presence of Europeans in the area and could be seen as rendering support to the colonial regime, which explains the subsequent silence about them in the postcolonial period.

1970s and Beyond

In the early 1970s the social life of Chettiars continued to revolve around the Sri Thendayuthapani Temple. Chettiars received visitors, held business meetings, fixed rates of interest and so on at the temple, and four services were held daily.[83] On Mondays the Chettiar community of Saigon held a common prayer at the temple and read the Shiva Purana.[84] The annual Thaipusam festival, when a statue of Murugan was taken around in a procession, continued to be popular, and the Thirukarthigai festival was also celebrated.[85] Chettiars maintained close connections to Tamil Nadu, and financed the activities of the Dakshinamurthy (great teacher) Swamigal in Thiruvarur in Tamil Nadu, while also supporting renovation projects for Buddhist shrines in Saigon.[86] The real estate of the temple as well as its jewels were valued at 50 million rupees (820,000 USD) in 1971 (the equivalent of 5 million USD in 2018).[87]

After the fall of Saigon in 1975 the majority of Tamils left Vietnam. Hindu temples were closed, and the premises used as warehouses, party workers' camps and so on.[88] The Mariamman Temple was turned in part into a factory for joss sticks, while one section was occupied by a seafood-export company.[89] In the early 1990s the Mariamman Temple and the Subramanian

Swamy Temple were renovated and were open to daily religious worship once again, through the intervention of a Vietnamese trading company.[90]

In 1994, in an article titled "Reviving temples. Recent Indian initiatives in Vietnam," published by a popular Indian magazine, the *Frontline*, M.A. Chidambaram, a prominent businessman in India, narrated a brief history of Indian presence in Vietnam. He wrote that "[n]early two hundred years ago, members of the Nattukottai Chettiars community [...] began trade links with Vietnam and other neighbouring countries. A large number of people from India, showing exemplary enterprise, settled down in Vietnam and engaged themselves in law-abiding trade activities."[91] According to him the Sri Thendayuthapani Temple was the oldest of the three Tamil temples in Saigon and was established by the Nattukottai Chettiar community two hundred years earlier, in the late eighteenth century.[92] Thus he dated the temple a full century earlier than it actually was. Chidambaram thus not only implicitly claimed that the temple pre-dated French colonization, he also wrote out any presence of the British or French in the region, completely masking the fact that Indian migration into Southeast Asia was within the frameworks of first British, and secondarily French, imperial expansion. Rather than following the British flag into Southeast Asia, in other words, in Chidambaram's account Indians' migration and trade activities in the region predated European colonization. Thus he made the modern links between India and Vietnam seem much more autonomous and of longer duration than they were. Chidambaram's narrative emphasized the prosperous sector of the Indian emigrants engaging in trade, and also underlined—accurately—the links the Indian community maintained with India. However, he omitted the fact that the Chettiars of Cochinchina were the predominant bankers and moneylenders. Also, in stating that many Indians in Vietnam were "obliged to abandon all their life's possessions and return to India" in 1977 and 1978,[93] he glossed over the fact that the Chettiars had expatriated most of their wealth back to Tamil Nadu, and invested there rather than in Vietnam.

In other recent accounts, misinformation also abounds as to the origins of the Tamil temples of Ho Chi Minh City. This variance in claims as to the origins and the dating of the temples itself turns out to be a significant aspect of narratives about the history of Hindu temples in Ho Chi Minh City. A number of authors, like Chidambaram, claim that the Sri Thendayuthapani Temple was established at the end of the eighteenth century or beginning of the nineteenth century by the Nattukottai Chettiar community. Geetesh Sharma in *India-Vietnam Relations: First to Twentyfirst Century* (2004) states that Indians "started immigrating here since the birth of [Saigon in 1698]," and that "this fact is established by the presence of two Hindu temples—Subramanyam Swami temple and Mariyamman temple in the city," both of which are "minimum two hundred years old."[94] Thus Sharma dated the temples back to the early nineteenth century. This statement is patently inaccurate, since both of these temples were built a century later.[95] Sharma's claim also contradicts the assertions of Chidambaram that the Sri Thendayuthapani Temple is the oldest Tamil temple in Ho Chi Minh City. Like most other accounts from the Indian perspective, Sharma's account does not mention any role of the British or the French, thus eradicating the history of the emigration of Indians from India into French Indochina under the aegis of the colonial regime. Sharma repeats erroneous claims in his *Traces of Indian Culture in Vietnam* (2009), stating that the Subramanyan Swamy Temple and the Mariamman Temple were both built in the early nineteenth century.[96] Sharma then speculates that the earliest Hindus to arrive in Ho Chi Minh City must date back to three hundred years, since it might have taken two to three generations for them to establish and flourish their business.[97] Again, like Chidambaram, Sharma does not mention the presence of the French in Indochina at all. These claims add up to a patently wrong revisionist account of Indians' history in colonial Vietnam that erases the particular link between the diverse group of Indians and the French colonial regime.[98]

Unlike the Mariamman Temple and the Subramanian Swamy Temple, Chidambaram observed that the Sri Thendayuthapani Temple was, in 1994, still in a dilapidated condition, although the temple, located in a spacious tract of land in the heart of the city, has large properties, both lands and buildings, in and near Ho Chi Minh City.[99] Chidambaram noted that the temple also held "valuable jewelry consisting of gold ornaments embedded with stones" and other pieces used on festive occasions. When Indians had to leave Vietnam in 1978, the administrators of the temple handed over all the jewelry of the temple, "in the presence of representatives of the Indian Embassy in Hanoi, to the National Bank for safe custody."[100] Since the restoration of "normal conditions," members of the Nagarathar community who returned to India were seeking to renovate the temple and reactivate worship there, or bring the jewelry and precious stones to India.[101] "Because of the long association of the local Vietnamese with the Hindu religion, spread over several centuries," Chidambaram wrote: when daily worship was restored it was expected that the temple would draw a large number of devotees.[102] Chidambaram would turn out to be wrong in this regard.

The campaign to renovate the Sri Thendayuthapani Temple involved the governments of both India and Vietnam as well as the Nagarathar community of India and took negotiations over several years. Chidambaram, along with J.C. Sharma, the Indian ambassador, his successor S.L. Malik, and other Indian diplomats, met with Vietnamese officials and conveyed the Nagarathar community's request to "permit the revival of the temple" and also to bring a priest from India. However, this required obtaining approval from the Vietnamese government allowing foreigners to run a place of worship and manage its properties in Vietnam. The government set up a board of administration for the temple in March 1993, nominating three Indians, all non-Chettiars who had been in Vietnam for several decades. However, the Nagarathar community in India was willing to sponsor the renovation only if their nominees were appointed to the board. In one of his visits to Ho Chi Minh City, Chidambaram verified that the temple's jewelry remained in the National Bank.[103]

A photograph illustrating the article is very telling. Taken from outside the temple, only the top portion of the *vimana* is visible; the peculiar and enigmatic figurines, which would point to the influence of Europeans and also undermine the historical narrative claimed by the author, among other things, made the temple seem older than it is.[104]

Also in 1994, the Indian National Parliament heard, regarding efforts to protect Hindu temples in Vietnam, from the Minister of External Affairs (Shri Salman Khursheed) that "the jewels and some other items of Saigon's Thendayudhapani Temple belonging to the Chettiar community who left Saigon in the wake of the fall of Saigon in 1975 have been lying in the custody of the Industrial and Commercial Bank of Ho Chi Minh City," and that they have not been "handed over to the temple management committee, as per the wishes of the Chettiar Community."[105]

The temple was renovated by 2003. The 2003 edition of *Rough Guide to Vietnam*, clearly written before the renovation, notes that the "peaceful Sri Thendayyutthapani Temple" "manages a certain rag-tag charisma," and that on the "weather-beaten tower of deities" the "ranks have been infiltrated by two incongruous characters dressed like public schoolboys in braces, shorts and striped ties, and waving merrily." This is the only acknowledgment of the "incongruous characters" I have ever come across, including on the Internet.[106] An online article on Hindu temples in Vietnam by the editor of the *Aum Muruga Journal*, a Hindu periodical based in Australia, describes in great detail all the deities represented on the "beautiful gopuram" at the Sri Thendayuthapani Temple, but leaves out any description of the odd figurines, merely stating: "In addition to these carvings, there are several other statues."[107] Likewise, a website in Vietnamese describing the temple in detail, only refers to the *vimana* as a "stepped tower, with the god and other decorations."[108] And an English-language website urges not to miss the roof terrace, "where you have a good view of the surrounding streets, and can see some more statues of Hindu deities."[109]

Contemporary Devotion

Today the Mariamman Temple is by far the most frequented Tamil temple in Saigon, where most of the devotees are Vietnamese, the majority women. As the most visited religious institution in southern Vietnam, it receives a million visitors a year.[110] In front of the temple vendors sell incense and jasmine petals. Large numbers of working Vietnamese women pray there in early evenings.[111] The practice of the worship of Sri Mariamman as Bà Đen has been renewed.[112] The temple is reputed to have miraculous powers.[113] A Ho Chi Minh City government committee administers the temple.[114] Philip Taylor, noting the creative, eclectic, and flexible character of all forms of religious worship in Vietnam, observes that the goddess Mariamman, "brought to Saigon by Chettiar moneylenders in the early twentieth century, is regarded by some as Kuan Yin, the Chinese goddess of mercy, and by others as a Khmer goddess known as the Black Lady." This parallels the phenomenon of Quan Công, a third-century Chinese general who became famous through the Chinese historical novel *The Romance of Three Kingdoms* and is worshipped in some Buddhist temples as a symbol of loyalty, integrity, and courage, being seen by some in Vietnam "as an incarnation of Sakyamuni Buddha." Some even say Quan Công was reincarnated in the personage of Ho Chi Minh.[115] The names Chùa Ông (Subramanian Swamy Temple) and Chùa Ba (Mariamman Temple) themselves are signs of the local adaptation of Hindu deities, via Chinese popular religion. The "Lady" Temple (Chùa Ba) and the "Mr." Temple (Chùa Ông or Quan Công Temple) are found in every Vietnamese city as an integral part of the kinh (ethnic Vietnamese majority) worship system.[116] Thus, Vietnamese adaptation of Chinese temples for popular local devotion paved the way for the integration of the two Tamil temples into popular local religious beliefs.

The characteristics of adaptability and creativity are seen in the creation of the new religions, Cao Dai and Hoa Hao (a Buddhism-based religion established in 1939) in southern Vietnam. The popularity of Sri Mariamman fits also into a pattern of innovation within the Tamil diaspora, in which the

Tamil communities have used performances of different types of rituals—festivals, domestic rituals, the building of shrines and so on—as strategies to negotiate their boundaries.[117] More than 50,000 Vietnamese, almost all Buddhists, flooded the Mariamman Temple during the seven-day Tet (Lunar New Year) festival in 2012 observing both Hindu and Buddhist rituals, and during the Vietnamese New Year Day prayed at the temple through the day and the entire night.[118]

The status of all three Hindu temples discussed here not only as places of practising worship open to all but also as "important landmarks on the cultural map of Ho Chi Minh City"[119] seems secure. However, the Mariamman Temple stands out among the Tamil temples. While the Subramanian Swamy Temple receives steady stream of foreign visitors, especially from India, Nepal, and Malaysia, on certain special days each month, the Sri Thendayuthapani Temple remains the least frequented. The reasons for the absence of a Vietnamese congregation seem clear. Whereas the Mariamman Temple attracts devotees worshipping the "Black Goddess" for good health and fortune, the Sri Thendayuthapani Temple, which primarily has served the function of expressing the Tamil identity, and was widely known as the "Chetty temple," does not provide any compelling reason for Vietnamese devotion.

In *Include Me Out II* (2011), a photograph by the artist Vivek Vilasini, through digital alteration of "traditional carvings of deities, devotees and demons" on a gopuram are replaced by "everyday individuals of all walks of life, including several western tourists, the artist himself and his mother."[120] Vilasini's work, commenting not only on the social reality of present-day India but also the gopuram as a prominent symbol of Indian culture and a tourist attraction, resonates with the *vimana* of the Sri Thendayuthapani Temple, which featured some contemporary types. Whereas Vilasini's work imagines what a gopuram *could* look like *if* it featured contemporary people, and imagines how the result would look drastically different from actual *vimanas*, the *vimana* at the Sri Thendayuthapani Temple actually shows the result of such an imagination, albeit in an idealized and ambiguous form.

Conclusion

The Sri Thendayuthapani Temple and the Sri Mariamman Temple possess a complex history as well as symbolism that reveal rich layers of cultural exchange. Located in central Ho Chi Minh City, the contrasting characteristics and manners of devotion at the two temples are all the more remarkable, given their geographical proximity and common origins as temples established by Chettiar moneylenders hailing from Tamil Nadu. The main difference between the two temples can be encapsulated by the symbolism of the respective deities the temples are consecrated to: good health and fortune for Mariamman, and Tamil identity for Murugan.

The temples occupy distinct locations in the cultural, spiritual, and historical landscape of present-day Vietnam marked by diversity in religious practice. On the one hand, cross-cultural popular belief in the sacred power of Mariamman, a Hindu goddess, shows a great deal of continuity through various tumultuous ruptures in modern history. The Mariamman Temple represents an example of a thriving religious institution marked by distinct shared cultural heritage. Interconnected and re-interpreted Vietnamese, Indian, Khmer, and Chinese religious practices enabled certain temple spaces to become, over a long period of time, shared sacred spaces seen as housing deities of popular local religions (which in many cases were imported from elsewhere to begin with as in the case of Quan Công). Such long-term integration and adaptation of religious practices allowed the temple to overcome challenges posed by the closure of the temple for nearly two decades as well as the emigration of the majority of Indians after 1975.

On the other hand, the history and symbolism of the Sri Thendayuthapani Temple make it a very different sort of temple. The original purpose of the temple—that of expressing Tamil identity—makes it hard to be integrated into Vietnamese religious and spiritual practices. A history of widespread association of this temple with Chettiar moneylenders might make this integration further challenging (although this fact is not well known today), explaining why the drive to renovate the temple came from India rather than from local communities. This lack of interest by the Vietnamese has precluded any meaningful reinterpretation of the temple's *vimana*. Had the temple drawn Vietnamese devotees, the idiosyncratic *Kopurantanki*, which visibly and overtly point to the colonial legacy, could be creatively reinterpreted. The lack of interest in the *vimana* contrasts to the flourishing of Cao Dai and its temple in Tây Ninh in syncretic architecture.

The *vimana* does not fit well into postcolonial Indian perspectives. Some accounts from the Indian postcolonial or nationalist perspectives have sought to revise or outright erase the complex colonial legacy, and the intertwining of the history of Indians in Southeast Asia with the colonial history, creating problematic distortions as can be seen in the wildly varying accounts about the origins of the three Hindu temples. The circulation of such revisionist narratives endangers a clear understanding of the temples' history. Further, for now there is only collective silence, a curious absence of narratives and commentaries from both Vietnamese and Indian perspectives, about the odd and transgressive features of the *vimana*, whether the boys are to be interpreted as human interlopers visiting the *vimana*, or agents of modernization through the adoption of cross-cultural identities. However, the act of renovating the temple (which had been left in a degraded condition longer than the other two temples) already acknowledged the inclusion of the temple into the landscape of cultural heritage in Vietnam and the Indian diaspora.

Notes

1. Thanks to Samuel K. Parker for sharing his expertise on Tamil temples, Caroline Herbelin, Mitch Aso, and Gerard Sasges for taking photos, and Pascal Bourdeaux, Vimalin Rujivacharakul, Philippe Peycam, and Janet Hoskins for their comments and suggestions. All translations are mine unless otherwise noted.
2. Trung tâm Luu trữ Quốc gia [National Archives] [hereafter TTLTQG] 2, file Conseil Privé 8372 "Arrêté du Gouvernement concédant un immeuble domaniale ... aux Indiens sectateurs de Brahme pour y construire un temple 1881;" TTLTQG 2, file Goucoch D9-15 "L'organisation, statuts des pagodes Mariammane et Sri-Soubramniassmy des indiens bouddhistes de Saigon 1918–1942," letter to the Head of the Service of Immigration and Identity, 14 May 1928. This letter notes that Hindu temples exist in Saigon since the 1880s but does not specify which temples were established in the 1880s. The Sri Thendayuthapani Temple was established around 1880 according to "Seminar on Chettiars and Hinduism in South-East Asia," *Bulletin of the Institute of Traditional Cultures* (University of Madras) (July–Dec. 1972), 109; Natasha Pairaudeau, *Mobile Citizens: French Indians in Indochina, 1858–1954* (Copenhagen: NIAS-Nordic Institute of Asian Studies, 2016), 95–6; A. Bouinais and A. Paulus described the presence of "a central prison, a hospital, a botanical garden, two mosques, a pagoda, a Hindu ['brahamanique'] temple, an observatory," and a theater in Saigon. A. Bouinais and A. Paulaus, *La France en Indo-chine* [France in Indo-China] (Paris: Challamel aîné, 1886), 212. The plaque at the entrance of the temple reads: "Sri Thenday Yutthapani Temple. Chùa Ấn Giáo [Hindu Temple]."
3. Unlike the Tamil temples dating from the modern period, the Hindu temples built in the Cham period in Central Vietnam have long been seen by scholars, colonial authorities, and Vietnamese authorities as possessing artistic and archeological significance. One of the few books that have reliable information on the temple is Quang Ninh Lê and Stéphane Dovert, *Saigon, 1698–1998: Kiến Trúc, Quy Hoạch = Saigon, 1698–1998: architectures, urbanisme* [Saigon,

1698–1998: Architecture, Urban Planning] (Ho Chi Minh City and Lyon: Uy Ban Nhân Dân, Communauté urbaine de Lyon and Consulat général of France in Ho Chi Minh City, 1998).

4. Fred W. Clothey, *Ritualizing on the Boundaries: Continuity and Innovation in the Tamil Diaspora* (Columbia, SC: The University of South Carolina Press, 2006), 5.
5. Clothey, *Ritualizing on the Boundaries*, 7.
6. Nayan Chanda, "Indians in Indochina," in Kernial Singh Sandhu, *Indian Communities in Southeast Asia* (Singapore: Institute of Southeast Asian Studies, 1993), 32.
7. The majority were from southern India though there were also Sindhi and Gujarati businessmen. Sudhir Devare, "Rising India and Indians in Cambodia, Laos and Vietnam," in *Rising India and Indian Communities in East Asia*, ed. K. Kesavapany, A. Mani, and Palanisamy Ramasamy (Singapore: Institute of Southeast Asian Studies, 2008), 288; *L'Indochine*, numéro spécial, hors série (Dec. 1922): 4.
8. Nasir Abdoul-Carime, "Note introductive," [Introductory Note] "Réimpression de l'article de G. Vidy: 'La communauté indienne en Indochine'," [Re-issue of the article by G. Vidy: 'The Indian community in Indochina'] *Sud-Est* (November 1949) n. 6, AEFEK: 4 http://aefek.free.fr/iso_album/vidy.pdf [accessed 20 May 2012].
9. Abdoul-Carime, "Note introductive," 4.
10. Ibid., 5.
11. There were 60 students at the Simon Jean School in 1923, and 48 in 1927. "Session ordinaire de 1923," *Rapports au Conseil de gouvernement* ["Ordinary session of 1923," Report to the Government Council] (1923 Part 1): 336; "Session ordinaire de 1927," *Rapports au Conseil de gouvernement* (1927 Part 1): 590.
12. Natasha Pairaudeau, "Vietnamese engagement with Tamil migrants in colonial Cochinchina," *Journal of Vietnamese Studies* 5, no. 3 (2010): 1.
13. Abdoul-Carime, "Note introductive," 5.
14. Clothey, *Ritualizing on the Boundaries*, 2.
15. *L'Indochine*, numéro spécial, hors série (Dec. 1922) : 4.
16. "Session ordinaire de 1927. Part 1," *Rapports au Conseil de gouvernement* (1927): 581.
17. *Annuaire administratif de l'Indochine* [Administrative Yearbook of Indochina] (1926): 141–76; (1928): 170–211; (1929):175–215. These numbers leave out naturalized Indians (French citizens) plus Indians who were not counted separately but included in "Various." For example, in 1929 in the Can-Tho province there were 132 "Naturalized" (likely naturalized Indians) among 199 Europeans, and 477 "Various." *Annuaire administratif de l'Indochine* (1929): 185. It is hard to get reliable figures for ethnic Indians in Saigon and Cholon,

where Indians were included in "Asiatic foreigners" who were majority Chinese.

18. *Annuaire administratif de l'Indochine* (1926): 252; (1929): 309; (1931): 341. There were also 30 "Métis indiens" (mixed Indian-Vietnamese) in Hanoi in 1929. *Annuaire administratif de l'Indochine* (1929): 309.
19. Chanda, "Indians in Indochina," 32.
20. Pairaudeau, "Vietnamese Engagement," 8.
21. In 1929, members of the Hindu Mutual Aid Association of Cochinchina were all French citizens and mostly functionaries or employees of commerce. That some of them had French last and first names make it hard to identify them as Tamils in sources. TTLTQG 2, file GC Divers 2997 "Mutuelle Hîndoue de la Cochinchine 1935," Letter dated 31 October 1929 to the Governor of Cochinchina.
22. TTLTQG 2, file IIA.45/252 (1) "API. Elections municipals, 1935–37," Report from Pagès to Robin, 13 May 1935.
23. Sunil S. Amrith, *Migration and Diaspora in Modern Asia* (Cambridge: Cambridge University Press, 2011), 93.
24. Amrith, *Migration and Diaspora*, 93; David West Rudner, *Caste and Capitalism in Colonial India: The Nattukottai Chettiars* (Berkeley: University of California Press, 1994), 1.
25. Claude Markovits, "The Colonised as Global Traders: Indian Trading Networks in the World Economy, 1850–1939," *The Foundations of Worldwide Economic Integration: Power, Institutions, and Global Markets, 1850–1930*, ed. Christof Dejung and Niels P. Petersson (Cambridge: Cambridge University Press, 2013), 165. On Chettiars, see also Pairaudeau, *Mobile Citizens*, esp. 67–8, 93–8, 215–16, 223, 269–71.
26. "Session ordinaire de 1915. Quatrième séance, 8 Oct. 1915," [Ordinary Session of 1915. Fourth Meeting, 8 Oct. 1915] *Procès-verbaux du Conseil Colonial* (1915): 168.
27. Puits-Martin, "Réflexions d'un Indochinois," [Reflections by an Indochinese] *Revue des questions coloniales et maritimes* (May–July 1916): 88.
28. "La question agraire en Cochinchine," [The question on Cochinchina's agriculture] *Bulletin fiduciaire d'Indochine* (April–June 1934): 97.
29. Geoffrey C. Gunn, *Rice Wars in Colonial Vietnam: The Great Famine and the Viet Minh Road to Power* (Lanham, MD: Rowman & Littlefield, 2014), 37.
30. Le Manh Hung, *The Impact Of World War II on the Economy of Vietnam 1939–45* (Singapore: Eastern Universities Press by Marshall Cavendish, 2004), 73; Michael G. Vann, "The Good, the Bad, and the Ugly: Variation and Difference in French Racism in Colonial *Indochine*," in *The Color of Liberty: Histories of Race in France*, ed. Sue Peabody and Tyler Stovall (Durham: Duke University Press Books, 2003), 198. It should be noted that during the financial crisis of the early 1930s the Bank of Indochina was also severely criticized for exploiting the plight of hard-pressed peasants. The members of the Grand

Council of Economic and Financial Interests of Indochina charged that the Bank of Indochina, "in violation of its status, shamefully abused its sovereign privilege, [acting] monstrous and intolerable," that the bank's actions were "inhumane, inflexible, hard, merciless, never agreeing to sacrifice anything for the unfortunate" who collectively allowed the bank to make a great fortune. "Dix-neuvième séance plénière," *Recueil des procès-verbaux des séances plénières du Grand Conseil des intérêts économiques et financiers de l'Indochine* [Nineteenth Plenary Session, Collection of the Minutes of Plenary Sessions of the Grand Council of Economic and Financial Interests of Indochina] (21 Dec. 1934): 236.

31. Devare, "Rising India and Indians," 288.
32. "Chettiars and Hinduism in Southeast Asia," *Bulletin of the Institute of Traditional Cultures* (July–Dec. 1972): 82.
33. Philip Taylor, *Goddess on the Rise: Pilgrimage and Popular Religion in Vietnam* (Honolulu: University of Hawai'i Press, 2004), 3.
34. Nguyễn Phương Thảo, "Văn hón dân gian miền Nam Việt Nam [The Culture of Worship in the South of Vietnam]," (n.p., 1997), 214, cited in Pairaudeau, *Mobile Citizens*, 220.
35. Thảo, "Văn hón dân gian miền Nam Việt Nam," [Folk Culture of South Vietnam] 214, cited in Pairaudeau, *Mobile Citizens*, 220. On the Black Lady, see also Taylor, *Goddess on the Rise.*
36. Pairaudeau, *Mobile Citizens*, 221. On Vietnamese absorption of Khmer deities, see L. Malleret, "Cochinchine, terre inconnue," *Bulletin de la Societé des Etudes Indochinoises* 3/18 (1943): 9–26; L. Malleret, *L'Archéologie du delta du Mékong* [Archeology of the Mekong Delta] (Paris: Ecole Française d'Extrême Orient, 1959); Tho, "Vn hón dân gian," 185, 214; Taylor, *Goddess on the Rise*, 3, 82.
37. Nguyen-Hoang, "La renaissance du bouddhisme en Cochinchine. L'inauguration de la Bibliotohèque et de la salle de lecture de la pagode Linh-Son, à Saigon," [The Renaissance of Buddhism in Cochinchina. Inauguration of the Library and Reading Room of the Pagoda Linh-Son in Saigon] *L'Écho annamite*, 21 Dec. 1929: 1.
38. M.A. Chidambaram, "Reviving Temples: Recent Indian initiatives in Vietnam," *Frontline* 11, no. 10 (7–20 May 1994): 75.
39. "Seminar on Chettiars and Hinduism in South-East Asia," *Bulletin of the Institute of Traditional Cultures* (University of Madras) (July–Dec. 1972): 85. K.K. Pilay was the director of this seminar. Lord Thendayuthapani has hundreds of other names such as Balasubrahmanyan, Shanmukhan, Swaminathan, Vallimanalan, Palaniandavar, Arumugan, Saravanan, and Sevar Kodiyon.
40. See "Making Temples/Making Selves: Essentialism and Construction in the Identity of the Traditional South Indian Artist," *South Asian Studies* 19 (2003).
41. Ibid.

42. "Nghề mới," *L'Echo annamite*, 1 Oct. 1924: 2; *Annuaire général de l'Indo-Chine française* (1912): 697; TTLTQG 2, file Goucoch D9-15 "L'organisation, statuts des pagodes Mariammane et Sri-Soubramniassmy des indiens bouddhistes de Saigon 1918–1942," letter to the Head of the Service of Immigration and Identity, 14 May 1928.
43. *Guide pratique, renseignements et adresses. Saïgon* (Saigon: J. Aspar, 1934), 3. A Madrolle guide also listed a "Temple des Chettys." *Indochine du Sud. De Marseille à Saïgon; Djibouti, Ethiopie, Ceylan, Malaisie, Cochinchine, Cambodge, Bas-Laos, Sud-Annam, Siam* (Paris: Librairie Hachette, 1926), 7.
44. *Annuaire général de l'Indo-Chine française* (1912): 697.
45. *Annuaire général de l'Indo-Chine française* (1912): 697; "Hindoue Tamoule Djana Sangam, *Indochine-Inde*, 8 March 1936;" *Les adresses* (1913): 286, cited in Pairaudeau, *Mobile Citizens*, 98.
46. Pairaudeau, *Mobile Citizens*, 96.
47. TTLTQG 2, file Conseil Privé 8372 "Arrêté du Gouvernement concédant un immeuble domaniale ... aux Indiens sectateurs de Brahme pour y construire un temple 1881."
48. TTLTQG 2, file Goucoch D9-15 "L'organisation, statuts des pagodes Mariammane et Sri-Soubramniassmy des indiens bouddhistes de Saigon 1918–1942," meeting minutes of the General Assembly of the Hindu Indians of Cochinchina, 21 Aug. 1942; letter from the Head of the Service of Immigration and Identity to the Cabinet of the Governor of Cochinchina, 28 Nov. 1918. By the late 1930s the Indians referred to themselves as "Indiens bramaniques." Ibid., meeting minutes of the General Assembly of Brahmanic Indians of Cochinchina, 19 May 1939.
49. Thanks to Pascal Bourdeaux for this information. Metropolitan decrees of 29 March 1880, applied to colonies by a decree of 4 April 1880, required all congregations or religious associations to request authorization. *Collection complète des lois, décrets, règlements et avis du Conseil d'État* [Complete Collection of Laws, Decrees, Regulations and Opinions of the State Council] (1880), 18. On Christian missions, see Caratini Marcel and Grandjean Philippe, *Le Statut des missions en Indochine* [The Statute of the Missions in Indochina] (Hanoi: IDEO, 1939). On Chinese congregations, see Tracy C. Barrett, *Chinese Diaspora in South-East Asia: The Overseas Chinese in IndoChina* (New York: I.B. Tauris & Co Ltd, 2012).
50. TTLTQG 2, file Goucoch D9-15 "L'organisation, statuts des pagodes Mariammane et Sri-Soubramniassmy des indiens bouddhistes de Saigon 1918–1942," Central Commissioner's report to the Mayor of Saigon, 29 April 1918.
51. This festival was still celebrated in the early 1970s. "Seminar on Chettiars and Hinduism in South-East Asia," *Bulletin of the Institute of Traditional Cultures* (University of Madras) (July–Dec. 1972): 85.
52. "Fête des Chettys," *L'Echo annamite*, 13 Jan. 1921: 1.

53. "Fête des Chettys," *L'Echo annamite*, 9 Feb. 1925: 4.
54. "La fête des chettys," *L'Echo annamite*, 29 Jan. 1926: 2.
55. "Seminar on Chettiars," 109.
56. Dr. R. Vitroz, "Etude zootechnique de l'élevage et de l'exploitation des Bovins du Sud-indochinois en Cochinchine," [Zootechnical Study of the Cattle Industry of the Southern Indochinese in Cochinchina] *Bulletin économique de l'Indo-Chine* (1933): 965.
57. By 1886 there were two mosques. Bouinais and Paulus, *La France en Indo-chine*, 212.
58. Thanks to Samuel Parker for this information.
59. TTLTQG 2, file Goucoch D9-15 "L'organisation, statuts des pagodes Mariammane et Sri-Soubramniassmy des indiens bouddhistes de Saigon 1918–1942," letter to the Head of the Service or Immigration and Identity, 14 May 1928.
60. "Pour Recevoir Tagore," [Reception for Tagore] *Réveil Saigonnais*, 1 July 1924, cited in Pairaudeau, *Mobile Citizens*, 250.
61. "En l'honneur de Tagore," [In Honor of Tagore] *L'Écho annamite*, 2 July 1924: 1.
62. Un Hindou, "Un appel aux Hindous!," [An Appeal to Hindus!] *Réveil Saigonnais*, 2 June 1924, cited in Pairaudeau, *Mobile Citizens*, 250; "Un savant hindou á Saigon," [A Hindu Scholar in Saigon] *Réveil Saigonnais*, 17 July 1924, cited in Pairaudeau, *Mobile Citizens*, 251.
63. "Rabindranath Tagore à Saigon," *Le Merle mandarin. Satirique hebdomadaire*, 28 June 1929, 2. On Tagore's visit of Saigon, see Chi Pham, "The Rise and the Fall of Rabindranath Tagore in Vietnam," unpublished Masters Thesis, U.C. Riverside (2012); H. Hazel Hahn, "Tagore as a Celebrity Tourist?: Urban Planning, Tourism, and Architecture in Colonial Saigon," in *Southeast Asia's Modern Architecture: Questions of Translation, Epistemology and Power*, ed. Jiat-Hwee Chang and Imran bin Tajudeen (Singapore: NUS Press, 2019), 25–57.
64. "Rabindranath Tagore à Saigon," *L'Echo annamite*, 18 June 1929: 1.
65. "Un thé en l'honneur de Tagore," *L'Echo annamite*, 24 June 1929: 2.
66. Pham, "The Rise and the Fall," 15.
67. Ibid.
68. "Rabindranath Tagore à Saigon," *Le Merle mandarin*, 28 June 1929: 2. This part of Tagore's speech is my translation from the French text published in *Le Merle mandarin*, rather than Tagore's original English text which I have not located.
69. *La Tribune indochinoise*, 21 June 1929; Nguyen-Dang-Thuc, "Tagore and Vietnam," in *Rabindranath Tagore: A Centenary Volume 1861–1961*, ed. S. Radhakrishnan (New Delhi: Sahitya Akademi, 1961), 362.
70. Supryia Roy, "Rabindranath Tagore: Stopover at Saigon," unpublished paper, conference on Tagore held in Hanoi, Nov. 2011, cited in Pham, "The Rise and the Fall," 10.

71. William Radice, "Introduction," *Rabindranath Tagore, Selected Poems* (London: Penguin, 1994), 23.
72. Rabindranath Tagore, *The Message of India to Japan: A Lecture* (New York: The Macmillan Company, 1916), 20.
73. Janet Hoskins's *The Divine Eye and the Diaspora: Vietnamese Syncretism becomes Transpacific Caodaism* notes the influences of Tagore and Gandhi on Cao Dai (Honolulu: University of Hawai'i Press, 2015).
74. Thanks to Samuel Parker for this information.
75. Lê and Dovert, *Saigon, 1698–1998*, 167. The *vimana* is referred to as a gopuram in the book. A *vimana* is frequently confused with a gopuram. G. Vidy calls the *vimana* at this temple a "miniature gopuram." G. Vidy, "Réimpression de l'article de G. Vidy," 13.
76. Krishna G. Rampal, *Sacred Structures: Artistic Renditions of Hindu Temples in Malaysia and Singapore* (Singapore: Bluetoffee, 2008), 60.
77. Ibid.
78. Within the complex there is also a shrine dedicated to Murugan.
79. There are some differences in colors between the two *vimanas*, but colors are the most superficial aspects from the religious perspective and could be easily changed.
80. Samuel Parker, "The Matter of Value Inside and Out," *Ars Orientalis* 22 (1992): 101.
81. On Chéret and the poster, see among others Ruth Iskin, *The Poster: Art, Advertising, Design, and Collecting, 1860s–1900s* (Dartmouth: Dartmouth College Press, 2014); H. Hazel Hahn, *Scenes of Parisian Modernity: Culture and Consumption in the Nineteenth Century* (New York: Palgrave Macmillan, 2009), Ch. 9.
82. *Indochine hebdomadaire illustré*, 23 Sept. 1943.
83. "Chettiars and Hinduism in Southeast Asia," *Bulletin of the Institute of Traditional Cultures* (July–Dec. 1972): 85, 109.
84. "Chettiars and Hinduism in Southeast Asia," 109.
85. Ibid.
86. "Chettiars and Hinduism in Southeast Asia," 109–10.
87. Ibid., 110.
88. Devare, "Rising India and Indians," 291.
89. Nick Ray, Peter Dragicevich, and Regis St. Louis, *Lonely Planet Vietnam* (Victoria, Australia: Lonely Planet, 2007), 344.
90. Devare, "Rising India and Indians," 291; Chidambaram, "Reviving temples," 76.
91. Chidambaram, "Reviving Temples," 75.
92. Ibid., 76.
93. Ibid., 75.
94. Geetesh Sharma, *India-Vietnam Relations: First to Twentyfirst Century* (Kolkata: Dialogue Society, 2004), 39.

95. Vietnamese websites tend to date the establishment of the Mariamman Temple to the late nineteenth century.
96. Geetesh Sharma, *Traces of Indian Culture in Vietnam* (New Delhi: Banyan Tree books Pvt. Ltd., 2009), 85–6.
97. Sharma, *Traces of Indian Culture*, 85.
98. French authors also often distorted the history of Indian presence in Indochina. Eugène Lagrillière-Beauclerc's book published in France in 1900, commissioned by the French Minister of the Colonies, noted that a Hindu temple existed in Saigon, that while Hinduism was scarcely present in "Indo-Chine," "dethroned everywhere by Buddhism, some followers of Shiva and Vishnu, and Indian monks remain[ed] in Cochinchina," giving the erroneous impression that the Indians of Saigon were direct descendants of the Hindus of the sixth century rather than recent arrivals. Eugène Lagrillière-Beauclerc, *Etudes coloniales. A travers l'Indo-Chine: Cochinchine, Cambodge, Annam, Tonkin, Laos* [Colonial Studies. Across Indo-China, Cochinchina, Cambodia, Annam, Tonkin, Laos] (Paris: C. Tallandier, 1900), 12; *Bulletin de l'École française d'Extrême-Orient* mocked this misrepresentation, *BEFEO* 1 (1901): 38.
99. Chidambaram, "Reviving temples," 76.
100. Ibid.
101. Ibid.
102. Ibid.
103. Ibid.
104. Ibid., 54.
105. India Parliament. Rajya Sabha, *Parliamentary Debates: Official Report* 171, no. 8 (3 Aug. 1994): 114.
106. Jan Dodd, Mark Lewis, and Ron Emmons, *Rough Guide to Vietnam* (London: Rough Guide, 2003), 93. In the Dec. 2003 issue of *India Perspectives*, a photograph of a new, restored *vimana* was published. The caption erroneously stated: "Entrance to the Yutthapani temple." Rama Gaind, "A Bit of India in Vietnam!," *India Perspectives* 16 (Dec. 2003): 35.
107. The Editor, *Aum Muruga Journal*, "Hindu Temples in VIETNAM," www.shaivam.org/siddhanta/toivietna.htm [accessed 3 May 2012]. This article states that Tamils from Pondicherry built the Mariamman Temple in the late nineteenth century, but wrongly claims that the other two Hindu temples, including the Sri Thendayuthapani Temple, were built in the mid-twentieth century.
108. Đăng Anh, "Đền Sri. Thenday Yutthapani," 9 April 2012. http://livelivego.wordpress.com/2012/04/19/dn-hindu-giao-p-1-dn-sri-thenday-yutthapani/ [accessed 5 May 2012].
109. "Sri Thendayyutthapani Temple," http://ho-chi-minh.cityseekr.com/sri-thendayyutthapani-temple/tourist-attractions-sightseeing/venue/247888 [accessed 7 May 2012].

110. Taylor, *Goddess on the Rise*, 3.
111. Walter Mason, *Destination Saigon: Adventures in Vietnam* (Crows Nest, NSW: Allen & Unwin Pty Ltd, 2010), 212. Mason erroneously states on p. 210 that Chua Ong is a Hindu temple at 66 Tôn Thất Thiệp Street. Actually Chùa Ông is the Subramanyan Swamy Temple.
112. Pairaudeau, *Mobile Citizens*, 220.
113. Ray, Dragicevich, and St. Louis, *Vietnam*, 344.
114. Devare, "Rising India and Indians," 291.
115. Taylor, *Goddess on the Rise*, 3.
116. Dong Vinh, "The Cult of Holy Mothers in Central Vietnam," *Vietnamese Studies* 131, no. 1 (1999): 20–35; Nir Avieli, *Rice Talks: Food and Community in a Vietnamese Town* (Bloomington: Indiana University Press, 2012), 82.
117. Clothey, *Ritualizing on the Boundaries*, 2.
118. Saibal Dasgupta, "Vietnamese celebrate New Year at Hindu temple," *The Times of India*, 24 January 2012, http://articlcs.timesofindia.indiatimes.com/2012-01-24/rest-of-world/30658872_1_hindu-temple-temple-premises-vietnamese-buddhistsMagh Shukla 4, Kaliyug Varsha 5113 [accessed 3 March 2012].
119. Devare, "Rising India and Indians," 291.
120. *City Dwellers: Contemporary Art from India*, exhibition booklet, Seattle Art Museum, 2014, n.p.

CHAPTER 6

French *Nhà Rường* and a Vietnamese Palace for the Governor?: Architectural Exchange in Colonial Vietnam[1]

Caroline Herbelin

"Empire-builders," "creators of the overseas," and especially the famous "colonizing is building": these are all expressions that can be readily found in a number of works touting "the colonial endeavor." This extended analogy at first glance could seem trivial; nevertheless, it reveals a certain confusion in the study of construction in a colonial context through the link it posits between the act of building and that of colonizing. This view of architecture as a metonymy of colonial policy has led to, in historiographic terms, a hypertrophy of research on architecture as an expression of colonial power. Though this approach is partially justified, it fails to reveal the complexity of the interactions at work in colonial constructions because it examines the process vertically and considers all those involved as belonging to homogeneous groups: there are the colonizer-"builders" and the colonized who must endure the imported architecture. Moreover, such a conception is partial in its outlook because it generally focuses on administrative and official buildings. In recent years, studies have tended to consider architecture as more than a "form of dominance"[2] by way of a more complex and heterogeneous system; they restore the diversity of actors involved and their motivation by highlighting the range of interactions. These studies notably show the processes of negotiation and re-appropriations undertaken by the colonized.[3]

Defining architecture in a colonial situation leads us to consider its corollary: the contact between two cultures and their interactions. From this point of view, recent research in the anthropology of art has opened up perspectives that have yet to be explored. Through their focus on exchanges, anthropologists, such as Arjun Appadurai[4] and Nicholas Thomas,[5] have demonstrated the complexity of values associated with objects and the diversity of social meanings attached to them. Albeit based on a different logic, a certain branch of art history in the wake of Alfred Gell[6] has come to these same conclusions. Wishing to demystify art, this branch defines it as both agent and product of a system of social interactions. In so doing, it frees art from a reductive aesthetic and symbolic definition and restores its etymological sense from the Latin *ars*: anything materially made by man. These theories, by claiming the relativity of the meanings assigned to artifacts, have profoundly changed the question of cultural differences. In determining the role of material culture with stakes defended by the social groups involved, the relative and evolving nature of these issues requires a more detailed analysis of the actors and contexts. This in turn leads us to go beyond the idea of two opposing homogeneous cultural blocks, as H. Hazel Hahn does in this volume regarding a Tamil temple in Ho Chi Minh City by highlighting the role of a complex minority group and its influence in varied sectors of colonial and postcolonial society, or Arnout H.C. van der Meer does by illuminating divisions among the colonizers as well as the colonized in colonial Java.

However, the application of these new theoretical perspectives has mostly focused on the significance of the circulations themselves and on their actors rather than the artifacts. In this regard, Dawn Odell's chapter in this volume provides an exemplary case study on how new meanings of artistic artifacts are produced through spatial processes. Studying the role of "finished" objects in social system rarely includes the study of their creation. To consider the "social life"[7] of these objects, we must not start with the history of their possession; as this would evacuate a part of what constitutes the very specificity of the artifacts. By definition, they are created objects with an intrinsic material logic that needs to be kept in mind. In other words, the material should no longer be considered as simply a given but also the result of a process. This conceptual leap offers another dimension to the issue of cultural contact by inserting the question of exchanges within the very core of the artifact. This allows us to raise the issue of hybridity without the restriction of "exterior" material circulations. In summary, social processes manufacture the meaning of the objects, but the objects are also produced by the same social processes, within an interactive loop. From a methodological perspective, this implies that we must deconstruct both the social processes and the manufactured objects. Considering the architectural object, which specifically concerns us here, leads to differentiating the issues of techniques, style, and use of space.[8]

Using new research in the history of architecture in colonial situations and in the anthropology of art, we will study cross-cultural exchanges through an architectural analysis of two examples from colonial Indochina. The first is the Palace of the Governor General in Hanoi. The second example includes the so-called "French" homes built by wealthy Vietnamese in rural Cochinchina in the 1930s. These two seemingly disparate examples will allow us to uncover shared mechanisms in the manufacture of inter-culturalism; they demonstrate a shared process of inter-culturalism, or an active, complex cultural exchange that allows both sides to impact each other. The aim of this chapter is to rethink the relationship between the "colonial" and "local." This reflection echoes Sarah Moser's chapter in this volume, which rethinks this matter in a diachronic way by studying the intentions and ideologies embedded in the built environment. My chapter considers this relationship in a synchronic way, by studying the social and technical elements at stake in culture exchanges, it demonstrates that they can't be considered as the mere confrontation of two homogenous cultural blocks, a dominant "French culture" imposing its features over the colonized, and a passive "Vietnamese culture" slowly being dissolved in the culture of the colonizer.

I. Anatomy of a Site of Colonial Power: The Palace of the Governor General of Indochina in Hanoi

The first example is the palace of the Governor General in Hanoi, built from 1900 to 1907.[9] It appears to be an object taken directly from the collection of buildings in the metropole and imposed onto the colony. This paradigm of colonial building is often cited as an example of the colonizers' architectural arrogance. This object is typical of the architecture of the French Third Republic (Fig. 6.1). By its size and style, it seems to flout the old Vietnamese city, long restricted by imperial edict to a single story in height[10] and still largely composed of straw huts when the Palace was built.

Through its aggressive differentiation from the surrounding landscape, it seems to be a symbol of assimilative colonization, which tries to impose the so-called cultural superiority of the colonizers. In official correspondence, both from engineers of the Public Works Department and from the General Government, everyone continually emphasizes the "French" and "prestigious" characteristics the building should take on.

Figure 6.1: Palace of the Governor General, Hanoi.

It would thus seem that it is through the affirmation of its purely "French" identity, in other words its imported nature, that this building is made a tool of colonial power. Without completely refuting this thesis, I would like to qualify it by suggesting a new reading of colonial administrative buildings through the architectural analysis of this example. Thus, even though the building's identity is proclaimed by the colonizers as "French," its reality is more complex. In fact, believing that this building asserts its power through its French identity is to focus only on the intentions and discourses of the colonizers. In the same vein, a certain confusion needs clearing up. Any administrative building, whether colonial or not, is by nature a place of power, since this is its primary function. Demonstrating that the Palace of the Governor General is a place of power is simply a tautology. This chapter is more interested in how exactly the process takes place.

Techniques and Materials

In terms of technology, we can say that overall, the building complies with French norms and taste. The builders were clearly not all from metropolitan France. However, the rare Vietnamese and Chinese builders were assigned to secondary work and were probably not employed for their technical know-how.[11] The methods used were thus very similar to those in the metropole.

However, the same cannot be said for the materials, which were generally sourced locally. The General Government of French Indochina, which had launched a prospecting policy soon after the start of the conquest, recommended materials be ordered from China when not available on site. An incredibly precise picture of the different resources available in Indochina and their characteristics is available for 1900, the onset of construction.[12] For example, in the specifications of the palace, the chief architect recommended Phu Ly (*sic*) or Keso (*sic*) marble tiles or *lim* wood, an indigenous tree.[13] Only elements made of metal, zinc and iron, which were still of poor quality in the colony, were imported directly from France. Unable to build such an edifice in stone as would have been the case in France, the walls were made of brick and covered with plaster that imitated stone and molded decorations. This process reveals that the appearance of French techniques was deemed important, even though they were in reality subjected to unavoidable modifications.

The Spatial Organization of the Building: Public vs Private

The spatial analysis of the building and its furnishings also suggest that the building cannot be conceived as a mere French "transplant." Certainly the exterior displays no sign of any local influence. The façade with its Beaux-Arts style displays pediments, moldings, and cornices that are in no way Vietnamese (Fig. 6.1). Only a portico at the rear of the building,[14] in the portion of the garden that communicates with the adjacent botanical garden, is inspired by traditional Vietnamese architecture (Fig. 6.2). Inside the building, the first or "noble" floor, the most public portion, the reception hall, and the hall of the Government Council display a mixture of different styles (Fig. 6.3). The range extends from Louis XV to the Empire style, all of which are classically French and without any visible reference to the colony. However, the upper floor, the one reserved for the Governor General and his family, shows a more complex arrangement. The semi-public spaces include a handful of elements referring to local culture: a stylized ideogram

Figure 6.2: Portico between the Palace of the Governor General and the botanical palace (Social Science Library, Hanoi [SSLHN]).

Figure 6.3: Palace of the Governor General, reception hall.

representing the word *Thọ* (longevity) appears in mosaic in the hallway (Fig. 6.4), antiques in the cabinet and the Governor's office (various bronze, tripod vases, and old paintings of high dignitaries), and an imposing bell similar to those found in temples stands majestically in the hallway leading to the private apartments (Fig. 6.5). Although discrete, these objects are all unequivocal references to Vietnamese culture. Finally, the decor in the most private space, the Governor's bedroom, is almost entirely devoid of references to classical European culture. It is in fact composed almost exclusively of furniture with patterns inspired by Vietnamese art: a carved dragon, a pierced frieze with stylized clouds and ideograms, and screens inspired from traditional painting (Fig. 6.6).[15] The furniture, despite its clear Asian reference, is not traditional. Rather, the pieces are clearly manufactured by the colony's art schools.

This organization certainly demonstrates the circumscription of references to French or local cultures to specific locations determined by their function. Local elements multiply as we enter increasingly private spaces. Such references are also tolerated in transitional spaces leading to areas with functions other than power. The gate towards the botanical garden is an example announcing a space whose main functions are leisure and knowledge.[16] To rephrase it differently: places with weaker functions of power are more inclined to accept local references under specific forms.

Figure 6.4: Palace of the Governor General, second floor corridor (SSLHN).

Figure 6.5: Palace of the Governor General, hallway leading to the private apartments (SSLHN).

Figure 6.6: Palace of the Governor General, the room of the Governor (SSLHN).

A Matter of Taste

Far from being anecdotal, the relationship between the public and private spheres highlighted in this example illustrates that a serious discussion of colonial culture cannot focus exclusively on its "official" expression if it does not wish to only partially understand the processes at work. The public and the private spheres, or more precisely the different social groups within which individual functions, interact either through similarities or differences. This observation opens up the perspective of a history of colonial taste (especially a history of the reception of aesthetic exchanges). Here, "taste" should be conceived not as the expression of an arbitrary subjectivity, but as an expression of social usage.[17]

A history of taste also implies that the analysis should be located chronologically and in context. Indeed, it is necessary to keep in mind that the above-described relationships varied over time. Thus, although the exact date of these photographs is not known, they can be situated between the late 1910s or early 1920s.[18] We can thus wonder whether the furniture belonged to Albert Sarraut during his second term as Governor General of Indochina from 1916 to 1919. As harbinger of the policy of "association" and the "Franco-Annamite Collaboration,"[19] it is interesting to consider the palace furnishings in light of his policies. The palace's configuration was changed in the 1940s when Governor General Admiral Decoux decided to modernize his apartments. He entrusted the task to a Vietnamese architect Nguyễn Cao Luyện, who redecorated the apartments entirely in an Art Deco style. Although they both implicated a Vietnamese element, the aims of these two examples are not the same. In the first example, the goal was to acknowledge in a limited fashion a certain aesthetic value in Vietnamese culture. In the second, it involves recognizing the value of local expertise[20] in terms of architecture, but paradoxically through Western aesthetics.

The Advantages of a Comparative Study

After considering the Palace of the Governor General as a whole, it is helpful to analyze comparatively. Here we will focus on the Beaux-Arts style and the use of neo-classical motifs in the building, which are often criticized because they evoke the building's arrogance. The engineer Georges Espitallier (1849–1923) commissioned to build military buildings in the Haiphong concession, recounts with humor the reasons the "Neoclassical style" was so massively used in early colonial buildings.

> Project monuments displayed neo-Greek attributes that reek of the School's traditional teachings. Engineers who were thrown into architecture always went through a period of Greek Revival. Sometimes, they free themselves later on; but they all start there.[21]

This assessment suggests that this style is the product of a certain technical system, that of colonizers at the beginning of the century. In other words, is it possible that to a certain extent, the colonizers applied the "Neoclassical" style because they did not know how to apply any others? They could of course have integrated elements of Vietnamese architecture. This was the case with the birth of "Indochinese style" in the 1920s; it was a style that aimed to be culturally relevant to the country's context and was used for a handful of official buildings. However, we must remember that the style was the result of a collaboration between one of the most important urban planning experts of the time, Ernest Hébrard (1875–1933), and knowledgeable architects who had long resided in Indochina.[22] Twenty years earlier, the Beaux-Arts style was a prestigious solution that also required the least effort and cost.

The measure of investments (both economic and labor) is fundamental because it provides an index for quantifying the involvement in various projects and offers an opportunity to compare programs of differing natures. Thus, if we compare the Palace of the Governor General with proposed draft projects, we note that the final draft is far from the most megalomaniac.[23] Budgetary considerations very quickly overcame initial aspirations that could be three times more imposing than the final realization. Nevertheless, reduced costs were relative when compared with the investments that could have been made to other fields. Thus, in a similar example, Dr. Montel, who would later become the head of Health Services of the City of Saigon, protested when the construction of the municipal theater consumed one-fifth of the city's budget in 1911. All the money could have been invested in assistance and hygiene, especially in favor of "natives," a much more urgent priority according to Dr. Montel.[24] Translating these buildings in terms of investment and priority does not minimize their importance but rather provides a useful scale with which to measure the "megalomania" evoked by Gwendolyn Wright in her discussion of architecture in Indochina.[25]

Finally, the most illuminating comparisons are probably those that exist outside of the colony. Recontextualized within the framework of buildings built in France under the Third Republic, the Governor's palace is stylistically consistent with its contemporary equivalents. Its arrogance thus appears relative; it is not ridiculous to compare its size to that of a town hall or prefecture in an important provincial town. This architecture, in its functioning, is therefore as much if not more tied to Republican architecture than to a specifically colonial one, with all the issues this entails. Indeed, one example among many is *La quinzaine coloniale* that published in 1910 an article on the absurdity of using statues that belong to the vocabulary of Republican street furniture in colonial buildings.[26] The journal of the "colonial party" draws attention to the fact that these allegories utterly failed to signify France's greatness, as they conveyed a message the colonized could not possibly understand. This concurs with Lawrence J. Vale's analysis of capitals in various colonial and non-colonial contexts and his analysis of how such buildings were received by various populations. He points out that part of the message contained in these locations is aimed at the society that built them.[27] The message conveyed by colonial buildings was destined for the "natives" as well as for the European community in the colony, for the metropole, and for other colonial empires.

Finally, we must remember that by the early twentieth century, this "Neoclassical" style and all derivatives using various references to Greco-

Roman antiquity were no longer the prerogative of the old continent and its colonies. Several famous examples can be found throughout Asia. The *Yuanming Yuan*,[28] the Summer Palace in Beijing, before its destruction in 1860 during the Second Opium War, boasted a style inspired by the Versailles Palace and was built with the help of the Jesuits. In Bangkok, King Rama V (1853–1910) called on European architects to build several palaces in a "Neoclassical" style.[29] More belatedly, the National Assembly in Japan,[30] rejecting projects highlighting more local architecture, eventually adopted in 1936 a project reflecting the monumental historicist style of the 1930s, a modern variation of the classical order. The scope of this chapter does not allow for a history of how these references were used in architecture and how they spread. However, their evocation helps underline the fact that the colonial power was not only in using the "Neoclassical" style to assert a certain form of authority; other royalties and non-French empires also used this attribute for the same reasons.

To conclude this section, we can state that administrative buildings were undeniably the colonial power's "new clothes." As uniforms identify a soldier or a cassock designates a priest, so architecture equips the social function of a building. Official buildings visually signify their function of power through their ornamentation. However, this should not prevent us from considering how this function is expressed and how it coexists with other less visible ones. This offers a certain distance from colonial discourse concerning these buildings, and measures the gap between the intentions at the onset of construction and the reality of the finished construction.

II. The Agency of the Colonized as Seen in the Architecture of Rural Homes in Southern Vietnam in the 1930s

Recent research has demonstrated how architecture and urban planning in colonial cities were not the unilateral product of colonizers' vision, but rather a joint production where the colonized played a very large part. The essential role of the local elite—architects and engineers—often formed by colonial institutions (in the metropole or in the colony) has been particularly underlined.[31] For Vietnam, the architects of the Ecole de Beaux-Arts of Indochina mentioned earlier,[32] by summarizing local knowledge and exogenous influences, were "cultural purveyors" who were instrumental in the creation of Vietnam's urban landscapes in the 1930s and 1940s as well as in the post-colonial era. As the role of these local elites is relatively well documented, we chose to focus here on an example that demonstrates that cultural exchanges were not limited to scholarly architecture. It can be the result of spontaneous exchanges and can affect categories of the colonized population other than the educated elite.

Our second example seems diametrically opposed to the previous one. Far from the pomp of the Republican palace in the colonial capital, the evolution of rural houses in Cochinchina (now southern Vietnam) in the 1930s deserves attention. These changes took place under the dual influence of urbanization and westernization. These homes are particularly interesting because they have yet to be studied as examples of architecture produced during the colonial period. Indeed, though the rural habitat has been the subject of several studies, notably by Pierre Gourou, research has been limited to Tonkin and Annam (respectively present-day northern and central Vietnam).[33] The geographer explains that he did not include Cochinchina because he considers that the rural habitat, being open to Western influences, was "bastardized" there. For him, these houses are "devoid of style and originality."[34]

Little would have been known about these houses if they had not been described in the survey conducted by the Guernut Committee of 1937 which, at the request of Popular Front government in France, had begun to take stock of the French colonies. In Indochina, one of these systematic surveys focused on habitats.[35] The investigators (the majority of who were low-ranking Vietnamese civil servants) classified these habitats as "French," "modern," or "Franco-modern." These homes are interesting because they offer an exemplary expression of the agency of the colonized. Indeed, one can speak of a "heist." Western architectural motifs were used without any direct intervention by the colonizers, who disapproved of these exchanges which they considered were undertaken at the expense of the traditional habitat.

Materials and Techniques

As part of Cochinchina's extraordinary economic development in the 1930s—some spoke of a Cochinchinese *Far West*—brick buildings multiplied in the region. Until that point, the use of brick and cement had been limited to royal palaces, temples, and merchant houses in the cities. In the countryside, the use of brick was mainly reserved for the homes of a few officials, and even there it was restricted to the gabled walls, while the façades remained composed of columns and wooden panels. In the 1930s, this changed, and homes were entirely built of bricks covered with plaster. This development favored manufactured goods, as wealthy home owners turned their backs on traditional craftsmanship deemed inferior. This trend in Cochinchina encouraged the creation of small and medium-sized industrial brickworks, run by Vietnamese or Chinese industrial figures because the French factory, Tuileries de l'Indochine, could not meet this new clientele's growing demand.[36] These companies also specialized in the construction of roof tiles and decorative architectural ceramics, railings, and floor or wall tiles. The use of industrial and even reinforced concrete, also became more common since the 1899 opening by the Pila group of the cement factory Portland Artificiels de l'Indochine.[37] With this stronger building material came the possibility of creating a wider range of shapes. In particular, reinforced concrete was used to replace ornamental wood carvings. This practice saddened certain Westerners, who saw it as a threat to traditional architecture.[38] This "hardening" of the habitat took place not so much because brand new techniques were introduced but rather thanks to the improved quality and an accrued availability of existing ones.

Due to costs, the use of these materials was reserved for the wealthiest. Construction methods were the first criteria used by investigators to socially classify housing and respond to the instructions of the Guernut Commission. Habitat types needed to be addressed so as to "reflect the conditions of various fortunes." The ranking that resulted almost invariably resembled the following: masonry and industrially produced flat tiles indicated a wealthy home; traditionally produced wood and hollow roof tiles meant a well-to-do home; a hut made of straw or cob corresponded to a poor home.

Although they entailed a dramatic transfiguration in the appearance of homes, a closer look reveals that the habitat did not radically change in principle. The frame remained traditional (Fig. 6.7), the roof supported by columns and kingposts. It is this element that distinguishes these homes from their Western counterparts. The columns support the vertical thrust of the frame without redistributing its weight to the walls, which consequently are not weight-bearing. The brickwork thus dressed the wood frame rather than replacing it.

Material and technical developments in these rural homes cannot be referenced without mentioning a less visible transformation whose impact on the lifestyle of the inhabitants was significant. We are referring to all of the technical arrangements meant to improve the comfort of homes such as toilets, lighting, and even the use of rain gutters. These amenities were perceived as Western derivatives as evidenced by the many comments in survey reports such as: "These homes tend to resemble European homes more and more. Some have a toilet, a bathroom, and are lit by gas lamps."[39]

Figure 6.7: Lamp post, symbol of technical progress and wealth in the countryside (Archives Nationales d'Outre-Mer, Aix-en-Provence [ANOM]).

Vietnamese Homes, Western Trappings

Just as with technical transfers, the spatial organization of homes reveals less radical changes than partial ones. The direct result of using a structure built on columns is that the house maintains its organization in rows (*gian*), and with it the traditional determination of different spaces. Simply stated, after the reception area at the entrance, came the private rest area with on either side of the altar of the ancestors a space reserved for each sex. However, whereas the living space was normally completely open, there are several cases in which the appearance of walls between the columns defined bedrooms, a previously unknown concept in rural homes (Fig. 6.8). This was a sign of social changes underway at the time. In rare cases, it was specified "parents' room," "children's room" and even "guest room." These denominations are surprising because traditionally, the rest area was organized by gender and not the social status of the person using the space. Such a shift also reflects the changes in family habits within Vietnamese society.[40] In general, spaces became more specialized and less versatile as seen on the blueprints with the appearance of rooms such as an office, a den, a hall, or a sewing room, which seem less related to the emergence of new spatial functions than to the fact that previously existing functions were assigned a space.

This selective use of Western elements can also be seen in the furniture, the simplest and most effective markers to determine the uses of various spaces. Among the wealthiest individuals, the following phenomenon can be observed: "modern," streamlined pieces of furniture were combined with traditional, ornate armchairs and tables that were sculpted and featured mother-of-pearl inlays. Behind the apparently chaotic disorder, the former were in fact more present near the entrance, in public spaces, while the latter were clustered around the altar for ancestors. This transitional area leading to private spaces thus retained its traditional design.

The most radical changes did not take place on the inside but on the outside of these homes. Traditional homes asserted themselves with the volume of their sober, majestic roofs, which almost entirely covered the entrance wall, made up of columns and wooden doors. In contrast, the new middle-class houses boasted front walls with exuberant decorations that almost entirely hid the roof behind the façade (Fig. 6.9). The arcade porch became the central visual element of the house, proudly topped by pediments that sometimes displayed the owner's name. Medallions, friezes, capitals, parapets, balustrades, and colorful ceramic tile inlay (Fig. 6.10) were used to identify and individualize homes. The style was eclectic; Rococo shells were blended with Art-Deco motifs, but there was a clear preference for the Neoclassical.

Thus "French" façades were added, like a screen, over homes that in reality bore very relative traces of Westernization. The general processes at work in these homes were more an overlay than a substitution of elements. This hypothesis is confirmed with testimony from the survey that explained how certain owners, when modernizing their homes, only altered the front façade. Jean-Yves Claeys, a former architect of the Public Works Department of Indochina who subsequently became an archaeologist at the Ecole Française d'Extrême-Orient (EFEO), personally witnessed the construction of one of these homes. He recounts how the structure was first erected according to tradition, guided by the watchful guidance of a geomancer. However, once the frame was in place, the construction underwent a clear change.

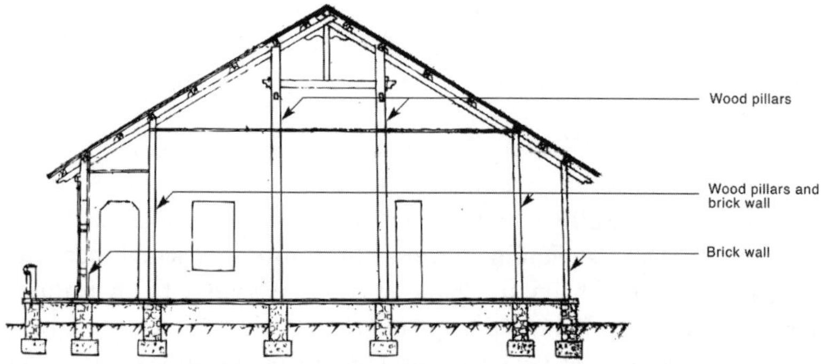

Figure 6.8: A traditional framework despite some simplifications (Redrawn from a document held at ANOM, legends translated).

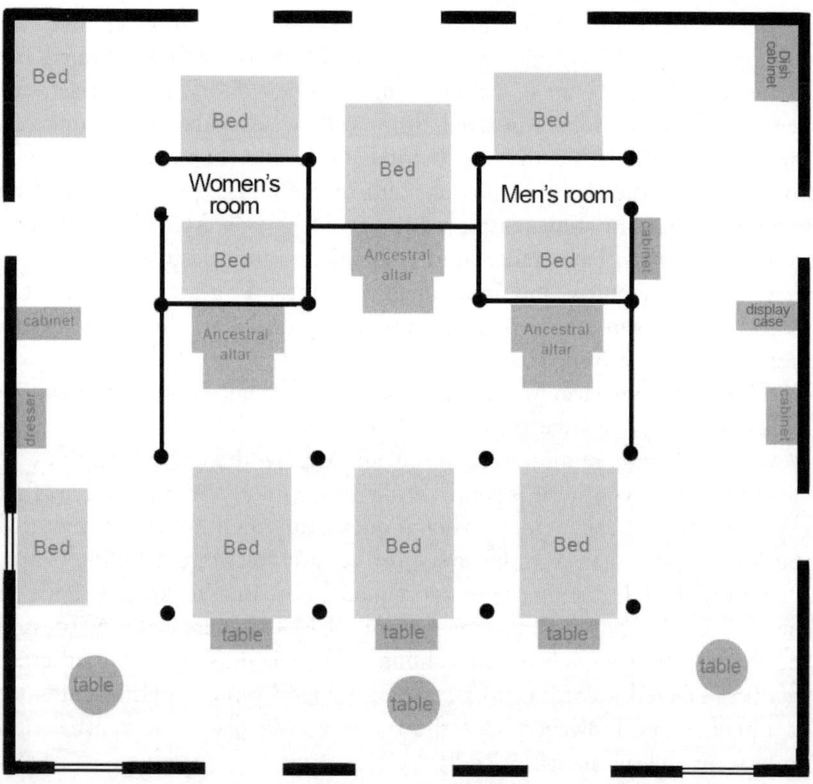

Figure 6.9: A spatial organization showing moderate changes (Redrawn from a document held at ANOM, legends translated).

Figure 6.10: A façade with element of western design (ANOM).

> Having accomplished the rituals, [the owner] was suddenly seized with a kind of itch for improvement. Instead of a beautiful wrap-around veranda with a multitude of squeaky doors, she ordered a wall to be built around the house with very few, very narrow windows. On the facade, she added a pavilion with a peristyle.

The architect then related the satisfaction of the owner's husband, a remark that certainly best summarizes the process underway. "It's still a success. With a '*nhà rường*,'[41] my wife [...] managed to make a house that looks like a European villa ... Quite a beauty, isn't it?"

As with the Palace of the Governor General, an analysis of these "Franco-modern" homes reveals two processes at work. It is clear that the appearance of these homes is linked to an affirmation of social status; the heavily decorated façades offered a chance to express one's wealth and individuality.[42] The goal was to differentiate oneself from the rest of the village, to create a distinction. These houses clearly reflect the emergence of a new social class, notably landowners who acquired their wealth during the rapid development of trade and agriculture in Cochinchina. Though trends in appearance were highly modified, the moderate changes in the internal organization of homes show that the impact of colonization on lifestyles needs to be more nuanced. It should be added that this form of borrowing continues in a certain fashion with the French-style houses still being built in present-day Vietnam.[43] It is not uncommon for today's project managers to request contractors to use certain details taken from old colonial buildings. These modern homes are as eclectic as the examples wc have just seen. Moreover, they are still disdained by Westerners as well as certain Vietnamese, especially intellectuals and former notables (who prefer to revive traditional wooden houses). This confirms that issues of taste are influenced by culture and class.

Conclusion

At first glance, a common denominator does not seem to exist between the imposing and solemn Palace of the General Governor of Indochina and the ostentatious homes of the wealthy in rural Cochinchina. Yet, once past the façades, a study of practices and techniques for both the frame and interior decoration suggests that exogenous influences function in both cases with similar mechanisms. The appropriations exist on symmetrically opposite paths. The Governor's palace publicly affirms its identity and borrows from the "Other" in more intimate spaces. Rural homes on the other hand, display their appropriations publicly while the private sphere remains stable with a clear preference for vernacular references. However, in both cases, stating one's taste also means positioning oneself on the social stage. Understanding references to the "Other" as a primarily social strategy is critical for understanding the mechanisms involved in cultural exchanges. The question of hybridity can thus be identified as a specific instance within a broader process of social distinction, reflected in the relationships between the endogenous and the exogenous, but it can just as easily express issues of class or temporal relationships (for example in the use of "neo" or "retro"). This explains the ubiquitous use of both "French" or "modern" to designate these rural homes. In reality, the referent is less important than the differentiation for which it makes room. This is what explains the very relative importance of authenticity. In the Palace of the Governor General, it is irrelevant whether the furniture is truly the kind used by the Vietnamese themselves. What is more important is that it appears "local" to potential visitors or the primary user of the domestic space. Similarly, the homes in rural Cochinchina have very little in common with French villas. What matters is that the reference is readily understood by those who see the façade of these homes. The goal therefore is to distinguish oneself from one's social group rather than trying to strictly resemble the "Other." The question of influences can therefore no longer be regarded as simply the exercise of an external relation of subordination. Internal factors are just as important as external ones in cultural exchanges.[44]

This also explains why it is difficult to use precise terminology for the different styles at work here. Of course Vietnamese art historians have produced typologies on the evolution of decorative directories in architecture (with particular reference to the various degrees of sinicization of art depending on the periods or by stating regional specificities).[45] We could have also discussed more extensively and accurately references to various Western styles in the Cochinchinese homes. However, the question that begs to be asked is to what extent a more precise typology would further enlighten the mechanisms involved at the time. In other words, is it useful to use categories of scholarly classification that were not significant as such? The operative distinction in colonial society was often reduced to a distinction between traditional and modern, French and Indochinese, and even Western and Eastern. These simplistic distinctions have also influenced the classification of architecture in the postcolonial period. Among other things, this has led to difficulty in the conceptualization of the validity of architecture seen as "colonial" or "French" that do not easily fit into new narratives about Vietnamese heritage. The question is valid more generally beyond the confines of this chapter. Thus the use of the neoclassical style in the West poses the same problem. Few know the precise decorative references of the different styles and periods used in this syncretic style; what matters is the general reference to antiquity.

To complete the presentation of cultural exchange processes in buildings, it should be noted that social issues were not their only driving force. Construction choices were also conditioned by the specificities of the manufactured materials. Indeed, cultural borrowing motivated by social strategies can be hampered by material constraints. It can fail or be modified due to insufficient funds, lack of technical know-how, or simply because the deciders do not wish to adopt the practices or lifestyles it necessitates. It is thus necessary to consider the issue of investment. How much are we willing to invest in these areas to remain true to ourselves in an exogenous environment, or inversely, to differentiate ourselves from our own environment? Conceiving contact no longer only influence and dominate but as a wider range of analytical categories allows us to consider these exchanges in a more nuanced manner and to grasp the diversity of motivations by those engaged in such practices. Such nuanced interpretations would in turn contribute in the production of layered interpretations regarding both Vietnamese national heritage and the legacy of French heritage in Vietnam.

Notes

1. An extract of this chapter was published in "Etudier la diversité des échanges culturels, L'exemple de l'architecture au Vietnam en situation coloniale" [Studying the Diversity of Cultural Exchanges. The Case of Architecture in Colonial Vietnam] by Caroline Herbelin in *Cultures d'empires. Échanges et affrontements culturels en situation coloniale* [Cultural Exchanges and Confrontations in Colonial Situation], ed. Romain Bertrand, Hélène Blais, and Emmanuelle Sibeud (Paris: Editions Karthala, 2015). I thank Lylan Dill for the translation.
2. I am reformulating Nezar Al Sayyad's expression in *Forms of Dominance, on the Architecture and Urbanism of the Colonial Enterprise* (1992).
3. See Kathleen James-Chakraborty, "Beyond postcolonialism: New directions for the history of nonwestern architecture," *Frontiers of Architectural Research* 3, no.1 (March 2014): 1–9.
4. Arjun Appadurai, ed., *The Social Life of Things: Commodities in Cultural Perspective* (Cambridge: Cambridge University Press, 1986).
5. Nicholas Thomas, *Entangled Objects: Exchange, Material Culture, and Colonialism in the Pacific* (Cambridge, MA: Harvard University Press, 1991).
6. Alfred Gell, *Art and Agency: An Anthropological Theory* (Oxford: Clarendon Press, 1998).
7. To borrow the title of the work directed by Appadurai, op. cit.
8. Here, we have adopted the method suggested by Phillippe Bruneau, "L'Echange d'art," [Exchanges in Art] *Ramage* 14 (2002): 123–32.
9. This study is based on files found at the Center n°1 of the National Archives of Vietnam in Hanoi (ANV1), Kiến Trúc collection, "Gouvernement Général de l'Indochine" box, from catalog number hp 1 h s 1 to hp 13 h s 219.
10. See article CLVI of the Gia Long Code "Contravention aux règlements sur les vêtements et les habitations," [Violation of Regulations on Clothes and Dwellings] trans. Philastre, *Le code annamite* [The Annamite Code] (Paris: Ernest Leroux editors, 1909), 658.
11. On the subject, see the various auctions and negotiated contracts on file in the Kiến Trúc collection mentioned above. On the discussion concerning the workers' choice over the decoration, see the National Overseas Archives (Aix-en-Provence) ANOM, GGI 7758 "Installation du Palais du Gouvernement général à Hanoi" correspondence between the Minister of Colonies and the Governor General of Indochina, May–June 1903.

12. See for example the "tableau récapitulatif des matériaux de construction," [Summary Table of Construction Materials] in Alfred Foulhoux, *Cours de construction pratique, Collège des stagiaires* [A Course on Building Practice], Saigon 1877, Manuscript, 54–61.
13. ANOM, TP 578 Box "Avant projet du palais du gouvernement général."
14. This analysis is based on iconography found in the old collection of the Ecole Française d'Extrême-Orient (EFEO), Library of Social Sciences in Hanoi. The documents are classified under the following shelf numbers: ô 47, 00111, Hanoi, Tonkin, portique asiatique à l'entrée du palais du Gouvernement général; ô 47, 00223, Hanoi, Tonkin, Véranda; ô 47, 00126, Hanoi, Tonkin, vestibule menant vers les appartements du gouvernement général; ô 47, 00067, Hanoi, Tonkin, le cabinet du gouvernement général; ô 47, 00072, Hanoi, Tonkin, le bureau du Gouverneur; ô 47, 00071, Hanoi, Tonkin, chambre à coucher du Gouverneur général.
15. Of course these objects should be analyzed as belonging to a whole, with all the specificities this implies a colonial environment, including the removal of the object from its original context to divert it for decorative purposes. Although this does not contradict our argument, this aspect has not been developed here as we consider these objects as pieces of furniture that contribute to the organization of architectural space.
16. This is why the majority of instances of hybrid styles in the colonies are located in sites of knowledge or cultural leisure: educational establishments or museums.
17. On the subject, several studies exist on taste as a social expression. To start, there is Bourdieu, *La Distinction. Critique Sociale du Jugement* [Distinction: A Social Critique of the Judgement of Taste] (Paris: Éditions de Minuit, 1979), and Francis Haskell's liminal work, *La norme et le caprice* [Rediscoveries in Art] (Paris: Flammarion, 1996) (original edition in English, 1976). Among works on the sociology of art, there exists Leora Auslander's impressive tome, *Taste and Power: Furnishing Modern France* (1996), that focuses on similar processes in furniture, which is considered to be a tool for expressing social distinctions in France between the end of the seventeenth century and the beginning of the eighteenth century, and Herbert J. Gans's *Popular Culture and High Culture: An Analysis and Evaluation of Taste* (New York: Basic Books, 1999).
18. Although these photographs were not precisely dated, it is possible to estimate, thanks to the series they belong to, that they were taken during the 1910s and 1920s. On the use of objects and "exotic" architectural decors in European taste and their meaning, see Mercedes Volait, *Fous du Caire : excentriques, architectes, et amateurs d'art en Égypte (1867–1914)* [Crazy about Cairo: Eccentrics, Architects and Art Lovers in Egypt] (Paris: L'archange Minotaure, 2009).
19. Charles Fourniau, *Vietnam. Domination coloniale et résistance nationale (1858–1914)* [Vietnam. Colonial domination and national resistance (1858–1914)] (Paris: Les Indes Savantes, 2002), 845.

20. Using Mercedes Volait's expression as found in *Architectes et architectures de l'Egypte moderne, 1830–1950: genèse et essor d'une expertise locale* [Architects and Architecture in Modern Egypt, 1830–1950: Origins and Development of a Local Expertise] (Paris: Maisonneuve et Larose, 2005).
21. Georges Espitallier, *Class notes*, mimeographed manuscript, s.d., p. 22, Bibliothèque nationale de France.
22. Caroline Herbelin, *Architectures du Vietnam colonial. Repenser le métissage* [Architectures of Colonial Vietnam. Rethinking Hybridity] (Paris: INHA/CTHS, 2016).
23. The ANOM has conserved one of the first of these pre-projects in its collection, Travaux Publics des colonies, 1 TP 578 9, map dated 1895 and the second is at the ANV1, collection Travaux Publics du Tonkin (TPT), 4614, dated 1899 and submitted by Henri Vildieu. The project that was eventually built is a third to a quarter smaller in volume.
24. Montel Marie Georges-Hippolyte, *La ville de Saigon, étude de démographie et d'hygiène coloniale* [The city of Saigon, study of demography and colonial hygiene], PhD thesis in Medicine (Bordeaux: Imprimerie moderne, 1911), 86.
25. Gwendolyn Wright, *The Politics of Design in French Colonial Urbanism* (Chicago: University of Chicago Press, 1991).
26. ANOM, "La nécessité d'une statuaire coloniale," [The Necessity of a Colonial Statuary] *La quinzaine coloniale* (10 Oct. 1910): 689–90. Concerning the Republican message as expressed through architecture, see Agulhon, "Imagerie civique et décor urbain dans la France du XIXe siècle," [Civic Imagery and Urban Decor in 19th-century France] *Ethnologie Française* 1–4 (1975): 33–56.
27. Lawrence J. Vale, *Architecture, Power, and National Identity* (New Haven: Yale University Press, 2008), 340.
28. Michèle Pirrazzoli-t'Serstevens, *Le Yuanmingyuan/Jeux d'eau et palais européens du XVIIIe siècle à la Cour de Chine* [The Yuanmingyuan/Water Effects and 18th-century European Palaces at the Chinese Imperial Court], Editions Recherche sur les Civilisations (ERC), Association pour la diffusion de la pensée française (ADPF), 1987 and Michèle Pirrazzoli-t'Serstevens, "The Emperor Qianlong's European Palaces," *Orientations* 19, no. 1 (1988): 61–71.
29. See Maurizio Peleggi, *Lords of Things: The Fashioning of the Siamese Monarchy's Modern Image* (Honolulu: University of Hawai'i Press, 2002).
30. Jonathan M. Reynolds, "Japan's Imperial Diet Building: Debate over Construction of a National Identity," *Art Journal* 55, no. 3 (Fall 1996): 38–47.
31. See for example Preeti Chopra, *A Joint Enterprise: Indian Elites and the Making of British Bombay* (Minneapolis: University of Minnesota Press, 2011) and Volait, *Architectes et architectures de l'Egypte Moderne.*
32. Caroline Herbelin, "Architects of the college of Fine Arts in Hanoi," in *Tạp Chí Nghiên Cứu Lịch Sử* [Journal of Historical Research] 2 (2007): 46–61. See

also Đoàn Đức Thành, *Thế Hệ Kiến Trúc Sư Việt Nam Đâu Tiên* [The First Generation of Vietnamese Architects] (Hanoi: Nhà xuất bản văn hóa, 2008). This work contains short biographies of these architects.

33. Pierre Gourou, *Les paysans du delta Tonkinois* [Peasants of the Tonkin Delta] (Paris: Les éditions d'art et d'histoire, 1936); Pierre Gourou, *Esquisse d'une Habitation annamite* [Sketches of Annamite Dwellings] (Paris: Les éditions d'art et d'histoire, 1936).
34. Gourou, *Esquisse d'une Habitation annamite,* 7.
35. This analysis is therefore based on the following archives: ANOM Commission Guernut, box 88.
36. Hồ, Văn Cầm, *Sụ bàn tính về việc lập một cái lò gạch máy tại Cần Thơ* [Project to Establish a Mechanical Brickyard in Cân Tho] (Cần Thơ: imprimerie de l'Ouest, 1928).
37. Jean-François Klein, *Ulysse Pila, "Vice-Roi de l'Indo-Chine China," Des routes de la soie au pouvoir impérial (1837–1909)* [Ulysse Pila "Vice-Roy of Indo-China," From the Silk Roads to Imperial Power (1837–1909)] (Lyon: Ed. du Zeugma, 2017).
38. On the ease with which the use of reinforced concrete in indigenous buildings in Indochina became widespread and the subsequent dismay of the Europeans, see George Groslier, "La fin d'une tradition d'art: les pagodes cambodgiennes et le ciment armé," [The End of an Art Tradition. Cambodian Pagodas and Reinforced Concrete] *L'Illustration* 175 (11 Jan. 1930): 50–3.
39. ANOM, Guernut 88, "Survey of Nguyen Van Nghe, province of Cholon, district of the center of Cho Lon, Canton of Long Hung Ha, Long Phu village."
40. On the changes in gender relations triggered by colonization within private spaces, see Ann Stoler, *Carnal Knowledge and Imperial Power: Race and the Intimate in Colonial Rule* (Berkeley: University of California Press, 2002).
41. The *nhà rường* is a type of traditional house characterized by the presence in each roof structure of two main columns linked by a single tie beam.
42. Daniel Hémery, "L'Homme, un itinéraire vietnamien. Humanisme et sujet humain au XIXe siècle," [Mankind, a Vietnamese itinerary. Humanism and Human Subject in the 19th Century] in Christian Culas and Jean-François Klein, eds., special issue "Viêt Nam. Histoire et perspectives contemporaines," [Viêt Nam. History and Contemporary Perspectives] *Moussons. Recherches en sciences humaines sur l'Asie du Sud-Est* 13–14, no. 1 (2009): 25.
43. Khuất Tân Hưng, "Cuộc 'xâm lăng' thứ bac của 'kiến truc pháp' vào Hà Nội" [The third invasion of French architecture in Hanoi], paper given at the School of Architecture of Hanoi, July 2008.
44. Philippe Papin has already underlined the importance of internal factors in the history of cultural exchanges: "Histoire des contacts: position du problème et hypothèses de recherches," [History of Contacts: Context of the Matter and Research Hypothesis] in *Liber Amoricorum. Mélanges offerts au Professeur*

Phan Huy Lê [Liber Amicorum, Miscellanies offered to Professor Phan Huy Lê], ed. Philippe Papin and John Kleinen (Paris: École Française d'Extrême-Orient / Thanh-Niên, 1999), 205–20.

45. See for example the monumental history of the architecture of Vietnam by Ngô Huy Quỳnh, *Kiến trúc Việt Nam* [Vietnamese Architecture] (Ho Chí Minh City: nhà xuat ban Thành pho Ho Chí Minh, 1986).

CHAPTER 7

Rejecting and Reproducing Colonial Urbanism in Putrajaya, Malaysia

Sarah Moser

After the end of the colonial era, the British left behind a legacy of new cities, architecture, and urban planning across the Americas, Africa, Asia, and the South Pacific. The creation of new cities and the strategic urbanization of the colonies was a key component of the imperial project designed to facilitate the extraction and export of resources and provide colonial administrative centers while bringing "civilization" to local populations. In the post-independence era, former colonies responded to their colonial urban past in a variety of ways. In some parts of the Commonwealth, many colonial-era buildings, city plans, and neighborhoods have been meticulously preserved or even expanded. In other contexts, colonial-era planning is adapted, neglected or transformed beyond recognition, such as Lagos, Nigeria, which rapidly outgrew the original British plans. In other former colonies, the urban legacy of the imperial British has been actively rejected in an attempt to break free of the perceived psychological burden associated with colonial cities, as can be seen in the broad destruction of or unwillingness to preserve colonial architecture.

Following independence in 1957, Malaya[1] embarked on a campaign of nation-building aimed at distancing itself from its colonial past and forging a new identity that would unite a diverse population.[2] Post-independence nation-building strategies shaped many dimensions of life including education,[3] religion,[4] language policy,[5] ethnic relations,[6] mass media,[7] and toponymics.[8] Nation-building was also embodied in the transformation of the built environment in a way that would reflect national values, aspirations, and perceptions of the nation.[9] Nationalistic building in Malaysia spans a wide range of projects, including new civic buildings, housing, state religious structures, new towns and suburbs, transportation infrastructure, and state-funded architectural spectacles.[10]

This chapter focuses on Putrajaya, Malaysia's new administrative capital, conceived in the 1990s by then-Prime Minister Mahathir to house all government ministries and foreign embassies. Putrajaya is part of an urban mega-development called the Multimedia Super Corridor (MSC) that includes Cyberjaya, an aspiring high-tech city, a new airport, and an LRT that connects Kuala Lumpur with the new developments within the MSC. The successor to this 1990s-era project is "Iskandar Malaysia," a mega-project three times the size of Singapore. Just as Putrajaya and the MSC are the legacy of Mahathir, Iskandar Malaysia was conceptualized by Abdullah Badawi, Mahathir's successor and rival.

Putrajaya is a lavish, master-planned city designed for 350,000 residents and 500,000 commuters at an estimated cost of US$9 billion.[11] Government officials have justified the creation of a new capital by claiming it was necessary in order to relieve pressure from Kuala Lumpur, a city of 1.7 million.[12] Putrajaya differs from earlier planned suburbs and satellite cities in several key ways. First, it is intended as a national and international showpiece with iconic architecture, extensive park systems, top-notch community facilities, and opulent government buildings. Second, Mahathir considered it crucial for Putrajaya to be a completely Malaysian effort, from the planning and engineering to the architecture, design, and marketing. This effort at utilizing local talent stands in stark contrast to other lavish state projects such as the Petronas Towers, the world's tallest buildings from 1998 to 2004, designed by international "starchitect" César Pelli, and symbolizes a desire to sever ties with "foreign experts" who have long shaped urban change in the region. Finally, Putrajaya has an overt pan-Islamic identity that contrasts with the secularism or indigenous identities of past national projects.

According to state rhetoric, the creation of Putrajaya and its completely new aesthetic was a concerted effort to break ties with the colonial past by pivoting away from the Western world and strengthening ties with the Middle East. However, despite careful attempts to differentiate independent Malaysia from its colonial past, Putrajaya demonstrates that the ruling elite have in fact internalized many values and ideas of colonial Britain, many of which have been long abandoned in Britain itself. As Caroline Herbelin and Hazel Hahn also emphasize in their chapters on colonial and postcolonial Vietnam in this volume, simplistic binaries constructed during the colonial era such as colonizer-colonized, and, in architectural styles, European-Asian or modern-traditional, continue to be used widely, obfuscating the complexity of patterns of cross-cultural exchange. In the urban sphere, Malaysia has continued to emphasize the importance that the colonial British placed on the construction of new cities as well as the inherent power dynamics in mega-developments, while perpetuating various colonial-era values and assumptions about race and design.

In the first part of the chapter, I provide a brief introduction to some of the priorities of tropical British colonial planning, followed by a discussion of the state planning and architecture that emerged in Malaya immediately after Independence. The main part of the chapter examines tangible ways in which colonial values and ideologies have been reproduced in Putrajaya, focusing on three main themes: ethnic segregation, exoticized "Orientalist" styles, and the revival of century-old British planning approaches.

Tropical British Colonial Planning

> Among history's imperialists the British were certainly not the greatest builders, but they were the greatest creators of towns. Conquerors since Alexander the Great had seen the strategic and cultural advantages of establishing their own cities across the world, but as the first modern industrial power, Britain was the chief exporter of municipalities, and through the agency of her empire broadcast them everywhere. Half the cities of the American East owe their genesis to the British Empire, most of the cities in Canada, many of the cities of Africa, all the cities of Australasia, and the tremendous city-states of Singapore and Hong Kong. Sporting pastimes apart, and the English language, urbanism was the most lasting of the British imperial legacies.[13]

British colonial city planning was an integral part of the imperial project and the effects of their legacy on former colonies cannot be overestimated. In fact, many cities throughout the former British Empire owe their existence to the colonial British, who created new cities to facilitate resource extraction and the export of materials and products back to Britain. Above all, the built environment in the colonies aspired to be "ordered, sanitized and amenable to regulation" with the aim of "civilizing" indigenous populations.[14]

To the colonial British, the "tropics" presented particular risks and rewards not found at home. While the European colonizers were lured to Asia, Africa, and the Caribbean to exploit the lucrative resources, the tropics posed extreme risks for the British, who viewed them as inherently dangerous, unsanitary, and populated by unhealthy and uncivilized people who carried an array of communicable diseases. British scientists, scholars, and professionals advanced areas of study that would enable and facilitate the colonial endeavor of extracting wealth and subduing native populations while exploiting their labor. Great care was taken to develop ways to safeguard the white population from the perils of the tropics, which were seen to take a particularly hard toll on the "white" body.[15]

The scientific expertise of doctors and town planners became increasingly important in assisting colonial expansion into the tropics. The peak of the British Empire coincided with the growing professionalization of medicine and planning, and their evolving theories about health, race, and human habitats were highly influential in shaping colonial policy and urban landscapes. According to Home,[16] in the late colonial era doctors and planners had an "unprecedented authority in public life" and provided a scientific approach to managing rapidly growing colonial cities. City planning and medicine became increasingly intertwined in the colonies and sanitation, public health, and the colonial urban landscape became the purview of doctors and planners.

As argued by Brenda Yeoh and others, concern about disease in the colonies was intimately linked to power relations between the rulers and the ruled.[17] Colonial doctors sought to determine how diseases spread and often assumed they originated in and were spread by locals, particularly children.[18] Doctors recommended a variety of interventions in the built environment that reflected their beliefs in how the spread of diseases could be prevented. For example, the creation of vacant zones between European and locals' housing was based on beliefs about how malaria was spread and the maximum flight of mosquitoes.[19] The spacing of homes, ventilation, and maintaining particular densities were believed to minimize the transmission of such diseases as cholera, which was seen as inherently linked to indigenous people and justified the separation of races rather than the provision of sanitary amenities to natives.[20]

Planners in the colonies not only sought to prevent the spread of disease to whites, but also aimed to impose a sense of "civilization" and order on indigenous peoples as a sort of uninvited exchange for giving up land, resources, and autonomy. Stamford Raffles was a key figure in the

British colonial bureaucracy and planning history whose ideas have left a significant imprint on the urban fabric of Singapore and Malaysia. While not trained as a planner, Raffles is seen as the modern founder of modern Singapore who implemented a series of urban guidelines with the aim of creating order in a growing and increasingly chaotic city.[21] The most lasting legacy is the colonnaded "shophouse," a rowhouse design with commercial space on the bottom and several residential storeys above, fronted by a five-feet wide contiguous covered sidewalk created by the overhang of the upper storeys of the buildings. This form was mandated in Singapore then spread throughout the British colonies in Southeast Asia. This colonial form is currently being reproduced in Putrajaya, as will be examined later in the chapter.

In Great Britain, the field of planning was becoming increasingly formalized in the late nineteenth century until the Town Planning Institute was formed in the UK in 1914. Until then, architects and other colonial administrators such as Raffles were laying out cities in the colonies throughout the nineteenth century. According to Home[22] "the town planning idea was vigorously exported to the colonies" and representatives of the Garden City movement traveled throughout the colonies to work on projects in various parts of Asia and Africa. Urban strategies and architecture idioms circulated throughout the empire through broad policies and individuals working in multiple colonies.

A number of pivotal events in the mid-1800s eroded the British sense of invincibility and inevitability as a colonial power. The most important of these was the so-called "Indian Mutiny" of 1857–58, which badly shook the confidence of the British and changed the nature of their relations with the colonized, resulting in greater spatial segregation between the British and Indians. As the Empire's right to rule was being increasingly challenged, a number of British planners and officials believed that planning and city-building could save the Empire.[23] Patrick Geddes, a key figure in British planning in the colonies, believed that town planning could convince the colonized to abandon nationalist sentiments.[24] In the late years of the Empire, many new towns were created in an attempt to address the deteriorating conditions for natives in urban areas and shore up support for the British.

In the context of late colonial Malaya, Petaling Jaya was created as the first new town. Started in 1953, just five years before the Independence of Malaysia, Petaling Jaya was a squatter resettlement strategy that reflected British planning philosophies of the time, particularly Ebenezer Howard's "Garden City" concept.[25] The "Garden City" (or at least interpretations of it) was influential in colonial urban planning throughout the British Empire and post-independence Commonwealth nations,[26] long after it had fallen out of favor in Britain itself.

As Lee[27] points out, Petaling Jaya was one of many satellite cities, suburbs, and new towns constructed around the country that demonstrate Malaysia as having one of the longest modern planning histories in Asia. The prioritization of planning urban mega-developments continued after independence and into the present, as evidenced by the current new cities under construction, including Putrajaya, Cyberjaya and the Multimedia Super Corridor, and the Iskandar Malaysia mega-development in Johor state. The long history of British planning experiments in colonial Malaysia continues to have a significant impact on contemporary planning, as will be examined later in the chapter.

Strategies, Characteristics, and Common Goals of Colonial Planning in the Tropics

Like many ruling powers, the colonial British used the built environment to create grand spectacles that address practical concerns while conveying power and identity and demonstrating their strength, superiority, and invincibility.[28] Colonial British planning can be broadly characterized by a number of strategies that were employed throughout much of the tropical colonies. This section explores some of the characteristics of tropical colonial planning with specific reference to Malaysia: racial segregation, a disregard for local tradition, particular urban features that aided the goals of order, sanitation and regulation, symbolism meant to exude power and a sense of permanence, and particular planning trends such as zoning and the "Garden City."

Social Darwinist theories, hierarchical racial classifications based on supposedly inherent racial attributes and understandings of health and disease of the day, found expression in the colonial built environment through segregationist planning and land-use policies.[29] The racial designations themselves were colonial categories that constructed race in an artificial and simplistic way that justified the subjugation of "natives" by whites and helped colonial authorities govern.[30] A variety of justifications were offered for segregating based on race in the colonies.[31] In South Africa, colonial authorities claimed that segregation was simply based on class.[32] In Singapore, Raffles claimed that separating ethnic groups was based on "respectability" and commercial success. The colonizers sought to order the physical landscape while influencing the "moral and social habits of the people."[33] Approaches to public health also sought to segregate based on race, and the fear of "native" diseases spreading to the white population was sufficient for policies of urban segregation.[34]

One of the key physical forms found throughout cities in the colonies is the wide street. In contrast to indigenous urban areas, which tended to be dense with narrow streets, the British laid out streets that were typically 100–150 feet wide, with no acknowledgement of the scorching heat. Wide streets had both social and symbolic functions: "they removed congestion, allowed the free movement of air, imposed a sense of order, facilitated police control, and broke up densely populated areas into manageable units."[35] They were justified on public health grounds, but were also designed to "impose a controllable public space upon societies which had different traditions."[36] Wide streets, over-sized public spaces and other grand gestures required great tracts of land to be expropriated from residents, causing tension and resentment of those residents who were forced off their land.

In some cases, the British actively rejected local building customs in favor of imposing a sense of European order and civilization. In other cases, they simply did not bother to explore indigenous tradition:

> The ideas and ideologies of colonial expansion generally disregarded the cultural traditions of the colonized peoples. Colonial settlement planning drew on European Renaissance and baroque models. In India, for instance, positivist ideology interpreted the indigenous populace as having no significant political principles or forms of government, only religious customs and domestic concerns, so that Indian culture was effectively depoliticized.[37]

In Malaysia, the British did not just ignore indigenous building techniques and materials, they actively pursued policies that would discourage indigenous architecture in central areas, leaving "Malayness" visible in peripheral, rural areas.[38]

While the British did not draw upon indigenous culture for their cities or architecture, they did attempt to engage local elites with an interpretation of local religion through lavish state buildings that employed a fantasy "Islamic" style. The popularity of this style was due in part to the effort at cultivating cultural sensitivity, a topic also explored by Matt Schauer and Arnout van der Meer regarding British Malaya and colonial Java respectively in this volume. In an attempt to appear sensitive to the religion of indigenous Malays, colonial administrative building took on a royal "British Raj" guise. British architects who had worked in India created similarly opulent, "Orientalized" buildings in Malaya, featuring domes, ogee arches, minarets and other fanciful details to decorate train stations and government buildings. The symbolic use of wide streets, in addition to other symbolic buildings and planning approaches, projected an "illusion of permanence"[39] and served to normalize British values and ideology that were based on supposedly sound "scientific" principles.[40]

In the twentieth century, the creation of new towns was seen to be the solution to Britain's urban problems relating to nineteenth-century industrialization. By the early 1970s, over 30 new towns had been built in Britain, with many planners calling for over 100 to be built.[41] At the time, these new towns attracted international attention and were widely viewed as modern, progressive and as global templates for handling urban growth. As a result, the new-town concept was enthusiastically adopted by planners in the colonies to address issues of rural-urban migration, overcrowding, and pollution.

New town supporters espoused a series of views on the ideal urban life that have fallen out of favor. For example, they facilitated the rapid growth in car ownership by designing new towns to accommodate a high level of everyday car use.[42] Planners of new towns believed in the segregation of home and work and supported the strict zoning of activities, which they contrasted favorably to older towns, in which the resident "lives, works and plays in a tightly knit, high-density architectural complex."[43] New town supporters argued that historical mixed-use urban forms were the products of a society that no longer exists and were built in ways that are "no longer relevant to the needs of an expanding industrial society."[44] While contemporary planners seek to recreate the density and pedestrian-friendly scale of pre-modern cities and are designing "live, work, play" environments to discourage long commutes, post-war new towns were encouraging a particular car-based interpretation of modern life in line with Garden City ideals.

The British obsession with zoning in new towns had a major impact in the colonies. Special zones or districts exclusively for residential, commercial, industrial or agricultural purposes were what most colonial British city plans sought to create. In the case of late colonial planning in Malaya, British planners sought to separate the shophouses from the "obnoxious trades"[45] and increasingly aimed to keep residential areas apart from businesses. Ironically, it was the planners of Putrajaya who fulfilled colonial aspirations of strict zoning just as the concept of zoning was reaching its nadir in the west, as will be discussed later in the chapter.

Post-Independence Urbanism and Architecture in Malaysia

Following independence from Britain in 1957, leaders of the new nation pursued a variety of strategies by which to differentiate independent Malaya from its former colonizer. In terms of the built environment, post-independence leaders and the planners and architects they employed, championed "International Modernism," a then-popular global style that was secular, unembellished and therefore free of historical baggage, and exuded a sense of optimism.[46] Post-war International Modernism in Malaysia was free of religious and ethnocentric references and was viewed in the architectural community as an inclusive, aspirational style.

However, as postcolonial scholars have demonstrated, independence did not create a clean break with the colonial era as British ideas, values and planning approaches continued to be reproduced in the urban environment. In the context of India, Judith Kenny observes that "colonial planning policies continue to influence modern Indians through the persistence of both the built structure of urban areas and colonial models of landscape."[47] The values, the systems of meaning, and the power relations by which the dominant elite bestowed legitimacy on projects in the built environment are still perpetuated decades after independence.

Immediately following World War II, around 50 British architects and planners were working in colonial administrations.[48] By 1959, this number rose to 450 and overseas branches of the Town Planning Institute were established in Malaya and other former colonies.[49] British consultants continued to work in former colonies and had a tremendous impact on Malaysian new towns and the direction of Malaysian urbanization. Furthermore, students from former colonies flocked to newly-created planning programs at British universities to study town planning and returned home to implement British planning philosophies.[50] Whether it was British planners or Malaysians educated in Britain, British planning approaches remained firmly entrenched in the urban landscape. New towns and satellite cities continued to be planned and were given precedence over the upgrading of infrastructure in existing cities. Highways were expanded, housing shortages were addressed through clusters of concrete apartment blocks, and districts were zoned according to use.[51] Large, public space in the form of open plazas captured the spirit of modernism but neglected the tropical climate.

These principles were embodied in Shah Alam, the first post-independence master-planned city, started in 1963.[52] Building on the success of

Petaling Jaya in providing housing and a "modern" environment, Shah Alam is a sprawling modernist industrial town and provincial capital with just 2,231 people/km^2, roughly one third the population density of Kuala Lumpur. Car ownership is a necessity for residents of Shah Alam; in fact one of the main employers in the city is Proton, Malaysia's primary car manufacturer. Shah Alam is divided into 24 sections and bifurcated by a freeway with cloverleaf onramps in the city center. Both the modernist sectioning of the city and the prioritization of cars is perpetuated in subsequent developments, including Putrajaya.

During the 1970s and 1980s, many Asian cities sought to emulate the "architectural gigantism" of Manhattan's skyline as the pinnacle of modern corporate power and economic virility, an architectural phenomenon Anthony King refers to as the "Manhattan transfer."[53] In Kuala Lumpur, the architecture of this period is marked by a proliferation of corporate skyscrapers, which, on one hand, broadcast Malaysia's modernity and readiness to be a global player, while on the other hand, eroded Kuala Lumpur's unique identity for some of its residents.[54] In contrast and in response to the placelessness of Kuala Lumpur, a distinctive "fantasy Middle Eastern" idiom[55] was prioritized in Putrajaya to give it a distinct "local" identity.

Putrajaya is one of Mahathir's ostentatious and expensive attempts to re-brand the country, turning the focus away from the west while embracing the Middle East as a land populated by fellow Muslims, as potential investors and as business partners. This pivot away from the West and courting of the Middle East has had some tangible impacts; Saudi investment alone is set to double to over $2 billion, and Malaysia is now the global leader in Islamic banking, a large portion of which is linked to Arab investment.[56] Several recent investments overtly reflect Arab-Malay cooperation, including "Arab City," a shopping and resort mega-development with a pan-Arab theme, complete with Dubai-style buildings featuring faux wind towers, an Arab Souk, and a Moroccan *hammam*.[57]

Putrajaya can be understood as anti-Kuala Lumpur.[58] Where Kuala Lumpur was founded and planned by the British and economically controlled by the Chinese, Putrajaya was intended to be a "pure Malay" city that represented and gave precedence to Muslim culture;[59] it is a city built by and for Malays. Rather than contracting the work out to foreign architecture and planning firms, all planning and architectural design was carried out in-house by government employees.[60] Mahathir and other politicians of the 1980s viewed Kuala Lumpur as tainted by a history that socially, economically, and spatially disadvantaged the Malay population. Putrajaya then was conceived as a symbol to right past wrongs and provide Malays with a city that they could proudly call their own.

Reproducing Colonial-Era Values and Ideology in Putrajaya

In many ways, Putrajaya feels like an elite new district of any Southeast Asian city. Pastel concrete apartment towers are clustered into estates filled with carefully tended tropical foliage. Traffic flows smoothly on wide highways and boulevards uncluttered by bicycles, rickshaws or other non-"modern" vehicles. Indonesian domestic workers wash cars and mind children, while Bangladeshi gardeners tend the tree-lined streets and flower beds lining sidewalks. Families eat in open-air food courts, drive to the shopping mall or equestrian facilities, and children take swimming lessons at brand new community centers. At Putrajaya's heart is a grand 4.2 kilometer-long formal axis designed as if for parades and military display. It has a sleepy, suburban feel with none of the chaos, noise, bustle, and diversity of Kuala Lumpur.

Putrajaya is clearly intended to be read against the colonial/Chinese city of Kuala Lumpur in a way that racializes the urban landscape. Kuala Lumpur has large colonial and Chinese districts set within an unplanned jumble of dirty and narrow streets and thus is an example of a city with a complex makeup that evolved gradually across colonial and postcolonial periods. It is comparable to Saigon and Hanoi, which were also expanded starting in the mid-1800s by another colonial power (the French) and significantly influenced by ethnic Chinese, covered in Hahn's and Herbelin's chapters. In comparison, Putrajaya is clean, spacious, orderly, and above all, meant to project a "pure" Muslim identity. The overall effect is an intended contrast between an ordered new Malay city and the relatively chaotic colonial/Chinese city. At the same time, Putrajaya echoes earlier colonial-era urban practices of constructing new, orderly European districts apart from and in contrast to older, non-European districts (for example, New Delhi vs. Old Delhi and new European districts inside Saigon and Hanoi).

Despite the originality of Putrajaya's fantasy Islamic idiom,[61] its exclusive use of Malaysian professionals, and its attempt to break with the past, it can be understood as an extension of the values and ideology vested in earlier "new towns." Beneath the sleepiness and immaculate landscaping of Putrajaya, there is an underlying cultural politics that reproduce modernist-era notions of town planning as heroic, something to be gifted by the ruling elite to the masses. Like the new towns that came before it, Putrajaya is a state experiment designed to showcase ideology, rationalized by colonial-era claims about new cities being required to address overcrowding and other urban problems.[62]

Maintaining Spatial Divisions between Ethnic Groups

During the colonial era, the formation of cities was a crucial instrument of racial dominance. Notions about race and strategies to spatially manage multi-ethnic populations have been internalized in former colonies, including Malaysia. Much like the British belief in a racial hierarchy, leaders in contemporary Malaysia[63] believe there are inherent qualities among "races" that make them more or less capable at particular pursuits.[64] According to former Prime Minister Mahathir, Malays are a weaker, more passive race than Chinese and Indians and therefore required special opportunities and protections that would nurture a class of Malay capitalists and leaders.[65] Such characterization of Malays is a direct extension of the colonial construction of the Malays as an ethnic category, and the perceived need to protect them as a weaker group, as discussed in Schauer's chapter in this volume. It is not the kind of in-depth understanding of pre-Islamic Malay history and culture that R.J. Wilkinson, as discussed by Schauer in this volume, was advocating that is emphasized by the current Malaysian government, but rather an Islam-centered reinterpretation of the past—which Wilkinson sought to discourage—that integrates aspects of British colonial built legacy.

Malaysia continues to be challenged by a desire to overcome racial divisions on one hand, and the deep entrenchment and internalization of colonial-era racial assumptions on the other. As a multi-cultural, multi-religious and multi-ethnic country,[66] the post-independence Malaysian state continues to debate about how to handle its diverse population. The state has generally had an uneasy relationship with the non-Malay minorities of the country. While government tourism material advertises a harmonious and diverse society, in reality local Muslim Malays, or *Bumiputra*, enjoy a privileged position[67] and benefit from official policies that seek to correct imbalances stemming from the colonial era, which favored ethnic Chinese.

Through its urban policy and design, Putrajaya is a manifestation of *Bumiputra* affirmative action policies that perpetuate the ethnic divisions of colonial cities. As I have argued elsewhere,[68] in contrast to the present-day multi-ethnic and multi-religious Kuala Lumpur, Putrajaya is designed as an expression of "pure" Malay and Muslim identity. Much like government and other secular buildings in Putrajaya that are topped with Islamic-looking domes, bridges, and parks also have an "Islamic" flavor through paving, design details, and landscaping. Facilities for Muslims to meet their religious obligations, including large mosques, neighborhood mosques and *suraus*, sidewalk *mushollas*, arrows indicating the direction of Mecca, Muslim washing facilities, and so on are found throughout the city. In contrast, no religious buildings for Hindus, Christians, or Buddhists have been built in Putrajaya.[69]

Putrajaya is a city created primarily for civil servants, who by no accident are overwhelmingly Malay. According to government statistics, of the 8,372 employees in the civil service, only 10 are ethnically classified as Chinese and 116 as Indians.[70] This means that Indians and Chinese make up 1.39 per cent and 0.12 per cent of the state civil service, respectively. In the Prime Minister's Department, there are about 31,297 Malays to 797 Chinese, which is about 2 per cent.[71] In other ministries, less than 1 per cent of employees are Chinese,[72] a reflection of decades of *Bumiputra* policies that have prevented non-Malays from participating in public life. The point of these statistics is not to explore the reasons for this systematic occupational bias in Malaysia, but to demonstrate the lack of diversity in Putrajaya despite government rhetoric and slogans[73] about national multi-culturalism and to illustrate the ongoing spatial separation of colonial racial categories.

In response to criticism that Putrajaya favors Malays/Muslims and excludes all others, planners in Putrajaya have suggested creating ethnic neighborhoods, namely a Chinatown and a Little India.[74] Districts differentiated by religion or ethnicity resurrect policies of spatial segregation based on racial identities found throughout colonial Asia and Africa,[75] and reveal a way of thinking about race and urban space that directly recalls colonial-era ideology.

There are three cemeteries found in and around Putrajaya designed to cater to its residents. They are spatially distinct and reify the racial politics and categories of the British: one is for Malays/Muslims, one for Indians/Hindus and another for Chinese (Buddhists/Confucians, not Christians). Putrajaya's Muslim cemetery is in a prominent location and, while mostly still vacant, is beautifully landscaped and tended carefully. There is some confusion about equivalent facilities for Hindus and Buddhists. A joint crematorium for Hindus and Buddhists has been constructed in a remote location along the southern boundary of Putrajaya but it is almost completely unutilized and most residents of Putrajaya are unaware of its existence. Older Chinese and Indian (Hindu) cemeteries are located just outside of Putrajaya in the nearby village of Dengkil. According to Muslim residents with whom I spoke, the Chinese and Indian cemeteries are located within the boundaries of Putrajaya and are viewed as equivalents to the Muslim cemetery (Fieldwork interview, June 2017). However, the Chinese and Indians I interviewed claimed that the cemeteries are in fact outside the official boundary of Putrajaya, they pre-date Putrajaya's existence, and are not national cemeteries. In contrast to the meticulous upkeep of Putrajaya and the Muslim cemetery, the Chinese and Indian cemeteries have poor signage, are unkempt, and have ad hoc unpaved parking next to the road, while the tall grass and weeds indicate that they are outside the domain of the Putrajaya gardeners.

Beyond urban planning policies, land allocation and maintenance, and bias in the civil service, there are more subtle but equally effective ways in which to racially segregate and privilege one group over another. As Njoh[76] points out in the colonial African context, there were not necessarily official policies of spatial segregation. The creation of subtly discriminatory building codes, separate and elite housing for whites, and the provision of facilities for those who had reached a particular socio-economic status meant that colonial powers effectively created obstacles to prevent the colonized from participating equally or living outside their racial group. For example, British colonial philosophies were instituted to shape the morals and habits of the population, including the imposition of curfews on the indigenous people and the regulation of drumming and dancing.[77] In order for the colonized to engage in drumming and dancing, an important element of ceremonies and special occasions, they needed to seek permission from the government and pay a fee, which only permitted them to perform on one evening per week. Controlling the times and locations of local dances in colonial African cities was a subtle but effective way of engineering behavior and supporting racial segregation. Municipal by-laws were also developed in many colonies to regulate building types, materials, and morphology as well as to force the colonized to conform to particular behaviors and routines.

Similarly, Putrajaya has a number of rules that restrict behavior to "Muslim" practices that limit cultural customs for non-Muslims. Within the boundaries of Putrajaya, but not in Malaysia in general, pork, alcohol, and dogs are banned. While they are considered forbidden or *haram* in Islam, they are not taboo for Malaysia's other main religious groups. Since religion is nearly interchangeable with race in Malaysia, imposing such bans in Putrajaya is a technique of racial bias that discourages non-Muslims from moving to the city and recalls the more subtle strategies used by the colonial British to privilege whites.

Exoticized "Orientalist" Styles

As mentioned, architects and politicians in the years following independence were drawn to the clean lines of International Modernism. This was a departure from the elaborate and Orientalized British Raj style and the other ornate styles the British used in colonial buildings, which were either romanticized, exotic versions of "Eastern" architecture or versions of architectural fashions found in Europe. Since the early 1990s, the Malaysian government has supported a national style that appears to resurrect the architectural aesthetic of the British Raj. Domes, arches, and minarets imported from Moghul India and other "exotic" corners of the (non-Southeast Asian) Muslim world have been replicated in Putrajaya. While exotic fantasy "Orientalized" styles are promoted in an effort to strategically appear more Muslim, local styles, materials, and craftsmanship are neglected.

One of the most prominent examples of this turn to an imagined Middle Eastern idiom and the rejection of local styles can be found in Putrajaya's Putra Mosque (Figure 7.1). Sitting on a piece of land that juts out into the artificial lake around which the city is built, Putra Mosque is the most visible and iconic landmark in the city. Rather than drawing inspiration from the tiered pagoda-like designs of mosques in the Malay world,[78] the Putra Mosque is an amalgamation of imported styles and is a prime example of the "High Islamic" fusion architecture[79] that the Malaysian state has adopted for national projects: the minaret is a replica of that in Baghdad's Sheikh Oman Mosque, one decorative wall is similar to Casablanca's King Hassan Mosque,[80] and other elements are taken from Arabian, Egyptian, Persian, and Turkish sources. Instead of providing space for a Malay *pasar* (market), designers have created what they call a "Souq" under the mosque, which is more accurately described as a Middle Eastern-themed mall and food court. Despite the many rich design traditions, elaborate wood carvings, and local building techniques that have evolved for over half a millennium in mosques in the region,[81] almost none of this heritage has been integrated into Putrajaya.[82] Instead, it is fantastical domes, arches, and minarets that dominate Putrajaya's skyline and geometric Islamic motifs that embellish government buildings, shopping centers, bridges, sidewalks, and parks.

Figure 7.1: The Putra Mosque in Putrajaya demonstrates an imagined Middle Eastern idiom and the rejection of vernacular Malay styles. Photograph by Sarah Moser.

The aesthetic parallel between the British Raj and the Malaysian ruling elite in Putrajaya is unmistakable. Neither styles draw inspiration from any indigenous architectural forms, materials, or techniques; both the British designers of government buildings of the Raj and the designers of Putrajaya look beyond Malaysia's rich variety of indigenous material cultures to the "great" civilizations of Islam, thereby positioning Malaysian Islam as inferior.[83] The British insensitivity to or disrespect for local Malay culture and their creation of grand "Islamic" buildings for the Muslims of Malaya is the result of colonial administrators naively seeking to pander to the indigenous Muslim elite within the context of a massive, rapidly expanding empire. Furthermore, the colonial architects sent to the Malayan colony to build infrastructure had been freshly relocated from India where the British Raj style dominated.

While the colonial case for importing Middle Eastern and Mughal architecture into Malaysia is understandable, the Malaysian government's rationale for selecting an exotic, fantasy Middle Eastern style for Putrajaya is more curious. The British Raj style had not been in use for a century and had in fact been cleansed from the Independence-era architectural palette, then it suddenly re-emerged in the 1990s under Prime Minister Mahathir. The motivations behind using a fantasy "Oriental" style may have been different for the British and for Mahathir, yet the result is the same. The colonial assumption that "true" Islam is located not in Malaysia but in the "great" Islamic civilizations is clearly demonstrated in Putrajaya's imported eclectic architecture.

The Perpetuation of Colonial-Era Planning Strategies

The power invested in late colonial planners and in the profession as a whole in imperial-era Britain left a lasting legacy in Malaysia. While planning has become a very different discipline in the "West" in recent decades and now generally prioritizes comparatively incremental change, community consultation, and less costly interventions, Malaysian planning has maintained the grandiose gestures and top-down approaches of late colonialism. This section examines some of the early twentieth-century British planning approaches embedded in Putrajaya's master plan.

The Garden City, Zoning, and the New Town

Putrajaya is divided into 20 *presints* (precincts) with separate zones for various activities. For example, there are precincts dedicated to entertainment, commerce, government, housing, embassies, and so on. This strict spatial division of uses draws on planning philosophies in vogue in the late colonial era among professional planners around the western world.

The distinctive colonial-era "shophouse" form legislated by Raffles is now considered a recognizably Malaysian part of the urban landscape.[84] While Shah Alam rejected the shophouse form in favor of lower density commercial urban fabric, and more recent developments have constructed malls as the main commercial buildings, Putrajaya has revived the colonial-era form in particular neighborhoods, complete with the five-foot covered walkway initially legislated by Raffles (Fig. 7.2).

Putrajaya has many oversized public areas despite the year-round temperatures of 32°C / 90°F. The wide ceremonial axis and the gigantic roundabout at the foot of the prime minister's office are coercive strategies intended to impress and remind the populace of the ruling elite's power (Fig. 7.3). Colonial British designed wide streets throughout their tropical colonies with the aim of providing ventilation, preventing the spread of disease and to aid in surveillance, and this is echoed throughout Putrajaya.

Figure 7.2: Planners have revived the colonial-era form of the shophouse and the five-foot covered walkway in particular neighborhoods in Putrajaya. Photograph by Sarah Moser.

Putrajaya fits into a long trajectory of new towns, a major British strategy in the late colonial period. Rather than focus resources on major infrastructure improvements, affordable housing, and other upgrades to Kuala Lumpur, satellite cities were built that started from scratch. After achieving independence, privileged British enclaves often survived and were even enlarged. In India, the local rajas internalized the exclusivity of British Garden Cities, which were maintained or even expanded for the benefit of local elites.[85] Colonial British versions of garden cities sought to relocate the population—or at least upper classes of the population—to new satellite garden suburbs as a way to escape the pollution and crowding of the main cities. While the Garden City concept fell out of favor with British planners decades ago, it has captured the imagination of many former colonies including Malaysia, with Putrajaya's motto being an "Intelligent Garden City." Petaling Jaya, the first new town in Malaya, was designed in accordance with British town planning and Garden City principles and versions of the concept have been implemented in other master-planned

Figure 7.3: A 4.2 kilometer-wide ceremonial axis forms the spine of Putrajaya which is intended to impress and remind the populace of the ruling elite's power. Photograph by Sarah Moser.

Malaysian cities including Shah Alam, Bangi, and more recently Putrajaya, Cyberjaya, and Nusajaya.[86] The Garden City concept always includes vast Botanical Gardens, which are a prominent feature of several new Southeast Asian cities.

Botanic Gardens

The large amount of land and resources allocated to the *Taman Botani* (Botanic Gardens) in Putrajaya indicate the prioritization of recreating a truly colonial concept.[87] Botanic gardens are a colonial invention that played a critical role in empire-building through "economic botany," the use of science to develop strains of plants that could become viable cash crops. Combining the romantic aesthetics of the landscape movement with leading-edge botany,[88] botanic gardens may seem benign and apolitical, yet they take root in Britain's imperialist expansion into the tropics when botany was a crucial and highly profitable science.[89] Botanic gardens were established throughout the empire in the 1880s and onwards in Calcutta, Ceylon, Java, Singapore, British West Indies, Kampala, Burma, Malaya, and others, while the main clearing house was London's Kew Gardens. Botanic gardens developed the technical knowledge to improve species, methods of cultivation and harvesting, and transmit knowledge to colonial planters. They were highly profitable and strategically important for colonial expansion and for the British Empire to compete with other colonial powers.[90]

Shifting economic forces away from economic botany towards manufacturing meant that botanic gardens no longer served as centers of scientific discovery for strategic economic purposes. Despite the lack of economic function, Putrajaya's planners decided to dedicate 92 hectares of land to what they purposefully called a "botanic garden," rather than a "city park" or "eco-park." The many parks built through Putrajaya range from urban pocket parks to city parks with recreational programming to vast wetlands that serve ecological functions. The variety of parks makes the prioritization of a *Taman Botani* particularly fascinating and reveals a clear connection to the colonial past.

While Putrajaya's *Taman Botani* claims to facilitate scientific research, it is unclear what is being studied by who and which educational institutions are using it. The gardens reproduce the British colonial botanic garden in a number of ways. Like the colonial botanic gardens, Putrajaya's *Taman Botani* are international and have only a minimal local species agenda. The gardens are a menagerie of global plants and have come to be a vehicle for showcasing the wealth, sophisticated tastes, power, and global reach of the state (Fig. 7.4).

The ruling elite in Malaysia have internalized the prestige attached to colonial botanic gardens. The massive tracts of land required signaled the unfettered power the British had to allocate land and determine its use. In colonial botanical gardens, the fence was an important feature designed to protect valuable property, both material and intellectual.[91] In Putrajaya, the fences have been reproduced, creating a distinctly elite feel, unlike a city park that would have multiple access points. The *Taman Botani* is not really a public park, as there is tightly controlled access through a single gate with an entrance fee. The British also believed that, like the "modern" cities they were creating in the colonies, botanic gardens promoted "'the gradual civilization' of the indigenous population."[92] The indigenous were meant to emulate British behavior and gain an appreciation for leisure gardens while admiring the capabilities of the British, who were able to construct such a grand place. Similar behavioral engineering occurs in Putrajaya's *Taman Botani*, where locals are informed through pervasive signage of the many rules of behavior within the gardens. Certain activities are acceptable (badminton, cycling, taking photos, reading informational signs about plants), while others are

Figure 7.4: Putrajaya's *Taman Botani*. Photograph by Adrian Cook.

not (listening to music, skateboarding, picnicking). *Taman Botani* retains the symbolism, exclusivity, behavioral engineering, and pedagogical ambitions of its colonial precedents without the scientific mission that drove colonial botanic gardens.

The Empire Lives On

In this chapter, I do not wish to suggest that there have not been innovations in Malaysian planning or that Putrajaya is simply an imitation of a colonial city. Nor do I wish to suggest that the colonial British are the only or even primary source of influence in contemporary Malaysian city-building. Malaysia's multiplicity of cultural, economic, political, and scholarly interactions with foreign governments, think tanks, and universities, all influence the built environment in a variety of complex ways.[93] While Putrajaya is certainly original in many ways and draws on a variety of both European and Asian precedents, the goal of this chapter is to explore the ways in which the values, assumptions, and planning styles of the colonial era have been reproduced in a contemporary Malaysian new city.

While the Malaysian state has actively sought to distance itself from its colonial past, I argue that the design of Putrajaya has in many ways inadvertently reproduced colonial values and priorities in a way that earlier post-independence efforts did not. The city-centric development agenda, ethnicized landscapes, the monumentality, the exotic "Oriental" idiom, the New Towns approach to urban development, and botanic gardens all serve to recall an imperial power based on distinct social hierarchies rather than reflect a multi-cultural, multi-lingual democracy.

Putrajaya affirms colonial aesthetics and perpetuates various policies aimed at separating the population based on categories of difference. The city confirms Malays as the sole legitimate rulers of Malaysia while discouraging non-Malays from living there. While the Malay ruling elite attempts to "intensify its own sense of itself by dramatizing distance and difference,"[94] I have demonstrated that British values, policies, and assumptions pervade Putrajaya's urban planning and many spaces in Putrajaya are designed not for the benefit of the public but for the purposes of projecting and sustaining power.

Notes

1. Later renamed Malaysia after Singapore left the union (or was expelled, according to the Singaporean perspective) and formed its own country in 1965.
2. The British imported thousands of Chinese and Indian workers to satisfy the demand for labor in rubber and tea plantations and other colonial enterprises. Malaysia's current population demographics reflect colonial labor demands: 61 per cent of the population is Malay, 24 per cent is Chinese, 7 per cent is Indian, and the remaining is 8 per cent.
3. Graham K. Brown, "Making Ethnic Citizens: The Politics and Practice of Education in Malaysia," *International Journal of Educational Development* 27, no. 3 (2007): 318–30; Sharom Ahmat, "Nation Building and the University in Developing Countries: The Case of Malaysia," *Higher Education* 9, no. 6 (1980): 721–41; J.K.P. Watson, "Cultural Pluralism Nationbuilding and Educational Policies in Peninsular Malaysia," *Multilingual and Multicultural Development* 1, no. 2 (1980): 155–74.
4. Kikue Hamayotsu, "Islam and Nation Building in Southeast Asia: Malaysia and Indonesia in Comparative Perspective," *Pacific Affairs* 75, no. 3 (2002): 353–75; Judith Nagata, "Ethnonationalism versus Religious Transnationalism: Nation-Building and Islam in Malaysia," *The Muslim World* 87, no. 2 (1997): 129–50.

5. Sarah Kaur Gill, "Language Policy in Malaysia: Reversing Direction," *Language Policy* 4, no. 3 (2005); Hock Guan Lee and Leo Suryadinata, *Language, Nation and Development in Southeast Asia* (Singapore: Institute of Southeast Asian Studies, 2007); Maya Khemlani and Subra Govindasamy, "Language Education and 'Nation Building' in Multilingual Malaysia," in *World Yearbook of Education 2003: Language Education*, ed. Jill Bourne and Euan Reid (London: Taylor & Francis, 2005); Geneive Abdo, *Mecca and Main Street: Muslim Life in America After 9/11* (New York: Oxford University Press, 2006).
6. Tan Chee-Beng, "Nation-Building and Being Chinese in a Southeast Asian State: Malaysia," in *Changing Identities of the Southeast Asian Chinese Since World War II*, ed. Jennifer Cushman and Wang Gungwu (Hong Kong: Hong Kong University Press, 1990), 139–64.
7. John Postill, *Media and Nation Building: How the Iban Became Malaysian* (Oxford/New York: Berghahn Books, 2008).
8. Lily Kong and Brenda Yeoh, *The Politics of Landscapes in Singapore: Constructions of "Nation"* (Syracuse, NY: Syracuse University Press, 2003); on education, see Brown, "Making Ethnic Citizens;" Ahmat, "Nation Building and the University."
9. Yat-Ming Loo, "'No Chinatown, Please!': Contesting Race, Identity and Postcolonial Memory in Kuala Lumpur," *The Journal of Architecture* 17, no. 6 (2012): 847–70.
10. Tim Bunnell, *Malaysia, Modernity, and the Multimedia Super Corridor: A Critical Geography of Intelligent Landscapes* (London: Routledge, 2004); J. Lepawsky, "Stories of Space and Subjectivity in Planning the Multimedia Super Corridor," *Geoforum* 36 (2005): 705–19; Beng-Lan Goh and David Liauw, "Post-Colonial Projects of a National Culture," *City: Analysis of Urban Trends, Culture, Theory, Policy, Action* 13 (2009): 71–9; Sarah Moser, "Globalization and the Construction of Identity in Two New Southeast Asian Capitals: Putrajaya and Dompak," in *Rethinking Global Urbanism: Comparative Insights from Secondary Cities*, ed. Xiangming Chen and Kanna (London/New York: Routledge, 2012).
11. Sarah Moser, *New Cities: Opportunities, Visions and Challenges – Cityquest KAEC Forum 2013: Summary and Analysis Report* (Paris: New Cities Foundation, 2014), bit.ly/Cityquest2013.
12. While government officials repeatedly state that Kuala Lumpur was overcrowded and chaotic, density numbers reveal Kuala Lumpur to have a slightly lower density than San Francisco (6,696/km^2 and 6,898/km^2, respectively) and is far less dense than comparable Southeast Asian capitals such as Manila (10,550/km^2), Singapore (8,350/km^2), and Jakarta (10,500/km^2). City Mayor Statistics <http://www.citymayors.com/statistics/largest-cities-density-125.html>
13. J. Morris and S. Winchester, *Stones of Empire: The Buildings of the Raj* (Oxford: Oxford University Press, 1983), 196, cited in R.K. Home, *Of Planting and*

Planning: The Making of British Colonial Cities (London and New York: Routledge, 2013), 1.
14. Home, *Of Planting and Planning*, 57.
15. David N. Livingstone, "Tropical Climate and Moral Hygiene: The Anatomy of a Victorian Debate," *The British Journal for the History of Science* 32, no. 1 (1999): 93–110.
16. Home, *Of Planting and Planning*, 46.
17. Brenda S.A. Yeoh, *Contesting Space in Colonial Singapore: Power Relations and the Urban Built Environment* (Kuala Lumpur: Oxford University Press, 1996); Francis G. Hutchins, *The Illusion of Permanence: British Imperialism* (Princeton: Princeton University Press, 1967); "Introduction: Disease, Medicine and Empire," in *Imperial Medicine and Indigenous Societies*, ed. David Arnold (Manchester: Manchester University Press, 1988); Nicholas Thomas, "Sanitation and Seeing: The Creation of State Power in Early Colonial Fiji," *Comparative Studies in Society and History* 32, no. 1 (1990): 149–70; Maynard W. Swanson, "The Sanitation Syndrome: Bubonic Plague and Urban Native Policy in the Cape Colony, 1900–1909," *Journal of African History* 18 (1977): 387–410; Daniel R. Headrick, *The Tools of Empire: Technology and European Imperialism in the Nineteenth Century* (Oxford: Oxford University Press, 1981).
18. Home, *Of Planting and Planning*.
19. Ibid.
20. Vijay Prashad, "Native Dirt/Imperial Ordure: The Cholera of 1832 and the Morbid Resolutions of Modernity," *Journal of Historical Sociology* 7, no. 3 (1994): 243–60.
21. Home, *Of Planting and Planning*.
22. Ibid., 50.
23. Home, *Of Planting and Planning*.
24. Ibid.
25. Ebenezer Howard, *Garden Cities of To-Morrow* (London: Faber and Faber, 1902).
26. Lee Boon Thong, "Petaling Jaya: The Early Development and Growth of Malaysia's First New Town," *Journal of the Malaysian Branch of the Royal Asiatic Society* 79, no. 2 (2006).
27. Ibid.
28. Lawrence J. Vale, *Architecture, Power, and National Identity* (New York: Routledge, 2008).
29. Syed Alatas, *The Myth of the Lazy Native: A Study of the Image of the Malays, Filipinos and Javanese from the 16th to the 20th Century and Its Function in the Ideology of Colonial Capitalism* (London: Frank Cass, 1977); Yeoh, *Contesting Space in Colonial Singapore*; William S.W. Lim, *Architecture Art Identity in Singapore: Is There Life After Tabula Rasa?* (Singapore: Asian Urban Lab, 2004).

30. Syed Alatas, *The Myth of the Lazy Native.*
31. Carl H. Nightingale, *Segregation: a Global History of Divided Cities* (Chicago: The University of Chicago Press, 2012).
32. Home, *Of Planting and Planning.*
33. Ibid., 127.
34. Ibid., 47.
35. Ibid., 59.
36. Ibid.
37. Karuna Mantena, *Alibis of Empire: Henry Maine and the Ends of Liberal Imperialism* (Princeton: Princeton University Press, 2010), cited in Home, *Of Planting and Planning*, 53.
38. R.K. Home, "Town Planning and Garden Cities in the British Colonial Empire 1910–1940," *Planning Perspectives* 5, no. 1 (1990): 23–37.
39. Home, *Of Planting and Planning*, 78.
40. Vale, *Architecture, Power, and National Identity.*
41. Hazel Evans, *New Towns: The British Experience* (New York: Halsted Press, 1972).
42. Ibid.
43. Evans, *New Towns*, 94.
44. Ibid.
45. Michael Roger Bristow, "Early Town Planning in British South East Asia: 1910–1939," *Planning Perspectives* 15, no. 2 (2000): 142.
46. Beng-Lan Goh and David Liauw, "Post-Colonial Projects of a National Culture;" T.N. Lim and L. Tay, *80 Years of Architecture in Malaysia* (Kuala Lumpur: Pertubuhan Akitek Malaysia, 2000).
47. Judith T Kenny, "Climate, Race, and Imperial Authority: The Symbolic Landscape of the Britih Hill Station in India," *Annals of the Association of American Geographers* 85, no. 4 (1995): 695.
48. Anthony D. King, *Urbanism, Colonialism, and the World Economy: Cultural and Spatial Foundations of the World Urban System* (London: Routledge, 1990).
49. Gordon E. Cherry, *The Evolution of British Town Planning* (Leighton Buzzard: Leighton Hill, 1974).
50. Ibid.
51. B.T. Lee, "New Towns in Malaysia: Development and Planning Policies," in *New Towns in East and South-East Asia*, ed. David R. Phillips and Anthony G.O. Yeh (Oxford: Oxford University Press, 1987).
52. Hafazah Abdul Karim, "The Satisfaction of Residents on Community Facilities in Shah Alam, Malaysia," *Asian Social Science* 4, no. 11 (2008): 131–7.
53. A.D. King, "Worlds in the City: Manhattan Transfer and the Ascendance of Spectacular Space," *Planning Perspectives* 11 (1996): 97–114.
54. Tim Bunnell, "Views from above and below: The Petronas Twin Towers and / in Contesting Visions of Development in Contemporary Malaysia," *Singapore Journal of Tropical Geography* 20 (1999): 1–23.

55. Sarah Moser, "Circulating Visions of 'High Islam': The Adoption of Fantasy Middle Eastern Architecture in Constructing Malaysian National Identity," *Urban Studies* 49, no. 13 (2012): 2913–35.
56. Hamim S. Ahmad Mokhtar, Naziruddin Abdullah, and Syed M. Al-Habshi, "Efficiency of Islamic Banking in Malaysia: A Stochastic Frontier Approach," *Journal of Economic Cooperation* 27, no. 2 (2006): 37–70.
57. Arab City, Melaka: http://www.myarabcity.com [accessed 5 June 2017].
58. Ross King, *Kuala Lumpur and Putrajaya: Negotiating Urban Space in Malaysia* (Copenhagen: NIAS Press, 2008).
59. Ross King, "Re-Writing the City: Putrajaya as Representation," *Journal of Urban Design* 12 (2007): 117–38; King, *Kuala Lumpur and Putrajaya.*
60. Sarah Moser, "Putrajaya: Malaysia's New Federal Administrative Capital," *Cities: The International Journal of Urban Policy and Planning* 27 (2010): 285–97.
61. Sarah Moser, "Circulating visions of 'High Islam': The Adoption of Fantasy Middle Eastern Architecture in Constructing Malaysian National Identity," *Urban Studies* 49 (2012): 2783–2805; Sarah Moser, "Malay(sian) National Identity in Contemporary Urban Mega-Projects," in *Urban Space, Place, and National Identity*, ed. Joshua Hagen and Alexander Diener (Lanham, MD: Rowman & Littlefield, 2018).
62. Standish Meacham, *Regaining Paradise: Englishness and the Early Garden City Movement* (New Haven/London: Yale University Press, 1999).
63. Also in Singapore, where the former Prime Minister, Lee Kuan Yew, has made a number of statements about his belief in eugenics. See Michael D. Barr, "Lee Kuan Yew and the 'Asian Values' Debate," *Asian Studies Review* 24, no. 3 (2000): 309–34; Michael D. Barr, "Lee Kuan Yew: Race, Culture and Genes," *Journal of Contemporary Asia* 29, no. 2 (1999): 145–66; C.K. Chan, "Eugenics on the Rise: A Report from Singapore," *International Journal of Health Services* 15, no. 4 (1985): 707–12.
64. Alison Bashford and Philippa Levine, *The Oxford Handbook of the History of Eugenics* (New York: Oxford University Press, 2010).
65. Mahathir Mohamad, *The Malay Dilemma* (Canberra: Asia Pacific Press, 1970).
66. Muslim Malays constitute 61 per cent of the population, Chinese 24 per cent, Indians 7 per cent and others 8 per cent. Religion mainly follows ethnic lines in Malaysia: Malays are Muslims, Indians are generally Hindus, and Chinese are generally a mix of Buddhist, Taoist, and Confucian.
67. Sharon Siddique and Leo Suryadinata, "Bumiputra and Pribumi: Economic Nationalism (indiginism) in Malaysia and Indonesia," *Pacific Affairs* 54 (1982): 662–87.
68. Moser, "Circulating Visions of 'High Islam': The Adoption of Fantasy Middle Eastern Architecture;" Moser, "Putrajaya: Malaysia's New Federal Administrative Capital;" Moser, "Globalization and the Construction of Identity."

69. Moser, "Putrajaya: Malaysia's New Federal Administrative Capital."
70. Nelson Benjamin, "Rep Says State Civil Service Has Only 10 Chinese and 116 Indians," *The Star Online*, 30 March 2010, http://www.thestar.com.my/story.aspx?file=%2f2010%2f3%2f30%2fnation%2f5960406&sec=nation.
71. Joseph Tawie, "Shocking Racial 'imbalance' in Civil Service," *Free Malaysia Today*, 20 Aug. 2011, http://www.freemalaysiatoday.com/category/nation/2011/08/20/shocking-racial-imbalance-in-civil-service/.
72. Criticism has been voiced about the low number of Chinese Malaysians in government positions since the 1930s. See C.M. Turnbull, "British Planning for Post-War Malaya," *Journal of Southeast Asian Studies* 5, no. 2 (1974): 239–54.
73. In recognition of recent brewing racial and religious tensions, the current government created the slogan "1Malaysia," standing for a belief in national unity—irrespective of race or religion. The 1Malaysia website is used as the official website of the Prime Minister (http://www.1malaysia.com.my/en).
74. Moser, "Circulating Visions of 'High Islam': The Adoption of Fantasy Middle Eastern Architecture."
75. Robert J. Ross and Gerard T. Telkamp, *Colonial Cities – Essays on Urbanism in a Colonial Context* (Dordrecht: Martinus Nijhoff, 1985).
76. Ambe J. Njoh, "The Segregated City in British and French Colonial Africa," *Race and Class* 49, no. 4 (2008): 87–95.
77. Ibid.
78. Imran bin Tajudeen, "Adaptation and Accentuation: Type Transformation in Vernacular Nusantarian Mosque Design and Their Contemporary Signification in Melaka, Minangkabau and Singapore," in *Pace or Speed? 4th International Seminar on Vernacular Settlement* (Ahmedabad, 2008), 143–62.
79. Moser, "Circulating Visions of 'High Islam': The Adoption of Fantasy Middle Eastern Architecture."
80. Putrajaya Holdings, *Pembinaan Putrajaya: Perspektif Pemaju: 1995–2002* [The Making of Putrajaya: The Developer's Perspective] (Putrajaya: Putrajaya Holdings, 2003).
81. Mohamad Haji Mohamad Tajuddin Rasdi, "Mosque Architecture in Malaysia: Classification of Styles and Possible Influences," *Jurnal Alam Bina*, 2007, http://eprints.utm.my/1780/; Abdul Halim Nasir, *Mosque Architecture in the Malay World* (Bangi: Penerbit Universiti Kebangsaan Malaysia, 2004); Mohamad Haji Mohamad Tajuddin Rasdi, *The Architectural Heritage of the Malay World: The Traditional Mosque* (Penerbit Universiti Teknologi Malaysia, 2000); Mohamad Haji Mohamad Tajuddin Rasdi, *Malaysian Architecture: Crisis Within* (Kuala Lumpur: Utusan Publications & Distributors, 2005).
82. Moser, "Circulating Visions of 'High Islam': The Adoption of Fantasy Middle Eastern Architecture."
83. Ibid.

84. Ho Kah Chun and Norizal M. Noordin, "An Influence of Colonial Architecture to Building Styles and Motifs in Colonial Cities in Malaysia," in 8th International Conference of the Asian Planning Schools Association, 2005.
85. Home, *Of Planting and Planning*.
86. Lee, "Petaling Jaya: The Early Development and Growth of Malaysia's First New Town."
87. Donald P. McCracken, *Gardens of Empire: Botanical Institutions of the Victorian British Empire* (London and Washington: Leicester University Press, 1997).
88. Ibid.
89. Lucile H. Brockway, *Science and Colonial Expansion: The Role of the British Royal Botanic Gardens* (New York: Academic Press, 1979).
90. Ibid.
91. McCracken, *Gardens of Empire*.
92. McCracken, *Gardens of Empire,* 168.
93. Many "developing" nations are looking for elite partners in urban research and development. The Malaysian government has recently formalized a relationship between the Massachusetts Institute of Technology and Universiti Teknologi Malaysia: http://dusp.mit.edu/epp/project/mit-utm-malaysia-sustainable-cities-program. Putrajaya and Iskandar Malaysia have also participated in the Cityquest KAEC Forum 2013, an international policy and design conference to explore challenges and opportunities posed by new cities: http://www.cityquest.net/kaec-forum-2013/.
94. Said, *Orientalism*, 55.

SECTION THREE
Leisure Exchange

CHAPTER 8

Context and Content: Colonial Photographs from Kandy, Ceylon

Benita Stambler

Many studies have examined nineteenth-century photographs of Asia in a colonial context.[1] Some of these focused on the photographers, the photographs, and the ideology through which these photographs were produced. While a few of the studies included colonial-era photographs taken in Ceylon[2] (now Sri Lanka), not many have examined the expositional contexts in which photographs of Ceylon were presented to the British public. The transnational transfer of images often added a layer of meaning in the form of visual and verbal commentaries and adjustments to photographs that contributed to the way they were perceived and, possibly, understood. This chapter examines selected photographs from Ceylon that arrived in England in an effort to explore period discourse surrounding photographs embedded in books, magazines, newspapers, and postcards. Although the web of imperial attitudes, interpretations, and responses was fraught with inconsistent elements, specific examples can provide insights into broader patterns.

Photographs are often thought to capture an incontrovertible reality, even as it may have existed for only an instant. However, photographic images may require additional information to be clearly understood. This is particularly true when photographs taken in one context are reproduced in another. Their intended meaning may be further distorted by accompanying texts. Moreover, the implications of the images may be unknown to viewers, who may be unfamiliar with the subject matter because of distance, culture or time.

Examples of cross-cultural misrepresentation are considered here through an examination of photographs of Kandy, the major center of the highland region in Ceylon, taken in the 1870–1910 period and transmitted to Britain in postcards, books, newspapers, and magazines. The subject matter of these particular photographs includes ethnicity, religion, status and ritual, cultural elements that might require explanation when viewed from outside their original social constructs. The texts that explained the content of the photographs may say as much about the interpreters as about the photographs. Since photographs of Ceylon are held in institutions and repositories throughout the world, such an examination provides a useful framework for ongoing clarification of their imagery.

Colonialism and Photography in Ceylon

The British arrived in Ceylon in 1796, gaining full control of the island and the independent kingdom of Kandy in 1815. In the next few decades, modern photography was born. The two forces of colonialism and photography developed along intertwined paths, reinforcing each other within an atmosphere of increased interest in ethnology and anthropology—as Matt Schauer's chapter in this volume shows—as well as archeology and tourism in the British Empire.[3] The contextualizing of these photographic representations of Ceylon provides a particular view of the island as a lush tropical landscape inhabited by people of various races, ethnicities and religions, with distinctive and exotic cultural beliefs and practices.

In 1839 the daguerreotype was invented in France; by 1840 photography had begun in India, and by the mid-1840s it was already being used commercially in Ceylon.[4] Since nineteenth-century cameras were cumbersome and the photographic process complex, travelers often did not personally carry cameras or take photographs, preferring instead to purchase photographs and albums from established purveyors.[5] By the end of the century approximately 25,000 to 30,000 visitors landed in Ceylon annually,[6] creating a substantial market for the products of photography firms.

The major photography firms in Ceylon produced a rich body of images in the second half of the nineteenth century. Local amateur photographers also took photographs, as did a few of the new breed of travelers who came to the island, either as a final destination or as part of a longer tour from Europe to Southeast Asia, China or Australia, particularly after the opening of the Suez Canal in 1869. The new medium was used to document aspects of life in Ceylon, ranging in subjects from the unfamiliar for the casual observer to official surveys of ancient ruins.[7] Photography began to be used in print media such as newspapers and magazines, gradually replacing the engravings that had been the staple of illustrations in these publications. The late nineteenth century saw this transition from drawings and engravings as the only illustrations in printed material, to engravings based on photographs to, finally, the inclusion of photographs, as emerging technologies of printing, photography, transportation, and transcontinental communications coalesced.[8]

Since many of the first known photographers in Ceylon were British, they provided a relatively consistent colonial vision of the island and its inhabitants. The photographic output of the major commercial photography firms collectively revealed, from the perspective of the colonizer, the ambivalent and complex relationships between the ruler and ruled, between the objective and subjective, and between a traditional paradise and a commerce-centered economy. The photographs represented not only personal memorabilia, but historical moments as well, imbued with attitudes and worldviews prevalent at the time.

The Environment for Photography

In Ceylon competition was a major factor affecting photography's commercial opportunities. Firms such as The Colombo Apothecaries' Co. Ltd. not only had a photography department, but also departments specializing in wines and whiskeys, drapery, hardware, haberdashery, and eyeglasses, as well as one for the pharmaceuticals of its name, a variety of pursuits to keep the company economically viable.[9] Large quantities of photographs were produced between the 1870s and 1910; books, magazines, and postcards in which they were reproduced were published at this time or somewhat later, up to about 1930. These photographs presented many different aspects of the island, from its railroad system to tropical species, as well as the local populace. Images of semi-nude indigenous peoples and snake charmers reinforced the notion of primitiveness in Ceylon, in contrast to the assumed civilization and sophistication of the British. Consumers for these photographs ranged from adventurous tourists in Ceylon to the island's elite to armchair travelers in Britain, who spread these images across the intervening oceans.

The Skeen family was initially among the prolific producers of photographs of Ceylon. The family first came to Ceylon from Britain when William Skeen (and later his son) was appointed as the official government printer in 1849. In 1860 William bought a photography firm for another son, W.L.H., who was then studying photography in London as a young man. The firm, which transitioned from Slinn & Co. to W.L.H. Skeen & Co., then later to F. Skeen & Co.,[10] was one of the premier photography firms on the island. Certain themes predominated; in 1898 an advertisement for the Skeen photography firm promoted photographs of their "specialty," "a very large collection of Native Types."[11] These individual portraits of the various ethnic and occupational communities of the island were later combined to create popular postcards which included representative inhabitants of the Kandy region—the Kandyan villager in the upper right corner, a Kandyan Sinhalese, a headman, two ladies, and a village girl (Fig. 8.1).

Distinctions in social status and ethnicity in Ceylon were illustrated by such postcards, which included many of the various groups and classes on the island, defined in this visual context mostly by their clothing and headgear. Skeen & Co. produced several different versions of this concept,

Figure 8.1: W.L.H. Skeen & Co., *Ceylon Natives: Types of Native Races met with in Ceylon* (postcard collage), c. 1891–1900. Author's personal collection.

each a composite created from their stock of individual photographs. Such a collage is consistent with imperial emphasis on ethnography and clothing (or lack thereof) worn by the local population, unfamiliar to the general British public. Visual impressions of Ceylon were created by the images selected by the photographers, based on their personal backgrounds, experience on the island, and commercial motivation, then acquired by collectors and travelers.

However, photographs of the exotic aspects of Ceylon did not accurately reflect the population as a whole. According to the 1881 census figures there were only 121 snake charmers[12] in all of Ceylon, out of approximately 2.95 million total inhabitants of the island.[13] Their preponderance in photographs and photograph collections is thus out of proportion to their percentage of Ceylon's general population. So, too, are Veddas, indigenous people portrayed wearing little more than a loincloth, who numbered fewer than four thousand at this time.[14] These images, however, appealed for various reasons, including a scientific curiosity regarding the primitive, an interest in the unusual, fulfillment of erotic fantasies, a need to document, a desire to civilize, and other attitudes of the period.

Creating Context: Photographs to the Public

While some photographs did make their way directly to England as souvenirs, individually and in albums, others were used as book illustrations, copied as engravings in newspapers, and reformatted as postcards. Guidebooks for Ceylon were illustrated with these photographs, not only those publications by George J.A. Skeen, government printer (1881 to 1906) and brother of photographer W.L.H. Skeen, who produced several volumes subtitled "useful alike to the visitor or resident,"[15] but those by other authors and firms as well. In the early 1900s the Ceylon photographic firm Plâté and Co. produced a book, *The Hundred Best Views of Ceylon,* including views of the Kandy region such as an elephant capture, palm trees and portraits, an alternative for those not wishing to create a personal photograph album.[16] Henry W. Cave's eponymous firm produced a number of guides to Ceylon between 1894 and 1912, both regional (such as his *Kandy and Peradeniya*) and comprehensive that incorporated photographs he took himself.[17]

Ceylon was not unique in having its picturesque elements packaged for the British public. Comparisons between Ceylon and India are inevitable, and certain consistencies in photographic subject matter are obvious from the historical record. John Falconer states, regarding India: "The photographing of racial types and the production of genre studies is continued in the work of all the major firms operating in India from the 1860s well into the present century."[18] Christopher Pinney also discusses the similar phenomenon in India, where a volume published in 1897 entitled *Typical Pictures of Indian Natives* was first intended for tourists, to document their travels.[19] Falconer wrote, speaking of India:

> The common factor in the work of all these photographers is their reliance on the conventions and attitudes of the earlier forms of visual art with which they coexisted for a time and finally superseded: the same themes, treated in almost identical fashion, recur again and again—snake charmers, fakirs, resplendent nobles, trades, customs and costumes, all familiar to the British vision of India, predominate: subjects which had illustrated travellers' memoirs and diaries over the whole period of British influence in the sub-continent. [20]

Similar subjects are found in the oeuvre of the photographers in Ceylon and across Southeast Asia. British photographers throughout the empire produced "native types" photographs, some more ethnographic, others more artistic, particularly because of the fluid national boundaries for photography. Even the Skeen family, relatively settled in Ceylon, had connections in other Asian countries. Frederick Skeen left the family firm in Ceylon in 1886 to move to Burma (now Myanmar), where he was instrumental in the establishment of Watts & Skeen, another successful photography firm, returning to Ceylon in 1903.[21] These connections produced thematic consistencies in photographs across the region.

Ceylon and Kandy

The city of Kandy is located in a particularly picturesque region of Ceylon, the hill country of the interior, and has been nicknamed the "mountain capital of Ceylon."[22] The periphery of the island had been controlled by the Portuguese—Ceylon's first European colonizers—at the end of the sixteenth century, followed by the Dutch. The centrally-located Kandy remained the only independent kingdom until its conquest by the British. Its relatively long-lasting sovereignty was attributable to a complex set of loyalties, interactions, and contentious identities, complicated by its geography.[23] With the fall of the Kandyan kingdom in 1815, the British extended their control over the entire island. Rebellions and riots ensued, but were ultimately unsuccessful. Almost two decades later the Colebrooke-Cameron Commission reforms eliminated the separate administration of Kandy,[24] integrating it more fully into the political sphere of the island, even as it kept certain social distinctions.

The dissolution of the Kandyan kingdom created a disruption in the status systems of the region, providing challenges for the traditional aristocracy. The failed attempts to overthrow the British left local administrative chieftains with little political power. The hereditary Kandyan aristocracy was thus forced to redefine its roles within a changing social structure. According to Seneviratne: "... the chiefs managed to preserve an indigenous aristocratic way of life even while certain spheres of their behavior were being steadily westernized. Further, although *de facto* privileges of the chiefs were removed by the British, they allowed certain ceremonial distinctions to be retained by the chiefs."[25] These distinctions included elaborate clothing for special occasions.

Kandyan Chieftains: Status and Clothing

The people of Ceylon were often defined in colonial encounters by their social background, differentiated in appearance by their clothing. One of the distinctive elements of the Kandyan aristocracy was their ceremonial dress. *The Illustrated London News* described the people at a celebration for the Duke of Edinburgh on his visit to Ceylon in 1870 visually and ethnically by their clothing: "Kandian [Kandyan] Headmen, with their singular pincushion coronets and crinoline-like robes; Buddhist 'ascetics,' in their saffron-coloured robes ... turbaned Tamils, funnel-capped Moormen, and Malays, all flocked to do honour to the son of the common Sovereign."[26]

The ceremonial clothing of the Kandyan chieftains was standardized during the British period to a *mul anduma*, a complete outfit which included a very full cloth wrap of many layers on the lower half of the body culminating in a knot at the waist, and trousers narrow at the bottom with a frill at the ankle. Other parts of the attire included various accessories, a decorative full-shouldered jacket, and a multi-peaked hat with semi-curved sides and a jeweled central ornament.[27] Although the power of the aristocrats deteriorated, the *mul anduma* remains a popular outfit for grooms and groomsmen at weddings, retaining its cultural associations without its political significance.

There are various opinions given regarding the origins of this outfit for the chieftains. According to J.C. Willis, the director of the Royal Botanical Gardens at Peradeniya, on the outskirts of Kandy:

> The great majority of costumes in Ceylon, other than the simple cloth, have been more or less hybridized with European dress, and one can very rarely see real native dress in the country. Even the extraordinary attire of the Kandyan chiefs is partly European, the hat—of a pincushion shape—being a form of the biretta or barett cap, one of which was given by a Portuguese captain to a king of Kotta [Kotte, a Ceylon kingdom overtaken by the Portuguese at the end of the sixteenth century], and the coat being European. The muslin worn round the middle, often making the body into a kind of peg-top shape, and the pantalettes, are rather of native origin, however.[28]

Others argue that the distinctiveness of the Kandyan chieftains' formal clothing could not be attributed to European sources, in contrast to the clothing patterns of low-country Ceylon.[29] Robert Knox's 1681 account of his forced stay in Ceylon provides an engraving of "Raja Singah, the King of Ceylon" [Rajasinghe II of the Kingdom of Kandy, reigned 1635–87] wearing full pantaloons, a slim jacket, and an elaborate tall-sided hat with a central plume, possibly also an early model for the dress adopted by the chieftains. Of this outfit, Knox stated: "His apparel is very strange and wonderful, not after his own country-fashion, or any other, being made after his own invention."[30] Regardless of its inspiration, this formal clothing retained its exotic characteristics during the colonial period when the chieftains were popular subjects in photographs.[31]

The text accompanying an engraving published in *The Illustrated London News* in 1870 states that it was created from a photograph by J. Lawton, presumably Joseph Lawton, who was assigned to take photographs documenting the visit of the Duke of Edinburgh when he visited Kandy on 13 April 1870 as part of his tour of Ceylon and India (Fig. 8.2). Other than the change in location of the chieftain on the left, possibly to improve the composition, the engraving at first appears to be a good likeness of the original photograph (Fig. 8.3). There is, however, a missing element: the finial-like ornamentation atop the hats of the male aristocrats, the *malgaha*, or royal flower tree. In the photograph from which the engraving was created, these decorative adornments are lost in the background of the trees and it is difficult, though not impossible, to see them. The engraving does not include this part of the formal attire. The artist reproducing the photograph was likely not familiar with this aspect of the official outfit. Such jewels atop hats, though, are included in the engraving of another photograph published on the same page, below the one discussed above (see Fig. 8.4). The ornaments were an integral aspect of this ceremonial dress, and their omission from the upper engraving renders it somewhat inaccurate. However, strict accuracy

Figure 8.2: "The Natives of Ceylon: High-Caste Ladies of Kandy," *The Illustrated London News*, 9 July 1870, p. 29.

Figure 8.3: Joseph Lawton, untitled photograph of Kandyan aristocrats, 1870. Photograph courtesy of James D. Julia Auctioneers, Fairfield, Maine, USA, www.jamesdjulia.com.

was not necessarily the main purpose of illustrations in the British Empire's popular press at this time.[32]

A.M. Ferguson, a newspaper publisher and editor called "the father of Ceylon journalism,"[33] wrote regarding an engraving he commissioned based on a photograph of an ancient site taken by Lieutenant Richard Warren Stewart of the Royal Engineers: "The engraver has done justice to Lieut. Stewart's beautiful photograph, while the artist who transferred the picture to the block has added additional truthfulness and animation to the scene by the introduction, at our suggestion, of a herd of elephants and a couple of aquatic birds, which did not, of course, stand to be photographed by the scientific officer."[34] Ferguson disparaged the veracity of the photographic process even further, criticizing the original photographs for their lack of clarity: "From the intense shade of the forest, and the action of the climate on the chemicals, probably, Lieut. Stewart's photographs were so excessively dark that great credit is due to the engraver for the fidelity with which he has represented the general effect of details which it required the aid of a strong magnifying glass to trace in the originals."[35] Thus, Ferguson expressed the belief that illustrations could be "improved" by the addition, or possibly subtraction, of compositional elements that were not clearly featured by the

Figure 8.4: "The Natives of Ceylon: Kandyan Chiefs," *The Illustrated London News*, 9 July 1870, p. 29.

photographer, and that the photographic process was not always capable of properly conveying images of the real world. Rather than authenticity, the appearance of authenticity, aided by creative license, was his aim.

This transition from photograph to engraving for publication was fraught with discrepancies between the original and its rendering. Changes to the original photographs in this process were not necessarily seen as flaws but as enhancements, embedded as they were with the attitudes and preferences of the period toward illustrations. Photographs were compromised by their transformation into engravings for illustrations, introducing levels of interpretation and human intervention. Manual engravings and photomechanical processes were used to transfer the content of photographs into a format compatible with printing techniques, sometimes losing details or even gaining them, as in the Lawton and Ferguson/Stewart examples above, in the transformation.

The Temple of the Tooth

One important symbol of Kandy, then and now, is its Temple of the Tooth, or *Dalada Maligawa*, housing a relic that is claimed to be the Buddha's tooth. As one of the most venerated Buddhist icons in Ceylon, the sacred tooth has functioned during the island's history as a symbol of political legitimacy and religious treasure to the invading Europeans, as well as to the indigenous inhabitants.[36]

One particular British interpreter of the significance of this temple and its tooth was Henry W. Cave (1854–1913). Cave began his life in Ceylon as a private secretary to the Bishop (Copleston) of Colombo. He left this career to found his own company to sell Christian religious literature in Ceylon in 1876. By the 1880s his company focused, among other interests, on publishing, with Cave himself writing several descriptive volumes on Ceylon. He became a fairly prolific author who took his own photographs to illustrate his books as a commercial enterprise. In his book *Picturesque Ceylon*, while discussing Kandy (Fig. 8.5), Cave wrote: "At what a price, then, did the Kandyans preserve their independence! Shut up from all intercourse with other countries, and suffering the worst forms of slavery and oppression, they yet lived in constant dread of being conquered by the nation which ultimately brought them the happiness of good government and the means of prosperity."[37] This makes his attitudes toward the Kandyans quite clear.

Figure 8.5: Henry William Cave, "Buddhist Temple, Kandy," *Picturesque Ceylon*, 1894, Plate XX.

Cave took photographs as he traveled throughout Ceylon, producing some published portraits. His photographs are often landscapes, some botanicals, and a few scenes that include individuals, in contrast to the photographs of the commercial photography firms that were so concerned with "native types." Thus, he did not generally comment on individuals and their clothing, but rather on their beliefs and customs. When Cave discussed the Temple of the Tooth, with its relic of the Buddha's tooth, he pontificated: "The tooth, for the possession of which bloody wars have been fought, and which is so carefully and reverently preserved, is very unlike a human tooth, indeed, so much so, that it strikes the visitor who is independent of the hereditary influence of Eastern superstition as ridiculous that any one should ever suppose it to be one. It exactly resembles a crocodile's tooth…."[38]

Cave used the opportunity presented by his photographs of the Temple of the Tooth to express the superiority of his own religious (and political) attitudes and to question the validity of the local Buddhist beliefs. He was apparently not alone in his attitudes. Cave's literary and photographic output was positively reviewed by *The Times* [London], *Overland Mail*, and *The Journal of the Royal Asiatic Society*, among others.[39] Given the civilizing and conversion goals of the British Empire regarding its colonies and Cave's past religious affiliations, his commentaries were not seen as overly opinionated explanations for his photographs.

Kandyan Dance

Certain special dances were once confined to the Kandy region, but have since become symbols of Sri Lankan national identity.[40] Originating in sacred rituals, the dances have moved into the public performative sphere through a national system of standardization and cooptation. In the late nineteenth and early twentieth centuries such dances were performed locally as part of rituals for religious purposes or for other special occasions.

Dancers and their elaborate clothing were presented as features of the exotic nature of Ceylon's culture, captured in photographs and postcards, and often labeled as "devil dancers" regardless of their localized tradition or religious significance (Fig. 8.6). This devil dance nomenclature seems to have been applied to any dancers in Ceylon who wore intricate attire and danced to the accompaniments of drums or other instruments. Although there were many distinctions among the dance traditions in Ceylon, the British press, and even the photography firms in Ceylon, labeled all as "devil dancers," as in Figure 8.6. The dancers in this photograph were specialists in a particular Kandyan tradition, wearing silver adornment on the head, large earpieces, a heavy belt, and upper-body bead ornamentation, the traditional *ves* outfit worn for specific ceremonies.

Figure 8.6: Colombo Apothecaries Co. Ltd., *Singhalese Devil Dancers* (postcard), c. 1890. Author's personal collection.

A.E. Souter in *The English Illustrated Magazine* reported on a *perahera*, a ritual procession in Kandy, in his article titled "A Sight the Duke of Cornwall and York Saw in Ceylon: Some Account of a Curious Festival." He characterized the dancers in the *perahera* as a "fearful band of devil-dancers, with their painted bodies and horrible masks representing the most satanic of demons."[41] He further described them:

> a band of devil-dancers performing their truly devilish figures and contortions to the deafening beat of tom-toms, the clashing of cymbals, and the blowing of horns and pipes. The object of this pandemonium, be it known, is to scare away all evil spirits: no doubt, it serves its purpose, for the occupants of the lower world, seeing themselves thus impersonated, would certainly turn tail and fly.[42]

This particular 1901 procession was a special one to celebrate the visit of the Duke, though similar *peraheras* had been held for previous visits of British royals to Kandy, such as for the Duke of Edinburgh in 1870 and the Prince of Wales in 1875.[43]

A photograph accompanying this article belies Souter's description (Fig. 8.7). From his narrative it is not clear if Souter was present at this procession.[44] Rather than a photograph of masked and painted dancers, a photograph of two dancers with neither paint nor masks is used to illustrate this aspect of the entertainment. This is a staged photograph taken most likely at an earlier date, and possibly selected to accompany the article because it was easily available. Such a discrepancy between image and text may be attributed to several possible causes. First, the photograph may have been selected for the publication with little attention paid to the specific description of the dancers in the text. Another possibility is that no photographs of masked dancers in a *perahera* were readily available. The article is introduced by the statement, "Photographs by kind permission of Messrs. Skeen and Co., Colombo and Kandy." Not many different photographs of masked "devil dancers" have been preserved in outstanding collections of Skeen photographs (though several different photographs of Kandyan dancers, as in Fig. 8.6, exist), suggesting that the masked dancers may not have been as common a subject for the Skeen firm as other dancers.

The Duke of Cornwall and York (later King George V of England) possibly saw masked dancers elsewhere. Accounts from other outlets of the British Empire press are inconclusive. *The Argus* of Melbourne describes groups at the station in Colombo, prior to the trip to Kandy, which included "the others in masks ... representative of the famous devil dancers of Ceylon."[45] This is similar to another account which also discusses masked

Figure 8.7: Skeen & Co., untitled photograph of dancers, originally c. 1890. Photograph courtesy of Dominic Sansoni Collection.

devil dancers entertaining the royals in Colombo,[46] much closer than Kandy to the lowlands where masked rituals were more commonly performed. Souter may have been confused by the headdresses worn as part of the *ves* outfit by Kandyan dancers in the festival procession. With their elaborate head and ear decorations (see Fig. 8.6), given the tumult described by Souter, the dancers may have been mistaken at a distance in low light levels for persons wearing masks.[47] The accompanying photograph would still have been inaccurate and does not account for Souter's version of the procession, though masked dancers may also have performed in Kandy for the royals.

The photograph of dancers that accompanies the Souter article is clearly a studio portrait, depicting those who are neither the dancers described by Souter nor the *ves*-costumed Kandyan dancers in the "devil dancers" photograph (refer to Fig. 8.6) but *pantheru* dancers, another style of Kandyan dance. Differences can be seen in the instruments and the upper body and head decoration. These Kandyan *pantheru* dancers hold *pantheruwa*, instruments resembling tambourines, dressed for a ritual to honor the goddess Pattini. They would not wear the masks that are part of other ritual traditions such as the *kolam*, a masked dance drama performed in the southern coastal region.[48]

According to David Scott, conversion to Christianity was a central component of the British influence on Ceylon, affecting the perception of religious rites deemed indigenous, and therefore pagan. Even use of expressions of demonism (such as "devil dancing") has been called into question by Scott as a colonial imposition of a framework on a ritual that is largely unexplained by such terms.[49] While Scott bemoans the colonial (lack of) understanding of these rituals, it is sufficient for our purpose to note that such dance forms were considered un-Christian by the British, and therefore probably did not require intense scrutiny of their differentiating features. Rather, the dances functioned as a platform for the imposition of Christian values and beliefs. It would not have been difficult for Souter, the Skeen firm, or *The English Illustrated Magazine* to conflate and confuse unique rituals, even ones with distinctive garments, instrumental accompaniment and purposes. Ethnographers and scientifically-oriented observers, in the meantime, would have focused more specifically on cultural characteristics and persons.[50] Souter, about whom nothing more is known, clearly had a purpose more suited to the popular press than to serious inquiry. Although several possibilities have been suggested, no definitive explanation can be provided for the discrepancy between the text and the photograph in his article. However, the dissonance between the two would have constrained an accurate understanding by the British public of not only this photograph, but also of Ceylon's rituals and customs.

Conclusion

Visible markers of social status, religion, custom, ritual, religion, and ethnicity were captured to create the photographic record of Ceylon in the late nineteenth century. Such imagery was embedded in diverse documents and transmitted across oceans to England and elsewhere. Although these photographs may have produced greater familiarity with the people and culture of Ceylon, the perceptions created were influenced by the contexts through which the photographs were presented to the British public, firmly situated within the prevailing period discourse. Additionally, the imposition of the technological and human constraints of the printing industry affected the reproduction and reformatting of photographs for publication. Thus, numerous opportunities for transnational miscommunication arose.[51]

James R. Ryan argues that photographs are "ambiguous images" because their meaning may be unclear to the viewer.[52] This is certainly the case for the images of the Kandy region of Ceylon examined here. Their underlying cultural significance became subsumed to the perceptions and attitudes of the authors whose texts surrounded them, misconstruing the content of the photographs and subjecting them to unintended interpretations. Such commentaries, without a closer examination of the photographs and a clear understanding of the social milieus in which they were taken, may have the final impact, rather than the imagery of the photographs themselves.

The reasons for the disjunctures between photographs and accompanying texts explored here include pre-existing attitudes that disregarded or denigrated the demographics and value systems of the colonies, an unfamiliarity with customs and clothing for clearly understanding the visual, artistic license in reformatting the photographic content, limitations associated with the technologies of the printing process, and discrepancies between the author of the text and the provision of its accompanying photographs. Regardless of the reasons for discontinuities between the images and their contexts, it is clear that period descriptions and explanations of colonial-era photographs portraying the social and religious customs of Ceylon must be considered with a certain degree of skepticism. While a variety of publications and formats served to popularize Ceylon in British settings, they also created colonial constructs at odds, deliberately or not, with the content of the photographs, complicating the representation and understanding of Ceylon's cultural imagery.

Notes

1. See for example John Falconer and Louise Hide, *Points of View: Capturing the 19th Century in Photographs* (London: British Library, 2009); James R. Ryan, *Picturing Empire: Photography and the Visualization of the British Empire* (Chicago: University of Chicago Press, 1998); Zahid R. Chaudhary, *Afterimage of Empire: Photography in Nineteenth-century India* (Minneapolis: University of Minnesota Press, 2012); Susie Protschky, ed., *Photography, Modernity and the Governed in Late-colonial Indonesia* (Amsterdam: Amsterdam University Press, 2015).
2. John Falconer, "Patterns of Photographic Surveys: Joseph Lawton in Ceylon," in *Traces of India: Photography, Architecture, and the Politics of Representation, 1850–1900,* ed. Maria Antonella Pelizzari (Montreal: Canadian Centre for Architecture, 2003), 156–73; Gael Newton, *Picture Paradise: Asia-Pacific Photography 1840s–1940s* (Canberra: National Gallery of Australia, 2008).
3. For consideration of photography and these subjects, see Eleanor M. Hight and Gary D. Sampson, *Colonialist Photography: Imag(in)ing Race and Place* (New York: Routledge, 2013); Christopher Pinney, "Classification and Fantasy in the Photographic Construction of Caste and Tribe," *Visual Anthropology* 3, nos. 2–3 (1990): 259–88; Ismeth Raheem, *Archaeology and Photography: The Early Years 1868–1880* (Colombo: The National Trust of Sri Lanka, 2009); Melissa Banta and Curtis M. Hinsley, "Nineteenth Century Visions of the Exotic: Travel and Expeditionary Photography," in *From Site to Sight: Anthropology, Photography, and the Power of Imagery* (Cambridge, MA: Peabody Museum Press, 1986).
4. Ismeth Raheem and Percy Colin Thomé, *Images of British Ceylon: Nineteenth Century Photography of Sri Lanka* (Singapore: Times Editions, 2000), Foreword.
5. See for example Alan Chong et al., *Journeys East: Isabella Stewart Gardner and Asia* (Boston: Isabella Stewart Gardner Museum, 2009).
6. John Ferguson, *Ceylon in 1903* (Colombo: A.M. & J. Ferguson, 1903), 117.
7. Stephen Montagu Burrows, *The Buried Cities of Ceylon: A Guide Book to Anuradhapura and Polonaruwa* (Colombo: A.M. & J. Ferguson, 1899).
8. Gerry Beegan, "Finding Florence in Birmingham: Hybridity and the Photomechanical Image in the 1890s," in *Visions of the Industrial Age, 1830–1814,* ed. Minsoo Kang and Amy Woodson-Boulton (Aldershot, England: Ashgate, 2008) and Gerry Beegan, *The Mass Image: A Social History of Photomechanical Reproduction in Victorian London* (Basingstoke, England: Palgrave Macmillan, 2008).

9. George J.A. Skeen, *A Guide to Colombo: A Handbook of Information, Useful Alike to the Visitor and Resident* (Colombo: A.M. & J. Ferguson, 1898), back matter (final advertisement section).
10. Raheem and Thomé, *Images of British Ceylon*, 58–65.
11. Skeen, *A Guide to Colombo*, front matter (introductory advertisement section).
12. John Ferguson, *Ceylon in the "Jubilee Year"* (London: John Haddon, 1887), 266. On page 287, the statistic is 120 snake charmers. In any case, their percentage of the total population was quite small.
13. Ferguson, *Ceylon in the "Jubilee Year,"* 10. Figure from the 1887 population.
14. John Ferguson, *Ceylon in 1903* (Colombo: A.M. & J. Ferguson, 1903), Appendix III, xlviii (Veddahs). Figure from the 1901 census.
15. Skeen, *A Guide to Colombo.* Also George J.A. Skeen, *A Guide to Kandy: A Handbook of Information, Useful Alike to the Visitor and the Resident* (Colombo: A.M. & J. Ferguson, 1903).
16. Plâté & Co., *The Hundred Best Views of Ceylon: From Photographs taken by the Publishers* (Colombo: Plâté & Co., n.d.).
17. Henry W. Cave, *The Book of Ceylon: Being a Guide to its Railway System and an Account of its Varied Attractions for the Visitor and Tourist* (London: Cassell, 1908). Combines Cave's volumes of Colombo and the Kelani Valley, Kandy, Nuwara Eliya, and the Northern Provinces. See also *Picturesque Ceylon: Kandy and Peradeniya* (London: Sampson Low, Marston & Co., 1894).
18. John Falconer, "Ethnographical Photography in India: 1850–1900," *Photographic Collector* 5, no. 1 (1984).
19. Christopher Pinney, *Camera Indica: The Social Life of Indian Photographs* (London: Reaktion, 1997), 56.
20. Falconer, "Ethnographical Photography in India."
21. Raheem and Thomé, *Images of British Ceylon*, 65.
22. A.M. Ferguson, *Souvenirs of Ceylon* (London: John Haddon, 1869), 166.
23. R.A.L.H. Gunawardana, "Colonialism, Ethnicity and the Construction of the Past: The Changing 'Ethnic Identity' of the Last Four Kings of the Kandyan Kingdom," in *Pivot Politics: Changing Cultural Identities in Early State Formation Processes*, ed. Martin van Bakel, Renée Hagesteijn, and Pieter van de Velde (Amsterdam: Het Spinhuis, 1994); L.S. Dewaraja, *The Kandyan Kingdom of Sri Lanka 1707–1782* (Pannipitiya, Sri Lanka: Stamford Lake, 2008); K.N.O. Dharmadasa, "The Sinhala Buddhist Identity and the Nayakkar Dynasty in the Politics of the Kandyan Kingdom 1739–1815," in *Sri Lanka: Collective Identities Revisited, Volume I*, ed. Michael Roberts (Colombo: Marga Institute, 1997); Michael Roberts, *Ethnicity after Edward Said: Post-Orientalist Failures in Comprehending the Kandyan Period of Lankan History* (Sri Lanka: International Centre for Ethnic Studies, 2001); Sujit Sivasundaram, "Tales of the Land: British Geography and Kandyan Resistance in Sri Lanka, c. 1803–1850," *Modern Asian Studies* 41, no. 5 (Sept. 2007): 925–65.

24. John D. Rogers, "Early British Rule and Social Classification in Lanka," *Modern Asian Studies* 38, no. 3 (July 2004): 625–47.
25. H.L. Seneviratne, *Rituals of the Kandyan State* (New York: Cambridge University Press, 1978), 117.
26. "Prince Alfred in Ceylon," *The Illustrated London News*, 11 June 1870: 614.
27. See Nira Wickramasinghe, *Dressing the Colonised Body: Politics, Clothing and Identity in Sri Lanka* (Hyderabad: Orient Longman, 2003), 130–4 for a chart, derived from a 1935 Ceylon Government Gazette, detailing the clothing associated with aristocratic chieftain ranks and the types of occasions that were appropriate for different forms of dress. Also H.W. Codrington, *Notes on Some of the Principal Kandyan Chiefs and Headmen, and Their Dresses* (Colombo: H.C. Cottle, 1910), who relied on a 1909 version of the Ceylon Government Gazette.
28. J.C. Willis, *Ceylon: A Handbook for the Resident and the Traveller* (Colombo: Colombo Apothecaries, 1907), 89. However, this European influence is in conflict with Cordiner's earlier attribution. He states, "it is evident that the form of no part of their attire is borrowed from that of Europeans." James Cordiner, *A Description of Ceylon (Volume 1), Containing an Account of the Country, Inhabitants, and Natural Productions with Narratives of a Tour Round the Island in 1800, the Campaign in Candy in 1803, and a Journey to Ramisseram in 1804* (London: Longman, Hurst, Rees & Orme, 1807), 132. While it is not completely clear which styles of clothing this phrase refers to, he does mention Kandyan chieftains in the immediately previous sentences. His description of the clothing of the Kandyan Adigaar [or Adigar], a hundred years earlier than Willis, is similar to their later attire, including a large wrap on the bottom (but no leggings), a "wide-sleeved" top, and a square hat.
29. K.D.G. Wimalaratne and Dian Gomes, *Costumes of Sri Lanka* (Sri Lanka, 2001), xvii.
30. Robert Knox, *An Historical Relation of the Island Ceylon* (London: Richard Chiswell, 1681), 34 (spelling modernized). The engraving is between pages 32 and 33.
31. On the popularity of the costumes and dances of the colonized, see also Susie Protschky's chapter in this volume.
32. Beegan, "Finding Florence" and *The Mass Image.*
33. Arnold Wright, *Twentieth Century Impressions of Ceylon, Its History, People, Commerce, Industries, and Resources* (London: Lloyd's Greater Britain Publishing, 1907), 302.
34. Ferguson, *Souvenirs of Ceylon*, 110.
35. Ibid., 111.
36. See Seneviratne, *Rituals of the Kandyan State,* for a historical perspective on the tooth's changing political meaning.
37. Cave, *Picturesque Ceylon: Kandy and Peradeniya,* 17.
38. Ibid., 76.

39. Henry W. Cave, *The Ruined Cities of Ceylon* (London: S. Low, Marston & Co., 1900), frontispiece.
40. Susan A. Reed, "Performing Respectability: The Beravā, Middle-Class Nationalism, and the Classicization of Kandyan Dance in Sri Lanka," *Cultural Anthropology* 17, no. 2 (May 2002): 246–77.
41. A.E. Souter, "A Sight the Duke of Cornwall and York Saw in Ceylon: Some Account of a Curious Festival," *The English Illustrated Magazine* XXV (April–Sept. 1901): 477.
42. Ibid., 477.
43. The public appearance of devil dancers is mentioned by Joseph Fayrer, *Notes of the Visits to India of their Royal Highnesses the Prince of Wales and the Duke of Edinburgh 1870–1875–6* (London: Kerby & Endean, 1879) and by William Howard Russell, who specifically mentions dancers with "masked and painted faces," *The Prince of Wales' Tour: A Diary in India* (New York: R. Worthington, 1878), 235, http://archive.org/details/princeofwalestou00russ. The *perahera* for the Prince is analyzed by H. Hazel Hahn, "Indian Princes, Dancing Girls and Tigers: The Prince of Wales's Tour of India and Ceylon, 1875–1876," *Postcolonial Studies* 12, no. 2 (2009): 173–92.
44. Corroborating evidence regarding this particular procession is limited. Sir Donald Mackenzie Wallace was the "assistant private secretary" to the Duke during this tour and produced what was considered the "authorized" account. (See the Prefatory Note, *The Web of Empire: A Diary of the Imperial Tour of their Royal Highnesses the Duke & Duchess of Cornwall & York in 1901*. London: Macmillan and Co., 1902.) His account contained mostly illustrations by prominent illustrators, with only a few photographs. One of the illustrators for the *perahera* at Kandy in this volume was S.P. Hall, or Sydney Prior Hall. The text makes no mention of a ceremony at the Colombo rail station as noted later, but does describe the Kandy *perahera*, including "bands of devil dancers in hideous masks" (p. 68). Hall's depiction of the procession shows Kandyan dancers wearing the *ves* costume, without masks. On another occasion, in a double-page illustration for *The Graphic*, in its 25 July 1885 issue (pp. 108–9), prior to the Duke of Cornwall and York's visit, Hall does portray masked dancers. Though Harry Price was on this 1901 trip with the Duke and Duchess, he does not comment on the *perahera*. See his *The Royal Tour, 1901: or, The Cruise of H.M.S. Ophir, Being a Lower Deck Account of Their Royal Highnesses, the Duke and Duchess of Cornwall and York's Voyage around the British Empire* (New York: William Morrow, 1980).
45. "The Royal Voyage: From Portsmouth to Albany: Magnificent Receptions Everywhere: The Life on Shipboard," 2 May 1901: 5, http://trove.nla.gov.au/ndp/del/page/325214. Maxwell mentions devil dancers in both Colombo and Kandy (pp. 30 and 35–6) but does not mention masks in either location. W. Maxwell, *With the Ophir Round the Empire: An Account of the Tour of the Prince and Princess of Wales 1901* (London: Cassels, 1902).

46. Edward Frederick Knight, *With the Royal Tour: A Narrative of the Recent Tour of the Duke and Duchess of Cornwall and York through Greater Britain, including His Royal Highness's Speech Delivered at the Guildhall on December 5, 1901* (London: Longmans, 1902), 44.
47. Susan A. Reed states in *Dance and the Nation: Performance, Ritual, and Politics in Sri Lanka* (2010) that dancers appeared in their *ves* costumes for the *perahera* at least as early as the visit of the Prince of Wales in 1875 (p. 100). Though probably not Kandyan dancers, James Emerson Tennent provides an account of being honored by "national dances" and "a band of devil dancers from an adjacent temple, with masks and grotesque dresses," in *Ceylon: An Account of the Island Physical, Historical and Topographical, with Notices of its Natural History, Antiquities, and Productions, Volume 1* (London: Longman, Green, Longman, and Roberts, 1860), 183. The participation of dancers is only briefly noted in the account of the *perahera* to honor the Duke of Edinburgh during his visit to Kandy in 1870 by John Capper, *The Duke of Edinburgh in Ceylon: A Book of Elephant and Elk Sport* (London: Provost, 1871), 62. The brevity may be attributable to Capper's focus on the hunting aspects of the visit. Slightly later, Governor Gregory was honored by a Kandy *perahera* upon taking office in 1872 in which "devil dancers" participated. See Lady Augusta Gregory, ed., *Sir William Gregory, K.C.M.G., Formerly Member of Parliament and Sometime Governor of Ceylon: An Autobiography* (London: John Murray, 1894), 280.
48. M.H. Goonatilleka, "Mime, Mask and Satire in Kolam of Ceylon," *Folklore* 81, no. 3 (Autumn 1970): 161–76.
49. David Scott, "Conversion and Demonism: Colonial Christian Discourse and Religion in Sri Lanka," *Comparative Studies in Society and History* 34, no. 2 (April 1992): 331–65.
50. Much of the more rigorous study of Ceylon during this period was published in *The Journal of the Ceylon Branch of the Royal Asiatic Society*, whose stated goal was "to institute and promote inquiries into the History, Religion, Literature, Arts, and Social Condition of the present and former Inhabitants of the Island, with its Geology, Mineralogy, its Climate and Meteorology, its Botany and Zoology," Royal Asiatic Society of Great Britain and Ireland, *Journal of the Ceylon Branch of the Royal Asiatic Society, 1848*, Volume II, Part I, no. 4 (1887): frontispiece.
51. For a consideration of the interactions between photography, illustrations, captions, and meaning elsewhere, see Andrew Jarvis, "'The Myriad-Pencil of the Photographer': Seeing, Mapping and Situating Burma in 1855," *Modern Asian Studies* 45, no. 4 (July 2011): 791–823.
52. Ryan, *Picturing Empire*, 16.

CHAPTER 9

Slipping into Something More Exotic: Transgressive Dress in Early Twentieth-century Java

Susie Protschky

This chapter examines cultural encounter between Europeans and Javanese through two vignettes on racially transgressive dress in late-colonial Java. The examples comprise two "portraits" of European females dressed as Javanese women. The first is a photographic portrait, taken in 1908, of two little Dutch girls dressed in *sarong-kebaya* (skirt and blouse), a costume with a complex history, but one that had become associated in the households of white, colonial elites with servants, especially nannies. The second is a written portrait, recounted in a memoir in which a brown-skinned Indo-European woman who, on a European study trip in the late 1920s, appeared in public to great acclaim dressed as a Javanese court dancer. Each vignette reveals how "dressing-up" as a Javanese woman at once familiar and exotic to these Europeans defined class, race, and age-specific colonial notions of femininity. I also trace a historical shift in Dutch evaluations of these cultural encounters through costume: from the early twentieth century, colonial context in which the portraits were seen by a small audience of contemporaries, to the late twentieth century, postcolonial milieu where spectators who often had no personal connection to the portraits formed a wider public.

I use the term "vignette" with purpose, for my examples capture and frame fragments from a vast spectrum of colonial representations, imposing stillness and focus upon fleeting moments in dynamic lives and encounters that differed substantially. Yet in sharing a common originating social context—Dutch colonial Java in the early twentieth century—these portraits of women provide important insights into the nature and limits of encounter between Europeans and Asians in this period. In drawing attention to the mode of each portrait, I argue that the meanings of dress were partly determined by the manners of their representation. Commemorative images and texts such as photographs and memoirs are shaped not just by their content but also by their audiences: those for which they were first intended, as well as those they circulate among long afterwards.[1]

As Jean Gelman Taylor and Elsbeth Locher-Scholten have demonstrated, close examination of the mutable act of dressing in the Netherlands Indies (colonial Indonesia) reveals how women's bodies in particular were key sites of cross-cultural encounter and, importantly, that Indies women actively negotiated complex, often unstable social identities in the act of deciding what to wear and when.[2] Colonial Javanese society in the early twentieth century was a heterogeneous blend of Asian, European, and Eurasian communities whose mingling extended at least as far back as the seventeenth century, when the Dutch East India Company established its capital on the island. These communities defied simple social categorizations based on language or skin color.[3] Mixed marriages between European men and Asian or Indo-European women remained common until the late nineteenth century, when women from Europe began to arrive in the colony in greater numbers. However, the legacy of Java's *mestizo* past—a high proportion of creoles and Indo-Europeans—continued to be evident in the European community until the very end of Dutch colonial rule. The legal question of paternity alone, then, could not settle the cultural question of "Europeanness" without reference to class indicators such as wealth, education, and occupation or ethnic markers such as language, food customs, and costume.[4]

European women occupied biologically and socially reproductive roles in colonial Javanese society as wives, mothers, educators, and caregivers whose encounter with Asian women occurred in public, in the street and the marketplace, and also in private, in the household, where servants were Asian and so were some family members. European women's bodies were thus important sites where social boundaries were fashioned and tested, for they were not just in daily exchange with culturally distant, "Other" women; they were often related to, imbricated with and intimately dependent on them. The vignettes examined here of European females dressing as Javanese women thus provide close analysis of how such acts demonstrated, in varying proportions, competence across cultures *and* acts of class and racial transgression.

Photograph: Two Little Dutch Girls in *Sarong-kebaya*

Figure 9.1 is a photograph of two little Dutch girls dressed in *sarong-kebaya*, replete with dolls borne in a *slendang*, a shawl that was often used to carry babies. The "cultural biography"[5] of this picture—its progress from the time of its creation more than a century ago to more recent contexts of display—illuminates the part that family photographs have played in articulating changing narratives of cultural exchange between Asia and Europe. The analysis that follows of the original, colonial milieu in which the photograph was made interrogates these narratives from a historical perspective that challenges more recent interpretations of the image.

The photograph was first published in the Netherlands in 1981 in a book titled *Baren en oudgasten* [Newcomers and oldtimers], a volume concerned with Indo-European society in the former Netherlands Indies. The book was the first in a three-volume series written in Dutch by Rob Nieuwenhuys (1908–99), titled *Tempo Doeloe – een verzonken wereld: Fotografische documenten uit het oude Indië 1870–1920* [The good old days – A sunken world: Photographic documents from the former Indies].[6] The books, originally published between 1981 and 1988, followed two earlier photo collections that had been the first to present a social history of the Indies in photographs for a wide audience.[7] The series augmented a longer career that Nieuwenhuys dedicated to writing about the Netherlands Indies in a country where, for decades following Indonesian independence in 1945, Dutch colonialism and its legacies were marginalized from national history.[8] In the words of E.M. Beekman, a Nieuwenhuys biographer, the *Tempo Doeloe* books became "melancholy icons of what was in the process of becoming a mythical time."[9]

Baren en oudgasten collated photographs that would have appealed specifically to Europeans with fond memories of colonial life. It showed the places Europeans frequented on Java—the grand parts of the capital, Batavia; the botanic gardens near the Governor-General's palace at Buitenzorg; hotels, swimming spots and hiking trails in the countryside. It showed Europeans at leisure—taking tea on the broad verandas of stately houses, attended by native servants; engaging in amateur theatrics; riding bicycles;

Figure 9.1: Etje Wilkens and Addy Bins, Semarang, 29 March 1908.
Source: KITLV Special Collections, Leiden University Libray, Album 110, Image 83316.

attending public festivals for the Dutch monarchy. It showed European modes of travel to and throughout the Indies, by steamship, train, and motorcar. And for governing men, it commemorated the public, ceremonial aspects of their work—meetings with indigenous officials (often in studio settings) where the contrast between the formal attire of Europeans and natives made for striking portraits. Other European subcultures appeared in the book: less well-to-do, Indo-European families, and the planters of Deli, the estate district of East Sumatra where tobacco and later rubber were grown for export and many fortunes were made and lost. A voyeuristic, masculine European view of Asian women is represented by photographs ranging from the pornographic nude to the artful studio portrait of the native belle. An intimate, sympathetic view of the European woman's lot ends the book. It shows the joys and sorrows of setting up house and starting a family in the tropics, including the death of beloved infants and other departures.

The nostalgic tone of *Baren en oudgasten* was set by the introductory chapter, "*Wat is tempo doeloe*?" (What is *tempo doeloe*?). Nieuwenhuys explored the colonial meaning of the Malay term, as used by Dutch writers who knew the Indies. From the mid-nineteenth century onward, he explained, each new generation of "newcomers and oldtimers" referred to the recent past as "*tempo doeloe*". Nostalgia was thus essential to Indies culture, and the best times were always already gone.[10] Nothing represents this bittersweet sentiment more clearly than the image that appears opposite the introduction, a full-page reproduction of the two little girls in *sarong-kebaya*. The children appear small and yet large, just one of the creative manipulations that Nieuwenhuys made to photographs throughout the volume.

For some (ex-)colonial Dutch viewers the photograph may well have encapsulated grief for many "sunken worlds": a childhood passed, the Indies lost, innocence gone. For others the photograph perhaps represented a small triumph, for it depicted a childhood they were at last permitted to remember—collectively as well as privately—in a context where the colonial period and Indo-European culture were, for the first time since Indonesian independence, no longer a matter of public shame.[11] The photograph of the two little girls in Nieuwenhuy's book comprised a poignant metaphor for the colonial past as a human life-cycle: an idyllic childhood (the colonial era) lost to a turbulent adolescence (the Japanese occupation and the Indonesian war of independence) and (postcolonial) adulthood.[12]

Although he was contemporaneous with and probably knew the (then) little girls in *sarong-kebaya* or their families personally, Nieuwenhuys did not name them in the book. Perhaps he chose to keep the girls anonymous to broaden their appeal, an aim enabled also by the portability of photographs as objects; their capacity to be flexibly deployed in various contexts for new audiences.[13] Another copy of the photograph exists in a public archive, the KITLV Collection at the Leiden University Library.[14] It is pasted into a family album donated in 1968 by one of its former owners, the girl pictured on the left of the photograph, Etje Wilkens. The original owners of the album were almost certainly Etje's parents, a woman named Valentine and a man referred to throughout the album only as "A." Born in 1904, Etje was around 4 years old when the photograph with Addy was taken. The album documented the life of her family in Semarang—the same port city on Java's north coast where Rob Nieuwenhuys was born in the year the photograph was taken—between 1900 and 1915. More particularly, the album focused on Etje's early life, following in chronological order her development as a toddler into an 11-year-old girl.

As a source for social history, the Etje-Addy photograph thus doubles—as do many family photographs from the former Indies—as a focus for the formation of postcolonial collective memories as well as a window into the colonial period itself.[15] In the latter regard, following Pamela Pattynama's reading of family photograph archives formed by Indo-Europeans in the Netherlands, the image testifies to the everyday, lived reality of a *mestizo* Indies culture that persisted until the very end of Dutch colonial rule, even despite the growing censure of the white, Eurocentric elite.[16]

Historic class, gender, and ethnic tensions are also captured in the costuming portrayed. The difference between the whiteness of the children and the brownness of their attire lies in the seismic transgression their dress represents: European children clothed as the servants they will have, not be, if their parents do their job properly. These tensions do not *disturb* the innocence of the two little girls; rather, they were *constitutive* of girlish innocence among white Europeans in late-colonial Java. Re-viewing the photograph in its original historical and material contexts—in a family album made in the early twentieth-century Indies—restores the complex tensions that were elided by the simultaneously new and nostalgic meanings it acquired in Nieuwenhuys' postcolonial publication. Transgressive dress of the kind commemorated in the Etje-Addy photograph instructed on early twentieth-century social boundaries that had to be identified, and from an early age, in order to be maintained.

Throughout the Wilkens album Etje was subject to parental manipulation, rather like the dolls she and Addy hold in their *slendang*. The family home, as I have discussed elsewhere,[17] functions in the album as a private photographic studio in which Etje's childhood was represented in ritual ways. This included the marking of time through records of Etje's engagement in a peculiarly Indies social activity (*thee-uurtje*, or tea time), but also through parental play with costumes. The *sarong-kebaya* outfit is not the only one that Etje appears in, almost certainly for the sole purpose of being photographed in it: she is also pictured in costumes that would have been impossible for a small child in the tropics to wear for very long, such as a European dress of heavy cloth and a tightly-wrapped Japanese kimono.

Etje appears very much the object of parental affection in the photographs, an adored object of her parents' gaze, but passive nonetheless—like a doll—to the ways in which she is being represented. With its surfeit of profile portraits, the album is pervaded by an unreciprocated parental look that permeates even the Addy-Etje photograph: here, the girls return a gaze, but not that of the photographer/viewer. Rather, they look up and to the side, to taller people outside the photograph's frame, probably the adults who orchestrated and were charmed by the scene. The adult gaze here is doubly elegiac, then, averting the eyes of the children for posterity even as it meets them in the moment, indirectly recording itself in captivation.

Most of the photographs of Etje in the album are full-length, much like the picture of her with Addy. Her diminutive, childish stature enables this perspective. The resultant focus is on Etje's body, and it is here that many of the tensions in the photograph are also situated: on the body of a girl-child who will become a woman— more specifically, a white woman in the Indies, a society where ethnic mixing was as old as European colonialism itself, but where an evaluative shift had occurred in the early twentieth century that not only regarded *mestizo* society in advantageous or neutral terms, but also in some circumstances, as "miscegenation"—as moral and biological degeneration.[18]

The history of Etje's costume encapsulates this shift in colonial morality. Before the mid-nineteenth century only Javanese royals wore clothing made of *batik*, a fabric (usually cotton) decorated with colored motifs using a hand-tooled, dye resist technique. Sumptuary codes strictly regulated the wearing of particular motifs to certain members of royal households. Commoner Javanese wore simple cottons and other ethnic groups wore costumes according to their own sartorial traditions. Following Dutch subjugation of Central Java's royal courts in the 1820s and the subsequent curtailment of their political powers, sumptuary codes governing dress became less rigorous. Further, in the 1840s tools were invented that enabled printed fabrics to be mass-produced for the first time and a market for cheaper, more diverse styles of batik was established, catered for by Chinese and Indo-European makers. As a result, in the mid-nineteenth century batik emerged as the "traditional" garment of *all* Javanese women, commoners as well as elites, an association that was later strengthened through the use of costume in studio photography.[19] European women in large numbers also began to wear *sarong-kebaya* in the mid-nineteenth century, as it was locally made, comfortable in the tropical climate, and signalled cultural facility with living in a *mestizo* idiom.[20] However, by the early twentieth century Europeans had cast aside *sarong-kebaya* for their public attire as the upper-class associations of batik became diluted and demographic changes permanently altered more than the composition of Indies society. The "European" elite became more Eurocentric with the arrival of recent migrants from the Netherlands, including, for the first time, large numbers of women. Advancements in communications and travel technologies meant that this new ruling class remained in constant contact with (indeed, frequently traveled to) Europe.[21] Maintaining competence in European customs now became a priority for the colonial elite, including adhering to western standards of dress. As a result, by the early twentieth century it was no longer deemed respectable for European women—certainly those living in large cities with substantial European populations like Semarang—to appear in public in *sarong-kebaya*. It was relegated to the status of *négligée*, something appropriate for the home and worn in the company of intimates.[22]

The authors of a history of (Indo-)European dress in the Indies have argued that in the early twentieth century "European girls wore the *sarong-kebaya* only in order to 'dress up'."[23] Indeed, in the vast majority of family photographs from the period, particularly formal portraits, European children wore forms of European dress. In informal family snaps, outfits that were specifically developed as playsuits for the tropics, such as the *tjelana monjet* (monkey suit), were also common. Photographs of European children dressed in *sarong-kebaya* are rare. In a search of some 5,000 digitized photographs in the KIT (Koninklijk Institute voor de Tropen, Amsterdam) and KITLV collections, I found only eight that showed European children dressed in the clothes of indigenous people. Only one showed children explicitly dressed up as household servants.[24] In all those examples, the blouse worn by girls is invariably the white variety that was the hallmark of (Indo-)European women.[25] The Etje-Addy photograph is exceptional in that it shows the girls wearing the patterned blouses worn only by commoner Javanese women—the kind of women who, in the domestic sphere of Europeans, were usually encountered as servants: cooks, seamstresses or nannies.[26]

The *babu* (nanny) was an ambiguous figure in the European imagination of the late-colonial era. On the one hand, Europeans who had been children in her care often remembered her fondly as a doting surrogate mother. By contrast, interviews conducted in the postcolonial era with former servants reveal that, in their own memory, their role in European households was as workers, not as family members.[27] Even the most touching photographic portraits of nannies with their young charges reveal how careful photographers and parents were to clarify that these women were far from equivalent with the (European) mother of the child in the household—in this instance, through posture and gaze (Fig. 9.2). While looked upon indulgently and held secure by her *babu*, the little girl confidently exchanges glances with the photographer. Moreover, she stands while the nanny sits (a standard representation of mistress-servant hierarchies in Javanese-colonial visual culture) and rests a hand on the woman's shoulder—an inversion of the body orientations that are more usually seen in European mother-daughter photographs of the period.

As Elsbeth Locher-Scholten and Ann Laura Stoler have explained, pamphlets and prescriptive literature for Europeans journeying to the Indies warned them against leaving children unsupervised with their servants. Nannies in particular were suspected of promiscuity, and of corrupting the innocence of European children through imparting inappropriate sexual knowledge. The medical literature of the period assumed that Javanese women—much like other indigenous women in equatorial colonies—were biologically and environmentally determined toward wantonness by virtue of their race and residence in the tropics.[28]

There is a friction, then, in the photograph of two ostensibly innocent white girl wearing *sarong-kebaya*, a dress associated with a subordinate, licentious class of "Other" woman whom they were supposed one day to employ and regulate, not emulate. That frisson is intrinsic to contemporary European representations of children. In the late nineteenth century, photography in Europe developed alongside a historically novel, utopian middle-class conception of childhood as innocent.[29] Photography captured youth before it "slipped away." The representation of children in photographs was thus, as Christopher Wright argues, "partially based on an awareness of the adult sexuality that is missing or latent."[30] Indeed, the sexuality of the *babu* referent-figure in the Etje-Addy photograph is heightened by the presence of the dolls, which evoke the reproductive potential of the little girls. While Etje and Addy's ethnic purity is maintained (the dolls are white,

Figure 9.2: Studio Charls & Co., Portrait of Antoinette Westerman and her *babu*, 1915/16. Source: KIT Tropenmuseum Amsterdam, inv. no. 60027454.

not brown), it is contingent, in the multi-ethnic Indies, on reproducing their whiteness and middle-class prospects even in the innocence of childhood.

Two things constrain the sexual burden of white colonial femininity that the children bear and makes their transgressive dress benign. The first is their tender age. Their minority exempts the girls from the more damaging connotations that the Javanese costume would have had for adult Dutch women of their class. The whole album works to labor the point of Etje's childhood, dwelling on the progress of time by dating the photographs that show her grow from infancy, before stopping abruptly when she reaches the age of eleven. Perhaps other albums treat her later years. In this "chapter" of her life, however, Etje's development is arrested at puberty, on the threshold between childhood and adulthood, before her reproductive potential becomes biological reality.

A motif of miniaturization is the second limit on the dangers of miscegenation and class slippage inherent in the costuming pictured. The diminutive size of Etje and Addy, the presence of the dolls (which serve as reminders of the girls' immaturity while representing small people themselves), and the framing of the moment in a hand-sized photograph are all repetitions on this theme. As Susan Stewart has demonstrated, miniaturization has a long history in European material culture, where it has been associated with nostalgia and expressions of power, chiefly through reducing, fixing, and manipulating properties.[31] In late-colonial culture, miniatures abounded: small-scale Indies villages were constructed for display at museums that trained Dutch officials bound for the colonies in ethnography, and at colonial exhibitions visited by an inquisitive European public.[32] People were similarly reduced. In 1893 a collection of dolls representing Indies natives "types" was given by elite Dutch and Javanese women from the Indies to the young Princess Wilhelmina to avail the future monarch of the ethnic groups that populated her oldest and most lucrative colony.[33]

In the Etje-Addy photograph, it is not indigenous people who are miniaturized for a colonial gaze. Rather, it is the nature of elite European femininity (and its alterity—in this context, subordinate Javanese womanhood) that is under scrutiny. In the photograph of the two children these ethnic, class, and gender categories are reduced (in both senses of the word: trimmed to their essences, stripped of their power)[34] and viewed together, as a paradox. The little girls and the photograph of them are smaller than life, manageable objects over which the parent/photographer has privileged oversight.[35] The Etje-Addy photograph captures transgressive dress under parental guidance, at a life-stage when Dutch girls in early twentieth-century Java were beginning their instruction in social boundaries, but not in the explicit modes that were suitable for older children. Rather, in a light-hearted spirit, where the class and ethnic dissonances of the costume against the bodies of Etje and Addy are the essence of the joke, and where disavowal of the Javanese is the object of the lesson.

Memoir: An Indo-European Woman as *Serimpi* Dancer

My second vignette involves a near contemporary of Etje Wilkens named Marguerite Lanzing who was born in 1907 near Kediri, East Java. Their closeness in age is where the similarities between the two girls' dalliances with Javanese costume ends. Marguerite was the brown-skinned daughter of a Dutch father and an Indo-European mother, and thus a member of Java's *mestizo* society. Her family were middle-class people who could afford to educate her well. Indeed, it was as a 20-year-old "finishing"[36] her schooling in Europe that she appeared twice in public dressed in a Javanese *serimpi* costume, an outfit worn by court dancers who performed at Central Java's palaces on special occasions (Fig. 9.3).[37] The class of Javanese woman Marguerite briefly passed as was therefore elevated far *above* the subordinate *babu* that Etje and Addy imitated.

By her own account—given in her autobiography, *Memoirs of an Indo Woman: Twentieth Century Life in the East Indies and Abroad* (1993)—Marguerite's appearance in the garb of a *serimpi* dancer was met with great acclaim among her European friends. The memoir recounted, in chronological order, her memories of an idyllic childhood; her education at the prestigious Dutch *Hogere Burger School* in Surabaya in the early 1920s; travel to Switzerland, Germany and England between 1926 and 1928; her secretarial work for the BPM (*Bataviasche Petroleum Maatschappij*) upon return to the Indies; her marriage in the mid-1930s to an Indo-European man, Henk Schenkhuizen; and the deprivations of the Japanese occupation in the early 1940s, during which first her husband and later, separately, she and her children were imprisoned. After the liberation from the Japanese the Schenkhuizen family was reunited, but then the revolution began. Marguerite passes relatively quickly over the Indonesian National Revolution and says little about the first years of the independent Republic. For her, the end of her "Indies" life commenced in 1957 when, during a family holiday to the Netherlands, President Soekarno's nationalization of Dutch assets and expulsion of Dutch passport-holders saw the Schenkhuizens barred from re-entering Indonesia. They joined the hundreds of thousands of other "repatriates" from the former Indies and lived for several years, unhappily, in the Netherlands, before emigrating to California in 1963.[38]

Marguerite Schenkhuizen's memoir, then, belongs to a category of postcolonial literature that recounts the often painful lived experiences of decolonization and diaspora, one shared by some 300,000 Europeans and Indo-Europeans from the former Netherlands Indies.[39] As I have detailed elsewhere,[40] despite its ostensibly simple narrative style and structure, Marguerite's memoir gives a complex account of what it was to be an Indo-European woman in both the late-colonial period and the recent post-colonial past. While she is careful to represent the first half of her life in the Indies as one that shaped her into a "modern," educated, worldly woman, and that endowed her with confident facility in both European and Indo-European society, a historically sensitive reading of the memoir reveals how the peculiarly colonial nature of her identity was profoundly challenged by

Figure 9.3: *Serimpi* dancers in the *kraton* (palace) of Paku Buwono X, Susuhunan of Surakarta, following a dance given in honor of the visit of Governor-General A.C.D. de Graeff, 22 May 1928. Source: KITLV Special Collections, Leiden University Library, Album 28, Image 11547.

the events that shattered her life when Dutch rule came to an end. During the Japanese occupation, for example, the European aspect of her heritage that had given her access to privileges in colonial society became a threat to Marguerite's life and liberty; at that moment, the physical trace of her Javanese ancestry—her dark skin—served her better, identifying her as "Indonesian" and keeping her out of the worst prison camps for Europeans. Further redefinitions of Marguerite's social status and self-conception occurred during the Indonesian revolution and her family's migration to the Netherlands and California.

Unlike the photographic parental gaze that represents the young Etje Wilkens, Marguerite Schenkhuizen represents herself textually, in autobiographical form, to recount her costuming episode. An adult, retrospective, consciously self-fashioning voice narrates her description of the events that occurred sometime between 1927 and 1928, when Marguerite stayed at a boarding house in Munich, Germany, and decided to attend a costume ball dressed as a Javanese court dancer. When the outfit arrived by mail, courtesy of her parents back in Java, Marguerite evaded paying a German import duty by persuading the customs officials that

> this was the way I dressed in the Indies, and that it was, in fact, my court costume. When they saw me, this brown-skinned, dark-haired girl, they believed me without question.... One day, when we were sitting together having a cozy chat, I shared this incident with Frau Mutti ["Mrs Mummy," the boarding house manager] and the other girls, and from then on I was "the Javanese princess," which flattered my ego no end.[41]

So pleased was Marguerite with the effect of her costume that she wore it a second time to a *künstlerfest* (artists' festival). This time, she also performed a version of the *serimpi* dance,

> ... albeit the way I had taught [it] to myself. Afterwards, I was literally mobbed by those artists. An Egyptian wanted to use me as a model for a sculpture; another man wanted to paint me; and a third wanted to teach me dance.
>
> The result was that a portrait of me in serimpi costume was hung in a collection of paintings, called the Pinacotheca [*sic*], in Munich.[42]

It is significant that Marguerite chose the dress not of a Javanese commoner for her German appearances, but of a courtier. While European anthropologists and ethnographers were certainly interested in the customs of ordinary farmers and villagers in the 1920s, such people were hardly glamorous examples for emulation at a costume ball, nor were they credible models for a young woman in Europe attempting to pass as authentically Javanese. An ordinary Javanese would not have had access to the education and social circle that Marguerite enjoyed. For a growing number of indigenous aristocrats and officials, on the other hand, participation in the European "migration circuit" through education and travel was, as Ulbe Bosma points out, increasingly common in the early twentieth century—but chiefly for men, very rarely their mothers, sisters or daughters.[43] Marguerite therefore chose the right class to imitate when she dressed as a Javanese courtier in Europe, but for those in the know her gender would have rendered the caper implausible. In elite colonial circles in the Indies and the Netherlands, Marguerite's costuming as a Javanese dancer would have appeared scandalously fraudulent the moment her commoner, Eurasian origins were revealed.

The success she met in Germany is accounted for by trends in European artistic and popular culture, where fascination for things Javanese was peaking in the 1920s. As Matthew Isaac Cohen has shown, Javanese dance in particular emerged in this period as a new way for Europeans to explore "Otherness."[44] A number of exotic dancers claiming to be Javanese (a false claim in all cases but one) made a name for themselves in Europe during the first three decades of the twentieth century, and as a consequence girls often attended fancy dress balls as Javanese dancers and princesses. A German-Dutch-Javanese dancer who performed under the name Takka-Takka was active in Germany when Marguerite Schenkhuizen was there. Soon after she left Europe a couple of films with Javanese themes were released, both starring Greta Garbo: *Wild Orchids* (1929), which was set on Java, and *Mata Hari* (1931), a film about the infamous Dutchwoman who was accused of espionage. Mata Hari (or Margaretha Geertruida Zella McLeod) was the most notorious of Javanese impersonators, having made her Paris debut as an exotic dancer in 1905. Unlike the other performers of her era, her claims to Javanese authenticity were at least partially supported by actual experience of the Indies, where she had lived as the wife of a colonial army officer between 1897 and 1902.[45]

In a climate where urbane European theater, film, festival, gallery, and dance-hall audiences eagerly sought encounters with Java (or rather, a particular idea of it), Marguerite Schenkhuizen's exotic appearance, direct experience of the "East," and access to "authentic" Javanese accoutrements—all tempered by her competence in European languages and customs—

amounted to a significant store of cultural capital that could be cashed for celebrity (albeit, in Marguerite's case, modest and short-lived).

Much has been written about the social vulnerability of Indo-Europeans who did not adequately demonstrate their "Europeanness" in public,[46] but Marguerite Schenkhuizen's triumphant story of skirting (quite literally) with racial alterity serves as a reminder of how the ambiguities of being Indo-European could also, in some contexts, be empowering. For women especially, deliberate "masquerades" as either European or Asian could indicate social agency through active negotiation of multiple possible identities.[47] Significantly, the prerogative of dressing either as "Native" or "European" in public was one that Indo-Europeans like Marguerite Schenkhuizen shared with male Javanese aristocrats and officials. Europeans, as discussed above, had barred themselves from wearing indigenous dress in public. For men of the civil service, this exclusion was even official. High-born, unmarried Javanese women with some western education could wear western frocks, but once they married they were expected to appear publicly in "traditional" attire. Only elite Javanese men, especially those who were western-educated and traveled in Europe, wore European costume frequently.[48] In the Javanese courts, John Pemberton has argued, the privilege of "dressing Dutch" (which was not reciprocated by Dutch officials "dressing Javanese") was "an act of cultural transvestitism" that empowered aristocrats and co-opted the Dutch into Javanese court ceremony, rather than the other way around.[49] More generally, Rosalind Morris has argued that, in the late-colonial period, sartorial flexibility was a mark of Southeast Asian kingship that almost never extended to male European viceroys or monarchs.[50]

Certainly, the public wearing of western dress was governed by protocols pertaining to audience and occasion, as Arnout H.C. van der Meer's chapter shows in this volume. These regulations rankled with some Javanese elites. Pangéran Ario Achmad Djajadiningrat (1877–1943), Regent of Serang and a founding member of the *Volksraad* (Council of the Indies), recorded one such resentment in his memoirs. In 1929 he fulfilled part of his father's dying wish by being granted an audience with Queen Wilhelmina in the Netherlands. The triumph was marred by one regret: that he was not able to wear the full ceremonial attire of a Sundanese Regent, as protocol demanded that he be received in European costume.[51]

For Indo-European women like Marguerite Schenkhuizen who belonged to a middle class and occupied a *mestizo* social realm, sartorial options were more flexible than for elite Europeans or Javanese aristocrats. And yet it was familiarity with both cultures that gave Marguerite social mobility in the colonial period, not just in the Indies but also in Germany, where her ability to pass as Javanese—however incredible it might have appeared to colonial "insiders"—was to her social advantage among "outsiders." She did not make the connection herself in the memoir, but Marguerite's cross-dressing episode can be read as a dress rehearsal for a more critical deception that she had to pull off to hostile outsiders. Her ability to pass as a Javanese woman to Japanese authorities in the 1940s not only extended her liberty by keeping her out of the "European" camps, perhaps it also saved her life.

Slipping Back into Something More Quotidian

The social acceptability of both costuming episodes I have examined here relied on the transience and alterity of the acts represented. The exotic clothes had to be exposed as belonging to "Other" women, and only temporarily. Although each example was transgressive, the shock of dissonance between costume and identity was neutralized by revealing the slippage—even in the absence of an actual costume change—from exotic (Javanese) to quotidian (European) in front of the contemporary audiences who viewed the photograph and the performance.

In the Etje-Addy photograph, this revelation was comic and nostalgic, and defined European femininity by constraint. The image of the two little girls in *sarong-kebaya* simultaneously heightened and contained the discrepancies between child and adult knowledge (about sexuality, gender roles, racial, and class hierarchies) and responsibilities the girls had yet to "grow into" (maintaining distinctions between white and brown, mistresses and servants). The vision of childhood's end—of little charges becoming mistresses in their own right—was at the core of the photograph's nostalgic appeal to doting parents. Later, it was at the heart of postcolonial reinterpretations of the image as a metaphor for a lost, colonial golden age.

In the *serimpi* vignette from Marguerite Schenkhuizen's memoir, the revelation of the exotic-to-quotidian slippage was amazing and amusing, and defined European femininity in more empowering terms. Although the persistent external imposition of racial classifications on Schenkhuizen's more complex understanding of herself proved oppressive later in her life, in this early instance, it was an exercise in agency that led to her dressing as a *serimpi* dancer. Significantly, unlike Etje Wilkens, Schenkhuizen succeeded in deceiving some of her audience into believing her to be a Javanese princess, and did not reveal in her book whether her "European" identity was ever entirely disclosed to those viewers most enchanted with her. In that regard, her costuming capitalized on an image of Java that was prevalent in Europe in the 1920s, rather than on the Java that she and other Indies intimates were familiar with. Her age (she was a young woman rather than a child), situation (living away from her parents in a country where things Javanese were exotic and in vogue) and authorial voice (she recounted the episode on her own terms in a memoir for a postcolonial audience) shape a triumphant narrative of transgressive dress, in which Schenkhuizen turned dark skin and experience with Javanese culture to her social advantage.

Notes

1. Pamela Pattynama, "Herinnerend Indië: Autobiografische teksten van Indische migrantenschrijvers," [Remembering the Indies: Autobiographical texts by Indies migrant writers] *Tydskrif vir Nederlands en Afrikaans* 10, no. 2 (2004): 270–84; Elizabeth Edwards, *Raw Histories: Photographs, Anthropology and Museums* (Oxford: Berg, 2001), 6, 14.
2. Jean Gelman Taylor, "Official photography, costume and the Indonesian Revolution," in *Women Creating Indonesia: The First Fifty Years*, ed. Jean Gelman Taylor (Clayton, VIC: Monash Asia Institute, 1997), 91–126; Jean Gelman Taylor, "Costume and gender in colonial Java, 1800–1940," in *Outward Appearances: Dressing State and Society*, ed. Henk Schulte Nordholt (Leiden: KITLV Press, 1997), 85–116; Jean Gelman Taylor, "Identity, nation and Islam: A dialogue about men's and women's dress in Indonesia," in *The Politics of Dress in Asia and the Americas*, ed. Mina Roces and Louise Edwards (Brighton and Portland: Sussex Academic Press, 2007), 101–20; Elsbeth Locher-Scholten, "Summer dresses and canned food: European women and western lifestyles" and "'So close and yet so far': European ambivalence towards Javanese servants," in *Women and the Colonial State: Essays on Gender and Modernity in the Netherlands Indie 1900–1942* (Amsterdam: Amsterdam University Press, 2000), 85–120 and 121–50, respectively. See also the important Dutch publication by Dorine Bronkhorst and Esther Wils, *Tropenecht: Indische en Europese kleding in Nederlands-Indië* [Authentically 'tropics': Indies and European clothing in the Netherlands East Indies] (Den Haag: Stichting Tong Tong, 1996).
3. Jean Gelman Taylor, *The Social World of Batavia: European and Eurasian in Dutch Asia* (Madison, WI: University of Wisconsin Press, 1983).
4. On the importance of class in determining "Europeanness" in the Indies, see Ulbe Bosma and Remco Raben, *Being 'Dutch' in the Indies: A History of Creolisation and Empire, 1500–1920*, trans. Wendie Shaffer (Athens, Ohio: Ohio University Press, 2008); Ulbe Bosma, *Indiëgangers: Verhalen van Nederlanders die naar Indië trokken* [Indies Emigrants: Stories of Netherlanders who journeyed to the Indies] (Amsterdam: Bert Bakker,

2010). On the nature of racial hierarchies in the Indies, see Ann Laura Stoler, *Race and the Education of Desire: Foucault's 'History of Sexuality' and the Colonial Order of Things* (Durham and London: Duke University Press, 1995); Ann Laura Stoler, *Carnal Knowledge and Imperial Power: Race and the Intimate in Colonial Rule* (Berkeley, Los Angeles, London: University of California Press, 2002). On the intersections between race, class, education, and employment in determining opportunity, see Bart Luttikhuis, "Beyond race: Constructions of 'Europeanness' in late-colonial legal practice in the Dutch East Indies," *European Review of History* 20, no. 6 (2013): 539–58.

5. Igor Kopytoff, "The cultural biography of things: Commoditization as process," in *The Social Life of Things: Commodities in Cultural Perspective*, ed. Arjun Appadurai (Cambridge: Cambridge University Press, 1986), 64–94. See also Arjun Appadurai, "Introduction: Commodities and the politics of value," in *The Social Life of Things: Commodities in Cultural Perspective*, ed. Arjun Appadurai (Cambridge: Cambridge University Press, 1986), 34.
6. The book was published by Querido (Amsterdam) in 1981, the photograph appeared on page 8. In *Baren en oudgasten*, Nieuwenhuys translates the Malay term *tempo doeloe* simply as "former times" (*tijd van vroeger* in the original Dutch): 9. It is more usually translated, however, as "good old days."
7. All five books were published by Querido (Amsterdam) and are as follows: under the pseudonym E. Breton de Nijs, *Tempo doeloe* (1961), and *Batavia, koningin van het oosten* (1976) [Batavia, Queen of the East]. The *Tempo Doeloe* series consists of *Baren en oudgasten* (1981, reprinted 1998), *Komen en blijven* [Coming and Staying] (1982), *Met vreemde ogen* [With Unfamiliar Eyes] (1988).
8. Nieuwenhuys wrote a classic survey of Dutch colonial literature and culture from the Indies, *Oost-Indische Spiegel: Wat Nederlandse schrijvers en dichters over Indonesië hebben geschreven, vanaf de eerste jaren der compagnie tot heden* (Amsterdam: Querido, 1978), published in English as *Mirror of the Indies: A History of Dutch Colonial Literature* (Amherst: University of Massachusetts Press, 1982), and an autobiography under the pseudonym E. Breton de Nijs, *Vergeelde portretten uit een Indisch familiealbum* (Amsterdam: Querido, 1954), published in English as *Faded Portraits* (Amherst: University of Massachusetts Press, 1982). On Nieuwenhuys, see Peter John Koets, *Rob Nieuwenhuys: Leven tussen twee vaderlanden* [Rob Nieuwenhuys: Living between two fatherlands] (Amsterdam: De Engelbewaarder, 1982); Gerard Temoirshuizen, "In memoriam Rob Nieuwenhuys, 30 June 1908–7 November 1999," *Bijdragen tot de Taal-, Land- en Volkenkunde* 158, 2 (2002): 147–67. On the social and political marginalization of Indo-Europeans in the Netherlands in the second half of the twentieth century, see Vincent J. Houben, "A torn soul: The Dutch public discussion on the colonial past in 1995," *Indonesia* 63 (1997): 47–66; Andrew Goss, "From *Tong-Tong* to tempo doeloe: Eurasian memory work and the bracketing of Dutch colonial history, 1957–1961," *Indonesia* 70 (Oct.

2000): 9–36; Lizzy van Leeuwen, *Ons Indisch erfgoed: Zestig jaar strijd om cultuur en identiteit* [Our Indies heritage: Sixty years of conflict over culture and identity] (Amsterdam: Bert Bakker, 2008).

9. E.M. Beekman, "Rob Nieuwenhuys/E. Breton de Nijs (born 1908): Making it stick," in E.M. Beekman, *Troubled Pleasures: Dutch Colonial Literature from the East Indies, 1600–1950* (Oxford, New York: Clarendon Press, 1996), 555.
10. Nieuwenhuys, *Baren en oudgasten*, 9. See also the important analysis on nostalgia in the *Tempo Doeloe* series in Paul Bijl, *Emerging Memory: Photographs of Colonial Atrocity in Dutch Cultural Remembrance* (Amsterdam: Amsterdam University Press, 2015), 135–63.
11. It was in the 1980s, when *Baren en oudgasten* appeared, that a second generation of Indo migrants in the Netherlands was beginning to stimulate public discussion about their heritage and on the Dutch colonial past more generally: Pattynama, "Herinnerend Indië," 276; Van Leeuwen, *Ons Indisch erfgoed*, 343. On the social and cultural impact of the *Tempo Doeloe* series more generally in the Netherlands, see Pamela Pattynama, "Collective memory: The interactions between literature, museums, cinema and photography," in *The Netherlands East Indies at the Tropenmuseum: A Colonial History*, ed. Susan Legêne and Janneke van Dijk (Amsterdam: KIT Publishers, 2011), 164–6; Pamela Pattynama, "*Tempo Doeloe* nostalgia and *brani* memory community: The IWI Collection as a postcolonial archive," *Photography and Culture* 5, no. 3 (2012): 274. An "answer" to the series, consisting of responses to the photographs from people acquainted with Nieuwenhuys, provides more recent reflections on their significance: A.N. Paasman and Rob Nieuwenhuys, eds., *Met andere ogen: Dertig vrienden over de fotoboeken van Rob Nieuwenhuys* [With other eyes: Thirty friends on the photo books of Rob Nieuwenhuys] (Amsterdam: Querido, 1998).
12. Bijl also notes the conflation of childhood with nostalgia in colonial photographs from the former Indies. *Emerging Memory*, 141.
13. Elizabeth Edwards and Janice Hart, "Introduction: Photographs as objects," in *Photographs, Objects, Histories: On the Materiality of Images*, ed. Elizabeth Edwards and Janice Hart (London and New York: Routledge, 2004), 1–15.
14. KITLV = *Koninklijk Institute voor Taal-, Land- en Volkenkunde* (Royal Netherlands Institute of Southeast Asian and Caribbean Studies).
15. Pattynama, "*Tempo doeloe* nostalgia."
16. Ibid., 267; see also Pamela Pattynama, "Interracial unions and the Ethical Policy: The representation of the everyday in Indo-European family photo albums," in *Photography, Modernity and the Governed in Late-Colonial Indonesia*, ed. Susie Protschky (Amsterdam: Amsterdam University Press, 2015), 133–63; Pamela Pattynama, *Bitterzoet Indië; Herinnering en nostalgie in literatuur, foto's en films* [Bittersweet Indies: Memory and nostalgia in literature, photographs and films] (Amsterdam: Prometheus, 2014), 184–215.

17. Susie Protschky, "Tea cups, cameras and family life: Picturing domesticity in elite European and Javanese family photographs from the Netherlands Indies, c. 1900–1942," *History of Photography* 36, no. 1 (2012): 54–8.
18. On the *mestizo* origins of Indies society and the shift toward Eurocentrism in the second half of the nineteenth century, see the classic study by Taylor, *Social World of Batavia*. On European conceptions of miscegenation in late-colonial society, see Stoler, *Race and Education of Desire*; Stoler, *Carnal Knowledge and Imperial Power*. For arguments that productively complicate Stoler's, see Luttikhuis, "Beyond race;" and Susie Protschky, "Race, class and gender: Debates over the character of social hierarchies in the Netherlands Indies, circa 1600–1942," *Bijdragen tot de Taal-, Land- en Volkenkunde* 167, no. 4 (2011): 543–56.
19. Susan Legêne, "Uitsparing en inkleuring: Batik en koloniale beeldvorming in Nederland," [Saving and colouring: Batik and colonial image formation in the Netherlands] in *Spiegelreflex: Culturele sporen van de koloniale ervaring* [Mirror reflex: Cultural traces of the colonial experience] (Amsterdam: Bert Bakker, 2010), 131. Taylor provides a nuanced analysis of the different kinds of batik worn by upper- and lower-class Javanese women in "Costume and gender in colonial Java," 103, 105.
20. Taylor, "Costume and gender in colonial Java," 103–7, 109.
21. Bosma and Raben, *Being 'Dutch' in the Indies*, xix, 17, 295, 339–42; Bosma, *Indiëgangers*.
22. Locher-Scholten, "Summer dresses and canned food," 126–31; Taylor, "Costume and gender in colonial Java," 114; Bronkhorst and Wils, *Tropenecht*, x, 29.
23. Bronkhorst and Wils, *Tropenecht*, 109.
24. KITLV Special Collections, Leiden, Album 478, inv. no. 86975. This photograph is unusual for including boys; with the exception of only two other photographs (KITLV inv. no. 154840, KIT inv. no. 60031642), all the photographs of this category of cross-dressing were of little girls.
25. Bronkhorst and Wils, *Tropenecht*, 36–7; Taylor, "Costume and gender in colonial Java," 90. For examples of little girls in *sarong* and white *kebaya*, see KITLV Special Collections, inv. nos. 118379, 30033526, 60053771, 10023886, 30007335.
26. Locher-Scholten, "'So close and yet so far'," 89–90; Ratna Saptari, "Domestic servants in colonial times," in *The Netherlands East Indies at the Tropenmuseum: A Colonial History*, ed. Susan Legêne and Janneke van Dijk (Amsterdam: KIT Publishers, 2012), 67–80.
27. Karen Strassler and Ann Laura Stoler, "Memory-work in Java: A cautionary tale," in Ann Laura Stoler, *Carnal Knowledge and Imperial Power: Race and the Intimate in Colonial Rule* (Berkeley: University of California Press, 2002), 162–204.

28. Locher-Scholten, "'So close and yet so far'," 94–5; Stoler, *Carnal Knowledge and Imperial Power*, 67, 133–6.
29. Carolyn Steedman, *Strange Dislocations: Childhood and the Idea of Human Interiority 1780–1930* (Cambridge, MA: Harvard University Press, 1995), 19; Rudolf Dekker, *Childhood, Memory and Autobiography in Holland: From the Golden Age to Romanticism* (London and New York: MacMilland Press Ltd and St. Martin's Press Inc., 2000), 10, 113–9. On the relationship between concepts of childhood and photography see Christopher Wright, "Supple bodies: The Papua New Guinea photographs of Captain Francis R. Barton, 1899–1907," in *Photography's Other Histories*, ed. Christopher Pinney and Nicolas Peterson (Durham and London: Duke University Press, 2003), 159.
30. Wright, "Supple bodies," 159.
31. Susan Stewart, "The miniature," in *On Longing: Narratives of the Miniature, the Gigantic, the Souvenir, the Collection* (Durham and London: Duke University Press, 1993), 37–69.
32. J.L.W. van Leur, *De Indische Instelling te Delft* (Delft: Volkenkundig Museum Nusantara, 1989), 55, 91–3; Marieke Bloembergen, *Colonial Spectacles: The Netherlands and the Dutch East Indies at the World Exhibitions, 1880–1931* (Singapore: Singapore University Press, 2006), 204; Janneke van Dijk, "Models and miniatures," in *The Netherlands East Indies at the Tropenmuseum: A Colonial History*, ed. Susan Legêne and Janneke van Dijk (Amsterdam: KIT Publishers, 2011), 155–7.
33. The dolls were exhibited in the Indies and then in the Netherlands, first when Wilhelmina received them and again for her fortieth jubilee, in 1938: Rita Wassing-Visser, *Koninklijke geschenken uit Indonesië: Historische banden met het Huis Oranje-Nassau (1600–1938)* [Royal gifts from Indonesia: Historical connections with the House of Oranje-Nassau] (Den Haag en Zwolle: Stichting Historische Verzameling van het Huis Oranje-Nassau, Waanders, 1995), 96–7.
34. "Minute description reduces the object to its signifying properties, and this reduction of physical dimension results in a multiplication of ideological properties:" Stewart, "The miniature," 47–8.
35. "The miniature, linked to nostalgic versions of childhood and history, presents a diminutive, and thereby manipulatable, version of experience, a version which is domesticated and protected from contamination:" Stewart, "The miniature," 69.
36. Middle-class European and Indo-European girls like Marguerite typically had their formal schooling in the Indies at Dutch grammar schools like the HBS (*Hogere Burger School*), and were sent to Europe for the "finishing touches." These included acquiring other European languages (French, German or English), vocational skills (such as typing), and socializing with other young people of "respectable" upbringing. For Europeans from wealthier families, education in Europe began much earlier, at the elementary level, and often

culminated at university, particularly for males destined for the civil service or judiciary: Bosma, *Indiëgangers*, 90, 187, 193, 218.

37. *Serimpi* enacts a *perang tanding*, a hand-to-hand battle between two warriors, in which each fighter is represented by two dancers. Symmetry is therefore an important characteristic of the dance, as is refinement. The battle is meant to signify the struggle of humans with their passions, and also the conflict between good and evil: Miriam J. Morrison, "The Bedaya-Serimpi Dances of Java," *Dance Chronicle* 2, no. 3 (1978): 189, 203, 206–10.
38. Some 60,000 Indo-Europeans emigrated to the United States, most of them settling in California: Greta Kwik, *The Indos in Southern California* (New York: AMS Press, Inc., 1989), 1–2.
39. Pattynama, "Herinnerend Indië;" Pamela Pattynama, "Postkoloniale Erinnerung an (Niederländisch)-Indien: Koloniale Vergangenheit, kulturelle Erinnerung und Literatur," [Postcolonial memory of (the Dutch) East Indies: The colonial past, cultural memory and literature] in *Kolonialismus und Erinnerungskultur. Die Kolonialvergangenheit im kollectiven Gedächtnis der deutschen und niederländischen Einwanderungsgesellschaft* [Colonialism and memory culture: The colonial past in the collective thought of the immigrant community of Germany and the Netherlands], ed. Helma Lutz and Kathrin Gawarecki (Münster: Waxmann Verlag, 2005), 111–26.
40. Susie Protschky, "The flavour of history: Food, family and subjectivity in two Indo-European women's memoirs," *Journal of the History of the Family* 14 (2009): 369–85.
41. Marguerite Schenkhuizen, *Memoirs of an Indo Woman: Twentieth Century Life in the East Indies and Abroad*, ed. and trans. Lizelot Stout van Balgooy (Athens, OH: Ohio Centre for International Studies, 1993), 122.
42. Schenkhuizen, *Memoirs of an Indo Woman*, 122. Marguerite goes on to say that the painting was later sold, but she had no idea what happened to it after the Second World War.
43. Bosma, *Indiëgangers*. The vast majority of Indonesians studying in the Netherlands in the 1920s and 1930s were males: Harry A. Poeze, *In het land van de overheerser: Indonesiërs in Nederland 1600–1950* [In the country of the overlord: Indonesians in the Netherlands 1600–1950], Vol. 1 (Dordrecht: Foris, 1986), 166–7, 222–3.
44. Matthew Issac Cohen, "Dancing the subject of 'Java': International modernism and traditional performance, 1899–1952," *Indonesia and the Malay World* 35, no. 101 (2007): 10.
45. Ibid., 13, 14, 20. The only genuinely Javanese dancer performing in European during this period was Raden Mas Jodjana, an aristocrat who was active in Paris, Berlin, and Amsterdam from 1914 until the 1930s. He choreographed novel pieces inspired by traditional dances.
46. See especially Stoler, *Race and the Education of Desire*; Stoler, *Carnal Knowledge and Imperial Power*.

47. For a feminist development of the notion of "masquerade," see Pamela Pattynama, "Assimilation and masquerade: Self-constructions of Indo-Dutch women," *European Journal of Women's Studies* 7 (2000): 281–99.
48. Taylor, "Costume and gender in colonial Java," 97–101, 109, 112; Taylor, "Official photography, costume and the Indonesian revolution," 106–11, 117.
49. John Pemberton, *On the Subject of "Java"* (Ithaca and London: Cornell University Press, 1994), 59.
50. Photographs of the Thai King Rama IV, or Mongkut of Siam (r. 1855–68), who exchanged portraits with Queen Victoria, serve to illustrate: Rosalind C. Morris, "Photography and the power of images in the history of power: Notes from Thailand," in *Photographies East: The Camera and its Histories in East and Southeast Asia*, ed. Rosalind C. Morris (Durham and London: Duke University Press, 2009), 121–60; see also Maurizzio Peleggi, "Dressing for power: Dress and bodily practices in Thai nation-building," in *The Politics of Dress in Asia and the Americas*, ed. Mina Roces and Louise Edwards (Brighton and Portland: Sussex Academic Press, 2007), 65–80.
51. Achmad Djajadiningrat, *Herinneringen van Pangeran Aria Achmad Djajadiningrat* [Memoir of Pangeran Aria Achmad Djajadiningrat] (Amsterdam and Batavia: G. Kolff & Co., 1936), 19. My research using a protocol governing private access to Queen Wilhelmina, drafted sometime after 1918, reveals the Queen's advisors were keen to allow only the highest born indigenous elites to maintain their customary privileges in her presence, and to otherwise enforce uniformity and, arguably, subordination on other indigenous elites by restricting their sumptuary trappings: Koninklijk Huisarchief, The Hague, A50 XXa 355.

CHAPTER 10

Jazz and the British Empire: The Rise of the Asian Jazz Professional

Frederick J. Schenker

In November 1927, a former English soldier named Walter B. Harris took an eight-month tour of Southeast Asia. Throughout his trip, Harris complained vigorously about the inescapable presence of jazz, the common name for popular music in the decade after World War I. "In such British colonies as I visited," he writes, "it was ubiquitous." Harris grumbled about the noise of jazz bands in public spaces and the cacophony of gramophones playing the latest hit records in hotel rooms. "When the traveler wants jazz," he writes, "let him have the opportunity of finding it in suitable surroundings and at suitable times, but do not thrust it down his throat at all hours of the day and night. It is not conducive to the creation or maintenance of brotherly love."[1] Harris's complaint was far from unusual.[2] Many English citizens both in England and throughout the empire were concerned about the changing social mores represented by the new sounds and movements of jazz.[3] Jazz "caused offence," as John Baxendale argues, "because it latched on to the most sensitive social issues of the time—sexuality, race, [and] class."[4] The jazz craze, marked by new styles of both music and social dance, was a youth movement that seemed to reject older, established styles of social interaction. These same qualities, though, were what made jazz so desirable throughout the British Empire: jazz was the sound of a new and changing society. Consuming jazz was the latest form of leisure practice and provided a medium for the performance of the newest forms of modernity that, in a colonial setting, could signify European-ness. Dancing to jazz in cities such as Calcutta, Singapore, or Hong Kong allowed British audiences to reproduce European leisure practices and to demonstrate their supposed racial superiority by engaging with contemporary trends of Europe.

This demand for jazz, though, also resulted in new opportunities for numerous Asian musicians. In addition to the traveling white and African American bands present throughout the region, Goan, Filipino, Chinese, and Japanese performers played jazz throughout colonial Asia, entertaining American, European, and Asian dancers. Goan and Filipino musicians in particular were able to capitalize on racial stereotypes about musical talent and the desire for live bands by finding employment in many colonial cities and treaty ports throughout Asia, especially those regions within the British Empire.

In this chapter, I explore the imperial spread of jazz and propose some ways to begin thinking about its various meanings for two particular groups: European dancers and Asian performers in colonial Asia. While the interaction between these two groups might not reflect the full complexity of the jazz age in colonial Asia—especially, for example, the situation in the late 1920s when growing numbers of Asian dancers began taking over dance floors—it offers a critical lens through which to explore the various meanings of jazz as an imperial form. As with many other chapters in this volume, I grapple with how the global circulation of cultural forms—jazz in this case—can generate new meanings as they garner new participants and audiences, and work their way into various colonial cultures. This chapter examines two related facets of Asia's jazz age, the first of which concerns the actual mechanisms for musical circulation. Much of the current work on US popular culture in Asia focuses almost exclusively on the structure of US capital and American imperialism in the Philippines.[5] While the formal presence of the US in Asia as a military and imperial power was critical for the circulation of American popular culture, the British Empire was also highly influential for its dissemination throughout Asia. Without diminishing the influence of US imperialism, then, this chapter explores the ways in which the British Empire facilitated the dispersal of British audiences and markets throughout the globe provided an important matrix for the spread of jazz.

The music and dance craze of jazz followed the path of empire but it also became a medium for the performance of imperial ideologies. In particular, jazz became a way for European audiences to attempt to domesticate foreign spaces through acts of leisure, reproduce practices of Europe, and participate in a version of what they imagined to be Western modernity. The British demand for live jazz performance also created a market setting in which Asian musicians, especially Filipinos and Goans, took part in this performance of modernity by providing the latest music for European dancers. Asian musicians used this same medium as means for profitable employment that complicated their positions as seemingly static, immobile, colonized subjects. Numerous Asian musicians became jazz professionals, a category of worker that stands in stark contrast to the demanding physical work performed by other colonial laborers, whether pulling rickshaws or working in various plantations.[6] I seek to illuminate how the participation of Asian jazz musicians produced new meanings of jazz not only for these musicians, but also more broadly for the colonial societies.

Routes of Global Jazz and Its Meanings

Jazz was present throughout much of the British Empire by the conclusion of World War I. While most descriptions of jazz today depict it as an American music, and a distinctly African-American music at that, during the 1920s, jazz was not only the popular music of the US; it was also the popular music of the Anglophone empire, heard in urban centers on every populated continent. The reason for its global presence was due both to the post-WWI emergence of the US as global power and also to the well-established demand for US popular culture that was present in communities throughout the British Empire. From the mid-nineteenth century to the first decades of the twentieth, British audiences were ardent fans of American popular music.[7] In the mid-1830s, US performers brought American-style blackface minstrelsy to Britain, sparking an interest in popular entertainment from the US that only increased in intensity through the first decades of the twentieth century.[8] Along with specific music genres crossing the Atlantic Ocean, such as ragtime and Tin Pan Alley songs, modes of music consumption also moved overseas. During the 1910s, a social dancing craze struck the US and English audiences were quick to follow.[9] Dancers in England moved to the sounds of the newest hit songs from the US, creating a large market for US recordings, sheet music, and performers. By the time World War I ended, there was already a well-established trans-Atlantic circulation of sheet music, performers, and recordings of US popular music. Even the ships carrying passengers between the US and Europe were home to jazz bands, and offered an easy way for American musicians to reach an English market.[10]

After the war, British dancers were keen to have their own jazz revolution. Jazz, a term that broadly referred to most forms of popular dance music, was wildly popular among the British youth eager for a diversion after the horrors of war.[11] While jazz was mostly popular with college students and working class youth, the music gained several famous adherents who boosted the music's visibility, including the crown prince, future King Edward VIII, who was known throughout the empire both as an amateur drummer and a great lover of jazz dance.[12] The popularity of jazz in Britain was also supported through formal trans-Atlantic links. A licensing arrangement between the British Gramophone Company and the American Victor Company, for example, insured a steady supply of American Victor recordings available in Britain.[13] Successful American ensembles, such as the Original Dixieland Jazz Band, noted the demand for jazz performances in Britain. In 1919, at the height of their popularity in the US, they traveled to London for a brief tour.[14] During the 1920s, jazz changed from a novelty of noise and shock to a common form of music heard in dance halls throughout the country.

This desire for American popular song did not stop at the outskirts of London. Popular song had accompanied British travelers and colonists around the globe throughout the history of the British Empire. When British colonists first settled in the relatively remote regions of Australia and New Zealand, for example, they did their best to replicate familiar forms of popular culture and entertainment. In the mid-1800s, brass bands sprung up immediately in these two regions, providing British colonists a way to hear and perform songs from home.[15] Within several years, gold rushes and other economic opportunities drew more and more settlers to corners of the empire. By the late 1800s, many of these communities were large enough to support professional entertainers alongside their own amateur performers. Performers in Britain took note of these new audiences and began traveling the empire in hopes of reaching new markets. Touring groups that had once moved from city to city within Britain began to set out on one- to two-year tours along the imperial shipping routes to entertain colonial audiences. They followed the routes of global sea transport to form an imperial entertainment circuit that included stops throughout British India, Australia, New Zealand, and South Africa. As Michael Booth and Pamela Heckenberg argue, by the late 1800s, British groups were bringing the latest trends in popular entertainment "everywhere there was red on the maps of Empire."[16] This circuit was made possible by the British Empire: it provided both the infrastructure for travel and organization as well as the audiences eager for British entertainment. This circuit was not exclusive to British performers, though. Theater groups, minstrel shows, circuses, opera companies, and classical musicians from the US, Europe, and Russia also entertained British settlers from India to Australia.[17] While some of these performers toured the circuit because they were unsuccessful at home, hugely popular figures such as John Philips Sousa also embarked on triumphant tours of the British Empire.[18] This imperial entertainment circuit meant that when European tourists in the early 1900s took part in the popular round-the-world tours they heard music from the US at almost every port at which they stopped.[19] The empire functioned as a medium for the circulation of American popular culture mediated through British demand.

After World War I, jazz was the newest form of popular culture to circulate throughout the empire.[20] By early 1919, for example, customers could purchase Paul Whiteman records in Blantyre, Nyasaland, listen to Victor records of American musicians in Bulawayo, Rhodesia, and learn the latest jazz dances in Mafeking, South Africa.[21] In other parts of the empire, jazz followed the movements of British soldiers and civilians to urban centers and remote sites. In the early 1920s, the British press reported accounts of jazz throughout its broad empire, from an outpost in the deserts of present-day Iraq, where a group of British soldiers hauled a drum set and saxophone to their camp to entertain themselves with the latest jazz hits, to the rubber plantations of northern Borneo, where a local jazz band played for weekend dances.[22] The music also spread to cities with British populations, such as Yokohama, Japan, or Beira, Mozambique.[23] While the British Empire was hugely important for this early global circulation of jazz, it was also present throughout the American empire, much of Europe, and some of the larger cities of South America.[24] In non-British Southeast Asia, jazz was common in the Dutch East Indies and the Philippines but, because many shipping routes largely bypassed French areas, seems not nearly as widespread in French Indochina.[25] The British Empire was critical for the global spread of jazz because of its sheer size and scale as well as its organization: the infrastructure of empire allowed for the relatively easy circulation not only of fans and performers, but also of recordings, sheet music, and news of Europe's latest fads.

Jazz was especially prominent among the many urban centers along the Asian coast of the British Empire. Ships carrying passengers, goods, and ideas from Europe to the eastern edge of the British Empire formed tangible connections between various ports.[26] This route eastward was especially well traveled. European passengers traveling to Asia for work or pleasure would sail from the Mediterranean, through the Suez Canal, to Bombay or Colombo. At either of these locations, visitors would be able to dance to the latest popular music from the US played by orchestras in venerable hotels.[27] From Colombo, ships would travel either to Calcutta, Rangoon, or Singapore, from which point passengers could continue on to Hong Kong, Manila, and Shanghai. At each of these ports, as Harris noted above, travelers would find jazz. Indeed, while its presence stood out to Harris because it likely disrupted his sleep, for others its ubiquity was barely worth noting. When the Dutch novelist and poet Louis Couperus described a hotel in Hong Kong in 1923, he mentioned "a white enameled hotel bathroom, a closed-in verandah with large basket-chairs ... evening dancing and a jazz-band." Couperus felt obliged to explain why he bothered making this list. These features were, he wrote, "the usual details of a hotel deluxe, which, although you may sniff in disdain at its banality, nevertheless appeals to you as you come from the limited space of your boat."[28] Other readers, Couperus imagined, would have already assumed that a hotel would have nice furniture and a jazz band. Travelers would find jazz even outside of the port cities of Asia, far from the urban hotels, cabarets, and social clubs. In more remote areas, such as the rubber plantations of Malaya, British dancers might not be able to hire a band to perform for them, but they could move to the beat of a gramophone.[29] Thanks to the rise of portable machines, European explorers who ventured out into even more rural or unpopulated areas of Asia would commonly bring a selection of popular hits with them.[30]

Reproducing the Sounds of Empire

The spread of jazz along the routes of the British Empire was not merely a side effect, but, rather, was a critical part of the imperial project. Jazz functioned as a medium that could also help maintain and strengthen imperial structures, especially in its consumption. During the 1920s, jazz was more than just music, as it is commonly understood today. It was also a dance, an attitude, and a social practice. In the 1910s, couples dancing grew into a hugely popular practice for the youth of the US and much of Europe, a practice that became even more popular as the music and dance became known as jazz in the late 1910s. Similarly, throughout the urban centers of colonial Asia, European dancers attended hotels, cabarets, social clubs, and private homes to move together to the sounds of jazz. During one week in early December 1921, for example, Calcutta was home to a Fancy Dress Ball at the Saturday Club, a ball at the Conservatoire de Musique, nightly dances at The Dancing Club, regular Tea Dansants at the Grand Hotel, and dancing at The Exclusive Club. In addition to these events, the public could also hire dance teachers or attend concerts that quite likely also included dancing.[31] Similarly numerous dancing options could be found in cities along the Asian littoral. Throughout the urban centers of British Asia were hotels, social clubs, and cabarets, most of which were exclusive sites where white Europeans and Americans could dance to bands or recorded music. With the exception of the Philippines, where Filipino dancers embraced public jazz dancing from its first appearance in the late 1910s, white dancers formed the largest market for jazz until the late 1920s, when Asian audiences in Japan and China began to appear in public dances in large numbers.[32]

For many Europeans in colonial Asia, spending an evening dancing was likely primarily a way to relax, but I suggest that this act of pleasure also had larger symbolic implications. Namely, dancing also became an important way to try to control foreign space by recreating the leisure practices of home in a new territory. As Vicente Rafael argues, a central element in the project of empire was "colonial reproduction."[33] Europeans and Americans alike sought to transform various lands and peoples by implementing practices and habits of their home country. Along with attempting to transplant ideologies of efficiency, racial hierarchies, religion, bureaucracy, and industrial techniques, the English often struggled to maintain the social practices of home even when they were abroad. As one of George Orwell's characters in *Burmese Days* wryly notes, "Our motto, you know is, 'In India, do as the English do'."[34] These practices of reproduction, which included shaping architecture to recall English buildings and towns, resulted in a visual landscape that could look startling similar to English locales, especially in Australia and New Zealand. As Sarah Moser's chapter in this volume also demonstrates, creating cities and towns that emphasized order and sanitation was also an integral part of the British imperial process.

Historian Jeffrey Auerbach explores how these practices of reproduction, as well as the exaggerated expectations of exoticism formed by travelogues, created a culture of "imperial boredom."[35] The empire was so familiar by the late 1800s, he writes, that it ceased to be a place of excitement and exoticism for colonial bureaucrats and tourists alike. The domesticating work of these colonial reproductions, though, situates Auerbach's boredom, and leisure practices such as jazz dancing, as explicit parts of the imperial project throughout colonial Asia. Indeed, the common complaints about what one Manila resident called "the monotony of life," were the result of remaking the foreign into something familiar.[36] As Rafael argues, Europeans and

Americans transformed areas of Asia into spaces of routine, of ease and leisure, creating lives of "predictability" through the violent control, subjugation, and transformation of colonial people and places.[37] Indeed, as Auerbach writes, the complaints of boredom arose only after the task of violent subjugation turned to more mundane affairs of bureaucratic administration. Europeans and Americans turned to jazz dancing only after they found that they no longer had to spend their time dealing with more time-consuming aspects of imperial governance and control. Boredom, then, was the sign of successful domestication and subjugation. When no longer required to engage in acts of violence, military excursions, or even feel the slightest hint of danger or uncertainty, European colonials complained of their regular routine and sought to pass the time through evenings of drinking and pleasure. Dancing to jazz was a leisure practice that was both a symptom and cause of imperial boredom, of the relative success of imperial control. It was a symptom of the complete routinization and domestication of the foreign.

The endless dinner dances, *thé dansants*, and balls that occurred at fancy hotels, social clubs, and private homes not only provided a way to pass the time but also allowed colonists to continue their participation in what they imagined as Western modernity and to perform their Europeanness through the careful movement of their bodies. As various scholars have demonstrated, the notion of modernity was central to empire even as imperial violence was a critical part of modernity.[38] This engagement with modernity and European civilization took many forms. Keeping up-to-date with the latest fads of Europe, such as jazz, was an important way for Europeans in the colonies to demonstrate a continued participation in the modernity of Europe. During the first decades of the twentieth century, dance fads shifted with startling rapidity; keeping current with the latest steps and songs gave Europeans a way to perform their sophistication by showing that they were not succumbing to the tropical climate and the distance from Europe. When Europeans living in Asia first heard of jazz via newspaper reports from New York and London in the late 1910s, they eagerly awaited the arrival of this latest music and dance craze. They expected European fashions to travel quickly, so much so that even though a group of American jazz musicians performed in Singapore in July 1919, a Singaporean journalist complained that, in the Straits Settlements, "the Jazz Craze came in late."[39] Dancing to jazz not only allowed settlers to reproduce English leisure practices, but also provided them with a means to perform their participation in the latest form of Western modernity.

The Rise of the Asian Jazz Professional

Jazz, though, was not merely a medium to perpetuate the Anglophone Empire. The demand for jazz dancing also led to the creation of a new category of cosmopolitan labor: the Asian jazz professional, an often-mobile performer, whose job depended on his or her ability to stay up-to-date with the latest trends from the US and Europe. While jazz provided a way for Europeans to reproduce colonial leisure practices and perform their engagement with fashions from home, it also became a way for Asian musicians to perform their own familiarity with modernity, and to earn a profit from doing so. While couples might host intimate dance parties that relied entirely upon recorded music, large venues had to do better: they needed a jazz band. In some of the cavernous dance halls live bands were not only louder than recordings, but also were more exciting for dancers. They could provide a visual spectacle as well as sonic one and carefully tailor their performances to the dancers.

During the first decades of the twentieth century, the major hotels, cabarets, and social clubs of colonial Asia from Mumbai to Yokohama each employed their own dance orchestras to provide music for weekly dances and special events. In addition to these house bands, venues would hire musicians who were traveling through the region on tours or as bands for one of the many ships that passed through the ports. These performers came from a variety of different backgrounds and included British and Australian musicians, some of whom were returning to the region where they had been stationed during World War I. White Americans also toured through the region, including the ship orchestras made up of college youth on summer vacation who would play short engagements from Yokohama to Manila.[40] Russians fleeing their country's revolution comprised a large part of the popular music scene in Harbin and Shanghai, China, but they also traveled throughout the whole region.[41] Likely fewer than two dozen African-Americans worked in Shanghai and Manila in the early 1920s but their numbers began to increase in the second half of the decade. With a few exceptions, these groups usually featured male musicians with female singers and dancers.[42]

The supply of these British, Russian, and American ensembles, though, could not fill the demand for live bands in colonial Asia. Dancing establishments, especially those that could not afford more expensive white performers or that entertained an Asian clientele, also hired Asian musicians. In some areas, these local musicians performed for dancers exclusively within their own regions. Japanese musicians, for example, stayed within

Japan to play jazz in cities such as Tokyo, Osaka, Kobe, and Yokohama.[43] In Shanghai, the huge number of cabarets led to the employment of Chinese bands, but these groups rarely performed outside of China.[44] In contrast to these local performers, though, Goan and Filipino musicians played widely throughout colonial Asia, from Tokyo to Bombay. These musicians were in high demand both because of their familiarity with Western music traditions, learned from their long history of colonization, and their low rates. Goan musicians performed primarily in India and the Straits Settlements and went on to play an important role in spreading jazz throughout India.[45] Not surprisingly, given the long history of African-Indian interaction across the Indian Ocean, Trevor Herbert and Margaret Sarkissian also cite several examples of brass bands in British East Africa hiring Goan bandleaders.[46] Along with Goans, Filipinos were among the most ubiquitous performers of popular music across Asia. They played everywhere from Hawaii to India, including the Dutch East Indies. Similar to Goans, they largely took the less glamorous jobs in hotel dance orchestras and movie theater bands, but individual Filipino musicians were also hired to be part of European and American-led bands.[47] The American musician Claude Lapham, who was based in Shanghai during the 1930s, noted "Filipino musicians … almost inundate the East."[48] Filipinos were by far the best-known and widespread of Asian jazz musicians.[49]

Goan and Filipino musicians were popular in part because their musical skills were cast as a racial quality of natural musicality. There are countless examples of Europeans or Americans visiting Asia in the nineteenth and twentieth centuries who, similar to the American soldier Mack P. Cretcher, describe Filipinos as "a musical people."[50] American listeners, in particular, saw their ability to perform Western music not as a product of centuries of exposure to music through the Portuguese and Spanish, but as an inborn musical talent. When the Philippine Constabulary Band performed in New York City in 1909, for example, the long history of brass bands in the Philippines and Western classical music from the Spanish period was largely ignored in favor of an interpretation that favored claims of racially-based musical ability: "Men Who Seven Years Ago Had Never Seen an Instrument," one article announced, "Now Play Wagner and Beethoven."[51] In colonial Asia, these stereotypes of musical ability functioned as a kind of guarantee or mark of quality assurance that helped Filipinos and Goans secure jobs throughout the empire. Their reputations meant that they were treated almost interchangeably in areas where both could be found, specifically in India and the Straits Settlements.[52]

To be clear, though, Filipinos' race-based reputation for musicality was often supported by their skills in performance. For example, when, in July 1921, a ten-piece Filipino jazz band ended their two-year engagement at the Oriental Hotel in Kobe, Japan, the European patrons missed their musical facility.[53] The Filipino group was replaced by a band of Japanese musicians but this group only lasted two months before the Filipinos were brought back. A reporter from Kobe noted that the white patrons who danced at the hotel were not impressed with the new Japanese band: "Having been accustomed to music of highly experienced Filipino musicians, it was a matter of disappointment."[54]

The demand for dance bands and the competitive advantage of racially-based reputations, while highly problematic, provided a number of opportunities for Filipino musicians. For many poor Filipinos, playing dance music was an important way to make money. Several Filipinos who went on to become famous composers described how, in the 1920s, they played in dance bands to support their siblings and parents. The composer Felipe de Leon recalled that, when he was younger, he sought employment with a Manila dance band. He describes how he "decided that I must learn jazz. I had to learn it. I needed the money."[55] De Leon stayed in Manila to work with the Malayan Orchestra, but other Filipino musicians traveled to cities such as Shanghai, Hong Kong, and Tokyo, or played in dance bands on cruise ships to support their families.[56] While these jobs could be quite grueling, they provided Filipino musicians with economic opportunities that could carry a degree of autonomy and financial success.[57] These Asian musicians were often cosmopolitan laborers, moving from city to city, from hotel to cabaret, experiencing and helping to create spaces of leisure even though they did so as workers who catered to the demands of managers and audiences and were contractually tied to specific locations for predetermined amounts of time.[58]

Asian jazz professionals performed the sounds that could be associated with a Western modernity, creating the spaces of leisure in which Europeans and Americans would perform their supposed imperial superiority. When British dancers performed their embodiment of modernity, then, they were regularly doing so to the sounds that had been produced and reshaped by Filipinos. This empire of US and European popular culture was not applied in a unilateral direction but rather was mediated and informed by the colonial subjects of Asia. Filipino musicians participated in the production of this imperial soundscape in a number of ways, disseminating songs through the region in both public and private settings, often staying ahead of Europeans and Americans in their adoption and knowledge of the latest trends. This embrace of US popular song began decades before the jazz craze of the 1920s. For example, when American Florence Russel went to Cebu in the early 1900s, she describes her astonishment at hearing Filipinos humming a song that, she thought, "with rag-time words ...would be vastly popular in American vaudeville." When she shared her excitement with her more worldly companions, they explained that the song the Filipinos were humming was actually already a Tin Pan Alley hit titled "Hello Ma Baby, Hello Ma Honey."[59] Filipino musicians regularly played this role of experts of US and European culture and over the next decades it was not uncommon for Filipinos to serve as the producers and keepers of Western musical modernity in Asia.[60] Filipinos demonstrated that jazz was a medium that they could shape and influence; it was not a medium of empire and modernity exclusive to Europeans.

These musicians also subtly challenged imperial hierarchies in the ways in which they took advantage of the demand for jazz. They implicitly rejected other forms of imperial labor and used the infrastructure of empire to aid in their movement from city to city. By working as musicians, entertainers chose not to take part in the large pool of physical laborers working on sugar plantations and in the rubber industry. During the 1920s, tens of thousands of Filipinos worked as part of the imperial circuit at the sugar plantations in Hawaii, the fields of California, or the canneries of Alaska. Hawaii was especially enticing, and thousands of Filipinos struck out for the islands every year.[61] When they arrived, though, they often found poor working conditions that inspired regular strikes and caused many would-be laborers to return home or try to find other means of employment.[62] In comparison, the life of a musician could offer better wages and more flexibility. While long nights of performing with few breaks day after day can grow wearisome, the quality of this labor was in stark contrast to that of agricultural worker, the most common form of employment for Filipinos outside of the Philippines. Filipinos in the sugar cane plantations relied on their physical abilities and brute force, but musicians employed their specialized musical skills to participate in and produce the soundscape of modernity.

Conclusion

The infrastructure of the British Empire and the constant need to perform and maintain imperial ideology aided in the profusion of jazz throughout colonial Asia. The demand for dance music led to the rise of Asian jazz professionals who were able to use popular music as one medium to negotiate the modern world and to show their capability for self-rule. While, as the ethnomusicologist Mary Talusan has shown, actions such as these were commonly misinterpreted as demonstrating the success of Western cultural imperialism, music was nonetheless a powerful realm for challenging imperial ideologies.[63] Because of music's ability to simultaneously sound out multiple and contesting meanings, popular music has long been a site for ideological struggle, especially in colonial settings. The Asian jazz professional was able to use music performance to demonstrate his or her ability to participate in and produce a modern vernacular, to take part in and help produce the global circulation of empire and capital.

Notes

1. Walter B. Harris, *East for Pleasure: The Narrative of Eight Months' Travel in Burma, Siam, The Netherlands East Indies and French Indo-China* (London: Edward Arnold & Co., 1929), 120.
2. Much of the early writing on jazz is negative and anxious. For example, see Robert Walser, ed., *Keeping Time: Readings in Jazz History* (New York: Oxford University Press, 1999); Karl Koenig, ed., *Jazz in Print (1856–1929): An Anthology of Selected Early Readings in Jazz History* (Hillsdale, NY: Pendragon Press, 2002).
3. The upper-class of England was especially wary of jazz. Hilary Moore, *Inside British Jazz: Crossing Borders of Race, Nation and Class* (Burlington, VT: Ashgate Publishing, 2007), 17–36.
4. John Baxendale, "'… into Another Kind of Life in Which Anything Might Happen…': Popular Music and Late Modernity, 1910–1930," *Popular Music* 14, no. 2 (May 1995): 148.
5. See, for example, the special issue on American pop culture in Asia: *Inter-Asia Cultural Studies* 13, no. 4 (2012).
6. I estimate that likely close to 1,000 Filipinos were active traveling musicians between 1910 and 1930. See Frederick J. Schenker, "Empire of Syncopation: Music, Race, and Labor in Colonial Asia's Jazz Age," PhD diss., University of Wisconsin, 2016.
7. Catherine Parsonage, *The Evolution of Jazz in Britain, 1880–1935* (Burlington, VT: Ashgate Publishing, 2005).
8. Michael Pickering, *Blackface Minstrelsy in Britain* (Burlington, VT: Ashgate Publishing, 2008).
9. Albert McCarthy, *The Dance Band Era: The Dancing Decades from Ragtime to Swing, 1910–1950* (London: November Books Ltd., 1971).
10. Susie Sexton, "Paul Whiteman Made Jazz Contagious," [*American Magazine*, June 1924], in *Jazz in Print*, ed. Koenig, 320.

11. For histories of jazz in Britain, see Parsonage, *The Evolution of Jazz in Britain*; George McKay, *Circular Breathing: The Cultural Politics of Jazz in Britain* (Durham, NC: Duke University Press, 2005); Jim Godbolt, *A History of Jazz in Britain 1919–50* (London: Quartet, 1985); Chris Goddard, *Jazz Away From Home* (London: Paddington Press, 1979).
12. See for example "Late Mail News," *The Singapore Free Press*, 1 March 1922: 4.
13. Geoffrey Jones, "The Gramophone Company: An Anglo-American Multinational, 1898–1931," *Business History Review* 59, no. 1 (Spring 1985): 76–100.
14. "Home Again from London," *The Metronome* (Feb. 1921): 96; Parsonage, *The Evolution of Jazz in Britain.*
15. Trevor Herbert and Margaret Sarkissian, "Victorian Bands and their Dissemination in the Colonies," *Popular Music* 16, no. 2 (May 1997): 165–79; Duncan Bythell, "The Brass Band in the Antipodes: The Transplantation of British Popular Culture," in *The British Brass Band: A Musical and Social History*, ed. Trevor Herbert (New York: Oxford University Press, 2000), 217–44.
16. Michael R. Booth and Pamela Heckenberg, "Touring the Empire," *Essays in Theatre* 6, no. 1 (Nov. 1987): 59.
17. Matthew Wittmann, "Empire of Culture: U.S. Entertainers and the Making of the Pacific Circuit, 1850–1890," PhD diss., University of Michigan, 2010.
18. Paul E. Bierley, *The Incredible Band of John Philip Sousa* (Urbana: University of Illinois Press, 2006); John Philip Sousa, *Marching Along: Recollections of Men, Women, and Music* (Boston: Hale, Cushman & Flint, 1941).
19. Travelers commonly mentioned hearing familiar songs in various cities along their trips: for example, Mack P. Cretcher, *A Tenderfoot in the Tropics* (Topeka, KS: Crane & Company, 1918), 32; Edgar Allen Forbes, *Twice Around the World* (New York: Fleming H. Revell Company, 1912), 122; E.W. Howe, *Daily Notes of a Trip Around the World* (New York: Minton, Balch & Company, 1927), 177.
20. Much of this story has yet to be written. For literature on early jazz in South Africa and Australia, see David Coplan, *In Township Tonight!: South Africa's Black City Music and Theatre* (Chicago: University of Chicago Press, 2008); Christopher Ballantine, *Marabi Nights: Early South African Jazz and Vaudeville* (Johannesburg: Ravan Press, 1993); Andrew Bisset, *Black Roots, White Flowers: A History of Jazz in Australia* (Sydney: Golden Press, 1979); Bruce Johnson, *The Inaudible Music: Jazz, Gender and Australian Modernity* (Sydney: Currency Press, 2000).
21. "Blantyre Printing and Publishing Co. ad," *The Nyasaland Times*, 5 April 1922: 4; "Laurence and Cope ad," *The Bulawayo Chronicle*, 19 Sept. 1919: 3; "Mems," *The Mafeking Mail and Protectorate Guardian*, 29 April 1919: 2.
22. "The Desert Patrol's Commander," *The Singapore Free Press*, 3 Sept. 1925: 11; "North Borneo Notes," *The Singapore Free Press*, 21 Oct. 1925: 11.

23. E. Taylor Atkins, *Blue Nippon: Authenticating Jazz in Japan* (Durham: Duke University Press, 2001); "English Character: A German Reading," *The Beira News*, 7 Nov. 1919: 3.
24. Richie Quirino, *Pinoy Jazz Traditions* (Manila: Anvil, 2004); Mark Miller, *Some Hustling This! Taking Jazz to the World, 1914–1929* (Toronto: The Mercury Press, 2005); Bruce Johnson, "The Jazz Diaspora," in *The Cambridge Companion to Jazz*, ed. Marvyn Cooke and David Horn (Cambridge: Cambridge University Press, 2003), 33–54; Matthew Jordan, *Le Jazz: Jazz and French Cultural Identity* (Urbana: University of Illinois Press, 2010); Michael Kater, *Different Drummers: Jazz in the Culture of Nazi Germany* (New York: Oxford University Press, 2003); Susie Sexton, "Paul Whiteman Made Jazz Contagious," *Jazz in Print*, 319–20; Brown, *Babylon Girls*, 238.
25. Journalist Burnett Hershey mentions hearing jazz in Saigon in 1922, but musicians traveling along the British imperial circuit rarely ventured to Indochina. "Jazz Latitude," *The New York Times Book Review and Magazine* (25 June 1922): 8–9 [Reprinted in Robert Walser, ed., *Keeping Time: Readings in Jazz History* (New York: Oxford University Press, 1999)].
26. For more on shipping routes, see George Music, *Canadian Pacific: The Story of the Famous Shipping Line* (Toronto: Holt Rinehart and Winston of Canada, 1981); John Niven, *The American President Lines and Its Forebears, 1848–1984: From Paddlewheelers to Containerships* (Newark: University of Delaware Press, 1987); E. Mowbray Tate, *Transpacific Steam* (New York: Cornwall Books, 1986).
27. Howe, *Daily Notes of a Trip Around the World*, 181.
28. Louis Couperus, *Eastward*, trans. J. Menzies-Wilson and C.C. Crispin (New York: George H. Doran Company, 1924), 285.
29. R.H. Bruce Lockhart, *Memoirs of a British Agent* (New York: Putnam, 1932), 24.
30. Norden Hermann, *From Golden Gate to Golden Sun: A Record of Travel, Sport and Observation in Siam and Malaya* (London: H.F. and G. Witherby, 1923), 20.
31. "Amusements," *The Statesman* [Calcutta], 4 Dec. 1921: 5.
32. For more about the Chinese dancing scene in Shanghai, see Andrew David Field, *Shanghai's Dancing World: Cabaret Culture and Urban Politics, 1919–1954* (Hong Kong: Chinese University Press, 2010); Andrew Jones, *Yellow Music: Media Culture and Colonial Modernity in the Chinese Jazz Age* (Durham: Duke University Press, 2001).
33. Vicente L. Rafael, *White Love and Other Events in Filipino History* (Durham: Duke University Press, 2000), 56.
34. George Orwell, *Burmese Days* (New York: Harcourt, Brace and Company, 1950), 147.
35. Jeffrey Auerbach, "Imperial Boredom," *Common Knowledge* 11, no. 2 (2005): 283–305.

36. Adjutant E. Hannaford, *History and Description of the Picturesque Philippines* (Springfield, OH: The Crowell & Kirkpatrick Co., 1900), 87.
37. Rafael, *White Love and Other Events in Filipino History*, 58.
38. Enrique Dussel, *The Underside of Modernity: Apel, Ricoeur, Rorty, Taylor, and the Philosophy of Liberation,* trans. and ed. Eduardo Mendieta (Atlantic Highlands, NJ: Humanitics Press, 1996), 50–3.
39. "Salaries, Sterling and Otherwise," *The Singapore Free Press*, 27 May 1920: 3.
40. For example, see "Troubadors," *The Capital Times* [Madison, WI], 28 Sept. 1923: 8.
41. Field, *Shanghai's Dancing World*; Jones, *Yellow Music*; Hon-Lun Yang, "The Shanghai Conservatory, Chinese Musical Life, and the Russian Diaspora, 1927–1949," *Twentieth-Century China* 37 no. 1 (Jan. 2012): 73–95.
42. Exceptions included all-female ensembles such as the Tully Sisters, a group of four American sisters who performed along the Asian and Australian circuit beginning in 1924. "Tullys Strong For Manila," *The Manila Times,* 29 Oct. 1924: 4.
43. Atkins, *Blue Nippon.*
44. Some Chinese entertainment troupes did travel from Shanghai to Hong Kong and beyond but they were not always successful. See, for example, Jones's discussion of the failed Asian tour of Li Jinhui. Jones, *Yellow Music*, 92.
45. Bradley Shope, "Anglo-Indian Identity, Knowledge, and Power: Western Ballroom Music in Lucknow," *The Drama Review* 48, no. 4 (Winter 2004): 167–82; Naresh Fernandes, *Taj Mahal Foxtrot: The Story of Bombay's Jazz Age* (New Delhi: Lustre Press/Roli Books, 2012).
46. Herbert and Sarkissian, "Victorian Bands and their Dissemination in the Colonies," 173.
47. For example, Henry Stonor, "They Played at Raffles," *Storyville* 42 (Aug.–Sept. 1972): 217–29.
48. Claude Lapham, "China Needs American Bands," *The Metronome* (July 1936): 13, 39.
49. For a broader view of Filipino musicians, see meLê yamomo, "Brokering Sonic Modernities: Migrant Manila Musicians in the Asia Pacific, 1881–1948," *Popular Entertainment Studies* 6, no. 2 (2015): 22–37; Peter Keppy, "Southeast Asia in the Age of Jazz: Locating Popular Culture in the Colonial Philippines and Indonesia," *Journal of Southeast Asian Studies* 44, no. 3 (Oct. 2013): 444–64; Lee Watkins, "Minstrelsy and Mimesis in the South China Sea: Filipino Migrant Musicians, Chinese Hosts, and the Disciplining of Relations in Hong Kong," *Asian Music* 40, no. 2 (Summer 2009): 72–99.
50. Mack P. Cretcher, *A Tenderfoot in the Tropics* (Topeka, KS: Crane & Company, 1918), 95.
51. "Hearty Cheers for Philippine Band," *The New York Times,* 8 March 1909: 4.
52. "Classified Ads," *The Straits Times*, 21 March 1916: 28; "Committee's Report on Band Proposal," *Singapore Free Press,* 28 Aug. 1924: 7.

53. "Social and General," *The Japan Advertiser*, 27 July 1921: 5.
54. "Hotel Gets Orchestra," *The Japan Advertiser*, 14 Oct. 1921: 3.
55. Helen F. Samson, *Contemporary Filipino Composers: Biographical Interviews* (Quezon City: Manlapaz Publishing Co., 1976), 113.
56. Tony Joaquin, *Simple Glories: A Memoir* (Pasig City, P.I.: Anvil Publishing Inc., 2000), 39.
57. S. James Staley gives a bleak account of playing in Shanghai in the mid-1930s. He describes bands playing as long as nine hours with very limited breaks and poor wages: "Is It True What They Say About China?" *The Metronome* (Dec. 1936): 17, 47–8.
58. For a similar discussion of the cosmopolitanism of foreign workers in Malaysia's exclusive resorts, see Mark Davis, "At the resort: Southeast Asian tourist workers and regimes of global citizenship," *Inter-Asia Cultural Studies* 12, no. 1 (2011): 165–72.
59. Florence Kimball Russel, *A Woman's Journey Through the Philippines* (Boston: L.C. Page and Company, 1907), 116.
60. Such as when, in 1934, Filipino musicians formed the jury for a Hot Jazz Competition in Jakarta, doling out advice and prizes to the participating European bands: Allard J.M. Möller, *Batavia, A Swinging Town!: Dansorkesten en jazz bands in Batavia, 1922–1949* (The Hague: Moesson, 1987), 47–8.
61. Rick Baldoz, *The Third Asiatic Invasion: Empire and Migration in Filipino America, 1898–1946* (New York: New York University Press, 2011).
62. Amando Calleja, "Dream and Reality," *The Independent* (20 Sept. 1924): 3–4.
63. Mary Talusan, "Music, Race, and Imperialism: The Philippine Constabulary Band in the 1904 St. Louis World's Fair," *Philippine Studies* 52, no. 4 (2004): 499–526.

Contributors

George Dutton is Professor in the Department of Asian Languages and Cultures at UCLA and Director of the UCLA Center for Southeast Asian Studies. He is a specialist in early modern Vietnamese social and intellectual history, and has written on Vietnamese Catholicism, social movements, historiography, and colonial era print culture. He is the author of *A Vietnamese Moses: Philiphe Binh and the Geographies of Early Modern Catholicism* (University of California Press, 2017), winner of the inaugural Fondação Oriente Book Prize for 2017, and *The Tay Son Uprising: Society and Rebellion in Eighteenth Century Vietnam* (University of Hawai'i Press, 2006). He is also editor of *Voices of Southeast Asia* (M.E. Sharpe, 2014), a sourcebook of literary texts spanning a millennium of Southeast Asian history and co-editor of *Sources of Vietnamese Tradition* (Columbia University Press, 2012), which was named a *Choice* outstanding title.

H. Hazel Hahn is Professor of History at Seattle University. She is the author of *Scenes of Parisian Modernity: Culture and Consumption in the Nineteenth Century* (Palgrave Macmillan, 2009) and co-editor of *Architecturalized Asia: Mapping a Continent through History* (Hong Kong University Press & University of Hawai'i Press, 2013), named a *Choice* outstanding title. She is writing a monograph on nineteenth-century travel cultures, and another monograph on the urban history of French Indochina. Her publications include: "Rounded Edges: Modernism and Architectural Dialogue in Ho Chi Minh City," *ABE Journal: Architecture Beyond Europe* (2017); and "Transportation Catastrophes and Travel Imaginaries in the French Mass Illustrated Press, 1890–1914," in *Tourism Imaginaries at the Disciplinary Crossroads: Place, Practice Media*, ed. Maria Gravari-Barbas and Nelson Graburn (Ashgate, 2016).

Caroline Herbelin is Assistant Professor of Asian History at Université de Toulouse 2-Jean-Jaurès. She is the author of *Architectures du Vietnam Colonial*

(INHA-CTHS, 2016), which won the 2017 Alf Andrew Heggoy Book Prize. She is editor and co-editor of several volumes including *Indochine, des territoires et des hommes* (Gallimard, 2013), *Arts du Vietnam, Nouvelles Approches* (Presses Universitaires de Rennes, 2015), and a special issue of the journal *Architecture Beyond Europe*, focused on Southeast Asia (2017). Her publications include: "In Search of 'Indochinese Style': Between Southeast Asian Synecdoche and Colonial Boundaries," in *Architecturalized Asia*, ed. Vimalin Rujivacharakul et al. (2013), and "Changements et opportunités dans l'architecture en Indochine pendant la période de Vichy," *French Colonial History* (2013).

Sarah Moser is Associate Professor of Geography at McGill University. Her research examines how national, religious, and ethnic identities shape cities in Southeast Asia and the Muslim world more broadly. Her current work investigates the global emergence of supra-national religious and ethnic identities and how they are manifested in urban form and used to serve secular nation-building purposes. In particular, she examines emerging pan-Islamic identity, the "Arabization" of Muslim identity and the effect these broad trends are having on urban areas. Her publications include *New Master-Planned Cities, Islam, and Identity* (Routledge, 2019); *The Research Handbook on Asian Cities* (Edward Elgar, 2018); and "Forest City, Malaysia, and Chinese Expansionism," *Urban Geography* (2018).

Dawn Odell is Associate Professor of Art History at Lewis & Clark College. Her research focuses on the exchange of material goods and artistic practices between Asia and Europe in the early modern period, with particular emphasis on the Dutch engagement with China. Recent publications include essays on the domestication of Chinese porcelain in the Netherlands, Chinese poetic painting and Dutch book arts, and material culture in eighteenth-century Jakarta. She is currently working on a book about the art collecting practices of Andreas Everardus van Braam Houckgeest, an employee of the Dutch East India Company and naturalized citizen of the United States. The project focuses on the display of van Braam's collection of Chinese art in eighteenth-century Philadelphia.

Susie Protschky is a Senior Lecturer in Modern History at Monash University (Melbourne, Australia). She researches on colonialism and visual culture, with a special focus on photography. She is the author of *Images of the Tropics: Environment and Visual Culture in Colonial Indonesia* (KITLV

Press/Brill, 2011) and editor of *Photography, Modernity and the Governed in Late-Colonial Indonesia* (Amsterdam University Press, 2015). Her last project focused on monarchy and empire, and the forthcoming monograph is *Photographic Subjects: Monarchy, Mass Photography and the Dutch East Indies* (Manchester University Press). Her current project, supported by an Australian Research Council Discovery Grant (2017–19), is "Disasters, Human Suffering and Colonial Photography."

Matthew Schauer is Assistant Professor of History at Oklahoma State University since 2015. He was a Post-Doctoral Fellow at Boston College from 2013 to 2015. He received his PhD in History at University of Pennsylvania in 2012. His book project examines how administrators in British Malaya, during the late nineteenth and early twentieth centuries, used amateur ethnological knowledge and policy models from adjacent colonies to inform imperial social engineering programs involving the domestic education of Malay girls, public health initiatives, and "handicrafts" education. He has published on gender and education in British Malaya and the Philippines in the *Journal of World History* and on popular ethnology and exploration in Sarawak, Borneo.

Frederick J. Schenker is a Postdoctoral Teaching Fellow in Music at St. Lawrence University. He received a PhD in ethnomusicology at the University of Wisconsin-Madison in 2016. His current book project is based on his dissertation, "Empire of Syncopation: Music, Race, and Labor in Colonial Asia's Jazz Age," which received the 2016 Wiley Housewright Dissertation Award from the Society for American Music. His publications include "Jazz Freedoms: Balkan Rhythm, Race, and World Music," *Jazz Perspectives* (2016) and a forthcoming article in the *Journal of the Society for American Music.*

Benita Stambler served as the Asian Art Coordinator at The Ringling Museum of Art in Sarasota, Florida from 2010 to 2016, where she researched and curated an exhibition of photographs from Ceylon. She has an MA in Asian Studies from New York University and a PhD from the University at Albany. She was an adjunct faculty member in the Cultural Studies Department of the Center for Distance Learning, Empire State College, State University of New York from 1996 to 2013, teaching courses on Asia. In 2012 she was awarded a grant to conduct research on colonial-era photography in Sri Lanka. Her articles on photography in Ceylon have appeared in *Trans-Asia Photography Review* and *The Journal of Early Popular Visual Culture*.

Arnout H.C. van der Meer is Assistant Professor of History at Colby College. He received his PhD in History from Rutgers University in 2014 and is specialized in Global and Comparative History, Indonesian History, and the History of European Colonialism and Imperialism. His book manuscript, titled "Performing Colonialism: Hegemony, Culture, and Resistance in Late Colonial Indonesia," explores the public performances through which colonial dominance was legitimized, maintained, negotiated, and contested. His current research focuses on the proliferation of colonial fairs in Southeast Asia in the first half of the twentieth century as sites of interaction and discursive spaces where Western modernity was displayed, embraced, and questioned.

Selected Bibliography

Abdo, Geneive. *Mecca and Main Street: Muslim Life in America After 9/11.* New York: Oxford University Press, 2006.

Alam, Muzaffar and Sanjay Subrahmanyam. *Indo-Persian Travels in the Age of Discoveries, 1400–1800.* Cambridge: Cambridge University Press, 2007.

Alatas, Syed. *The Myth of the Lazy Native: A Study of the Image of the Malays, Filipinos and Javanese from the 16th to the 20th Century and Its Function in the Ideology of Colonial Capitalism.* London: Frank Cass, 1977.

Alberts, Tara and D.R.M. Irving, eds. *Intercultural Exchange in Southeast Asia: History and Society in the Early Modern World.* London: I.B. Tauris, 2013.

Alpers, Edward A. *The Indian Ocean in World History.* Oxford: Oxford University Press, 2013.

Al Sayyad, Nezar, ed. *Forms of Dominance, on the Architecture and Urbanism of the Colonial Enterprise.* Aldershot: Avebury, 1992.

Allsen, Thomas T. *Commodity and Exchange in the Mongol Empire: A Cultural History of Islamic Textiles.* Cambridge: Cambridge University Press, 1997.

________. *Culture and Conquest in Mongol Eurasia.* Cambridge: Cambridge University Press, 2001.

Amrith, Sunil S. *Migration and Diaspora in Modern Asia.* Cambridge: Cambridge University Press, 2011.

Andaya, Barbara Watson and Leonard Y. Andaya. *A History of Early Modern Southeast Asia, 1400–1830.* Cambridge: Cambridge University Press, 2015.

Anderson, Benedict. *Language and Power: Exploring Political Cultures in Indonesia.* Ithaca, NY: Cornell University Press, 1990.

________. *The Spectre of Comparisons: Nationalism, Southeast Asia and the World.* New York: Verso, 1998.

Anderson, Jaynie, ed. *Crossing Cultures: Conflict, Migration and Convergence.* Melbourne: Miegunyah Press, 2009.

Appadurai, Arjun, ed. *The Social Life of Things: Commodities in Cultural Perspective.* Cambridge: Cambridge University Press, 1986.

Arnold, David, ed. *Imperial Medicine and Indigenous Societies.* Manchester: Manchester University Press, 1988.

Auslander, Leora. *Taste and Power: Furnishing Modern France.* Berkeley: University of California Press, 1996.

Avcioglu, Nebahat. *Turquerie and the Politics of Representation, 1728–1876*. Farnham, Surrey, England and Burlington, VT: Ashgate Publishing, 2011.

Bakel, Martin van, Renée Hagesteijn, and Pieter van de Velde, eds. *Pivot Politics: Changing Cultural Identities in Early State Formation Processes*. Amsterdam: Het Spinhuis, 1994.

Baldoz, Rick. *The Third Asiatic Invasion: Empire and Migration in Filipino America, 1898–1946*. New York: New York University Press, 2011.

Ballantine, Christopher. *Marabi Nights: Early South African Jazz and Vaudeville*. Johannesburg: Raven Press, 1993.

Banta, Melissa and Curtis M. Hinsley. *From Site to Sight: Anthropology, Photography, and the Power of Imagery*. Cambridge, MA: Peabody Museum Press, 1986.

Beegan, Gerry. *The Mass Image: A Social History of Photomechanical Reproduction in Victorian London*. Basingstoke, England: Palgrave Macmillan, 2008.

Barrett, Tracy C. *Chinese Diaspora in South-East Asia: The Overseas Chinese in IndoChina*. New York: I.B. Tauris & Co Ltd, 2012.

Bashford, Alison and Philippa Levine. *The Oxford Handbook of the History of Eugenics*. New York: Oxford University Press, 2010.

Bayly, C.A. *The Birth of the Modern World, 1780–1914*. Oxford: Wiley-Blackwell, 2003.

Beekman, E.M. *Troubled Pleasures: Dutch Colonial Literature from the East Indies, 1600–1950*. Oxford and New York: Clarendon Press, 1996.

Belmessous, Saliha, ed. *Empire by Treaty: Negotiating European Expansion, 1600–1900*. Oxford: Oxford University Press, 2014.

Bentley, Jerry H. *Old World Encounters: Cross-Cultural Contacts and Exchanges in Pre-Modern Times*. New York: Oxford University Press, 1993.

Benton, Lauren. *Law and Colonial Cultures: Legal Regimes in World History, 1400–1900*. Cambridge: Cambridge University Press, 2001.

________. *A Search for Sovereignty: Law and Geography in European Empires, 1400–1900*. Cambridge: Cambridge University Press, 2009.

Biedermann, Zoltán. *(Dis)connected Empires: Imperial Portugal, Sri Lankan Diplomacy, and the Making of a Habsburxfg Conquest in Asia*. Oxford: Oxford University Press, 2018.

Biedermann, Zoltán and Giorgio Riello, eds. *Global Gifts: The Material Culture of Diplomacy in Early Modern Eurasia*. Cambridge: Cambridge University Press, 2017.

Bierley, Paul E. *The Incredible Band of John Philip Sousa*. Urbana: University of Illinois Press, 2006.

Bijl, Paul. *Emerging Memory: Photographs of Colonial Atrocity in Dutch Cultural Remembrance*. Amsterdam: Amsterdam University Press, 2015.

Bisset, Andrew. *Black Roots, White Flowers: A History of Jazz in Australia*. Sydney: Golden Press, 1979.

Black, Jeremy. *Italy and the Grand Tour*. New Haven: Yale University Press, 2003.

Bloembergen, Marieke. *Colonial Spectacles: The Netherlands and the Dutch East Indies at the World Exhibitions 1880–1931*. Singapore: Singapore University Press, 2006.

Blussé, Leonard. *Strange Company: Chinese Settlers, Mestizo Women and the Dutch in VOC Batavia*. Dordrecht, Holland and Riverton, NJ: Floris Publications, 1983.

Bolton, Andrew with John Galliano, Adam Geczy, Maxwell K. Hearn, Homay King, Harold Koda, Mei Mei Rado, and Wong Kar Wai. *China through the Looking Glass*. New York: Metropolitan Museum of Art, 2015.

Bosker, Bianca. *Original Copies: Architectural Mimicry in Contemporary China*. Honolulu: University of Hawai'i Press, 2013.

Bosma, Ulbe and Remco Raben. *Being 'Dutch' in the Indies: A History of Creolisation and Empire, 1500–1920*. Trans. Wendie Shaffer. Athens, Ohio: Ohio University Press, 2008.

Bourdieu, Pierre. *Distinction: A Social Critique of the Judgement of Taste*. Trans. Richard Nice. Cambridge, MA: Harvard University Press, 1987.

Britto, Karl Ashoka. *Disorientation: France, Vietnam, and the Ambivalence of Interculturality*. Hong Kong: Hong Kong University Press, 2004.

Brockway, Lucile H. *Science and Colonial Expansion: The Role of the British Royal Botanic Gardens*. New York: Academic Press, 1979.

Brownlee, John M. "Colonial Knowledge and Indigenous Power in the Dutch East Indies." *Explorations in Southeast Asian Studies* 2, no. 1 (1998): 19–29.

Bunnell, Tim. *Malaysia, Modernity, and the Multimedia Super Corridor: A Critical Geography of Intelligent Landscapes*. London: Routledge, 2004.

Burbank, Jane and Frederick Cooper. *Empires in World History: Power and the Politics of Difference*. Princeton: Princeton University Press, 2011.

Burton, Antoinette. *At the Heart of the Empire: Indians and the Colonial Encounter in Late-Victorian Britain*. Berkeley: University of California Press, 1998.

Burton, Antoinette, ed. *After the Imperial Turn: Thinking with and through the Nation*. Durham and London: Duke University Press, 2003.

Cavanaugh, Alden and Michael Yonan, eds. *The Cultural Aesthetics of Eighteenth-Century Porcelain*. Farnham, Surrey, England and Burlington, VT: Ashgate Publishing, 2010.

Chakrabarty, Dipesh. *Provincializing Europe: Postcolonial Thought and Historical Difference*. Princeton: Princeton University Press, 2000.

Chaudhary, Zahid R. *Afterimage of Empire: Photography in Nineteenth-Century India*. Minneapolis: University of Minnesota Press, 2012.

Checkland, Olive. *Japan and Britain after 1859: Creating Cultural Bridges*. London and New York: Routledge Curzon, 2003.

Cherry, Gordon E. *The Evolution of British Town Planning*. Leighton Hill: Leighton Buzzard, 1974.

Chong, Alan and Noriko Murai with Christine M.E. Guth, Louise Allison Cort, Greg M. Thomas, Stanley Abe, Haejeong Hazel Hahn, and Pedro Moura Carvalho. *Journeys East: Isabella Stewart Gardner and Asia*. Penzance, UK: Periscope Publishing, 2009.

Clémentin-Ojha, Catherine and Pierre-Yves Manguin. *A Century in Asia: The History of the École Française d'Extrême-Orient, 1898–2006*. Trans. Helen Reid. Singapore: Editions Didier Millet; Paris: Ecole française d'Extrême-Orient, 2007.

Clothey, Fred W. *Ritualizing on the Boundaries: Continuity and Innovation in the Tamil Diaspora*. Columbia, SC: The University of South Carolina Press, 2006.

Codell, J.F. and D.S. Macleod, eds. *Orientalism Transposed: The Impact of the Colonies on British Culture*. Farnham, Surrey, England and Burlington, VT: Ashgate Publishing, 1998.

Codell, Julie F., ed. *Transculturation in British Art, 1770–1930*. Farnham, Surrey, England and Burlington, VT: Ashgate Publishing, 2012.

Coppel, Charles. *Ethnic Chinese in Indonesia*. Singapore: Singapore Society of Asian Studies, 2002.

Cooke, Marvyn and David Horn, eds. *The Cambridge Companion to Jazz*. Cambridge: Cambridge University Press, 2003.

Coplan, David. *In Township Tonight!: South Africa's Black City Music and Theatre*. Chicago: The University of Chicago Press, 2008.

Corrigan, Karina, Jan van Campen, and Femke Diercks with Janet C. Blyberg. *Asia in Amsterdam: The Culture of Luxury in the Golden Age*. New Haven: Yale University Press, 2016.

Crowley, John E. *Imperial Landscapes: Britain's Global Visual Culture, 1745–1820*. New Haven: Yale University Press, 2011.

Curtin, Philip D. *Cross-Cultural Trade in World History*. Cambridge: Cambridge University Press, 1984.

Cushman, Jennifer and Gungwu Wang, eds. *Changing Identities of the Southeast Asian Chinese Since World War II*. Hong Kong: Hong Kong University Press, 1990.

Daly, Patrick and Tim Winter, eds. *Routledge Handbook of Heritage in Asia*. Abingdon, UK and New York: Routledge, 2012.

Das Gupta, Ashin. *India and the Indian Ocean World: Trade and Politics*. Uttar Pradesh, India: Oxford University Press, 2004.

Davies, Simon, Daniel Sanjiv Roberts, and Gabriel Sánchez Espinosa, eds. *India and Europe in the Global Eighteenth Century*. Oxford: Oxford University Press, 2014.

Dejung, Christof and Niels P. Petersson, eds. *The Foundations of Worldwide Economic Integration: Power, Institutions, and Global Markets, 1850–1930*. Cambridge: Cambridge University Press, 2013.

Dekker, Rudolf. *Childhood, Memory and Autobiography in Holland: From the Golden Age to Romanticism*. London and New York: MacMilland Press Ltd and St. Martin's Press Inc., 2000.

Dewaraja, L.S. *The Kandyan Kingdom of Sri Lanka 1707–1782*. Pannipitiya, Sri Lanka: Stamford Lake, 2008.

Dikötte, Frank. *Exotic Commodities: Modern Objects and Everyday Life in China*. New York: Columbia University Press, 2006.

Doel, H.W. van den. *De Stille Macht: Het Europese Binnenlands Bestuur op Java en Madoera, 1808–1942* [The Silent Power: The European Colonial Administration on Java and Madura]. Amsterdam: Bert Bakker, 1994.

Dohmen, Renate, ed. *Empire and Art: British India*. Manchester: Manchester University Press, 2018.

Dussel, Enrique. *The Underside of Modernity: Apel, Ricoeur, Rorty, Taylor, and the Philosophy of Liberation*. Ed. and trans. Eduardo Mendieta. Atlantic Highlands, NJ: Humanities Press, 1996.

Dutton, George E. *A Vietnamese Moses: Philiphe Binh and the Geographies of Early Modern Catholicism*. Berkeley: University of California Press, 2016.

Dutton, George E., ed. *Voices of Southeast Asia: Essential Readings from Antiquity to the Present*. London: Routledge, 2014.

Eaton, Natasha. *Mimesis across Empires: Artworks and Networks in India, 1765–1860*. Durham: Duke University Press, 2013.

Edwards, Elizabeth. *Raw Histories: Photographs, Anthropology and Museums*. Oxford: Berg, 2001.

Edwards, Elizabeth and Janice Hart, eds. *Photographs, Objects, Histories: On the Materiality of Images*. London and New York: Routledge, 2004.

Eliëns, Titus M. and Monique van de Geijn-Verhoeven. *Domestic Interiors at the Cape and in Batavia, 1602–1795*. Zwolle; Waanders; Den Haag: Gemeentemuseum, 2002.

Elisseeff, Vadime, ed. *The Silk Roads: Highways of Culture and Commerce*. Oxford: Berghahn Books, 2000.

Evans, Hazel. *New Towns: The British Experience*. New York: Halsted Press, 1972.

Falconer, John and Louise Hide. *Points of View: Capturing the 19th Century in Photographs*. London: British Library, 2009.

Fernandes, Naresh. *Taj Mahal Foxtrot: The Story of Bombay's Jazz Age*. New Delhi: Lustre Press/Roli Books, 2012.

Field, Andrew David. *Shanghai's Dancing World: Cabaret Culture and Urban Politics, 1919–1954*. Hong Kong: Chinese University Press, 2010.

Findlen, Paula, ed. *Early Modern Things: Objects and their Histories, 1500–1800*. London: Routledge, 2013.

Fourniau, Charles. *Vietnam. Domination coloniale et résistance nationale (1858–1914)* [Vietnam. Colonial Domination and National Resistance]. Paris: Les Indes Savantes, 2002.

Foxwell, Chelsea and Anne Leonard, eds. *Awash in Color: French and Japanese Prints*. Chicago: Smart Museum of Art, The University Of Chicago, 2012.

Fusaro, Maria, Mohamed-Salah Omri, and Colin Heywood, eds. *Trade and Cultural Exchange in the Early Modern Mediterranean: Braudel's Maritime Legacy*. New York: Taurus Academic Studies, 2010.

Gans, Herbert J. *Popular Culture and High Culture: An Analysis and Evaluation of Taste.* New York: Basic Books, 1999.

Gell, Alfred. *Art and Agency: An Anthropological Theory*. Oxford: Clarendon Press, 1998.

Ghosh, Durba. *Sex and the Family in Colonial India: The Making of Empire.* Cambridge: Cambridge University Press, 2006.

Ghosh, Durba and Dane Kennedy. *Decentring Empire: Britain, India and the Transcolonial World.* Hyderabad: Orient BlackSwan, 2006.

Gompel, Dave van, Joost Hoving, and Reinier Klusener. *Furniture from the Netherlands East Indies 1600–1900: A Historical Perspective based on the Collection of the Tropenmuseum*. Amsterdam: KIT Publishers, 2013.

Gouda, Frances. *Dutch Culture Overseas: Colonial Practice in the Netherlands Indies 1900–1942.* Amsterdam: Amsterdam University Press, 1995.

Gouda, Frances and Julia Clancy-Smith, eds. *Domesticating the Empire: Race, Gender, and Family Life in French and Dutch Colonialism.* Charlottesville: University of Virginia Press, 1998.

Gordon, Stewart. *When Asia was the World: Traveling Merchants, Scholars, Warriors, and Monks who Created the "Riches of the East"*. Cambridge, MA: Da Capo Press, 2008.

Gravari-Barbas, Maria and Nelson Graburn, eds. *Tourism Imaginaries at the Disciplinary Crossroads: Place, Practice, Media*. Farnham, Surrey, England and Burlington, VT: Ashgate Publishing, 2016.

Greenblatt, Stephen, ed. *Cultural Mobility: A Manifesto.* Cambridge: Cambridge University Press, 2009.

Gunn, Geoffrey C. *First Globalization: The Eurasian Exchange, 1500 to 1800.* Lanham: Rowman & Littlefield, 2003.

________. *History Without Borders: The Making of an Asian World Region, 1000–1800.* Hong Kong: Hong Kong University Press, 2011.

________. *Rice Wars in Colonial Vietnam: The Great Famine and the Viet Minh Road to Power*. Lanham, MD: Rowman & Littlefield, 2014.

Grijns, Kees and Peter J.M. Nas, eds. *Jakarta-Batavia: Socio-cultural Essays*. Leiden: KITLV Press, 2000.

Ha, Marie-Paul. *French Women and the Empire: The Case of Indochina*. Oxford: Oxford University Press, 2014.

Hagen, Joshua and Alexander Diener, eds. *Urban Space, Place, and National Identity*. Lanham, MD: Rowman & Littlefield, 2018.

Hahn, H. Hazel. "Indian Princes, Tigers and Dancing Girls: The Tour of the Prince of Wales through India and Ceylon, 1875–1876." *Postcolonial Studies* 12, no. 1 (June 2009): 173–92.

________. *Scenes of Parisian Modernity: Culture and Consumption in the Nineteenth Century*. New York: Palgrave Macmillan, 2009.

________. "Heroism, Exoticism and Violence: Representing the Self, the 'Other' and Rival Empires in French and British Illustrated Press, 1880–1905." *Historical Reflections / Réflexions Historiques* 38, no. 3 (2012): 62–83.

________. "Tagore as a Celebrity Tourist?: Urban Planning, Tourism, and Architecture in Colonial Saigon," in *Southeast Asia's Modern Architecture: Questions in Translation, Epistemology and Power*, ed. Imran bin Tajudeen and Jiat-Hwee Chang. Singapore: NUS Press, 2018.

Hall, Catherine. *Civilising Subjects: Metropole and Colony in the English Imagination 1830–1867*. New York: Polity Press, 2002.

Hall, Catherine and Sonya O. Rose, eds. *At Home with the Empire: Metropolitan Culture and the Imperial World*. Cambridge: Cambridge University Press, 2006.

Hall, Kenneth R., ed. *Secondary Cities and Urban Networking in the Indian Ocean Realm, c.1400–1800*. Lanham, MD: Lexington Books, 2008.

Handler, Sarah. *The Austere Luminosity of Chinese Classical Furniture*. Berkeley: University of California Press, 2001.

Haneda Masashi, ed. *Asian Port Cities, 1600–1800: Local and Foreign Cultural Interactions*. Singapore: NUS Press, 2009.

Haskell, Francis. *Rediscoveries in Art: Some Aspects of Taste, Fashion, and Collecting in England and France*. Ithaca: Cornell University Press, 1976.

Headrick, Daniel R. *The Tools of Empire: Technology and European Imperialism in the Nineteenth Century*. Oxford: Oxford University Press, 1981.

Henriot, Christian and Wen-hsin Yeh, eds. *Visualising China, 1845–1965: Moving and Still Images in Historical Narratives*. Leiden and Boston: Brill, 2012.

Herbelin, Caroline. *Architectures du Vietnam colonial. Repenser le métissage* [Architectures of Colonial Vietnam. Rethinking Hybridity]. Paris: INHA/CTHS, 2016.

Herbert, Trevor, ed. *The British Brass Band: A Musical and Social History*. New York: Oxford University Press, 2000.

Herzfeld, Michael. *Anthropology Through the Looking-Glass: Critical Ethnography in the Margins of Europe*. Cambridge: Cambridge University Press, 1987.

Hight, Eleanor M. and Gary D. Sampson. *Colonialist Photography: Imag(in)ing Race and Place*. New York: Routledge, 2013.

Hitchcock, Michael, Victor T. King, and Michael Parnwell, eds. *Heritage Tourism in Southeast Asia*. Honolulu: University of Hawai'i Press, 2010.

Hodacs, Hanna. *Silk and Tea in the North: Scandinavian Trade and the Market for Asian Goods in Eighteenth-Century Europe*. Basingstoke, UK: Palgrave-Macmillan, 2016.

Hoganson, Kristin L. *Consumers' Imperium: The Global Production of American Domesticity, 1865–1920*. Chapel Hill: The University of North Carolina Press, 2007.

Hoang Anh Tuan. *Silk for Silver: Dutch-Vietnamese Relations, 1637–1700*. Leiden and Boston: Brill, 2007.

Home, R.K. *Of Planting and Planning: The Making of British Colonial Cities*. London and New York: Routledge, 2013.

Honig, Elizabeth Alice. "The Space of Gender in Seventeenth-Century Dutch Painting," in *Looking at Seventeenth-Century Dutch Art: Realism Reconsidered*, ed. Wayne Franits. Cambridge: Cambridge University Press, 1997.

Hung, Wu. *The Double Screen: Medium and Representation in Chinese Painting*. London: Reaktion Books, 1997.

Hutchins, Francis G. *The Illusion of Permanence: British Imperialism*. Princeton: Princeton University Press, 1967.

Iskin, Ruth. *The Poster: Art, Advertising, Design, and Collecting, 1860s–1900s*. Dartmouth: Dartmouth College Press, 2014.

Jackson, Anna and Amin Jaffer, eds. *Encounters: The Meeting of Asia and Europe, 1500–1800*. London: V & A, 2004.

Jay, Martin and Sumathi Ramaswamy, eds. *Empires of Vision: A Reader*. Durham: Duke University Press, 2014.

Jennings, Eric. *Imperial Heights: Dalat and the Making and Undoing of French Indochina*. Berkeley: University of California Press, 2012.

Johnson, Bruce. *The Inaudible Music: Jazz, Gender and Australian Modernity*. Sydney: Currency Press, 2000.

Jones, Andrew. *Yellow Music: Media Culture and Colonial Modernity in the Chinese Jazz Age*. Durham: Duke University Press, 2001.

Jones, Eric. *Wives, Slaves and Concubines: A History of the Female Underclass in Dutch Asia*. DeKalb: Northern Illinois University Press, 2010.

Jordan, Matthew. *Le Jazz: Jazz and French Cultural Identity*. Urbana: University of Illinois Press, 2010.

Kang, David C. *East Asia before the West: Five Centuries of Trade and Tribute*. New York: Columbia University Press, 2010.

Kang, Minsoo and Amy Woodson-Boulton, eds. *Visions of the Industrial Age, 1830–1814*. London: Routledge, 2008.

Kartini, Raden Adjeng. *Letters of a Javanese Princess*. Kuala Lumpur: Oxford University Press, 1976.

Kater, Michael. *Different Drummers: Jazz in the Culture of Nazi Germany*. Oxford: Oxford University Press, 2003.

Kaufmann, Thomas DaCosta and Michael North, eds. *Mediating Netherlandish Art and Material Culture in Asia*. Amsterdam: Amsterdam University Press, 2014.

Kennedy, Dane. *The Imperial History Wars: Debating the British Empire*. London: Bloomsbury Academic, 2018.

King, Anthony D. *The Bungalow: The Production of a Global Culture*. London: Routledge & Kegan Paul, 1984.

Knapp, Ronald G. *China's Living Houses: Folk Beliefs, Symbols, and Household Ornamentation*. Honolulu: University of Hawai'i Press, 1999.

King, Anthony D. *Urbanism, Colonialism, and the World Economy: Cultural and Spatial Foundations of the World Urban System*. London: Routledge, 1990.

King, Ross. "Re-Writing the City: Putrajaya as Representation," *Journal of Urban Design* 12 (2007): 117–38.

________. *Kuala Lumpur and Putrajaya: Negotiating Urban Space in Malaysia*. Copenhagen: NIAS Press, 2008.

Kitson, Peter J. *Forging Romantic China: Sino-British Cultural Exchange 1760–1840*. Cambridge: Cambridge University Press, 2013.

Knapp, Ronald G. and A. Chester Ong. *Chinese Houses of Southeast Asia: The Eclectic Architecture of Sojourners and Settlers*. Tokyo: Tuttle, 2010.

Koenag, Karl, ed. *Jazz in Print (1856–1929): An Anthology of Selected Early Readings in Jazz History*. Hillsdale, NY: Pendragon Press, 2002.

Kong, Lily and Brenda Yeoh. *The Politics of Landscapes in Singapore: Constructions of "Nation"*. Syracuse, NY: Syracuse University Press, 2003.

Kuklick, Henrika. *The Savage Within: The Social History of British Anthropology 1885–1945*. Cambridge: Cambridge University Press, 1993.

Kuklick, Henrika, ed. *A New History of Anthropology*. Oxford: Blackwells, 2008.

Kuruppath, Manjusha. *Staging Asia: The Dutch East India Company and the Amsterdam Theatre*. Leiden: Leiden University Press, 2016.

Lasansky, D. Medina, ed. *Archi.Pop: Mediating Architecture in Popular Culture*. London: Bloomsbury Academic, 2014.

Le Manh Hung. *The Impact of World War II on the Economy of Vietnam 1939–45*. Singapore: Eastern Universities Press by Marshall Cavendish, 2004.

Lê, Quang Ninh and Stéphane Dovert. *Saigon, 1698–1998: Kiến Trúc, Quy Hoạch = Saigon, 1698–1998: Architectures, urbanisme* [Saigon, 1698–1998: Architectures, Urban Planning]. Ho Chi Minh City and Lyon: Uy Ban Nhân Dân, Communauté urbaine de Lyon and Consulat général of France in Ho Chi Minh City, 1998.

Lee, Hock Guan and Leo Suryadinata. *Language, Nation and Development in Southeast Asia*. Singapore: Institute of Southeast Asian Studies, 2007.

Lees, Lynn Hollen. *Planting Empire, Cultivating Subjects: British Malaya, 1786–1941*. Cambridge: Cambridge University Press, 2017.

Legêne, Susan and Janneke van Dijk, eds. *The Netherlands East Indies at the Tropenmuseum: A Colonial History*. Amsterdam: KIT Publishers, 2011.

Levine, Philippa. *The Amateur and the Professional: Antiquarians, Historians, and Archaeologist in Victorian England, 1838–1886*. Cambridge: Cambridge University Press, 1986.

Lewis, Martin and Kären Wigen. *The Myth of Continents: A Critique of Meta-geography*. Berkeley: University of California Press, 1997.

Liebersohn, Harry. *The Return of the Gift: European History of a Global Idea*. Cambridge: Cambridge University Press, 2011.

Lieu, Samuel N.C. and Gunner B. Mikkelsen, eds. *Between Rome and China: History, Religions and Material Culture of the Silk Road*. Turnhout, Belgium: Brepols, 2016.

Lim, T.N. and L. Tay. *80 Years of Architecture in Malaysia*. Kuala Lumpur: Pertubuhan Akitek Malaysia, 2000.

Lim, William S.W. *Architecture, Art, Identity in Singapore: Is There Life After Tabula Rasa?* Singapore: Asian Urban Lab, 2004.

Linden, Bob van der. *Music and Empire in Britain and India: Identity, Internationalism, and Cross-Cultural Communication*. New York: Palgrave Macmillan, 2013.

Liu, Lydia. *Translingual Practice: Literature, National Culture, and Translated Modernity—China, 1900–1937*. Stanford: Stanford University Press, 1995.

Liu, Xinru. *The Silk Road in World History*. Oxford: Oxford University Press, 2010.

Locher-Scholten, Elsbeth. *Ethiek in Fragmenten: Vijf Studies over Koloniaal Denken en Doen van Nederlanders in de Indonesische Archipel, 1877–1942* [Ethics in Fragments: Five Studies on Dutch Colonial Theory and Practice in the Indonesian Archipelago, 1877–1942]. Utrecht: HES Publishers, 1981.

________. *Women and the Colonial State: Essays on Gender and Modernity in the Netherlands Indie 1900–1942*. Amsterdam: Amsterdam University Press, 2000.

Logan, William. *Hanoi: Biography of a City*. Seattle: University of Washington Press, 2000.

Manguin, Pierre-Yves, A. Mani and Geoff Wade, eds. *Early Interactions Between South and Southeast Asia: Reflections on Cross-Cultural Exchange*. Singapore: Institute of Southeast Asian Studies, 2011.

Mantena, Karuna. *Alibis of Empire: Henry Maine and the Ends of Liberal Imperialism*. Princeton: Princeton University Press, 2010.

Marchand, Suzanne. *German Orientalism in the Age of Empire: Religion, Race, and Scholarship*. Cambridge: Cambridge University Press, 2009.

McAleer, John and John M. MacKenzie, eds. *Exhibiting the Empire: Cultures of Display and the British Empire*. Manchester: Manchester University Press, 2015.

McCarthy, Albert. *The Dance Band Era: The Dancing Decades from Ragtime to Swing, 1910–1950*. London: November Books Ltd., 1971.

McCracken, Donald P. *Gardens of Empire: Botanical Institutions of the Victorian British Empire*. London and Washington: Leicester University Press, 1997.

McKay, George. *Circular Breathing: the Cultural Politics of Jazz in Britain*. Durham: Duke University Press, 2005.

Meacham, Standish. *Regaining Paradise: Englishness and the Early Garden City Movement*. New Haven: Yale University Press, 1999.

Moon, Suzanne. *Technology and Ethical Idealism: A History of Development in the Netherlands East Indies*. Leiden: CNWS Publications, 2007.

Meer, Arnout H.C. van der. "Performing Colonial Modernity: Fairs, Consumerism, and the Emergence of the Indonesian Middle Classes." *Bijdragen tot de taal-, land- en volkenkunde / Journal of the Humanities and Social Sciences of Southeast Asia* 173 (2017): 503–38.

Meisterernst, Barbara. *The Silk Roads: Silk Road Culture: Languages, Art, Material Culture, Archaeology*. London: Routledge, 2017.

Miller, Mark. *Some Hustling This! Taking Jazz to the World, 1914–1929*. Toronto: The Mercury Press, 2005.

Möller, Allard J.M. *Batavia A Swinging Town! Dansorkesten en jazz bands in Batavia, 1922–1949*. The Hague: Moesson, 1987.

Moore, Hilary. *Inside British Jazz: Crossing Borders of Race, Nation and Class.* Farnham, Surrey, England and Burlington, VT: Ashgate Publishing, 2007.

Morley, Ian. *Cities and Nationhood: American Imperialism and Urban Design in the Philippines, 1898–1916*. Honolulu: University of Hawai'i Press, 2018.

Morris, J. and S. Winchester, *Stones of Empire: The Buildings of the Raj*. Oxford: Oxford University Press, 1983.

Morris, Rosalind C. *Photographies East: The Camera and its Histories in East and Southeast Asia*. Durham and London: Duke University Press, 2009.

Moser, Sarah. "Circulating Visions of 'High Islam': The Adoption of Fantasy Middle Eastern Architecture in Constructing Malaysian National Identity." *Urban Studies* 49, no. 13 (2012): 2913–35.

________. "Globalization and the Construction of Identity in Two New Southeast Asian Capitals: Putrajaya and Dompak," in *Rethinking Global Urbanism: Comparative Insights from Secondary Cities*, ed. Xiangming Chen and Kanna. London and New York: Routledge, 2012.

________. *New Cities: Opportunities, Visions and Challenges – Cityquest KAEC Forum 2013: Summary and Analysis Report*. Paris: New Cities Foundation, 2014.

Music, George. *Canadian Pacific: The Story of the Famous Shipping Line.* Toronto: Holt Rinehart and Winston of Canada, 1981.

Nasir, Abdul Halim. *Mosque Architecture in the Malay World.* Bangi: Penerbit Universiti Kebangsaan Malaysia, 2004.

Newbury, C.W. "Patrons, Clients, and Empire: The Subordination of Indigenous Hierarchies in Asia and Africa." *Journal of World History* 11, no. 2 (2000): 227–63.

Newton, Gael. *Picture Paradise: Asia-Pacific Photography 1840s–1940s.* Canberra: National Gallery of Australia, 2008.

Ngô Huy Quỳnh. *Kiến Trúc Việt Nnam* [Architecture of Vietnam]. Ho Chí Minh City: nhà xuat ban Thành pho Ho Chí Minh, 1986.

Nguyen-Marshall, Van, Lisa B. Welch Drummond, and Danièle Bélanger, eds. *The Reinvention of Distinction: Modernity and the Middle Class in Urban Vietnam.* Heidelberg: Springer, 2011.

Niemeijer, Hendrik E. *Batavia: Een koloniale samenleving in de 17de eeuw* [A Colonial Society in the 17th Century]. Amsterdam: Balans, 2005.

Nightingale, Carl H. *Segregation: A Global History of Divided Cities.* Chicago: The University of Chicago Press, 2012.

Niven, John. *The American President Lines and Its Forebears, 1848–1984: From Paddlewheelers to Containerships.* Newark: University of Delaware Press, 1987.

Njoh, Ambe J. *Tradition, Culture and Development in Africa: Historical Lessons for Modern Development Planning.* Farnham, Surrey, England and Burlington, VT: Ashgate Publishing, 2006.

________. "Colonial Philosophies, Urban Space, and Racial Segregation in British and French Colonial Africa." *Journal of Black Studies* 38, no. 4 (2008): 579–99.

________. "The Segregated City in British and French Colonial Africa." *Race and Class* 49, no. 4 (2008): 87–95.

________. *French Urbanism in Foreign Lands*. Heidelberg: Springer, 2016.

Nordholt, Henk Schulte, ed. *Outward Appearances: Dressing State and Society*. Leiden: KITLV Press, 1997.

North, Michael, ed. *Artistic and Cultural Exchanges Between Europe and Asia, 1400–1900*. Farnham, Surrey, England and Burlington, VT: Ashgate Publishing, 2010.

Ooi, Keat Gin and Hoang Anh Tuan, eds. *Early Modern Southeast Asia, 1350–1800*. London: Routledge, 2016.

Osterhammel, Jürgen. *The Transformation of the World: A Global History of the Nineteenth Century*. Princeton: Princeton University Press, 2014.

________. *Unfabling the East: The Enlightenment's Encounter with Asia*. Princeton: Princeton University Press, 2018.

Otsuka, Ronald and Donna Pierce, eds. *Asia and Spanish America: Trans-Pacific Artistic and Cultural Exchange, 1500–1850*. Denver: Denver Art Museum, 2009.

Pairaudeau, Natasha. *Mobile Citizens: French Indians in Indochina 1858–1954*. Copenhagen: NIAS Monographs, 2015.

Palmier, Leslie H. *Social Status and Power in Java*. London: University of London, Athlone Press, 1960.

Parthesius, Robert. *Dutch Ships in Tropical Waters: The Development of the Dutch East India Company (VOC) Shipping Network in Asia 1595–1660*. Amsterdam: Amsterdam University Press, 2010.

Papin, Philippe and John Kleinen. *Liber Amicorum, Miscellanies Offered to Professor Phan Huy Lê*. Paris: École Française d'Extrême-Orient / Thanh-Niên, 1999.

Park, Hyunhee. *Mapping the Chinese and Islamic Worlds: Cross-Cultural Exchange in Pre-Modern Asia*. Cambridge: Cambridge University Press, 2012.

Parker, Charles H. *Global Interactions in the Early Modern Age, 1400–1800*. Cambridge: Cambridge University Press, 2010.

Parsonage, Catherine. *The Evolution of Jazz in Britain, 1880–1935*. Burlington, VT: Ashgate Publishing, 2005.

Peleggi, Maurizio. *Lord of the Things, The Fashioning of the Siamese Monarchy's Modern Image*. Honolulu: University of Hawai'i Press, 2002.

Pelizzari, Maria Antonella, ed. *Traces of India: Photography, Architecture, and the Politics of Representation, 1850–1900*. Montréal and New Haven: Canadian Centre for Architecture, Yale Center for British Art and Yale University Press, 2003.

Pelley, Patricia M. *Postcolonial Vietnam: New Histories of the National Past*. Durham: Duke University Press, 2002.

Phillips, David R., Anthony G.O. Yeh, and Kwi-Gon Kim. *New Towns in East and South-East Asia: Planning and Development*. Singapore: Oxford University Press, 1987.

Pickering, Michael. *Blackface Minstrelsy in Britain.* Farnham, Surrey, England and Burlington, VT: Ashgate Publishing, 2008.

Pieterse, Jan Nederveen. *Globalization and Culture: Global Mélange*, 3rd edition. Lanham, MD: Rowman & Littlefield, 2015.

Pinney, Christopher. *Camera Indica: The Social Life of Indian Photographs.* London: Reaktion, 1997.

Pinney, Christopher and Nicolas Peterson, eds. *Photography's Other Histories.* Durham and London: Duke University Press, 2003.

Pirrazzoli-t'Serstevens, Michèle. *Le Yuanmingyuan/Jeux d'eau et palais européens du XVIIIe siècle à la Cour de Chine* [The Yuanmingyuan / Water Effects and 18th-century European Palaces at the Chinese Imperial Court]. Paris: Éditions Recherche sur les Civilisations, 1987.

________. "The Emperor Qianlong's European Palaces." *Orientations* 19, no. 1 (1988): 61–71.

Ponsavady, Stéphanie. *Cultural and Literary Representations of the Automobile in French Indochina: A Colonial Roadshow.* New York: Palgrave Macmillan, 2018.

Postill, John. *Media and Nation Building: How the Iban Became Malaysian.* Oxford and New York: Berghahn Books, 2008.

Prakash, Gyan, ed. *After Colonialism: Imperial Histories and Postcolonial Displacements.* Princeton: Princeton University Press, 1995.

Protschky, Susie. "The flavour of history: Food, family and subjectivity in two Indo-European women's memoirs." *Journal of the History of the Family* 14 (2009): 369–85.

________. *Images of the Tropics: Environment and Visual Culture in Colonial Indonesia.* Leiden: KITLV Press, 2011.

________. "Race, class and gender: Debates over the character of social hierarchies in the Netherlands Indies, circa 1600–1942." *Bijdragen tot de Taal-, Land- en Volkenkunde* 167, no. 4 (2011): 543–56.

Protschky, Susie, ed. *Photography, Modernity and the Governed: Re-viewing the 'Ethical' Era in Late-Colonial Indonesia.* Amsterdam: Amsterdam University Press, 2014.

Quirino, Richie. *Pinoy Jazz Traditions.* Manila: Anvil Publishing, 2004.

Rafael, Vicente L. *White Love and Other Events in Filipino History.* Durham: Duke University Press, 2000.

Raheem, Ismeth. *Archaeology and Photography: The Early Years 1868–1880.* Colombo: The National Trust of Sri Lanka, 2009.

Raheem, Ismeth and Percy Colin Thomé. *Images of British Ceylon: Nineteenth Century Photography of Sri Lanka.* Singapore: Times Editions, 2000.

Rajagopalan, Mrinalini and Madhuri Desai, eds. *Colonial Frames, Nationalist Histories: Imperial Legacies, Architecture and Modernity.* Surrey, England and Burlington, VT: Ashgate Publishing, 2012.

Ramachandran, Ayesha. *The Worldmakers: Global Imagining in Early Modern Europe.* Chicago: The University of Chicago Press, 2015.

Ramaswamy, Sumathi. *The Goddess and the Nation: Mapping Mother India.* Durham: Duke University Press, 2010.

________. *Terrestrial Lessons: The Conquest of the World as Globe.* Chicago: The University of Chicago Press, 2017.

Rampal, Krishna G. *Sacred Structures: Artistic Renditions of Hindu Temples in Malaysia and Singapore.* Singapore: Bluetoffee, 2008.

Rappaport, Erika. *A Thirst for Empire: How Tea Shaped the Modern World.* Princeton: Princeton University Press, 2017.

Ray, Nick, Peter Dragicevich, and Regis St. Louis, *Lonely Planet Vietnam.* Victoria, Australia: Lonely Planet, 2007.

Reed, Marcia and Paola Dematte, eds. *China on Paper: European and Chinese Works from the Late Sixteenth to Early Nineteenth Century.* Los Angeles: Getty Research Institute, 2011.

Reid, Anthony. *Charting the Shape of Early Modern Southeast Asia.* Chiang Mai: Silkworm Books, 2000.

Richardson, David and Filipa Ribeiro da Silva, eds. *Networks and Trans-Cultural Exchange: Slave Trading in the South Atlantic, 1590–1867.* Leiden: Koninklijke Brill NV, 2015.

Reynolds, Jonathan M. "Japan's Imperial Diet Building: debate over Construction of a National Identity." *Art Journal* 55, no. 3 (Fall 1996): 38–47.

Riello, Giorgio and Prasannan Parthasarathi, eds. *The Spinning World: A Global History of Cotton Textiles, 1200–1850.* Oxford: Oxford University Press, 2009.

Riello, Giorgio and Tirthankar Roy, eds. *How India Clothed the World: The World of South Asian Textiles, 1500–1850.* Leiden: Koninklijke Brill NV, 2009.

Roberts, Michael, ed. *Sri Lanka: Collective Identities Revisited, Volume I.* Colombo: Marga Institute, 1997.

Roberts, Michael. *Ethnicity after Edward Said: Post-Orientalist Failures in Comprehending the Kandyan Period of Lankan History.* Sri Lanka: International Centre for Ethnic Studies, 2001.

Roces, Mina and Louise Edwards, eds. *The Politics of Dress in Asia and the Americas.* Brighton and Portland: Sussex Academic Press, 2007.

Roodenburg, Herman, ed. *Cultural Exchange in Early Modern Europe vol. 4, Forging European Identities, 1400–1700.* Cambridge: Cambridge University Press, 2007.

Ross, Robert J. and Gerard T. Telkamp. *Colonial Cities – Essays on Urbanism in a Colonial Context.* Dordrecht: Martinus Nijhoff, 1985.

Rudner, David West. *Caste and Capitalism in Colonial India: The Nattukottai Chettiars.* Berkeley: University of California Press, 1994.

Rujivacharakul, Vimalin, ed. *Collecting "China": The World, China, and a Short History of Collecting.* Lanham, MD: University of Delaware Press, 2011.

Rujivacharakul, Vimalin, H. Hazel Hahn, Ken Tadashi Oshima, and Peter Christensen, eds. *Architecturalized Asia: Mapping a Continent through History.* Hong Kong: Hong Kong University Press; Honolulu: University of Hawai'i Press, 2013.

Ryan, James R. *Picturing Empire: Photography and the Visualization of the British Empire.* Chicago: The University of Chicago Press, 1998.

Said, Edward. *Orientalism.* New York: Pantheon Books, 1978.

Salomon, Nanette. *Shifting Priorities: Gender and Genre in Seventeenth-Century Dutch Painting.* Stanford: Stanford University Press, 2004.

Sandhu, Kernial Singh. *Indian Communities in Southeast Asia.* Singapore: Institute of Southeast Asian Studies, 1993.

Saurma-Jeltsch, Lieselotte E., and Anja Eisenbeiss, eds. *The Power of Things and the Flow of Cultural Transformations: Art and Culture between Europe and Asia.* Berlin: Deutscher Kunstverlag, 2010.

Savoy, Daniel, ed. *The Globalization of Renaissance Art: A Critical Review.* Leiden: Brill, 2017.

Schauer, Matthew. "Industrious Women and Lost Traditions: Gender, Imperial Exchange, and Handicrafts Education in British Malaya 1916–1932." *Journal of World History* 28, no. 3–4 (Dec. 2017): 493–524.

Schenker, Frederick J. "Jazz Freedoms: Balkan Rhythm, Race, and World Music." *Jazz Perspectives* 9, no. 3 (2015): 217–39.

Schmidt, Benjamin. *Inventing Exoticism: Geography, Globalism, and Europe's Early Modern World.* Philadelphia: University of Pennsylvania Press, 2015.

Sears, Laurie J. *Shadows of Empire: Colonial Discourse and Javanese Tales.* Durham: Duke University Press, 1996.

________. *Situated Testimonies: Dread and Enchantment in an Indonesian Literary Archive.* Honolulu: University of Hawai'i Press, 2013.

Sen, Tansen. *India, China, and the World: A Connected History.* Lanham: Rowman & Littlefield, 2017.

Shatzmiller, Joseph. *Cultural Exchange: Jews, Christians, and Art in the Medieval Marketplace.* Princeton: Princeton University Press, 2013.

Snodin, Michael and Nigel Llewellyn, eds. *Baroque Style in the Age of Magnificence, 1620–1800.* London: V&A Publishing, 2009.

Stambler, Benita. "Coming to America: Re-inventing and re-using the 1903 Delhi durbar." *Congent Arts and Humanities* (2 September 2016) https://doi.org/10.1080/23311983.2016.1225419

Steedman, Carolyn. *Strange Dislocations: Childhood and the Idea of Human Interiority 1780–1930.* Cambridge, MA: Harvard University Press, 1995.

Stewart, Susan. *On Longing: Narratives of the Miniature, the Gigantic, the Souvenir, the Collection.* Durham and London: Duke University Press, 1993.

Stoler, Ann Laura. *Race and the Education of Desire: Foucault's 'History of Sexuality' and the Colonial Order of Things.* Durham and London: Duke University Press, 1995.

________. *Carnal Knowledge and Imperial Power: Race and the Intimate in Colonial Rule.* Berkeley: University of California Press, 2002.

Stoler, Ann and Frederick Cooper, eds. *Tensions of the Empire: Colonial Cultures in a Bourgeois World.* Berkeley: University of California Press, 1997.

Streets-Salter, Heather. *World War One in Southeast Asia: Colonialism and Anticolonialism in an Era of Global Conflict.* Cambridge: Cambridge University Press, 2017.

Subrahmanyam, Sanjay. *Merchant Networks in the Early Modern World.* Aldershot: Variorum Books, 1996.

________. "Connected Histories: Notes towards a Reconfiguration of Early Modern Eurasia." *Modern Asian Studies* 31, no. 3 (1997): 735–62.

________. *Courtly Encounters: Translating Courtliness and Violence in Early Modern Eurasia*. Cambridge, MA: Harvard University Press, 2012.

________. *Europe's India: Words, People, Empires, 1500-1800.* Cambridge, MA: Harvard University Press, 2017.

________. *Empires Between Islam and Christianity, 1500–1800.* Ranikhet: Permanent Black; Albany: SUNY Press, 2018.

Sutherland, Heather. *The Making of a Bureaucratic Elite: The Colonial Transformation of the Javanese Priyayi.* Singapore: Heinemann Educational Books, 1979.

Sweda, Jennifer Erica, ed. *Exploring Travel and Tourism: Essays on Journeys and Destinations*. Cambridge: Cambridge Scholars Press, 2012.

Szanton, David L., ed. *The Politics of Knowledge: Area Studies and the Disciplines.* Berkeley: University of California Press, 2004.

Tagliacozzo, Eric. *Chinese Circulations: Capital, Commodities, and Networks in Southeast Asia*. Durham: Duke University Press, 2011.

Tate, E. Mowbray. *Transpacific Steam.* New York: Cornwall Books, 1986.

Taylor, Jean Gelman. *The Social World of Batavia: European and Eurasian in Dutch Asia.* Madison: University of Wisconsin Press, 1983.

________. *Global Indonesia*. Abingdon, Oxon, UK and New York: Routledge, 2012.

________. *Indonesia: Peoples and Histories*. New Haven: Yale University Press, 2004.

Taylor, Jean Gelman, ed. *Women Creating Indonesia: The First Fifty Years*. Clayton, VIC: Monash Asia Institute, 1997.

Taylor, Philip. *Goddess on the Rise: Pilgrimage and Popular Religion in Vietnam.* Honolulu: University of Hawai'i Press, 2004.

Terwen-De Loos, J. *Het Nederlands-koloniale meubel: studie over meubels in de voormalige Nederlandse koloniën Indonesië en Sri Lanka* [Dutch Colonial Furniture: Study of Furniture in the Former Dutch Colonies of Indonesia and Sri Lanka]. Franeker: T. Wever, 1985.

Thomas, Nicholas. *Entangled Objects: Exchange, Material Culture, and Colonialism in the Pacific*. Cambridge, MA: Harvard University Press, 1991.

Trüper, Henning, Dipesh Chakrabarty, and Sanjay Subrahmanyam, eds. *Historical Teleologies in the Modern World.* London: Bloomsbury, 2015.

Vale, Lawrence J. *Architecture, Power, and National Identity*. New Haven: Yale University Press, 2008.

Vann, Michael G. "The Good, the Bad, and the Ugly: Variation and Difference in French Racism in Colonial *Indochine*," in *The Color of Liberty: Histories of Race in France,* ed. Sue Peabody and Tyler Stovall. Durham: Duke University Press, 2003.

Veen, Sytze van der. *Brill: 325 Years of Scholarly Publishing.* Leiden: Brill, 2008.

Vickers, Adrian. *A History of Modern Indonesia.* Cambridge: Cambridge University Press, 2005.

Victoir, Laura A. and Victor Zatsepine, eds. *Harbin to Hanoi: The Colonial Built Environment in Asia, 1840 to 1940.* Hong Kong: Hong Kong University Press, 2013.

Volait, Mercedes. *Architectes et architectures de l'Egypte moderne, 1830–1950: genèse et essor d'une expertise locale* [Architects and Architectures of Modern Egypt, 1830–1950: Genesis and Rise of a Local Expertise]. Paris: Maisonneuve et Larose, 2005.

Walser, Robert, ed. *Keeping Time: Readings in Jazz History.* New York: Oxford University Press, 1999.

Wang, Gungwu. *Anglo-Chinese Encounters since 1800: War, Trade, Science, and Governance.* Cambridge: Cambridge University Press, 2003.

Ward, Kerry. *Networks of Empire: Forced Migration in the Dutch East India Company.* New York: Cambridge University Press 2009.

Wedema, Steven. *"Ethiek" und Macht: Die Niederländisch-Indische Kolonialverwaltung und Indonesische Emanzipationsbestrebungen, 1901–1927* [Ethics and Power: The Netherlands Indies' Colonial Administration and the Indonesian Emancipation Movement, 1901–1927]. Stuttgart: F. Steiner, 1998.

Whitfield, Susan. *Silk, Slaves, and Stupas: Material Culture of the Silk Road.* Oakland: University of California Press, 2018.

Wickramasinghe, Nira. *Dressing the Colonised Body: Politics, Clothing and Identity in Sri Lanka.* Hyderabad: Orient Longman, 2003.

Wilson, Kathleen, ed. *A New Imperial History: Culture, Identity and Modernity in Britain and the Empire, 1660–1840.* Cambridge: Cambridge University Press, 2004.

Wright, Ashley. *Opium and Empire in Southeast Asia: Regulating Consumption in British Burma.* Basingstoke, UK, and New York: Palgrave Macmillan, 2014.

Wright, Gwendolyn. *The Politics of Design in French Colonial Urbanism.* Chicago: The University of Chicago Press, 1991.

Yang, Chi-ming. *Performing China: Virtue, Commerce, and Orientalism in Eighteenth-century England, 1660–1760.* Baltimore: Johns Hopkins University Press, 2011.

Yeh, Wen-hsin. *Shanghai Splendor: Economic Sentiments and the Making of Modern China, 1843–1949.* Berkeley: University of California Press, 2007.

Yeoh, Brenda S.A. *Contesting Space in Colonial Singapore: Power Relations and the Urban Built Environment.* Honolulu: University of Hawai'i Press, 2003.

Index